The
Third Texas Cavalry
in the Civil War

The
Third Texas Cavalry
in the Civil War

Douglas Hale

University of Oklahoma Press
Norman and London

By Douglas Hale

The Germans from Russia in Oklahoma (Norman, 1980)
The Third Texas Cavalry in the Civil War (Norman, 1993)

Library of Congress Cataloging-in-Publication Data
Hale, Douglas.
    The Third Texas Cavalry in the Civil War / Douglas Hale.
        p.   cm.
    Includes bibliographical references and index.
    ISBN 0-8061-2462-8 (alk. paper)
    1. Confederate States of America. Army. Texas Cavalry
Regiment, 3rd. 2. Texas—History—Civil War, 1861–
1865—Regimental histories. 3. United States—History—
Civil War, 1861–1865—Regimental histories. I. Title.
E580.6 3rd.H34   1993
973.7'464—dc20   92-54153
                                                            CIP

The paper in this book meets the guidelines for permanence
and durability of the Committee on Production Guidelines for
Book Longevity of the Council on Library Resources, Inc. ∞

        1   2   3   4   5   6   7   8   9   10

For Otis A. Singletary

Contents

Illustrations

Maps

Tables

Preface

THIS BOOK began as a simple act of filial piety: I set out merely to discover and record the circumstances of service by my great-grandfather Gustavus A. Jarvis in the Confederate army. But the project quickly got out of hand when I became intrigued with the story of his regiment, the Third Texas Cavalry, in the Civil War. As I followed my curiosity into the labyrinth of unresolved questions involving the character and background of the soldiers, the motivation for their long and arduous service, their steadfastness in a dubious cause, the reasons for their gradual diminution in numbers, and the impact of the conflict on their Southern communities, I discovered to my amazement that there might still be room for one more book about the Civil War.

To be sure, there are hundreds of regimental histories already available, but few focus upon the daily life of the common soldier. Most chronicle the battles, recall anecdotes of derring-do, and offer hagiographical tributes to valiant commanders, but generally treat the experiences of the regiment in isolation, without explaining the relationship between the unit's own little war and the conflict as a whole. I have attempted, on the other hand, to explore the civilian background of the troops in the ranks and provide a socioeconomic profile of those who served. I hope further to show how their regional cultures shaped their reaction to a long war and their ultimate defeat. I have tried to tell the story of the Third Texas Cavalry in the context of the great strategic issues in the struggle, so that its otherwise meaningless litany of marches and countermarches, victories and defeats, becomes part of the larger history of the war. Whenever possible, I have allowed the common soldier to speak for himself.

While my studies have focused upon life and death among a mere handful of some eleven hundred men, the soldiers of the Third Cavalry were in many respects representative of that entire generation of young Southerners who went to war in 1861. Though they sprang from an isolated corner of East Texas, their campaigns carried them through more than seventy engagements all the way from the Great Plains to the flanks of the Appalachian Mountains. They served under some of the most notable (and controversial) commanders of the era, including Price, Van Dorn, Forrest, and Hood. While I have attempted to convey accurately the story of their battles and marches and to assess objectively their effectiveness as fighting men, I have focused also on the often appalling conditions of their lives in camp and their attrition through disease, desertion, and death in battle. I trust that the microcosmic perspective of these soldiers' experiences will prove of interest to the general reader as well as to the specialist in military history.

Throughout this enterprise, I have been the grateful recipient of generous assistance from dozens of people far more knowledgeable than I concerning various aspects of the story of the Third Texas. Some were kind enough to grant me access to precious family records, letters, or diaries, without which I could not have proceeded with my research. To Virginia Carroll, W. D. Cater, Dorothy Craver, Jane J. Greer, Ralph O. Harvey, Jr., Richard R. Hrabchak, David D. Jackson, Alice L. Raymond, Mary Sylvester, and John A. Templeton, I am profoundly grateful.

Others with detailed knowledge of regional and local history guided me expertly through the thicket of names, relationships, and localities on the roster of the regiment. They include:

Bobby T. Alexander	Leila B. LaGrone
Marie Arnold	Max S. Lale

J. L. Bryan	Andrew L. Leath
James R. Caldwell	Louise Martin
John Dulin	McXie Martin
Mary F. Dunn	Judson Milburn
Hilda M. Gaut	Frances Russell
Jean Gilley	Justin M. Sanders
Colleen Green	Mary L. Taylor
Mrs. Don Hudson	Susan Weaver
Marcille Hughes	J. Dale West
Ruthmary Jordan	Bonnie Wolverton

I am deeply indebted to them for their help.

Staff members of the Barker Texas History Center, University of Texas; the Dallas Public Library; the East Texas Baptist University Library; the Edmund Low Library, Oklahoma State University; the Jefferson Historical Museum; the Longview Public Library; the U. S. National Archives and Records Administration; and the Western History Collections at the University of Oklahoma, cheerfully assisted me in my research. I am especially grateful to Gayle E. Maxwell, Department of Geography, Oklahoma State University, for her excellent maps.

In addition, the following archivists, librarians, and curators were particularly helpful: Donaly E. Brice and Michael R. Green, Texas State Library and Archives; Julius A. Buchanan, Smith County Historical Society; Sally Harper, Tyler Public Library; Inez H. Hughes, Harrison County Historical Museum; Mary Hummer, Family History Center, Stillwater; Linda C. Nicklas, East Texas Collection, Stephen F. Austin State University; Donna Rich, Texas Confederate Museum; the late Harold B. Simpson, Confederate Research Center, Hill College; Fred S. Standley, Oklahoma Historical Society; and Richard J. Summers, U.S. Army Military History Institute. I appreciate their kindness very much.

Philip A. Bevers, Randolph B. Campbell, LeRoy H. Fischer, David D. Jackson, Joseph A. Stout, and Emory M. Thomas read part or all of various drafts of my manuscript, and their trenchant comments have spared me many embarrassing blunders. Any errors of fact or interpretation that remain are of course my own. Finally, I am ever grateful to my wife Lou for her encouragement and confidence in this project.

Stillwater, Oklahoma   DOUGLAS HALE

The
Third Texas Cavalry
in the Civil War

CHAPTER 1

Texas Leaves the Union, 1860–1861

THE MEN of the Third Texas Cavalry blundered into their first battle fifty-seven days after they enlisted in the Confederate army. As volunteers in Brigadier General Ben McCulloch's ten-thousand-man army, they rolled out of their blankets before daybreak beside a sparkling Ozark stream, called Wilson's Creek, on the morning of August 10, 1861. The troopers had their first intimation that this day might well be their last as Yankee cannon suddenly thundered in their rear; canister shot rattled through the trees and rained down on them as they boiled their coffee under the oaks and hickories along the creek bank. After momentary panic and considerable confusion, these farm boys from East Texas eventually fell into ranks, extricated themselves from the Union field of fire, mounted a ragged charge against their declared enemy, and, with the exception of six of their number, managed to survive that morning of sanguinary violence, which left some 2,500 men lying dead or wounded on the battlefield.

That night, "the evidences of the desperate and terrible fighting . . . were on every hand. The dead, dying and wounded . . . were scattered thick along the road and on the hills."[1] Sam Barron, a twenty-six-year-old sergeant from Cherokee County, reflected somberly as he surveyed the carnage: "Thus ended our first battle. Would to God it had been our last, and the last of the war!"[2]

But the war went on and on. Three and a half years later a tattered remnant of this regiment fought its final engagement along the banks of another obscure watercourse, Sugar Creek, which flowed astride the Tennessee-Alabama border. Serving as the rear guard for General John Bell Hood's shattered Rebel army as it fled south ahead of its victorious Yankee pursuers, the Third Texas ambushed the enemy in the early-morning mist and held him long enough for Hood's ragged command to cross the Tennessee River. Barron was there, too, peering through the dense fog as the Rebel infantry suddenly plunged forward across the creek with a terrifying yell, throwing the head of the enemy column into confusion. Then the Texans "charged them . . . at a gallop and pressed them back two or three miles. *And this*," recalled Barron, "*was the last fight I was ever in!*"[3] It was the last fight of the Third Texas Cavalry as well.

The men of the regiment spent the war far from their East Texas homes, amid appalling hardships and hazards, and still remained remarkably active campaigners throughout the conflict. They participated in two of the most decisive campaigns of the Civil War—Vicksburg and Atlanta—and acquitted themselves with courage and remarkable fortitude. Considering what was expected of these men and the circumstances under which they served, the soldiers of the Third Texas compiled an honorable record of sacrifice and endurance. Their story is one worth telling, if only as an exemplary account of tenacity in the face of overwhelming odds.

But there is a larger dimension to the history of the regiment as well: the day-to-day experiences of this little band of eleven hundred men provide a personal perspective on the Civil War as a whole. By placing these soldiers in the context of the larger issues that shaped the great struggle, the true meaning and character of the war attain immediacy and precision. For however differing in detail, the fate of these volunteers from a remote corner of the South was in many ways typical of the three million men who bore arms for both the Union and the Confederacy. They shared fully in the privation and suffering that the

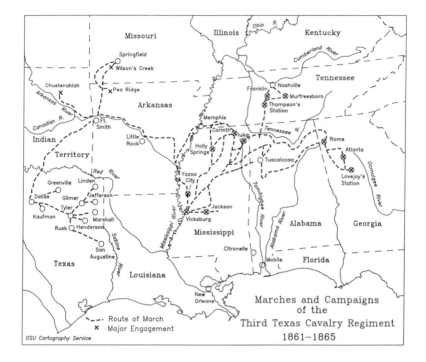

Marches and Campaigns
of the
Third Texas Cavalry Regiment
1861–1865

- - - Route of March
× Major Engagement

OSU Cartography Service

conflict entailed; their attitudes and behavior reflected the prevailing values held by their Confederate compatriots both at
home and in the ranks; in most respects, these Texans were
representative of their generation of Southerners.

In other ways, however, the men of the Third Texas were
more fortunate than the majority of Civil War soldiers. They
were cavalrymen, after all: an elite minority. They belonged to
a branch of service that, though surrounded by an aura of glam-
our and prestige, played but an ancillary role in the four years
of fighting. The Confederacy as a whole raised only one cavalry
regiment for every five regiments of infantry sent into battle;
Texas was the only state that enlisted more horsemen into the
service than foot soldiers. Since the men provided their own
horses and equipment, cavalrymen were most often drawn from

those more prosperous elements of society that could afford the considerable expense involved. The men of the Third Texas were disproportionately representative of the well-to-do.

The regiment was exceptional also because its men were the first to volunteer from their various localities early in the war. Their enthusiasm, morale, and tenacity were therefore probably higher than that of later recruits. Furthermore, they had the good fortune of being spared participation in the most costly of the war's battles, and the casualties they suffered were correspondingly less severe than the norm. On their horses, they enjoyed more freedom of movement, greater respect from the civilian population, and wider access to the scarce necessities of life. Finally, they were Texans: the homes they defended remained relatively untouched by the worst ravages of the conflict. Deservedly or not, these Texans enjoyed a reputation for bold combativeness, and they generally shared in this high opinion of themselves. In these respects, the men of the Third Texas were atypical of ordinary Civil War soldiers.[4]

Keeping in mind these exceptional characteristics of the regiment, I hope in the following pages to address three major concerns. First, through an examination of the prewar status of the 1,097 men who joined the unit at the time of its organization, I hope to identify their regional, economic, and political backgrounds. Whether they sprang from humble or affluent circumstances and the degree to which they represented substantial investments in slave property are factors of considerable significance in sketching a profile of the regiment. Was success as a soldier in any way predetermined by wealth or class? Did these men share a fairly homogeneous Texas frontier environment, or did they exhibit instead a wide diversity of localized cultures? Consideration of these questions can lead us to a fuller understanding of the character of antebellum Texas as well as the social origins of these East Texas volunteers.

The motivations that impelled these men to flock so eagerly to the banner of the Third Texas provide the second focus of the study. What inspired Texans as a whole to choose secession and war in the spring of 1861, and to what degree did the troops in the ranks share these convictions? Did their morale fluctuate in response to the varying fortunes of the Confederacy? How did their friends and loved ones view their service so far away from home? My emphasis throughout is upon the life of the common soldier. When the sources permit, I have let these men speak for themselves as they express their evolving attitudes toward their service and their cause. I am particularly interested, for example, in their opinions about their various commanders, their treatment of African-American troops in the Union army, and their reactions to defeat.

Most of the following pages will focus upon the third objective of this book: to recount the military record of a Confederate cavalry regiment throughout the war and evaluate its performance. Though the Third Texas occupies center stage in the drama, I have tried to portray its role in the context of the larger struggle as a whole. Since the unit participated in many of the major engagements in the western theater of the war, it is necessary to comprehend the broader strategies in which the regiment represented but a minor pawn. In assessing the military effectiveness of the unit, the whole question of the obsolescence of cavalry as a decisive arm of battle must be addressed. I have given attention to the quality of its leadership, the sufficiency of its supplies and equipment, and how effectively it was used by the Confederate command. I have also explored the incidence and impact of casualties in battle and attrition through disease and desertion.

If one is to understand the young men of the Third Texas, one must begin with an account of how and why Texas slid precipitously into war in the spring of 1861. Not only did these soldiers share fully in the values and prejudices of their elders, but their own behavior also reflected the impact of events at home immediately prior to the conflict. The volunteers were inspired by the paradoxical, but not uncommon, coupling of profound moral indignation with a reckless pugnacity that demanded action without undue thought to its consequences. So motivated, they were typical of Texans as a whole.

On the one hand, many of the young recruits of the Third Cavalry affirmed their moral imperative to sacrifice all, if need be, to defend their homeland. Shortly after enlisting, Private

Ben Long wrote his cousin that, though "it may fall my lot to be one among the slain . . . , I will willingly lay down my life to keep the northern vandals from polluting the southern soil with their unhallowed footsteps."[5] At about the same time, Lon Cartwright expressed to his father the hope that "by brave and generous deeds" he and his comrades might earn the privilege "of living under the banner of liberty and independence."[6] Doug Cater, a young Henderson music teacher, volunteered, he said, because "my country had called and I was obeying that little word, duty, which meant so much."[7]

On the other hand, most of the Texans went off to war in a jubilant, light-hearted mood, "rarin' for a fight"—an attitude that belied the lofty purposes elsewhere ascribed to their crusade. Clearly, they were out to enjoy the great adventure that a beneficent Providence had placed before them. As one grizzled veteran of the regiment ruefully observed, "Had our embryo warriors been asked for what purpose they were going to war, doubtless the only reply in many instances would have been: 'To whip the Yankees!' "[8] They marched off to war full of "merriment and good cheer," as frolicsome and carefree as if they were headed for two weeks at summer camp instead of four years of gnawing hunger, disease, exhaustion, pain, and the stench of death.[9]

In their brash bravado as well as the high moral tone in which they justified their action, the amateur soldiers of the Third Cavalry merely reflected the attitudes of their elders. The vast majority of the people of the Lone Star State went to war in 1861 under the delusion that their cause was a just and necessary one, that the conflict would be short and relatively innocuous, that courage and determination would be the crucial keys to victory, that with their sister states of the Confederacy they could prevail over the material advantages of their Northern adversaries, and finally, that the resort to war merited its cost. That these dubious propositions were enthusiastically shared and given the sanctity of Holy Writ, and that they fueled a hopeless effort through four years of ruinous war, suggest that by the spring of 1861 Texas politics had ceased to follow the path of rational calculation. Indeed, in the preceding year a series of events and a concatenation of forces had the effect, in the words of Sam Houston, of "stilling the voice of reason" in the Lone Star State and transforming the public mood from ardent American nationalism to outright rebellion.[10]

As late as the summer of 1860 most Texans held firm to the Union. They were acutely aware of the advantages of belonging to a powerful nation whose army could fend off the hostile Indians of their western plains or march against turbulent Mexico to the south. Texas merchants and planters recognized that continued prosperity depended upon selling their cotton, hides, and sugar in the great emporium of the United States. Slavery, the paramount issue, was economically insignificant in wide reaches of the state. Black bondsmen, who comprised less than one-third of the 604,215 inhabitants of Texas, constituted a smaller proportion of the population than in any other Confederate state except Tennessee and Arkansas. The reins of political leadership, with Governor Sam Houston, the legendary hero of San Jacinto, as its cynosure, remained in the hands of moderate Unionists until the eve of secession.

Yet in the space of a few short months a complex series of developments created an atmosphere that rendered most Texans suspicious of or hostile toward the Union and ready to accept war as the final arbiter, if it came to that. This transformation of public opinion was primarily the work of a once insignificant minority of ardent secessionists who succeeded in creating a popular consensus for their cause by generating and then skillfully exploiting a sense of impending crisis.

Their campaign was facilitated by subtle but powerful secular changes in the demographic and economic dimensions of the population. In the first place, the target audience for the secessionist appeal became ever more susceptible to the message as settlers with cultural ties to the Deep South came to constitute an increasing proportion of the population of Texas. The cotton plantation economy became dominant in East Texas, and the societal values and perceived interests of the Lower South came to prevail there. Though only one in four white families in the state owned slaves, this minority constituted the politically influential and economically potent segment of that agrarian society. Every black bondsman represented an investment of about $765 to his owner; in that era of cheap land, slaves were the primary measure of wealth and prestige. The interest in preserving and expanding this wealth was broadly shared even among those who had not yet acquired it.[11]

Furthermore, the dominant Texas Democratic Party came under the control of states' rights extremists; former political leaders who advocated a more moderate course on the slavery question lost the advantage of a strong political network through which to disseminate their views. The old moderates rather suddenly found themselves disorganized and powerless to define the terms of the bitter debate or to influence substantially the popular consensus. Without a party organization to give their appeal breadth and coherence, Unionist politicians were left to express their views as isolated individuals.

A third precondition that determined the outcome of the secession crisis in Texas was the increasingly strident demand for absolute conformity of opinion and expression on the issue of slavery. Growing apace with abolitionist attacks on their "peculiar institution," Southerners gradually developed a siege mentality. Conscious that many of their countrymen held them in contempt for perpetuating and profiting from human bondage, they reacted with bitter justifications and rationalizations that brooked no argument. Typical of this extravagant self-vindication was the declaration by a Harrison County district judge that "I have no more doubt of the right of a civilized and christian nation to capture the African . . . and subject him to labor, enlightenment, and religion, than I have of one of our people to capture a wild horse on the prairies of the West, and domesticate and reduce him to labor."[12]

To question slavery upon any ground—its economic efficiency or its potential viability in the western territories, for instance— came to be viewed as an act of criminal treason. In this paranoid atmosphere, Texans lost their capacity to draw distinctions where the issue of slavery was concerned: mild expressions of disagreement quickly degenerated into vituperation. To many ardent Southerners, merely to advocate the perpetuation of the Union became tantamount to a betrayal of their way of life. No wonder that prudent individuals remained silent as the bold and reckless stepped forward.

The retreat from Unionism occurred amid sensational events that created an ever growing sense of crisis. Developments far removed from the Lone Star State took on ominous symbolic significance while incidents closer to home stirred passions beyond control. First in the long train of emotion-packed events was John Brown's raid on the federal arsenal at Harper's Ferry, Virginia, in October 1859. His quixotic effort to incite a slave insurrection received the enthusiastic approval and support of such prominent Northern abolitionists as Ralph Waldo Emerson, who predicted that Brown's martyrdom would "make the gallows glorious like the cross."[13] Though Brown's escapade was executed in folly and ended in disaster, and though his call for a slave revolt went unheeded, the fiasco seemed to confirm the suspicions of many Southerners that a Yankee conspiracy had set out to destroy them.

In distant Texas the news of Brown's mad adventure pushed invective to hitherto-unscaled heights of bombast. Many towns held mass meetings to plan for their defense against the perceived threat of servile war, while newspaper editors throughout the state gave free rein to hyperbole. At Palestine, for instance, a citizens' committee excoriated the "covert, dark, unholy, and fanatical" plot by abolitionists to infiltrate the South in the guise of peddlers and teachers. Those in attendance at the meeting voted to seize and burn dangerous books, boycott antislavery firms in the North, scrutinize the records of teachers of Northern birth for subversive tendencies, and suppress all *music* adjudged to be "dangerous to and subversive of the Constitutional rights and liberties of the South."[14]

The incident at Harper's Ferry was enough to persuade many Texans that they had better move quickly to protect their way of life before its enemies struck it down. Some of these proslavery extremists belonged to a bizarre secret society called the Knights of the Golden Circle, organized in the 1850s to safeguard the future of black servitude. By uniting northern Mexico and Cuba to the Deep South by force of arms, its adherents believed they might provide a secure and permanent home for Negro slavery and for the profits realized by that system. Despite the extravagance of such goals, similar projects had been floated ever since the Mexican War. The KGC attracted into its ranks many prominent Texans, who organized chapters in at least twenty-seven Texas counties.

Beset by problems of finance and leadership, the KGC never successfully launched any of its grandiose schemes. The organization was nonetheless important to Texas in at least three respects. As fervent Southern patriots, KGC members provided the leadership for several of the first Confederate military units to be raised in the state. More important, the KGC assisted in shaping and solidifying secessionist opinion during the crisis of 1861. Its activities also gave color to Northern suspicions of a sinister slavocracy conspiracy, further inflaming emotions on both sides.[15]

As if to confirm the wildest fears of Texas slaveholders that abolitionist elements were out to destroy their way of life, a rash of disastrous fires broke out at widely scattered points across the state during the summer of 1860. On July 8 every store in Dallas was consumed by fire; on August 5 the town of Henderson lost a total of forty-three buildings to a conflagration that left the place a field of ashes. Numerous other towns either suffered severe damage or were seriously threatened by fire. For about six weeks the inhabitants of Texas lived in dread that their homes would be next. The preponderance of evidence suggests that the true cause of this widespread series of disastrous fires lay in the spontaneous combustion of the new phosphorous matches during the exceptional heat of that summer.[16]

But secessionist rabble-rousers were quick to ascribe the conflagrations to an abolitionist plot. A Dallas newspaper editor propounded a conspiracy theory; soon pro-slavery newspapers all over the state propagated his ideas and occasionally invented lurid details of their own. According to the *Texas Republican* of Marshall, these fires were "too numerous to have resulted from accident. . . . If we are to place any reliance in the testimony elicited by an examination of the negroes, all these outrages were the work of abolition emissaries."[17] The Democratic press warned that the wave of fires was but an opening salvo in a campaign to destroy northeastern Texas, assassinate the leaders of the region, and turn the whole area over to the blacks by means of a slave insurrection. While a few sober-minded citizens demanded some proof before swallowing this hypothesis, and Unionist politicians indignantly warned that the allegations had been hatched to influence the fall elections, Texas public opinion had been so poisoned by suspicion that many whites succumbed to panic and hysteria. Looking back upon the strange episode from a perspective of forty years, one East Texas veteran ruefully observed, "Such were the conclusions of a mad people."[18]

White mobs lashed out ferociously at anyone suspected of complicity in the imagined plot, lynching dozens of blacks as well as a number of whites thought to be responsible for fomenting discontent among the slaves. On June 17, Fort Worth vigilantes hanged two white men, one on suspicion of abolitionism, the other for allegedly distributing pistols to blacks. At Henderson a mob attacked another white resident who was believed to entertain antislavery opinions. These champions of order threw a loop around his neck, tied the rope to a saddle horn, and dragged the man to death around the public square. Then they hanged the corpse from a tree and shot it full of holes. Similar outrages occurred around the state. In Fayette County alone, mobs lynched more than twenty-five whites and fifty blacks between July and September. Such was the slave insurrection in Texas.[19]

Shortly, the weather cooled, the fires ceased, and the tide of hysteria ebbed as both press and public took a more sober view of the dubious evidence for the insurrection. But the manufactured crisis had done its work: it exacerbated Texans' fears of a Northern conspiracy and provided fuel for the firebrands preaching secession. Speaking at Tyler on September 3, United States Senator Louis T. Wigfall, the most reckless of the Texas rabble-rousers, warned that "an enemy is in our midst not with bayonet and broad sword, but with torch and poison."[20] The violent reaction provoked by the spurious insurrection intimidated many Unionists to the point that they became afraid to speak out on the issue and gave the victory to secessionism by default. Fears of a servile revolt, the imponderable passions of racism, the waning power of Unionist sentiment, the political impotence of its partisans, and the gathering momentum of a secessionist consensus must all be considered if one would understand why Texas left the Union.

In such a climate of anxious anticipation Texans faced the national elections in the fall of 1860. The balloting of November gave the voters the first of three clear opportunities to register their will as to the future of the Union. Three decades of sectional strife had left the American two-party system a shambles. The Democratic Party split over the issue of slavery in the territories, the Republicans nominated Abraham Lincoln on an antislavery platform attractive to the Northern electorate, and a group of former Whigs created a new party, the Constitutional Unionists, in the vain hope of reaching some sort of sectional compromise. With four major contenders in the field, and the electorate divided in sentiment according to sectional lines, the campaign of 1860 was confused, bitter, and fateful.

When the ballots were cast on November 6, the voters registered in numbers the alarming divisions of opinion in the nation. No single candidate received a majority of the popular vote. Lincoln garnered a scant 40 percent of the ballots, but his modest plurality, strategically concentrated in populous Northern states, translated into a comfortable majority in the electoral college, where he won the presidency. As far as most Southerners were concerned, the worst had happened.

Texas ballots featured but two choices for president: John C. Breckinridge, the nominee of the Southern wing of the Democratic Party; and John Bell, the candidate of compromise. Texans overwhelmingly supported the Southern rights, proslavery position, with 48,367 voters, or three-quarters of the men who went to the polls, casting their ballots for Breckinridge. Bell received 15,580 votes, chiefly in those districts where the old Whig tradition was still strong. Only 410 voters wrote in the name of Stephen A. Douglas, the Northern Democrat; not a single Texan voted for Lincoln.[21] In their first opportunity to register an opinion on the merits of sectional compromise versus dogged defiance, the Texas electorate arrayed themselves in the unyielding ranks of those who refused to compromise on the issue of slavery and were prepared to defy the federal government if necessary.

The fact remained, however, that Lincoln had been constitutionally elected president and would be duly inaugurated on March 4, 1861. For a long time many Southern leaders had threatened to take their states out of the Union rather than see their cherished institutions jeopardized through an accession to power by Lincoln and his "Black Republicans." Though the Republican platform stipulated that there would be no interference with slavery in those states where it already existed, and though Lincoln tried to reassure the South on this point, the more extreme Southern politicians were in no mood to calculate the true extent of abolitionist influence in the new administration or to remember that both the legislative and judicial branches of the federal government were still safely in the hands of Democratic majorities. The Southern fire-eaters preferred instead to trumpet the gospel of secession, and the more prudent voices of moderation, the cautious counsels to "wait and see," were drowned amid the torrents of defiant and bellicose rhetoric. Throughout the Deep South proslavery extremists seized the initiative and launched campaigns to lead their respective states out of the Union on the very morrow of the election.

In Texas, too, the election of Lincoln crystallized and focused the growing secessionist sentiment. For the next three months the state would revel in an orgy of debate on this issue until at last the people would decide. As the outcome of the balloting of November 6 became known, local worthies expressed their disgust and defiance by summarily replacing the flag of the Union with that of the Lone Star on public buildings. Mass meetings were held in many localities to discuss the implications of Lincoln's election. Already on November 16, for example, an assembly at Marshall called for immediate secession.[22] Among the speakers at this event was the state commander of the Knights of the Golden Circle, Elkanah B. Greer, who in six months' time would become the first commanding officer of the Third Texas Cavalry. He warned that it would be consummate folly "to wait for the North to inaugurate her withering, dishonoring, and diabolical policy. The overt act has been committed [in Lincoln's election]. Let the South speak out, or forever hold her peace."[23] In anticipation of impending secession,

Greer tendered to the state the services of his trained band of volunteers.

Throughout December, self-appointed secessionist leaders presided at public meetings and demonstrations, as crowds assembled to denounce the Union and hang Lincoln in effigy. Editors vied with each other in the violence of their invective. "The North has gone overwhelmingly for Negro *Equality* and Southern Vassalage!" charged one. "Southern men, will you submit to the degradation?"[24] The *Texas State Gazette* declared that the election of Lincoln had threatened the safety of Southern homes and the lives of Southern families with "the torch and the poison of the fanatic, the murderer, and the robber."[25] No matter how hasty the actions of state leaders might be, they could not come soon enough, according to the editor of that paper. The defenders of the South "should not postpone the day of resistance until the enemy shall become stronger and they shall become weaker."[26]

Indeed, proponents of secession wasted little time in shoving their respective states down the slippery slope toward war. After South Carolina voted to secede on December 20, the five other states of the Deep South followed in rapid succession. Mississippi, Florida, Alabama, Georgia, and Louisiana all passed secession ordinances by the end of January 1861. This avalanche of defiant and dramatic action inspired Texas politicians to hasten their deliberations, since no Texan was content to lag behind. The excitement occasioned by the departure of so many sister states from the Union, moreover, drowned out the sober admonitions of the Texas Unionists.

Though they counted among their number some of the ablest and most prominent men the state had produced, the Unionists were disorganized, divided as to strategy, and saddled with arguments that seemed tepid and uncertain when compared to the fiery certitudes of the partisans of disunion. Generally, they took the position that while Lincoln's election was unfortunate, the event was not of such magnitude to warrant the dissolution of the nation. As Houston put it, "Mr. Lincoln has been constitutionally elected, and, much as I deprecate his success, no alternative is left me but to yield to the Constitution."[27] The aging governor further argued that Texas could better serve its interests in the Union than out of it.

Consequently, when communities across Texas petitioned Houston to call a special session of the legislature or a state convention to act on the question of secession, he refused. Faced with the governor's stubborn opposition, a cabal of prominent secessionists took the extralegal step of issuing a call for a convention on their own initiative. They extended an invitation to the voters to send delegates to an extraordinary assembly to deal with the question of separation from the Union. By this audacious stroke, these self-appointed leaders gained a march over the Unionists, whose cautious strategy seemed hesitant and irresolute by comparison.

Responding to the call, the people of Texas took their second step down the road to war. Voters in ninety-two Texas counties elected 192 delegates to the impromptu convention on January 8. Since many Unionist electors simply boycotted the delegate selection, the men chosen as representatives were of a decidedly secessionist disposition. Their authority was considerably enhanced when Governor Houston at last bowed to public pressure to the extent of summoning a special session of the legislature. In a joint resolution, the Senate and the House sanctioned the competence of the convention to act on the matter of secession, with the proviso that its decision would be ratified by a popular referendum.

Thus, when the convention met in Austin on January 28, it had already received the imprimatur of the electorate and the legislature as well as the grudging acquiescence of the governor. In their perfunctory deliberations, the majority of the delegates defended the right of Texas to leave the Union on the grounds that the several states had entered upon a voluntary compact and were consequently free to dissolve that bond when the central government infringed upon the prerogatives of the individual members. Whatever the arguments advanced, most of those present had already made up their minds on the issue before they arrived in Austin, and they required only a day or two to reach a verdict. By a vote of 166 to 8, the convention adopted its Ordinance of Secession on February 1.[28]

The next day the majority composed a lengthy justification for their action to take home to the voters. They dispensed with abstruse concepts of political philosophy and concentrated instead upon the real motive behind their decision to leave the Union: racism. The convention charged that the federal government had attempted to impose upon them "the debasing doctrine of the equality of all men, irrespective of race or color—a doctrine at war with nature, in opposition to the experience of mankind, and in violation of the plainest revelations of the Divine Law." "The servitude of the African race," this document continued, "is mutually beneficial to both bond and free," whereas "the destruction of the existing relations between the two races, as advocated by our sectional enemies, would bring inevitable calamities upon both and desolation upon the fifteen slaveholding states."[29] Having delivered this weighty vindication, the convention adjourned, and its members returned to their districts to campaign among the ordinary voters. In electing these men to represent them in the Secession Convention, the people of Texas had enjoyed a second opportunity to choose between compromise and conflict. Their third and final chance was to come on February 23, when a referendum on the issue was to be held.

In the meantime, the shapers of opinion endeavored assiduously to help the voters make up their minds. While the convention delegates distributed twenty thousand copies of their "Declaration of Causes" around the state, pro-secession editors urged Texans to adopt a revolutionary mentality. "Lincoln and his party are pledged to our subjugation and threatens [*sic*] us with the sword [if] we dare to resist,"[30] warned one, while another admonished his readers to "show that Texans, in this revolution; as in the first, are an unbroken brotherhood."[31] The embattled Unionists issued a circular address in favor of compromise, and several Central Texas newspapers took their side in the campaign, but their feeble efforts were to little avail.

When the voters went to the polls on February 23 they repudiated the Union by a margin of three to one (46,153 to 14,747), almost the same proportion by which they had rejected the Constitutional Union Party and the spirit of compromise the previous November. Only 19 of the 122 counties reporting registered pro-Union majorities. Clearly, most white Texans had come to regard the federal government as their enemy. Their judgment, clouded by the emotional fog that enveloped the entire slavery issue, could no longer distinguish between subtle gradations of right and wrong, justice and injustice, but recognized only black and white. In the eyes of the people the partisans of the Union, divided and hesitant, had been vanquished in the contest over secession by the superior tactics and organization of the anti-Union forces. Warmly gratified by the enthusiastic endorsement given their work by the voters, the members of the convention reconvened at Austin on March 2. Three days later they voted to join the Confederacy.[32]

CHAPTER 2

Texas Goes to War,
February–May 1861

AS TEXAS united with the states of the Lower South to form the new Confederate government, the speed, ease, and general harmony by which it had been established inspired a deceptive euphoria. During these blossoming days of the Southern springtime, it was easy to imagine the infant Confederacy growing into a hemispheric power in its own right, as the editor of the *Texas State Gazette* predicted: "The child of today will live to see the boundaries of a Southern Republic gradually extended over Chihuahua, Sonora, and Lower California. Our ships will whiten the Gulf of California and the Pacific as well as of Mexico and the Atlantic."[1] Anyone who could entertain such extravagant visions could be equally persuaded that the bold resolve shown by Southerners would be sufficient to dissuade Lincoln and his minions from interfering while the United States dissolved into its constituent sections.

Like most other seceders, Texans were confident that war would not come, but if it did, Southern valor and prowess under arms would end it quickly and victoriously. The chief justice of the Texas Supreme Court concluded confidently that "we shall have no war," and even in the unlikely event that the new administration should challenge the Confederacy at arms, a few swift strokes of Southern gallantry would send the Yankees reeling.[2] Most Texans agreed with an influential editor's assessment that if the Northern abolitionists provoked a war, they would soon find their own country "entered triumphantly by a Southern Army."[3]

Such effusions of romantic bravado were unfortunately not confined to small-town editors. The illusion of Southern invincibility was generally shared despite its egregious inconsistency with well known facts and figures. If it came to war, the South could realistically expect to be outnumbered almost four to one. Of a total American population of 31.5 millions, the eleven states of the Confederacy could count but 8.7 million inhabitants, and 3.5 million of those were slaves. The North had a potential pool of 4 million fighting men; the South only 1.1 million. The industrial capacity of the Confederate states was negligible: both New York and Pennsylvania *each* produced twice as much in manufactured goods in 1860 as the entire South taken together. Of the 31,000 miles of railroad in the United States, only 9,000 miles of track ran through the Confederacy. Understandably, the ardent champions of secession ignored such unpleasant indices of disparity and seized instead upon intangibles like the superior quality of Southern valor and leadership to bolster their arguments.[4]

Otherwise sane and responsible people could entertain these illusions because fortune seemed to smile on the Texas secessionists during the early months of 1861. Through a combination of bold initiative by the Secession Convention and cautious hesitation on the part of the federal authorities, a few determined hotspurs successfully drove the United States military establishment out of Texas and confiscated several formidable federal arsenals almost without firing a shot. More than two weeks before President Lincoln took his oath of office, and almost two months before the fateful salvo at Fort Sumter, Texas Rebels seized the initiative to clear the state of Union troops.

The Secession Convention had set up a Committee of Public Safety to raise a military force for the state, and this body invited three veteran Texas Ranger captains—the brothers Ben and Henry McCulloch, and John S. "Rip" Ford—to organize cavalry regiments as the nucleus of a Texas provisional army. In the warlike atmosphere that prevailed during the spring of 1861, these bold captains easily recruited the men they needed. The units' objective was to occupy the nineteen United States Army posts that extended across Texas from Camp Cooper on the northern plains to Fort Brown at the mouth of the Rio Grande. About 2,700 Federal troops, or fully one-sixth of the United States Army, garrisoned these far-flung outposts and guarded the huge quantity of arms and supplies stored in them. They were all under the command of Major General David E. Twiggs, who maintained his headquarters at San Antonio. A native of Georgia, this seventy-one-year-old commander was in sympathy with the Southern cause, and in the interim between Lincoln's election and his inauguration, Twiggs was left without definite orders from Washington.

Assisted ably by Twiggs's desire to avoid bloodshed, Ford and the McCulloch brothers proceeded upon their mission with workmanlike efficiency. Confronted by Ben McCulloch's volunteers, Twiggs agreed to surrender all the federal posts in Texas to the state authorities on February 18. Meanwhile, Henry McCulloch's men rode into northwestern Texas to occupy the major Union forts between the upper Brazos and Colorado rivers. At about the same time, Rip Ford's recruits sailed down the Gulf Coast and captured Fort Brown. These troops later occupied various frontier posts from Brownsville to El Paso. In this way, the Texans drove the United States Army out of their state and confiscated Union arms and equipment to the value of some three million dollars. For surrendering his posts without resistance, Twiggs was dismissed from the army; he later became a major general in the Confederate forces.[5]

Ford and the McCullochs were astonishingly successful because throughout much of the secession crisis the federal government at Washington provided little guidance to its officials in Texas. In the four months between the November election and Lincoln's inauguration, the Northern reaction to the secession of the Deep South was confused and uncertain. Even Lincoln's inaugural address, delivered on March 4, offered few solid clues to the substance of his future policy. Preferring to keep as many options open as possible, the new president avoided committing himself to any specific course of action toward the seceding states beyond promising to execute the federal laws and "hold, occupy and possess" forts still in Union hands. Some Southerners read this as an ominous warning; others considered it to be but another expression of Yankee cowardice.

In the face of Lincoln's calculated ambiguity, Texas, like the six other original states of the Confederacy, busied itself with the minor alterations necessary to fit its government into the new nation. On March 14 the Secession Convention, which had assumed the legislative function in the state, decreed that all public officials must render an oath of allegiance to the Confederacy. When Governor Houston refused, the convention duly deposed the old warrior and replaced him with Lieutenant Governor Edward Clark.[6] Though Houston continued to urge caution upon those who would recklessly plunge the South into a war it might not win, "he might as well had been giving advice to the inmates of a lunatic asylum," admitted one of the objects of his counsel.[7] Embittered and humiliated, the discredited hero withdrew to his farm near Huntsville, made an uneasy peace with his Confederate compatriots, and died two years later.

After the Secession Convention finally adjourned on March 26, political affairs at Austin slipped into the background as the military mobilization of Texas assumed center stage. These initial state and local measures went forward concurrently with those of the Confederate authorities in their temporary capital at Montgomery, Alabama, but there was little coordination among them at first. Southern governors scrambled to reactivate their militias, offering commissions to almost any local worthy who could recruit and equip a company of volunteers. On March 6 the Confederate Congress authorized President Jefferson Davis to accept the enlistment of one hundred thousand volunteers. The seceding states faced an unprecedented challenge in organizing themselves for a modern war, however, and the raising and equipping of a Confederate army proceeded in a decidedly haphazard manner. Only gradually during the summer did a procedure evolve whereby the troops raised by the states were routinely mustered into Confederate service. The wonder was that by the end of the year the South actually succeeded in putting three hundred thousand men in the field.

In Texas many soldiers had originally volunteered to serve in the local patrols set up to deal with the imaginary threat of a slave rebellion the previous summer, and these units frequently became the nucleus of companies that would serve throughout the war. In April, Governor Clark issued an appeal for eight thousand volunteers for the Confederate army and appointed prominent citizens to recruit and train troops throughout the state. Soon dozens of independent companies seemed to spring out of the ground at almost every country crossroad.

Normally consisting of about one hundred men enrolled for a year, each company elected its own officers in accordance with traditional militia practice. These companies exhibited not only a motley appearance but carried a bewildering variety of arms, accouterments, and unit designations as well. As a rule, ten companies formed a regiment under the command of a colonel, and from four to six regiments made up a brigade, commanded by a brigadier general. Confederate cavalrymen were expected to supply their own weapons, equipment, and uniforms, as well as provide their own horses, for which they were promised a monthly stipend of twelve dollars, a sum equivalent to a private's wage. Given the simultaneous commitment of both public and private property for the cause of Southern defense, the variety of ammunition required, the chronic shortages of money and supplies, and the haste by which it was accomplished, the mobilization of the Texas communities presented countless scenes of utter but enthusiastic confusion.

In the midst of this tumult the news arrived that on April 12 Confederate guns had bombarded the Union garrison at Fort Sumter, South Carolina, forcing its surrender. The irrevocable act that Lincoln hoped to avert had at last occurred. Now that the Rebels had actually fired upon the American flag, Northern opinion rallied to the defense of the Union. Lincoln's first reaction to the fall of Sumter was to call upon the loyal states for seventy-five thousand volunteers to suppress the rebellion. This threat of coercion by the president was enough to provoke the secession of four states of the Upper South—Virginia, North Carolina, Tennessee, and Arkansas—and whip the bellicose mood in the new Confederacy to a fever pitch.[8]

The flow of eager recruits into the newly formed Texas companies now assumed the dimensions of a flood, and the authorities were soon swamped by more volunteers than they could organize, feed, equip, or train. Most Texans responded to the news from the East with their accustomed bravado. A Clarksville editor summed up the prevailing opinion that "it will not be Much of a war"; that the Northern fanatics would soon have their fill of playing soldier.[9] Governor Clark struck a properly defiant tone when he derisively pointed out that Lincoln had been conspicuously tardy in carrying out his threats. "All we ask," scoffed the governor, "is for them to come & give us a chance to *welcome* them."[10] Meanwhile, Clark cooperated with the Confederate authorities, who were trying to cope with the thousands of young, enthusiastic volunteers while working to develop a strategy whereby these recruits could be used with maximum effect. Should the Texans join in a triumphant march against the North, or should they be employed to defend their own state against invasion?

The organizers of the Third Texas Cavalry intended to accomplish both. The regiment owed its inception to the exaggerated fear that the most serious threat to the Lone Star State lay in Kansas. In the confusion of May 1861, Confederate authorities worried that hordes of fanatic Kansas abolitionists were poised to descend across the two hundred miles of Indian Territory to loot, burn, and destroy the defenseless towns and exposed farmsteads of North Texas. Antislavery guerrilla bands had already earned a fearsome reputation for their ruthless depredations along the Kansas-Missouri border before the war; the names of their leaders had become synonymous with the Yankee conspiracy to despoil the South. Many responsible Texans were convinced that these "Jayhawkers" were about to attack through Indian Territory, and the Confederate War Department acted early to secure the region.[11]

Indian Territory, which comprised the present state of Oklahoma, was the home of some 56,000 members of the Five Civilized Tribes—Cherokees, Choctaws, Chickasaws, Creeks, and Seminoles—who had settled the wooded uplands or cultivated the fertile valleys of the Arkansas, Canadian, and Red River basins in the eastern half of the territory. To the west, about 2,600 Plains Indians had been forced onto reservations in what is now western Oklahoma. With a settled population of less than 60,000 on about as many square miles, Indian Territory was an empty place indeed.

Yet because of the territory's strategic location, the new Confederate government launched both a diplomatic and a military initiative among the Indians. President Davis concluded a series of treaties of alliance with the tribes in the summer and fall of 1861. Concurrent with this diplomatic effort, the Confederacy encouraged the formation of Native American cavalry regiments to fight for the South, and four such units were soon raised. On May 13 the Confederate secretary of war commissioned Ben McCulloch a brigadier general, charged him with the defense of Indian Territory, and ordered him to set up his headquarters at Fort Smith, just across the Arkansas state line. The War Department promised to assign him a regiment of infantry, two regiments of cavalry, and two additional regiments of Indian troops just as soon as these volunteer forces could be raised.[12] Arriving at his duty station two weeks later, McCulloch was alarmed by reports that a dangerous Yankee guerrilla expedition was preparing to raid south from Kansas, and he urged his fellow Texans to "look to your arms and be ready for any emergency."[13]

Within a fortnight McCulloch's little army began to materialize as its various components marched to join their commander at Fort Smith. During the first weeks of June, Colonel Louis Hébert led his Third Louisiana Infantry into McCulloch's camp, and Colonel Thomas J. Churchill's First Arkansas Mounted Rifles reported for duty. In the meantime, Confederate recruiting officers back in Texas were mobilizing a regiment of volunteers for McCulloch who would fight the war together as the Third Texas Cavalry.

The organizer and commander of the new regiment was the same Elkanah Greer of Marshall who had spoken out so forcefully against Lincoln's election the previous fall. This thirty-five-year-old planter, son of a wealthy land speculator, had grown up in Holly Springs, Mississippi, and had served in Jefferson Davis's regiment during the Mexican War. For at least a decade he had stridently condemned what he called "the foul breath of Abolitionism" and the "diabolical impositions of the North on the free-born and liberty-loving Southerners."[14] Settling at Marshall in 1851, Greer married into the prominent Holcombe clan and repeatedly ran for public office as an ardent secessionist.

During the crisis of 1860 the fiery would-be politician served as a delegate to the Democratic convention at Charleston, South Carolina, recruited troops for the Southern cause, and as state commander of the Knights of the Golden Circle, conspired at an invasion of Mexico for the purpose of extending and perpetuating slavery.[15] He boasted that he had a thousand Knights "eager to take up the line of march,"[16] and promised his cohorts in the KGC that his Texas regiments were ready to "take possession of the States of Tamaulipas, Neuava [sic] Leon, Coahuila, and Chihuahua, and of them organize a Government, thereby forming . . . a nucleus around which our valiant Knights would soon rally."[17] Foiled in this Napoleonic design, Greer was still spoiling for a fight, and the Civil War came along just when he needed it.

The Confederate War Department issued him a colonel's commission and ordered him to raise a thousand volunteers for McCulloch's command. Through his fellow Knights scattered across East Texas, Greer could call upon a network of influential comrades who were in a position to rally to his banner the local volunteer companies then being formed. Moreover, his home town of Marshall, then inhabited by about four thousand people, was the commercial and political hub of East Texas and a vital link to New Orleans and the great world beyond. Consequently, when Greer issued his call for recruits, most of the men who eagerly responded came from those northeastern Texas counties that were economically and politically tributary to Marshall.

Having promulgated his appeal for volunteers, Greer repaired to Dallas, then "a pretty little town near the Trinity River," where his recruits were to rendezvous and muster into Confederate service.[18] Because he intended to join McCulloch in his campaign along the Kansas-Missouri border, Greer dubbed his still embryonic command the "South Kansas–Texas Regiment," in anticipation of its intended field of operations. Only later in the fall did the War Department assign the permanent designation of Third Texas Cavalry to the unit. By early June the dusty roads to Dallas were crowded by enthusiastic volunteers, hurrying to answer Greer's appeal and anticipating the first great adventure of their lives.

Each of the ten companies which began converging on the rendezvous point had been raised earlier as local defense forces in various parts of East Texas. These companies, which ranged in size from 96 to 115 officers and men, had chosen for themselves names suggesting prowess in battle or memorializing some local dignitary. The Harrison County volunteers called themselves "The Texas Hunters," for example; Smith County sent "The Ed. Clark Invincibles." All these colorful epithets would be superceded by more prosaic alphabetical designations as soon as the units arrived in Dallas.

At the head of each contingent rode its captain, generally the substantial citizen who had taken the initiative in raising and equipping the unit in the first place. All these local commanders were men of mature years and prominent leaders in their communities; most were wealthy, by the standards of their time and place. They enjoyed an average wealth of $21,596 each, almost three and a half times that of the general population at large. In a state where only one in every four white households owned slaves, all these original captains were slaveholders.[19]

Captain Thomas W. Winston organized Company A principally from the elite class of cotton planters in eastern Harrison County. Most of the men in Company B hailed from Rusk County and elected as their commander Captain Robert H. Cumby, a former legislator and one of the richest men in the area. Cherokee County recruits formed Company C, under the command of District Clerk Francis M. Taylor. The blackland prairie farms of Hunt and Fannin counties provided most of the troopers for Company D. These men elected Stephen M. Hale, a forty-seven-year-old farmer from Greenville, as their captain. Daniel M. Short, a Shelbyville lawyer, led 114 volunteers from San Augustine and Shelby counties to form Company E.[20]

Captain Isham Chism raised Company F primarily from the prairie counties of Kaufman and Dallas. The 107 men in Company G enlisted at Jefferson, the premier river port of Texas and the seat of Marion County. They chose Hinche P. Mabry, a local lawyer and legislator, as their captain. Company H's recruits from the forested hills of Upshur County elected Jonathan L.

Table 1. Original Command of the Third Texas Cavalry Regiment, August 31, 1861

CO.	NAME	RANK	AGE	PLACE OF BIRTH	COUNTY	OCCUPATION	WEALTH	NO. OF SLAVES
				Regimental Command and Staff				
	E. B. Greer	Col.	35	Tenn.	Harrison	Farmer	$12,000	12
	W. P. Lane	Lt. Col.	44	Ireland	Harrison	Merchant	9,000	6
	G. W. Chilton	Maj.	33	Ky.	Smith	Lawyer	5,500	5
	M. D. Ector, Adj.	Capt.	39	Ga.	Rusk	Lawyer	29,000	20
	H. Harris, Q.M.	Capt.						
	J. R. Armstrong, Com.	Capt.	38	Tenn.	Rusk	Lawyer	5,500	0
				Company Commanders				
A	T. W. Winston	Capt.	32	Ala.	Harrison	Farmer	36,470	31
B	R. H. Cumby	Capt.	35	Va.	Rusk	Farmer	60,600	30
C	F. M. Taylor	Capt.	33	Ala.	Cherokee	Dist. Clerk	10,300	7
D	S. M. Hale	Capt.	47	Va.	Hunt	Farmer	3,060	1
E	D. M. Short	Capt.	42	Del.	Shelby	Lawyer	15,000	10
F	I. Chism	Capt.	43	Miss.	Kaufman	Farmer	15,315	8
G	H. P. Mabry	Capt.	31	Ga.	Marion	Lawyer	17,000	2
H	J. L. Russell	Capt.	35	N.C.	Upshur	Farmer	4,220	2
I	J. A. Bryan	Capt.	42	Ala.	Cass	Farmer	13,000	12
K	D. Y. Gaines	Capt.	28	Fla.	Smith	Farmer	41,000	37
	Mean		37				$18,464	12

Sources: U.S. National Archives, Compiled Service Records of Confederate Soldiers Who Served in Organizations from the State of Texas (Washington, D.C., 1960). M No. 323, Rolls 18–23; U.S. National Archives, Population Schedules of the Eighth Census of the United States, 1860 (Washington. D.C., 1967). M No. 653. Rolls 1287–1308.

Russell, a former state senator, to lead them. Cass County mobilized 115 volunteers under the command of John Arthur Bryan to form Company I. Finally, David Y. Gaines, a twenty-eight-year-old planter, raised a Smith County contingent designated Company K.[21]

Like other Confederate volunteers, these men had to supply most of their own arms, uniforms, mounts, and equipment, often at considerable personal sacrifice. The father of Private John Long, for instance, admonished his son to "be careful of your money John; it has cost me about six hundred dollars to fit you to go out."[22] (That sum represented about one-tenth of the Long family's resources.) Since many of the men of Company B did not own horses, wranglers drove a herd of unbroken mustangs into the Rusk County seat, where the would-be cavalrymen could buy them cheap and break them on their own, often with agonizing results. Sympathetic citizens of a Cherokee County village all chipped in to supply Bugler Charley Watts with a horse and tack so he could ride off to the rendezvous with Company C.[23]

Each of the home counties scrambled to collect clothing, shoes, and blankets for the troops. As evidence of their patriotism, the Rusk County commissioners floated a $1,000 bond issue to supply Company B, while Marion County citizens pledged $10,000 for the cause. Less-affluent Van Zandt County cautiously committed itself for $200 per month. Kaufman County officials initially authorized an expenditure of $300 from their treasury for Company F; after a year of learning how expensive war could be, they would be forced to borrow an additional $10,000 for the purpose.

Since the troops were raised from so many localities and under such widely divergent circumstances, they presented a bewildering variety in their clothing, the arms they carried, and the quality of their leadership. A public subscription in prosperous Harrison County collected enough money to equip each of the men in Company A with a smart new uniform in cadet gray, but most of the regiment were not so lucky. The troopers of Company B had to purchase their own uniforms, and in so doing strove for style over function. They chose black coats, vests, hats, and boots, and acquired a quantity of heavy brown jeans from the Texas prison shops sufficient to put them all in breeches. They looked fine on parade, but their uniforms were stifling hot under the June sun. They grabbed whatever weapons they could find: a haphazard assortment of rusty carbines, ancient shotguns, and squirrel rifles, for the most part. Many of the recruits carried no firearms at all. The Rusk County volunteers, for example, had to be content with Bowie knives fashioned in a local blacksmith shop.[24]

Equally varied in terms of experience, competence, and talent, were the officers elected to command the individual companies. A few, like Lieutenant Jiles S. Boggess, of Company B, or Captain Short, of Company E, had seen action in the Texas Rangers or the Mexican War, but most were as blissfully ignorant of the ruthless nature of war as the men they commanded. Despite such inexperience, however, several of the officers quickly demonstrated a capacity for command. Lawyer Mathew D. Ector enlisted as a private in the spring of 1861; fourteen months later he found himself a brigadier general in the Army of Tennessee. He lived long enough to see a West Texas county named in his honor. Captain Mabry proved himself an intrepid officer who rose to lead a brigade.

Captain Taylor, of Company C, "a noble, brave, and patriotic man," was especially popular with his troops despite his reputation as a disciplinarian.[25] Hardly had his company been formed than he began to demonstrate the force of his personality. When Private George Buxton, a chronic drunk and inveterate brawler, involved himself in an altercation with civilians, Taylor subdued him by personally pinning the man down on a manure pile while his sergeant applied copious bucketsfull of cold water to Buxton's prostrate form. By constrast, the commander of Company D, Captain Hale, was better known for his rustic manners and irregular grammar. In comparatively modest circumstances, Hale inspired an affectionate condescension from his fellow officers of the planter-politician class. Hale's second-in-command, Lieutenant Daniel Deupree, was so unpopular with his men that they voted him out of office within two months.[26]

Despite the variety of uniforms, the deficiency in arms, and the disparity in the qualities of their leaders, all ten of the companies shared one common and indelible experience as they marched off to war: the solemn yet festive farewell they received from their loved ones who stayed behind. In each case, the departure of the local company from its little hometown was attended by a huge assemblage of well-wishers; patriotic speeches, the formal presentation of a company ensign, and frequently a barbecue formed the program.[27] The leave-taking of Company C from Rusk, county seat of Cherokee County, may serve as a case in point.

The governor had appointed Brigadier General Joseph L. Hogg, a veteran of the Mexican War, delegate to the Secession Convention, and most prominent political leader in the county, to recruit and train troops for the Confederacy. By May 1, Hogg had enlisted a hundred men, who styled themselves "The Lone Star Defenders." Some of the recruits dropped out before mobilization, but sixty-two Cherokeans remained in the unit to form the nucleus of Company C, and they enticed enough brothers, cousins, and neighbors into the unit to bring it up to a strength of 114 officers and men. Since Hogg himself was destined for a higher command in the Rebel army, the troops chose Captain Taylor as their commander in his stead.

On June 10, Taylor's company received a rousing send-off from the 395 people who made up the population of Rusk at that time. From the steps of a hotel on the courthouse square, General Hogg addressed the troops in a tone of high seriousness, reminding them that they faced a future fraught with uncertainty for their country as well as danger to themselves: "Don't ever jeer at or mock any of your comrades who cannot stand the fire of the enemy," he admonished them. "Some of you, perhaps, will find yourselves unable to do so."[28] Sobered by these reflections, the would-be cavalrymen accepted a flag from the hands of local women who had made it and received the tearful blessings of their loved ones. "Even rough, hard-faced men . . . [who] hadn't shed a tear since their boyhood boo-hoo'd and were unable to speak the word 'good-by'."[29] But once on the road to Dallas, the young men cantered northward in a carefree and sportive procession, fortifying their spirits occasionally with free drinks offered at saloons along the way. Thus the future troopers of the Third Texas Cavalry took leave of their homeland.

CHAPTER 3

The Boys from East Texas, June 1861

JOINED BY bonds of kinship, friendship, and local loyalty, each of the constituent companies in Greer's regiment had a character and identity of its own. Yet by examining what is known about the lives of these young recruits and the amateur officers who commanded them, it is possible to draw general conclusions about the regiment as a whole and about the region from which its members sprang. In sketching this composite portrait of the unit, one must consider the geographical, demographic, economic, and political dimensions of East Texas society as exemplified by these volunteers.[1]

Ninety-eight percent of the 1,097 original members in the regiment were residents of northeastern Texas in 1860. This region, a western outpost of the Deep South, was bounded on the west by the Trinity River, and stretched eastward about 160 miles to the Louisiana border, encompassing the area between the Red River on the north and the lower Neches River on the south. The volunteers' homes were widely scattered; all but two of the twenty-eight counties of northeastern Texas provided troops for Colonel Greer. Rusk County, the most populous in the state, led the way with 116 recruits.[2]

Before the war northeastern Texas seemed a land of promise. The great cotton boom of the previous decade had lured thousands of substantial farm families from the Lower South into the rich bottomlands of the Sabine, Neches, and Red rivers. In the ten years after 1850 the white population of East Texas more than doubled, and more than three-quarters of these people were directly engaged in agriculture. The amount of Texas land under cultivation quadrupled in the space of a decade; cotton production expanded more than sevenfold. When the war came, East Texas appeared to be riding a wave of unlimited prosperity generated by cotton and slave labor, and its people were confident of their future.

Recognizing the limitations inherent in defining rigid categories among the economic classes of antebellum society, it is useful nevertheless to identify four groups among the white population. At the apex of the pyramid stood those large planters who owned twenty or more slaves and the members of the various professions—lawyers, physicians, and merchants, for the most part—who were allied with them. Though constituting a minority of the white population (only 14 percent in Harrison County, for example), the planter class was disproportionately influential in the political life of the region. On the major issues of the age, the opinions and predilections of the elite minority generally prevailed.

A second group of slaveholders—prosperous landowners who held fewer than twenty slaves each—constituted an upper middle class that included about one-fifth of the white population. Yeoman farmers without slaves, who produced corn, livestock, and a little cotton through their own labor, made up the third and most numerous category of whites. Then there were the poor whites, defined for our purposes as those who owned real property worth less than $250 (about eighty acres at the time). Finally, of the quarter million Texans who lived east of the Trinity in 1860, almost a third were slaves.[3]

Despite the promising economic development of northeastern Texas in the prewar years, most of the region was still only a decade and a half removed from the frontier; crucial elements of its infrastructure, as well as important social amenities, were notably lacking. Wages were low, and capital was scarce in the state. A white farmhand might expect to earn $15.00 a month, while a carpenter's wage averaged $2.40 per day. The average worth of property per household was only $6,393 in 1860. There was but a single millionaire in all of Texas, and only 263 citizens owned more than $100,000 in property. San Antonio, the state's largest city, counted just 8,235 inhabitants.

In the northeastern quadrant of the state there was little manufacturing, save for an occasional sawmill, cotton gin, or blacksmith shop. Land was abundant but also cheap: it brought an average price of three dollars per acre. Transportation was almost as primitive as it had been on the eastern seaboard a century earlier. The numerous streams flowing across East Texas were too shallow to offer regular service by steamboat but sufficiently broad and muddy to impede overland traffic in that bridgeless age. Near the Louisiana border the towns of Marshall and Jefferson enjoyed relatively easy access to shipping on the Red River, and the lower reaches of the Sabine River provided a direct route to the Gulf of Mexico. But most people in the interior counties still did their traveling on horseback and hauled their cotton and corn to market by ox wagon. Unfortunately for the economic development of Texas, the onset of the Civil War interrupted its first real burst of railway building. Though some substantial lines had been completed along the Gulf Coast, the commencement of hostilities caught the northeast with only two short lines between Marshall and Jefferson and the Louisiana border.[4]

Perceptive sojourners from both the North and the South found Texas east of the Trinity to be a rude and undeveloped region still in transition between a raw frontier and a settled society. Though they would have agreed on little else, the Connecticut Yankee Frederick Law Olmsted and the Louisiana plantation belle Kate Stone were as one in the distaste they expressed for the squalid villages, dilapidated farms, and loutish inhabitants of East Texas in the years around 1860. Olmsted found the male population lazy and crude and the women worn out before their time by the rigors of their existence. As for cultivated minds, he encountered none. "In the whole journey through Eastern Texas," Olmsted complained, "we did not see one of the inhabitants look into a newspaper or a book."[5]

Forced to take refuge in East Texas during the Civil War, twenty-two-year-old Kate Stone was shocked by her first impressions of the place. "There must be something in the air of Texas fatal to beauty," she wrote. "We have not seen a good-looking or educated person since we entered the state. We are in the dark corner."[6] A transplanted Georgian lamented a few years later that northeastern Texas provided "society the poorest I ever saw." The inhabitants seemed to be "satisfied with their ignorance and rough new country customs."[7] East Texans still had a long way to go.

In the whole state there were no free public schools, although some twelve hundred subscription schools or private academies were scattered among the villages and towns. They may have reached perhaps half the white children of school age, and no formal education for slaves existed.[8] Though growing fast economically, East Texas was still an undeveloped region on the eve of the Civil War.

The homeland of Greer's recruits was by no means totally uniform in character, however. North Texas east of the Trinity consisted of three loosely defined subregions whose distinctiveness in topography, landscape, and economy could be easily recognized by a traveler riding westward from, say, Shreveport, Louisiana, to Dallas. The tier of counties along the Louisiana border were located in the piney woods whose low rolling hills rose above the fertile plains of the Red River and the Sabine. This area had been settled principally from Alabama and Mississippi; the market for its cotton lay down the Red River at New Orleans, and the spirit of that great emporium shaped its perceptions of the world.

In the piney woods the essence of the Deep South was most pervasive, and the plantation economy was most highly developed and prosperous. As a case in point, Harrison County listed 8,784 slaves among its total population of 15,001, more than any other county in the state, and ranked second among Texas counties as a cotton producer. Marshall, the county seat, was a hotbed of secessionist sentiment and the home constituency for both Senator Wigfall and Governor Clark. Only one out of every twenty Harrison County voters opposed secession in the February referendum.

Just to the west, a second tier of counties occupied parts of the post-oak belt, whose higher and more undulating terrain

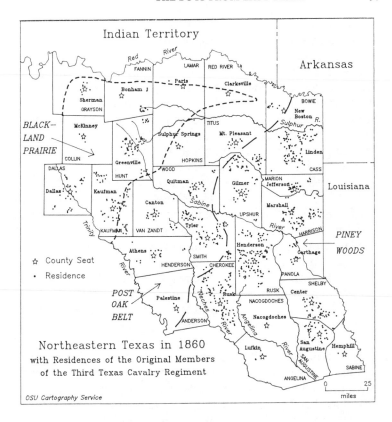

Northeastern Texas in 1860
with Residences of the Original Members
of the Third Texas Cavalry Regiment

OSU Cartography Service

rose along the upper reaches of the Neches, the Angelina, and
the upper Sabine rivers. These hill counties were originally covered by both pine and hardwoods; here were found loftier and
more panoramic vistas than those of the river plains to the east.
Yet the sandy soil was also less fertile, access to market was
more difficult, and the economy was less dominated by planta-
tion-style agriculture than in the piney woods. Farmers produced less cotton and owned fewer slaves. While the counties
of the post-oak belt were deeply Southern in sentiment, there
was a more even balance between independent small farmers
and large planters, and agriculture was more diversified, with a
heavy emphasis on corn to feed families and livestock. Still,
these people supported the states' rights position just as avidly

as did their neighbors to the east. In the referendum, for instance, only 4 percent of Smith County voters opposed the dissolution of the Union.

The third tier of counties situated just east of the upper Trinity River lay wholly or in part on the rich soil of the blackland prairie. This subregion had been settled chiefly by pioneers from the Upper South—Tennesseans for the most part—who had no tradition of large-scale cotton cultivation. They grew wheat instead. Though their black soil would later prove highly productive for cotton, little was grown on the prairie during the antebellum period, and few slaves were brought into the area. Only 142 of the 6,053 white Hunt Countians owned black bondsmen, but this slaveholding minority controlled almost half the wealth in the county and generally ran its affairs. A similar proportion prevailed in neighboring Van Zandt and Kaufman counties.

The blackland prairie was the realm of the self-sufficient yeoman farmer, who, though supportive of the institution of slavery, was generally cool toward the doctrine of secession. In the February referendum of 1861 the prairie voters registered a divided opinion on the issue. Some 45 percent of the electorate of Hunt County rejected secession; a majority of 58.2 percent of Fannin County voters did likewise. Yet when Colonel Greer issued his call to arms, hundreds of high-spirited young men abandoned their blackland farms to answer it. The reason for this apparent paradox, in which enthusiasm for war seemed to outpace economic interest and public commitment to the secessionist cause, lay in the disproportionate influence of the slaveholding minority among the population.[9]

Northeastern Texas, then, was relatively poor in the west, moderately well-off in the middle, and most prosperous in the eastern counties near the Louisiana border. The men in the regiment reflected the economic diversity of their region. Volunteers who hailed from the rich bottomland farms of the Sabine or Red River valleys tended to enjoy far more affluent backgrounds than those who enlisted from the forested hills or upland prairies farther west. Recruits from the piney-woods plantation zone came from households with mean property holdings worth about three and one-half times the state average.

Because they were raised largely from the planter class of Harrison, San Augustine, and Shelby counties, the soldiers in Companies A and E were the wealthiest in the regiment. Lon and Americus Cartwright, sons of a San Augustine merchant and land speculator, enlisted as privates in Company E. With half a million dollars' worth of property, their father was the seventh richest man in the state. Private J. W. Hood's father possessed assets in Harrison County worth almost a quarter-million dollars.

Yeoman farmers for the most part, volunteers from the post-oak belt came from families owning almost twice the state mean. Typical of this group were the men in Companies C and H, from Cherokee and Upshur counties, respectively. Only seven of the Cherokeans and five of the Upshurites lived in households worth more than $30,000. Private Calvin M. Roark's father, for instance, had immigrated from Tennessee in 1834 and surveyed much of East Texas for the early empresarios who colonized the area. In the process, the elder Roark had accumulated $20,000 worth of land and seventeen slaves on his own. The father of Private Thomas N. Pitts had come from Georgia to settle in Upshur County in 1854. By 1860 he had increased his holdings to property worth $33,250. While a few of the soldiers in Companies C and H came from households which listed no property at all in the 1860 census, most of the men sprang from yeoman farmer stock with moderate holdings in land or slaves.

Recruits residing in the blackland-prairie region came from poorer families owning less than the Texas average in property. But a handful were exceptions. For example, Lieutenant Dan Deupree ran a Fannin County store worth about $15,000. When his place of business burned down during the summer of 1860, he became a militant defender of the South and helped organize Company D. The Reverend T. P. Andrews, who owned $21,000 in property and ten slaves at Kaufman, sent two sons into Company F.[10]

Considered as a whole, the officers and men of the regiment came disproportionately from the wealthier classes in their society. After all, as cavalrymen they were dependent upon family resources substantial enough to supply their own mounts and equipment. On average, the officers and men together came from households worth $12,812, twice the mean holdings of all

Table 2. Original Members of the Third Texas Cavalry Regiment: Company Rolls of August 31, 1861

CO.	COUNTY OF ENROLLMENT	NUMBER ON ROLL	FOUND ON 1860 CENSUS		MEAN WEALTH PER HOUSEHOLD ($)		PERCENT OF HOUSEHOLDS OWNING SLAVES		MEAN NUMBER OF SLAVES PER SLAVE-OWNING HOUSEHOLD	
			NO.	%	OFF.	E.M.	OFF.	E.M.	OFF.	E.M.
A	Harrison	104	80	77	$38,012	$25,073	100%	76%	32	18
B	Rusk	112	103	92	30,150	13,664	100	54	15	16
C	Cherokee	114	102	89	9,240	8,082	50	51	6	10
D	Hunt and Fannin	115	98	85	4,902	4,869	50	26	4	5
E	Shelby and San Augustine	114	96	84	8,043	28,186	33	64	10	12
F	Kaufman	104	78	75	7,891	6,539	75	36	5	5
G	Marion	107	92	86	18,550	11,798	75	50	8	11
H	Upshur	96	70	73	17,240	7,308	100	45	7	10
I	Cass	115	101	88	13,348	10,480	100	53	14	13
K	Smith	110	109	99	12,975	10,718	50	64	21	12
	Reg. Command	6	5	83	12,200	—	80	—	11	—
	Total Regiment	1,097	934	85%	$15,470	$12,683	80%	52%	13	12
	Mean for all Officers and Enlisted Men				12,812		53%		12	

Sources: U.S. National Archives, Compiled Service Records of Confederate Soldiers Who Served in Organizations from the State of Texas (Washington, D.C., 1960). M No. 323. Rolls 18–23; U.S. National Archives. Population Schedules of the Eighth Census of the United States. 1860 (Washington, D.C.. 1967). M No. 653. Rolls 1287–1308.

Texas families. Seventeen percent of the original volunteers were identified with the elite class of planters and professional men; about four out of ten represented households employing from one to nineteen slaves. Approximately one-third of the troops came from nonslaveholding yeoman families owning more than eighty acres of land. Only 14 percent sprang from the ranks of the poor.[11]

Within the regiment there was a substantial correlation between economic class and positions of command, not least because the well-to-do enjoyed superior educational advantages. Although the men elected their own officers, the elite had greater chances for promotion than their poorer comrades. Twenty-three percent of the planter-professional group received commissions during their service, but only 11 percent of the men from households owning fewer than twenty slaves did so. Seven percent of soldiers from yeoman families became officers, while 6 percent of the poor were commissioned.[12]

The majority of the men who enlisted in Greer's regiment also had a personal stake in the future of slavery. Since land was so cheap, slaves were the chief measure of wealth, and almost half the property in northeastern Texas (46 percent) consisted of human chattels. More than half the original volunteers in the regiment (53 percent) came from slaveholding households. Some of these establishments were quite large. Private Neil Hall's father owned sixty black bondsmen, for example, and Sergeant James Stovall oversaw seventy-eight slaves on a plantation operated by a Confederate congressman. One hundred and six of the original volunteers came from households owning twenty or more slaves each. The median number of bondsmen per household was eight.[13]

The recollections of a few of these African Americans have been recorded and preserved, and from this record one can learn a little about the East Texans in their role as masters in a slave society. Given the conditions of their servitude—unremitting toil and occasional abuse—former bondsmen showed themselves remarkably free of bitterness and resentment toward their former masters, at least in the retrospective of old age. For example, Private J. W. Hood's father owned forty-nine slaves in Harrison County. From a perspective of more than seventy years, one of these black men recalled witnessing "one of my sisters whip 'cause she didn't spin 'nough. Dey pull de clothes down to her waist and laid her down on de stomach and lash her with de rawhide quirt." Yet this same witness remembered his master as "one de bes' bosses round dat country. . . . When dey need whippin' he done it, but when it come to feedin' he done dat right, too." [14]

The father of Private Iredell Thomas, of San Augustine County, also owned forty-nine slaves and was remembered by one of them as "kind and good . . . and wouldn't whip nobody without de cause." [15] Private Will Caven's father was recalled fondly as a paragon of affectionate paternalism by two of his twenty-nine blacks. [16] Captain Cumby, of Company B, worked thirty slaves on his Rusk County plantation. One of his former bondsmen, reflecting over his long life, acknowledged that he "allus had de good marster. He sho' was good to us, but you knows dat ain't de same as bein' free." [17]

By occupation, the officers and men of the regiment were not entirely typical of their agrarian society: while three out of four of all white Texans made their living from farming, just over half of the soldiers (54 percent) listed occupations in agriculture. Their occupational status was generally superior to the men of a typical Confederate regiment and far higher than that in the Union army. Four out of ten Union soldiers had been either a skilled or an unskilled laborer before the war; only 15 percent of Greer's troopers had been so employed. Only 8 percent of Union recruits followed white-collar, commercial, or professional pursuits prior to service, while almost one-fifth of the enlistees in Greer's regiment came from that class. There were two dozen lawyers, twenty-three schoolteachers, sixteen physicians, five "gentlemen," and one loafer on the original regimental rolls. [18]

Some two hundred men were heads of households with families to worry about. Their concerns could be considerable, as the following letter to Corporal Oyer Funderburgh, of Company K, attests. He had been in the Confederate army only nineteen days when his wife back in Smith County informed him of the birth of his second daughter and begged him to come home. "I am getting a long very well considring my mind being tor up the way it is," she wrote:

> Oh me, if you wer hear today my heart wold be releaved. To think of twelv long monthes. I canot stand it now hear, my two little children to think of. Por little Lillin . . . is calling you now. You now that maks me feel misebul indeed. . . . Oyer, think [of] the too little girles and come home. Forsake your Companey and all outher object. I think if you will reflect rightly you will. Oyer, I have prayed for you to reterne befor your time is out, and I hope my prear will be heard.[19]

Despite those pleas, Corporal Funderburgh did not forsake his company.

Far more carefree than the family men were the students who enlisted: they amounted to 10 percent of the volunteers. Virtually all these young men came from privileged backgrounds, their families enjoying about four times the average wealth of all Texas households. Fifteen of the recruits in Company C, for example, had studied at the Presbyterian college in Larissa, an oasis of genteel cultivation amid the piney hills of Cherokee County. Private Victor M. Rose was a student at Centenary College when the war began. Americus Cartwright was an alumnus of Kentucky Military Institute, while Harvey Gregg had attended Virginia Military Institute. Bugler Albert Blocker, the sixteen-year-old son of a wealthy Harrison County planter, was enrolled in boarding school when the call to arms went out.[20]

Lieutenant Dan Alley was a student at Upshur County's Murray Institute at the beginning of the war. Stirred by all the excitement, the headmaster of that academy addressed his charges in the following vein: "Young men, war has been declared. All you that desire to go in defense of his home and country can go with my best wishes, my sincere prayers for success. God bless you, guide and direct you safely through your perilous lives."[21] So inspired were his students that they immediately emptied the school, leaving its founder no choice but to close its doors. Alley himself rushed home to Jefferson to enlist in Captain Mabry's company.

The volunteers who flocked to Greer's banner were predisposed by heritage to fight for the South. Of those members of the regiment whose state of birth is known, six out of ten came from the Lower South; Alabama led in this regard with 211 natives. A third came from the Upper South. Tennessee, the birthplace of 155 recruits, was ahead in this category. Only forty-one men were natives of Northern states, and but twenty of the volunteers had been born abroad. Seven of these were native Norwegians from their settlements in Kaufman and Henderson counties.

The median age for privates in the regiment was twenty-three years, which conformed closely to the ages at enlistment of other Confederate units from Texas. A wide range of ages existed, however, from Nelson Walling, the oldest man in the regiment at sixty-three, to thirteen-year-old Walton Ector, who came along from Henderson with his father, Mathew.[22]

Just as the volunteers in Greer's new regiment generally represented families of substantial wealth, they also included a larger than normal proportion of the political elite. Some of the recruits were prominent in state government, others had occupied county or local elective office, and many had played an active role in the successful agitation for secession. Seven of the original members of the regiment had served in the state legislature; all but one of these mustered in as an officer. More than a dozen county and local officials enlisted as well. James Connally and Ben Durham, sheriffs respectively of Cass and Anderson counties, enrolled as lieutenants, while Dr. A. D. Rice, the former mayor of Dallas, enlisted as a private.[23]

Appropriately, many of those men who had campaigned most zealously for secession found their way into the regiment. Three former delegates to the Secession Convention joined Greer's unit; others had worked at the county level for separation from the Union. Though only twenty-five, Private John Coleman had been active in the secession movement in Harrison County and subsequently served with distinction as a Confederate soldier. Private Jim Farr, a Hunt County attorney, had been a secessionist leader in his area; Private Tom Greenwood, a lawyer from Athens, helped organize the Democratic Party in Texas.[24]

To be sure, most of the men in the regiment were too young

to have achieved much prominence themselves, but a large number came from families of considerable political influence. More than a dozen recruits were sons of men who had served in the Texas legislature. The father of Private Tom Jennings was a former state attorney general. John and Hillery Taylor's father was speaker of the state House of Representatives. The Gragard brothers, Nicholas and John, and the Reierson brothers, Christian and Otto, were heirs of prominent leaders in the movement for Norwegian immigration to Texas.[25]

Local and county office holders seemed to vie with each other in sending their offspring to the service, setting, it may be supposed, a patriotic example for their constituents. From Smith County, three commissioners and the treasurer dispatched their boys to the regiment; in Cherokee County, the judge, five current or former commissioners, and the sheriff did likewise. Judges in Cass and San Augustine counties, and the sheriffs of Harrison, San Augustine, and Shelby counties offered their youthful heirs to the cause. Assessor Nat Anderson and Treasurer J. H. Gee sent their sons out from Hunt County. Lieutenant Alley's father had established the town of Jefferson; that of Private Tom Pitts was the founder of Pittsburg; Private John W. Smith's father founded Jacksonville. Seven of the youths were sons of delegates to the Secession Convention, and Private John B. Reagan was the nephew of the Confederate postmaster general.[26] No wonder some of the young men thought of themselves as "the flower and the chivalry" of East Texas.[27]

The reception each company encountered along its route to Dallas and the extravagant welcome the men received at their rendezvous point only reenforced their exalted opinion of themselves as "the very flower of the land."[28] At every village on their way an adoring populace turned out in droves to regale the men with sumptuous banquets and flights of oratory celebrating their valor. At Dallas the mobilization of Greer's regiment was the biggest event that ever hit the place. Its 775 inhabitants turned out repeatedly with cheers and unstinting hospitality as the various companies arrived in their town, paraded around the courthouse square, and found campgrounds at well-watered and shady sites in the nearby countryside.[29]

None of the Dallasites were more delighted than the local

belles, who observed with fascination the sudden descent of hundreds of young cavaliers into their otherwise uneventful lives. The youthful troopers naturally reciprocated this admiration by the "Prairie Girls," and many a budding romance flourished in the soft June nights. A Cherokee County private confessed tactfully to his sister that in Dallas he found "some of the best-favored girls, nearly, I ever saw."[30]

Greer's regiment was the first to be organized for out-of-state service. To participate in the historic event and take advantage of the crowds it attracted, a gaggle of political celebrities accompanied the troops to the rendezvous. For those citizens who admired a good oration there was always someone ready to oblige. Oran Roberts, the president of the Secession Convention, was present to speak eloquently on every occasion, and Richard Hubbard, another champion of disunion, maintained his reputation as the "Demosthenes of Texas." Moreover, many of the local worthies who had enlisted in the various companies were campaigning hard for election to the regimental staff and contended vigorously with each other for a chance to talk. The Smith County contingent brought its own preacher along in the person of Lieutenant Williamson Milburn. Wasting no time in getting down to business, he organized a preaching at the Dallas Masonic Hall.[31]

On June 13, Milburn also assisted in a service at the fairgrounds in which the assembled troops observed the official Confederate Fast Day. The text chosen was Joel 2:5–12, whose verses speak of "a strong people set in battle array" before whom "the earth shall quake" and "the heavens shall tremble." The sermon presented in this service was focused upon the presumption that future historians of the war would conclude that "we were victorious because we were *right*, and because God himself was honored and worshipped by the men, women and children of the country."[32] As if summoned for the occasion, the "magnificent streamer of pure diaphanous luminosity" of the Great Comet of 1861 burst across the sky a few nights later.[33] There were many Americans that summer who regarded the celestial apparition as a portent of impending disaster, but the young volunteers and the enthusiastic crowds around them in that prairie village interpreted it as a sign of God's blessing on their endeavor.[34]

Against this continuo of inspirational rhetoric and celestial spectacle, Greer proceeded with the more prosaic business of organizing his regiment. The men were sworn into Confederate service on June 13, and they began in turn to elect their company and regimental officers. They chose as Greer's executive officer by a wide margin Walter Paye Lane, an Irish adventurer of forty-four who had already become a legend in his own time. He had seen service at the battle of San Jacinto and later commanded his own cavalry battalion in the Mexican War. For a decade thereafter, he had made and lost several fortunes in various western mining ventures before settling uneasily into the mercantile life of Marshall. Lane was a colorful fellow, full of blarney and bombast, but his courage and resourcefulness under fire would vindicate his own high opinion of himself.[35]

With somewhat less enthusiasm, the men elected George W. Chilton, of Tyler, to serve as their regimental major. Thirty-three years old, Chilton, who came from a prominent Kentucky family, had moved to Tyler in 1850 and had married well. There he practiced law and built a flourishing political career upon his fiery oratory and uncompromising proslavery stance. One of Greer's comrades in the Knights of the Golden Circle, Chilton took the position that the United States should reopen the African slave trade, outlawed since 1807, on the grounds that the South was languishing for lack of labor. Every white person should have a black slave to perform menial tasks so that the master race might concentrate its energies on self-improvement. As Chilton explained it, God had after all ordained physical labor for the blacks, and American slavery was in any case a distinct improvement over the African barbarism that the bondsmen had formerly known. Chilton owned five slaves, whose labor had doubtless made it possible for him to represent Smith County in the state legislature as well as serve in the Secession Convention.[36]

Greer had brought Captain Hannibal Harris, his quartermaster, with him from the temporary Confederate capital at Montgomery. Opinions differed about Harris: "No regiment in the service had . . . a better quartermaster"[37] was the verdict of one soldier, while another described him as "incompetent and worthless."[38] Greer appointed as his commissary officer Captain James Armstrong, a thirty-eight-year-old lawyer from Henderson and another veteran of the Secession Convention. Recognizing immediately the superior talents of Lieutenant Ector of Company B, Greer promoted him to the position of adjutant. Like the company commanders, the regimental staff of the newly formed regiment was drawn from the economic and political elite of East Texas.

Having successfully uprooted themselves from the familiar haunts of civilian life, the freshly minted soldiers chafed impatiently to begin their march to Fort Smith, where General McCulloch anxiously awaited them. They were obliged, however, to while away almost a month at Dallas in anticipation of the arrival of a shipment of vital supplies from San Antonio. The arms and equipment were part of the huge store of Federal materiel that McCulloch captured when he occupied the United States arsenal in the Alamo city the previous February. Especially crucial to Greer's calculations was the expected delivery of a battery of confiscated Yankee artillery, for he had none of his own. The gunners, organized by Captain John Good, of Dallas, and Lieutenant James Douglas, of Tyler, were ready; they awaited only the shipment of cannon to be off. Good's First Texas Battery would serve with Greer's regiment throughout the first year of the war.[39]

Acutely embarrassed by the long delay in the arrival of the wagon train from San Antonio with their supplies, Greer's officers blamed their inactivity variously on the incompetence of state or Confederate officials and used the time as well as they could to train their green and ill-equipped men. The recruits spent about half of each day in cavalry drill and the rest of their time loitering about their camp or around the Dallas square, playing foolish pranks on each other or admiring the local girls. Some used the opportunity to have their photographs taken, with pistol and knife prominently displayed.

Though life among the friendly people of Dallas County was pleasant enough, many of the troopers grew restive. In the army less than a month, they were "getting tired staying in one place so long." [40] A few of them simply went back home, where they became the butt of local contempt. Sheriff Long, of Rusk, thought it advisable to warn his son against the fate of one such miscreant: "Everyone is hissing him everywhere he goes," the father wrote. "John, I want you to go as far as the company goes & not to return till the company returns. . . . I would rather never see you again than for you to come off as he has." [41]

At last the three dozen freight wagons bearing the supplies from San Antonio began to straggle into Dallas on July 6. The equipment included Sibley tents, camp cooking gear, and a consignment of 1,550 brass-mounted pistols sufficient to arm most of the command. The prize delivery, however, consisted of a splendid battery of four six-pounder cannons with the mules and caissons necessary to move them. Greer assigned these pieces to Captain Good's artillery and distributed some of the small arms immediately, but many of his men would have to await arrival at Fort Smith to receive their weapons. [42]

The colonel, spurred on by urgent appeals from General McCulloch, had resolved that he could delay his march northward no longer. Without waiting for the formal presentation of the regimental flag by the ladies of Dallas, he roused his troops out of their pleasant encampments on July 9 and marched them to McKinney, thirty miles farther up the road. There the regiment remained only long enough to form up for its trek to the seat of war. With colors fluttering proudly, and supremely confident of their prowess, the still untested warriors resumed their march toward the Red River on July 13. Young Lieutenant Douglas assured his sweetheart back in Tyler, "We will all be at home by the first of November." [43]

CHAPTER 4

Wilson's Creek,
July–August 1861

GREER'S COLUMN plodded along the main road toward Colbert's Ferry on the Red River, from which it was to march across Indian Territory to Fort Smith. At the river crossing the troops encountered their first real adventure on July 16. While the ferryman transported their supply wagons and artillery across the river, the riders forded the stream at a shallower point a few yards above. By the middle of that sultry afternoon the men and mounts had reached the north bank of the river, and all but a few wagons and several pieces of artillery had been laboriously drawn across the channel. Suddenly and without warning, a flash flood in the upper watershed sent a wall of water ten feet deep roaring downstream, filling the once-placid river to its banks in a matter of minutes. A torrent of foam and debris swept past the astonished soldiers lounging on the bank. With every man hurriedly pressed into service to save the artillery, the regiment lost only one commissary wagon to the flood, and no one was injured. But the green recruits were powerfully impressed; some saw in their narrow escape a harbinger of perils to come.[1]

From their bivouac on the river the regiment followed the Texas Road across the Choctaw Nation. Rising out of the bottomlands along the river, past fields of ripening cotton and herds of fat cattle, their trail led them along the western foot-hills of the Ouachita Mountains. Covered with thick stands of fragrant pine and cut by clear, rocky streams, it was a realm of spacious vistas and awesome emptiness interrupted only occa-sionally by a cluster of cabins along the mail route or the clap-board plantation house of some Choctaw grandee. Having but recently returned from West Point, a Dallas officer avowed that the country "rivals the Hudson in its beauty, grandeur and magnificence."[2]

Already feeling a long way from home, the East Texas youths were more eager to catch a glimpse of the dark-eyed Indian damsels who were supposed to inhabit this land than to admire the scenery. Unfortunately, Colonel Greer was in a hurry, and he kept his men on the road all day, rendering them sufficiently exhausted to discourage any nocturnal rambles. Besides, most of the full-blood Choctaws led sequestered lives in the forests and avoided any unnecessary contact with whites traveling through their domain. The more assimilated mixed-bloods who operated farms along their route seemed very much like ordi-nary Southerners—cordial and pleasant enough, with Confed-erate flags over their gateposts—but not nearly as exotic as the young recruits had anticipated. Only once, as their column of twos plodded northward, did the boys have a sustained oppor-tunity to observe the celebrated charms of the Indian girls. De-murely but resolutely striding down the middle of the road, a young Chickasaw lass passed down the entire length of the regi-ment, which respectfully gave way on either side to permit her passage.[3]

At Boggy Depot, one of the chief towns of the nation, Choc-taw ladies presented the regiment with a flag on July 19. By this time Colonel Douglas H. Cooper, Jefferson Davis's emissary to the Indians, had organized Choctaw and Chickasaw volunteers into a regiment to support the Confederacy. Encamped on the Poteau River near Scullyville, these Indian allies staged a war dance for the edification of their wide-eyed Texas comrades. Captain Good described the scene for his wife: "One thousand tawny sons of the prairie drawn up in a vast circle . . . , heav-ing, whirling, racing round and round, singing, yelling the war whoop, firing pistols, all wild and delirious with excitement."[4]

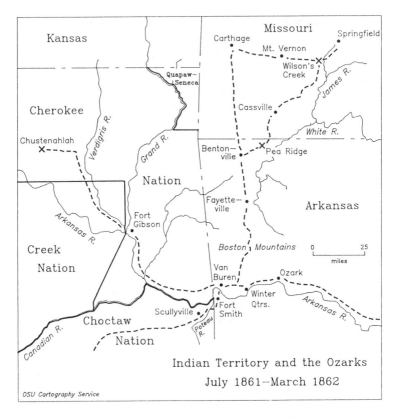

Indian Territory and the Ozarks

July 1861–March 1862

OSU Cartography Service

At the Poteau crossing the Texans swam their horses across the river and indulged themselves in a refreshing swim after their hot and dusty march.[5]

When Greer's volunteers at last arrived at Fort Smith on July 27, they discovered that General McCulloch had already led his forces northward, leaving orders for Greer to abandon his impedimenta and follow immediately. It required three days for the colonel to distribute arms and ammunition to his companies, replace horseshoes already worn out by the flinty ground, and ferry his men across the Arkansas River to Van Buren. Greer left his artillery and wagons and the sick behind, and McCulloch's quartermaster passed out an assortment of shotguns, carbines, and rifles to the Texans, leaving each company with a

mélange of weapons. Thus equipped, the troops from East
Texas struck out northward on July 31 towards McCulloch's
headquarters in southwestern Missouri.[6]

During the previous fortnight the Texas general had watched
the situation in Missouri reach a point of extreme crisis. He felt
compelled to intervene there despite his primary responsibility
to defend Indian Territory. The state was vital to the Confederate war effort; even cautious old Ben McCulloch was persuaded
to gamble on the outcome of his action. Though the strategic

Table 3. Arms and Accouterments of the Third Texas Cavalry
Regiment, August 31, 1861

CO.	ARMS	ACCOUTERMENTS
A	92 pistols,[a] 75 shotguns[b]	35 cartridge and cap boxes
B	160 pistols,[a] 107 shotguns[b]	100 cartridge and cap boxes
C	180 pistols,[a] 53 common rifles[c]	53 cartridge and cap boxes
D	220 pistols,[a] 44 shotguns[b]	44 cartridge and cap boxes
E	152 pistols,[a] 80 small common rifles[c]	100 shot bags, 48 powder flasks
F	152 pistols,[a] 74 common rifles[c]	Scant accouterments
G	144 pistols,[a] 76 common rifles[c]	85 cartridge and cap boxes
H	130 pistols,[a] 50 common rifles[c]	No accouterments
I	125 pistols,[a] 100 carbines[d]	Scant accouterments
K	192 pistols,[a] 52 Sharps rifles,[e] 19 percussion rifles[c]	86 cartridge and cap boxes

Notes: Though the designation of the weapons in the muster rolls was imprecise,
evidence from other sources suggests that they probably included the following types
of arms:

[a] Single-shot percussion pistols, model 1842, caliber .54.
[b] Brought from home by the individual soldiers.
[c] U.S. Army percussion rifles, model 1841, caliber .54.
[d] Sharps carbines, models 1851–59, caliber .52.
[e] Sharps carbines; the terms "carbine" and "rifle" were frequently interchanged.
Sources: Muster Rolls, National Archives and Records Administration, Record Group
109. The invaluable assistance of David D. Jackson in compiling this inventory is gratefully acknowledged.

aims of both sides were still in a state of flux so early in the war, it was already evident that the nature of the conflict would be determined by the Confederacy's primary goal: to defend its territory from the Federal armies sent to conquer the rebellious states and force them back into the Union on Northern terms. Since the war would be fought on Southern ground, the geography of that section came to shape Northern strategy, and Missouri formed an important part of that geography.

The South comprised three great regions that became the main theaters of the war. The eastern theater revolved around the 120-mile-long axis between Washington, D.C., and Richmond, Virginia, which had become the Confederate capital on May 29. The western theater embraced all that vast expanse of Southern landscape between the Mississippi River and the Appalachian Mountains. Finally, the trans-Mississippi theater was composed principally of Missouri, Arkansas, Louisiana, and Texas.

Contemplating the enormous stretch of land they were duty bound to invade and subdue, Northern strategists were at first bemused by the size of their task. Beyond the obvious necessity of defending the capital at Washington, there were divided counsels over where to concentrate their forces against the South. The Confederacy, too, faced its own dilemmas: confronted by formidable odds, should the Rebels withdraw their limited forces from vulnerable areas and concentrate their strength at easily defensible points? Indeed, should the South adopt this more economical defensive posture at all, or would its chances be enhanced by boldly and swiftly carrying the war into enemy territory?

Constrained by political considerations, Confederate planners chose to disperse their forces over a wide area and tried to defend the entirety of the South. Though the Rebels launched three major offensives during the course of the war, they generally maintained a defensive posture. This left the initiative largely in the hands of Lincoln and his generals. They ultimately evolved a grand strategy, but it emerged not so much in response to long-range planning as in reaction to targets of opportunity that arose as the war wore on.

One of the most crucial factors in determining where the war would be fought involved developments in the border states of Kentucky, Tennessee, and Missouri. In such places, where divided loyalties often rose to fratricidal ferocity among old neighbors and created a state of general anarchy, the schism in public opinion sometimes accommodated an entering wedge of Northern power. Typically such a tentative initiative expanded into a major strategic thrust by the Union, inspiring a hasty and frantic Confederate reaction.

So it went in Missouri. This most turbulent border state dominated the Mississippi River and thus was crucial to both the North and the South. Free states framed it on three sides, and the majority of its population were Union sympathizers. Yet many Missourians opposed the Republican administration's policy of coercion toward the South, while the partisans of slavery were powerful and influential. A vicious struggle developed between the Union and Confederate factions in the state, and four principal protagonists emerged to vie for its control.

The first was Governor Claiborne F. Jackson, a confirmed secessionist, who was determined to use the power of his office to carry Missouri into the Confederacy. His principal antagonist was Francis P. Blair, Jr., a Republican congressman and organizer of a Unionist Home Guard designed to thwart Jackson's plans. Blair's chief ally was the zealous Captain Nathaniel Lyon, who seized the contents of the United States arsenal at St. Louis to keep the weapons out of the hands of Jackson's state militia. The commandant of this force, Brigadier General Sterling Price, a former governor who enjoyed enormous popularity, found himself drawn inexorably into the proslavery camp of Governor Jackson.

By late spring sporadic violence had erupted all over Missouri. Lyon, now promoted to the rank of brigadier general, launched a military offensive designed to drive Governor Jackson from office and bring Missouri firmly under Union control. On June 15, Lyon's forces took the capital at Jefferson City and compelled Jackson and Price to retreat with the remnant of their militia toward the extreme southwestern corner of the state. Jackson then urgently pressed McCulloch to intervene in Missouri and save it for the Confederacy.[7]

Resolved to deliver the state from the "Northern yoke,"

McCulloch marched into Missouri on the Fourth of July. He effected a juncture with General Price's State Guards and some twelve hundred Arkansas troops under the command of Brigadier General N. Bart Pearce, and aided Governor Jackson in repulsing a Federal attack near Carthage. Having accomplished his immediate mission, McCulloch retired to a position in northern Arkansas to prepare his army for future operations.[8]

By the middle of July, Union and Confederate armies confronted each other near the westernmost end of the boundary between Missouri and Arkansas. Here magnificent oak and hickory forests flourished amid the steep hills and across the deep valleys of the Ozark Plateau. Oblivious to the charms of the landscape, each of the four generals—Lyon, Price, Pearce, and McCulloch—wrestled anxiously with his own logistical and strategic problems as he attempted to prepare his inexperienced and ill-equipped recruits for the impending collision.

Occupying the town of Springfield, and separated from his base of supply by more than a hundred miles, Lyon worried about the imminent expiration of the ninety-day enlistments of most of his Union volunteers. He knew that he must act immediately or retreat to the east. About eighty miles away, in the southwestern corner of Missouri, General Price organized and trained the thousands of ragtag Missouri State Guards who had drifted into his camp at Cowskin Prairie. A few miles farther south, near Maysville, Arkansas, General Pearce drilled his Arkansas militiamen and wrangled with his superiors over their transfer into Confederate service.[9]

With his force of two thousand men, McCulloch took up a position near Bentonville, Arkansas, and agonized over his inadequate supplies of arms and ammunition. He worried about Lyon's apparently overwhelming power at Springfield and the incompetence of his fellow generals. Though anxious to move against the Union concentration, McCulloch had developed a profound and ill-disguised contempt for the Missouri State Guards and for their commander, and he was reluctant to be sucked into an irredeemable disaster by Price's bluster and impetuous zeal. Finally consenting to a combined attack on Lyon's troops, McCulloch joined Price and Pearce in a cautious advance.

By the first of August the three commands had converged on

Crane Creek, about twenty miles southwest of Springfield. On the following day McCulloch's misgivings were confirmed when Lyon's cavalry surprised and routed a contingent of the Missouri militia in a sharp skirmish. In order to allay McCulloch's concerns and win his cooperation for the attack on Springfield, Price reluctantly concluded that he must give the dour Texan complete charge of the operation. After a stormy interview on August 4, the former governor ceded overall command to his rival, and McCulloch found himself at least nominally in charge of the Rebel armies in southwest Missouri.[10]

It was this rather tense atmosphere that greeted Greer's volunteers when they stumbled, exhausted, into the Crane Creek campground that same evening. For the past five days, ever since their departure from Van Buren, the troopers had been spurring their horses over the rough trails of the Ozarks, hastening to join McCulloch before he won the war without them. Marching day and night, with only brief intervals of rest, the East Texans found the fatiguing passage through the mountains replete with "steep hills, hard work, big rocks and clouds of dust."[11]

Yet it was a grand adventure for many of the lads, as rumors of an impending battle quickened the pulse and lent a sense of new excitement to their enterprise. At Van Buren a brass band had serenaded the troopers with "Dixie" for the first time, and the troops took up the song on the route of march. The entire population of Fayetteville, Arkansas, then a pleasant village of some two thousand souls, had cheered the regiment through the streets of their town. Among the charms of that place were two female seminaries, and the young ladies were particularly enthusiastic in the welcome they extended to the thousand "fine looking men from Texas, armed with shotguns and coming to defend them." One veteran recalled with pride that "those ladies felt safer when we had passed through the town and were between them and the Federal army."[12] All along the Telegraph Road (so called because the wire was strung along the roadway), the local citizenry had piled out of their houses to offer encouraging words.

The Texans needed all the encouragement they could get, for they arrived in the Rebel camp in a state of utter exhaustion.

"They were strewed along under every tree, some sick and vomiting and others weary with fatigue, and weakened by hunger."[13] But there was no time to rest: McCulloch had effected a temporary and volatile consolidation of three untried Rebel armies, and he had to move rapidly. He now had about 2,720 men in his own brigade, including Hébert's Louisiana infantry regiment and Greer's Texans. Pearce contributed a brigade of 2,234 Arkansans, and Price's Missouri State Guards numbered 5,221 soldiers, some still without weapons. In all, McCulloch enjoyed a numerical superiority with about ten thousand men and fifteen guns against Lyon's 5,400 Yankees. Believing that his enemy was encamped but a few miles up the road toward Springfield, McCulloch ordered his troops to advance at midnight in an effort to surprise Lyon with a dawn attack.

All that evening the untested troopers from East Texas scurried about, molding bullets and testing their unfamiliar firearms. Many were preoccupied with thoughts of impending death: They wrote their last letters home and left cherished watches and rings in the care of comrades, who, for one reason or another, they expected to survive them. This was to be their first battle, and most of them had a hazy notion of what it would be like, except that it would be dangerous. However, having expended all this emotional capital in preparation for eternity, and having further wearied themselves by stalking the enemy half the night and all the next day, General McCulloch's soldiers discovered that the Yankees had retreated all the way back to Springfield without being detected in the process. Disgusted by his inept intelligence, McCulloch led his troops a few miles north and camped on Wilson's Creek, ten miles southwest of Springfield.

His confidence further shaken by the enemy's successful withdrawal, "Old Ben" remained stationary in this position for four days. It was not a particularly advantageous site from a tactical point of view—a creek bottom surrounded by wooded hills—but it offered food and water for the hot, jaded, and hungry Rebel soldiers and their mounts. Wilson's Creek flowed almost due south at this point, carving a broad valley between the undulating hills that rose some five hundred feet above the stream bed. Most of these rocky slopes were covered by timber and brush, but ripe corn, a feast for famished man and beast, grew in the clearings scattered here and there above the creek. The Telegraph Road from Cassville ran north along the west bank of the creek for about a mile and then crossed the stream at a ford before turning northeast toward Springfield. Price's Missourians camped at the base of Oak Hill, which rose to the northwest of the creek, while Pearce and McCulloch posted their men on both sides of the road near the ford. Greer's troopers found a campsite just south of the ford, between the road and the creek. Conveniently located nearby, Joseph Sharp's cornfield occupied part of the cleared land that rose toward the wooded hills behind them.[14]

While the impulsive Price was anxious to attack the Union force in Springfield, McCulloch was in no hurry to launch such a gamble. While their generals debated and delayed, the troops had to satisfy themselves with sporadic scouting forays that occasionally exploded into minor skirmishes. Captain Frank Taylor led his Cherokee County horsemen on a raid into a nearby village and garnered booty in the form of one horse and seven tons of pig lead, more trouble to carry than it was worth. In the meantime new recruits straggled in, gradually augmenting the strength of the regiment by approximately three dozen. With the amused condescension characteristic of his age, sixteen-year-old Bugler Blocker observed that "old, gray-headed men came in, armed with their old squirrel rifles, a pouch of bullets, a string of patching already cut out, and a powder horn full of powder, to help the boys whip the Yankees when the fight came off."[15]

At last, on August 9, a petulant outburst from General Price finally goaded McCulloch into action. Having heard that Lyon was on the point of evacuating Springfield, the Missourian pressed his nominal superior to launch an immediate attack; otherwise, Price threatened to lead his State Guards against the Yankees independently. Faced with this ultimatum, McCulloch reluctantly ordered an advance to begin at 9 P.M.

As the hour approached, however, a gentle rain began to fall, while lowering skies and the roll of distant thunder threatened a downpour. Since most of his men carried their precious ration of cartridges in crude cotton bags, McCulloch feared that the soldiers would be effectively disarmed if the bags got wet. He consequently postponed the attack and left the troops standing under arms or lying about on the damp ground all night. They were strung out for about two miles in their camps along both sides of the road as it passed through the creek bottom. Though McCulloch had mounted sentries earlier in the evening to forestall surprise, these pickets had been called in when an advance seemed imminent and were not reposted when it was canceled. Inevitably, the surprise came the following morning.[16]

Outnumbered two to one, Lyon was acutely conscious of his perilous position in Springfield. While many of his troops were United States Army regulars, a large contingent consisted of volunteers whose enlistments were due to expire within a few days. Among them were 1,118 St. Louis Germans under the recently promoted Brigadier General Franz Sigel. Though enlisted for only three months, these troops counted many experienced soldiers among their number. Given the nature of his command, Lyon knew that he must either attack the Southern army before it surrounded him or retire to his base at Rolla. Consequently, the diminutive but audacious Yankee general ordered a dawn attack for August 10.[17]

He achieved complete surprise. Marching out of Springfield in the darkness, Lyon divided his command. He led four thousand men against Price's position on Oak Hill, while Sigel's Germans slipped around the Rebel right to fall upon McCulloch's command two miles to the south. (If the Rebel campgrounds along the creek are represented as the vertical trunk of a capital I, Lyon came down to cross it at the top, while Sigel's troops provided its base.) At 5:30 A.M., as Price and McCulloch were enjoying their breakfast, and while their men were boiling their coffee and washing their faces, the Yankees struck.

Price was suddenly shocked to glimpse swarms of his own men streaming over the crest of Oak Hill as they fled in panic before Lyon's advancing column. In the valley, McCulloch's soldiers were abruptly jolted out of their sleepy lethargy by the crash of artillery in their rear and the rattle of canister shot in the branches above their heads. Sigel had successfully dragged his cannon onto the heights that commanded the creek, began firing down directly into the camp of the South Kansas–Texas

Regiment, and took considerable satisfaction in the "'stirring' effect" that his cannonade exerted on the Rebel horsemen.[18] Each soldier from East Texas now faced the moment for which he had prepared, but no one was quite ready. Remarkably, most were preserved to profit from the experience of that day, despite its unpromising beginning.

The battle of Wilson's Creek fell into three phases. By their simultaneous assaults against opposite ends of the Rebel line, Lyon and Sigel administered a shocking surprise to their enemy and almost enveloped him. The Confederate response was confused and disorganized. "There was perfect panic at first, and not more than two regiments (of our troops) fought in any order," reported a Texas observer.[19] But in the second phase Price, on Oak Hill, and McCulloch, in the valley, were able to rally their men and stem the Yankee onslaught, largely owing to Sigel's failure to press his initial advantage and to the frequent cases of mistaken identity that plagued the Union commanders. Since some units on both sides were clad in various shades of gray, it was extremely difficult to distinguish friend from foe on the battlefield, and the outnumbered Yankees missed several opportunities for success. Finally, after knocking Sigel out of action, McCulloch freed his brigade to join Price's defenders on Oak Hill and repelled the enemy with heavy losses.

This eventual outcome seemed highly improbable, however, as Greer's men milled about in confusion on the creek bank, grabbing whatever arms they could lay hands upon and retrieving their tethered horses. In some cases this took time. Private B. L. Thomas, an Irish lad from Company A, had chained and padlocked his mount to a tree the night before, and in the confusion of the early morning cannonade, the trooper could not open his lock. While his horse remained chained to the tree amidst a storm of bullets, Thomas took to the woods, as did many of his comrades.[20] Some of the boys "skedaddled not less than three quarters of a mile before their officers could rally them."[21]

They were understandably rattled by their first exposure to enemy fire; a few had seen enough of the war already. There were two privates in Company D, for example, who had become notorious for their bravado on the march up from Texas, having bragged incessantly about what they would do to the Yankees when they caught them. But as their company moved out in the face of Sigel's artillery, both men found themselves overcome by a sudden indisposition. "Captain Hale," they cried, "Where must we go? We are sick." "Go to h[ell], you d[amned] cowards!" the disgusted captain replied. "You were the only two fighting men I had until now we are in a battle, and you're both sick. I don't care [where] you go."²²

Remarkably enough, however, most of Greer's men calmly followed their officers' orders. They formed up by companies in the open field adjacent to their campground, only a few hundred yards from Sigel's thundering guns on the heights above. With Lieutenant Colonel Lane at their head, they galloped off to find some concealment in the woods of the creek bottom.²³

As Greer assembled his regiment near the ford, the main focus of the battle was engaged on the southern slopes of Oak Hill, about a mile across the valley to the north. Price had rallied his raw Missourians from their camps along the creek and sent them against Lyon's attacking Yankees on the crest of the hill. Grappling at close range, these unlikely soldiers were able to stem the initial assault. McCulloch rushed his Arkansas and Louisiana infantry to reenforce the Missourians, and for six hours the battle raged amid the rocks and timber of Oak Hill and in the fields to the east of Wilson's Creek.

During a pause in the action McCulloch ordered Greer to lead his cavalrymen to the west around Oak Hill in support of Price, whose troops were bearing the brunt of Lyon's attack. By this time, however, the ford across the creek was clogged by abandoned wagons and hundreds of terrified Confederates fleeing south from the battlefield. Half of Greer's troopers became separated from their commander in the confusion, but sheltered by covering timber, Greer and the first five companies of his regiment clattered along the stony bottom of Skeggs Branch and out onto the western slopes of Oak Hill. Held in reserve, for five hours the Texans skulked through the brush-choked ravines just beyond the Yankee flank, while the battle raged fiercely on the hillside immediately to their right. Comparatively safe themselves, the East Texans cheered wildly as the Missouri Rebels

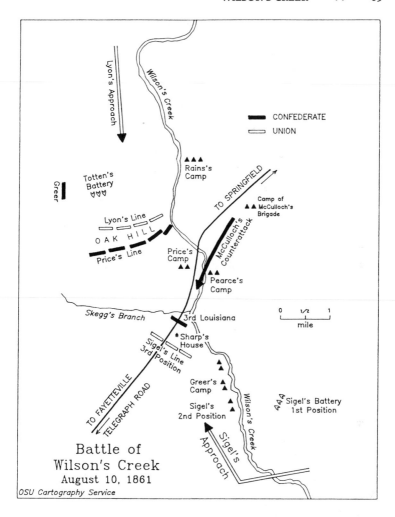

Battle of
Wilson's Creek
August 10, 1861

OSU Cartography Service

loosed volley after volley against their fellow Missourians under
Lyon.[24]

In the meantime, Lieutenant Colonel Lane, Major Chilton,
and Adjutant Ector encountered extreme difficulty in forming
up the five companies left behind near the ford when Greer
dashed off toward Oak Hill. Lane's horse was shot out from

under him; Ector's young son, Walton, became separated from his father in the confusion, and the adjutant agonized over him all morning. Chilton rallied two companies—Mabry's "Dead-Shot Rangers" (Company G) and Captain Russell's Company H—and they joined a battalion of Missouri cavalry to support the infantry on Oak Hill. Since the brush on the hillside was so dense, the Texans did not attempt a charge but merely occupied a position on the left flank of the enemy, where they dodged Minie balls most of the morning. Three companies (F, I, and K) were left in the valley to mingle with the other units tossed this way and that by the chaotic fighting.[25]

By midmorning Lyon's attackers began to waver, while their commander dashed frantically up and down the line, urging on his men. He could not understand why Sigel had failed to drive across the valley to support him. Desperately trying to rally his troops, Lyon rushed forward waving his hat in the air, and a Rebel soldier shot him dead. At this critical point of the battle, Major Samuel D. Sturgis succeeded the fallen general to command the Union troops on Oak Hill.

A mile to the south, everything had gone Sigel's way at first. Having begun his day by shelling the Rebel campground, he then led his brigade across Wilson's Creek, past Sharp's farm, and took a position across the Telegraph Road on the slope to the south of Skeggs Branch. From there his artillery sporadically fired across the valley at the Rebel concentrations on Oak Hill, while his infantry rounded up Confederate stragglers and looted their deserted camps. The Germans plundered everything Greer's men had left behind in their hasty departure that morning, including the colonel's baggage.[26]

Owing to the confusion over similarly colored uniforms, some of Sigel's prisoners never knew they were being captured until it was too late. Private Jim Eldridge, a Jefferson clerk in civilian life, became entangled in the harness lines of a team drawing artillery into position and obligingly cut himself loose when so requested by the driver. To his query, "Whose battery is that?" the driver replied, "Sigel's of Missouri," as the battery opened fire on Eldridge's own comrades.[27]

The Germans caught Private Brazille, of Company A, because he refused to be hurried at his breakfast. He had just settled down to roasting a dozen ears of corn when Sigel opened fire, and he refused to budge until his cooking was done, in spite of the crash of cannon shot and the departure of everyone else in his regiment. At last, with the still steaming corn under his arm, he mounted his horse and rode off in the direction he supposed his fellow Texans had taken, but blundered instead into one of Sigel's patrols. On being hailed down by a Yankee officer who inquired of his purpose, Brazille replied, with his mouth full of corn, "I'm gwine to ketch me a Dutchman, I am, you bet!"[28] The "Dutchmen" promptly disarmed him and sent him trudging back to Springfield as a prisoner of war.

Assuming that Lyon would drive the beaten Rebels toward his line, Sigel took no further action until midmorning, when he glimpsed what appeared to him the entire Confederate army streaming down the Telegraph Road as if in full retreat. And indeed, some of these men were Rebel soldiers in flight from Oak Hill. In the meantime, however, McCulloch had hastily collected scattered units of Missouri and Texas cavalry and Louisiana infantry in order to confront Sigel's threat from the south. Because Sigel believed the onrushing Louisianans to be part of the gray-clad First Iowa Infantry, he held his fire until McCulloch's troops were already swarming over his guns. Overrun, his infantry panicked and fled from the field.

The Germans scattered in all directions: some retreated south toward Fayetteville; others rushed pell-mell up the road they had taken from Springfield the night before. McCulloch's cavalry then took up the chase. Riding with a Missouri battalion, Mabry's and Russell's companies ambushed the retreating enemy at a ford about two miles up the road, where they "did terrible execution with their short-arms."[29] The Texans killed 64 and captured 147 of Sigel's men.

Now McCulloch reversed his field and rejoined the battle for Oak Hill. Though stunned by the death of their commander, the Union soldiers along the crest of the hill at first held firm against the most sustained Confederate attack of the day. "Masses of infantry fell back and again rushed forward. The summit of the hill was covered with the dead and wounded," McCulloch reported.[30] At this point he ordered Colonel Greer forward from the flank against a battery of guns commanded by Captain

James Totten, Second United States Artillery, and the line of Kansas infantrymen who supported him. Then, Bugler Blocker remembered, "Col. Greer pulled his sabre, waved it toward the enemy and shouted 'Draw your pistols, men, and charge!' "[31]

Unfortunately, the headlong assault that followed was less than a masterpiece of military precision. Amid the dense undergrowth of the ravine, most of the men could not hear their colonel's command, so that the riders emerged onto the hillside piecemeal, with only Taylor's Company C and a few others joining Greer at the head of the charge. Some of the men, moreover, were delayed by secondary considerations. Joe Welch, a sturdy Grimes County blacksmith, interrupted his charge down the slope when one of his precious pistols jolted out of its holster and fell to the ground. The frugal Welch reined in his horse, deliberately dismounted, retrieved his weapon, remounted, and rode after his galloping comrades.[32]

Still, for the young soldiers who made it, their first charge of the war was an unforgettable experience. As one veteran remembered it:

> With a yell we went toward that line of blue like the wind. . . . On we went, pouring lead into the blue line that was standing there 50 yards in front of us, with fixed bayonets, prepared to receive cavalry. The next moment that blue line was a mass of running, stampeding soldiers trying to get out of the way of that mass of horses and men that was bearing down on them.[33]

This assault, however, proved to be a momentary diversion. While many of the Yankee infantry panicked and fled, others merely took cover amid the trees and brush of the hillside and poured a lethal fire on their attackers. As soon as Totten's gunners realized how small the cavalry force was, they calmly waited until the East Texans were within about forty paces and opened fire. Greer suspended his assault and led his men back down into the sheltering woods to regroup.

With this volley the Yankee artillery levied its initial tribute in dead from Greer's volunteers. J. A. Wasson, whose father operated a plantation in Rusk County, was shot through the thigh. "The ball entered near the body, passed along and around the bone, and came out just above the knee."[34] Wash Cole, a young Cherokee County farmer, was also mortally wounded in the aftermath of the charge, while David Owens, the Episcopal minister's son from San Augustine, was killed as well.[35]

The sacrifice of these men did not materially affect the outcome of the battle, since Greer failed to dislodge the Yankee guns. Captain Totten, the officer against whom his effort had been directed, was starkly contemptuous of its effects. He reported that "this was the only demonstration made by [the Rebel] cavalry, and it was so *effete* and ineffectual in its force and character as to deserve only the appellation of child's play. Their cavalry is utterly worthless on the battle-field."[36]

The Texans would have bridled at his words, had they been privy to the Federal after-action reports. They regarded their charge as a glorious achievement, since they had already learned how difficult it was to persuade several hundred horses to gallop in the same direction at the same time. Their commanders, moreover, had yet to recognize the unpleasant truth that mounted charges had very limited effect amid the heavily wooded hillsides of the American South. In any case, the East Texans were not permitted a second chance to demonstrate their prowess, for McCulloch now ordered Greer to retrace the circuitous route from his camp and hold a line across the Telegraph Road south of the ford. There the five companies under his command waited tensely for about an hour.[37]

At eleven o'clock McCulloch launched his third attack of the day against Oak Hill. Though Major Sturgis rushed reinforcements into the threatened position, his men had exhausted their ammunition and were tormented by thirst. The Yankee commander therefore ordered a retreat to Springfield, and by noon he had withdrawn his men from the bloody hilltop. Dazed and exhausted themselves, the Rebels did not pursue them. "We watched the retreating enemy through our field glasses," reported Confederate General Pearce, "*and were glad to see him go.*"[38]

At the south end of the battlefield, on the other hand, McCulloch ordered Greer to pursue and harass any of Sigel's survivors who might still be on the road. The colonel collected his stray companies and followed the Union stragglers eastward, where the Texans found that Mabry's and Russell's men had already left "dead men in blue . . . strewn along the road in a horrible manner."[39] Terminating their pursuit at dusk, the cavalrymen returned to camp to learn that their supply train had finally arrived from Fort Smith, bringing letters from home. Too weary even to build a fire by which to read them, the exhausted troopers of the South Kansas–Texas Regiment dropped to the ground after their first battle. Though Price urged McCulloch to pursue the defeated enemy, the cautious Texan refused to order an advance that night on the grounds that his men were spent, his units disorganized, and his ammunition virtually exhausted.[40]

Moreover, his losses had been severe, including 279 men killed and 951 wounded. In that half day of combat on Wilson's Creek about 2,500 soldiers were killed, wounded, or missing on both sides—a casualty rate of some 23 percent of all engaged and a fairly normal attrition for a Civil War battle.[41] Considering the general carnage, Greer's regiment emerged from Wilson' Creek comparatively unscathed with only six men killed. The colonel noted with satisfaction that they "were buried as neatly as if they had been at home."[42] Among the slain was Willis Kilgore, fifty-six, whose body was never recovered. Private F. J. Willey, born in England, was the first Harrison County man killed in the Civil War. Cherokee County's Private Wash Cole paid with his life for his bravery on the battlefield, and a thoughtful comrade later presented his mother with the the the bullet that killed him. Twenty-three men were wounded, while six turned up missing.[43]

In their own eyes at least, the East Texans had aquitted themselves very well in spite of their initial disarray under Sigel's guns. On the following day the regiment got a chance to savor its victory when McCulloch finally ordered his troops to advance on Springfield. Lieutenant Colonel Lane led four companies ahead as a reconnoitering force. They found the Yankees gone; they were by now in full retreat toward their railway terminus at Rolla, and the streets of Springfield were crowded with jubilant Southern sympathizers. The courthouse served as a dismal haven for the Union wounded, the Stars and Stripes still floating defiantly above its cupola. Lane replaced the Union banner with the Lone Star flag of Texas and assured the helpless men inside that they would not be harmed. Shortly thereafter, the main body of McCulloch's army moved into town and set up camp nearby. Three days later Greer's regiment moved to a more spacious encampment near Mount Vernon, thirty miles to the west.[44]

Chustenahlah, August–December 1861

LYON'S DEFEAT and death at Wilson's Creek only thickened the pall of gloom that settled over the Union counsels in Washington late in the summer of 1861. For the failure in Missouri came only three weeks after the Union disaster at Manassas, when a Confederate army routed a Federal attacking force only twenty-five miles from the capital. Lincoln's government as well as its numerous critics saw this unexpected debacle at Wilson's Creek as confirmation of the ineptitude and incompetence of the Northern war effort.

The twin Confederate victories emboldened the South, of course. Back in East Texas, Matthew Cartwright wrote his sons in Company E that after Manassas, "We now have no fear of our ultimate success and hope for an early peace. I hope by 1st Nov. next."[1] Similarly, the "Glorious News" of the victory at Wilson's Creek so delighted Sheriff Long, of Cherokee County, that he sent his son John a new pistol. "You can kill a Dutchman [at] 150 yards with it," he quipped. "All I charge you for the pistol is to kill a Lincolnite or take his horse from him."[2]

Yet, while McCulloch had beaten the enemy, Confederate critics pointed out that given the initial surprise and general confusion of his troops, "the victory . . . under the circumstances was miraculous."[3] Enjoying a momentary advantage after the battle, McCulloch might have pursued the shaken Federals and cut them off before they reached the relative safety of Rolla. But, despite strident exhortations from Price, the "Big Captain" from Texas had wasted his opportunity, and Wilson's Creek proved not the first step in a decisive drive for Rebel control of Missouri but rather a prelude to four months of inconclusive campaigning that left Confederate forces in the trans-Mississippi arena even weaker than before.[4]

Having creditably undergone their baptism of fire south of Springfield, the men in the Rebel ranks became both witnesses and victims of three serious deficiencies that plagued the Confederate command throughout the war: discord among the commanders, costly epidemic disease, and wretched intelligence. The most inexcusable flaw in Confederate military leadership in the West was that the generals permitted personal pique and conflicting objectives to intrude upon the larger purposes of the war. Price and McCulloch exemplified this weakness.

In the first place, McCulloch was annoyed by the suggestion, even from normally friendly quarters, that he had left himself open to surprise and failed to follow up his victory. Furthermore, his contempt for the Missourians had not been allayed by their effusion of blood at Wilson's Creek, and he simply regarded Price as an incompetent. The prideful Texan was offended by Price's bombastic claims of precedence and his vainglorious report of the recent battle.

In this atmosphere of mutual hostility it became impossible for the commanders to agree on priorities or establish a unified command. Price first urged an immediate advance against the Yankees at Rolla and beyond; then he pleaded with McCulloch to join him in a campaign north toward the Missouri River. The Texan refused on both occasions, pointing out that he was short of both men and ammunition. He became increasingly uneasy about plunging into the dangerous maelstrom of local factionalism. Officially, Missouri was neither a Confederate state nor fully integrated into the Union; the state remained a chaotic battleground between bitterly contending factions in which no one could feel secure. The more McCulloch saw of Missouri, the less he liked it. "We had as well be in Boston as far as the friendly feelings of the inhabitants are concerned," he complained.[5]

Therefore, only a few days after their successful collaboration at Wilson's Creek, the Southern commanders parted company to pursue their own individual objectives. General Pearce led his men back to Arkansas, where the entire brigade of ninety-day volunteers promptly dispersed into the hills. The impetuous Price launched his militia northward to the Missouri River. Mc-Culloch, meanwhile, drew his forces back to the west to re-organize, drill, and resupply the troops. Encouraged by the success at Wilson's Creek, reinforcements continued to join his camp until McCulloch accumulated approximately 4,800 men present for duty, including the 992 members of Greer's regiment who were still available.

The East Texans spent the pleasant days of early autumn foraging for food and riding leisurely from encampment to encampment amid the brilliant colors and crystalline atmosphere of an Ozark fall. Still savoring their recent victory, they "lived off the fat of the land."[6] On September 12, McCulloch ordered Colonel Greer to select a camp for his men near Carthage, about fifty miles north of the Arkansas state line. Now designated officially as the Third Texas Cavalry, the regiment bivouacked in a pleasant grove just outside the town, where they remained for almost two months, munching Ozark apples and racing their horses for recreation. At first, it seemed an idyllic campsite on the banks of Spring River, in a friendly and fruitful land.

But here, in this ostensibly salubrious setting, the second besetting scourge of the Confederate army—disease—struck down hundreds of McCulloch's men. More lethal than Yankee bullets, the effects of measles, typhoid, and dysentery devastated the Rebel army and undermined the South's capacity to fight. During the course of the war as a whole some three-fourths of all Confederate fatalities were inflicted by disease rather than enemy action. Already by the middle of October half of McCulloch's command was sick; of the nearly one thousand troopers in the Third Texas, almost a third were absent from duty owing to severe illness.[7]

The local families of Carthage took these sick soldiers into their homes, turned their courthouse into a hospital, and gave the East Texans the best care they could devise. But knowing nothing of the causes of the maladies, and disposing only of the primitive medical treatments then available, they could do little to arrest or palliate the scourge. As the measles epidemic gave way to a siege of typhoid, troopers died, including the popular and cultivated Captain Taylor, commander of Company C, who succumbed in December after suffering weeks of debilitating fever. His men elected Lieutenant James Barker, of Rusk, to take his place. Besides Taylor, 18 members of the Third Texas died that fall as victims of disease, and 145 others were dropped from the rolls, most of them because they were too sick to serve.[8]

The scores of stricken men limping home to recuperate and their woeful accounts of the suffering of their comrades in Missouri tempered the tidings of victory in East Texas. Now Sheriff Long confided to his absent son, "I study all the time about you."[9] Or, "Your Ma is very lonely & speaks of you with tears in her eyes."[10] "If your health should not become good," Matthew Cartwright counseled his sick boy, "you will not be of much service in the army this winter. Therefore it would be better to return home."[11]

As they faced the prospect of their sons' absence for still more months to come, soldiers' families scoured the country for supplies to see them through the winter. When Sigel's troops had looted their camp on Wilson's Creek, many of the boys had lost both their money and their clothes. Captain Winston reported that his men were "nearly naked,"[12] and the good people of Rusk were shocked to learn that some of the members of Company C were so poorly clad that "they could not hide their person."[13] The folks at home collected shoes and blankets and dispatched wagonloads of clothing to the troops. The San Augustine ladies, for instance, were "doing every thing in their power for the soldiers; knitting, sewing, and fixing every thing that will conduce to their comfort," while a bevy of Dallas women were working tirelessly to the same end.[14]

Reluctant to plunge his depleted forces yet deeper into the uncertain waters of Missouri politics, McCulloch cast about for some useful employment for them before the frosty nights of late autumn confined his ill-clad troops to winter quarters. A possible target were the Union Jayhawkers, who repeatedly raided the border counties of Missouri from their base at Fort Scott, Kansas. "Claib" Jackson, the deposed secessionist governor of Missouri, established his temporary headquarters with the Third Texas on September 28 and singled out the Kansas guerrillas for condign punishment. In his harangue to the assembled troops, the governor summoned them in rolling biblical cadences to mount against Kansas "the most ruthless invasion known to man since the razing of Jerusalem to the earth, and burn their accursed land from Dan to Beersheba!" [15] McCulloch took up the project of a punitive expedition against the Jayhawkers; he proposed to his superiors that his men be employed in the task "of destroying Kansas as far north as possible." [16] With this draconian objective in mind, the Confederate general ordered his units to prepare to march against Fort Scott.

But before McCulloch had time to lay waste to Kansas, he was forced to look hastily to his own defense. A massive Union offensive forced a change in plans and brought about another episode of uneasy collaboration between the impulsive Price and the skeptical McCulloch. On September 26 the Federal commander in Missouri, Major General John C. Frémont, launched his army of 38,000 men on an ambitious campaign from St. Louis westward. He forced Price to retreat from his position on the Missouri River all the way to the extreme southwestern corner of the state once again, and the Union army reoccupied Springfield on October 27. Their forces depleted, lacking ammunition and clothing, and fearful that Frémont would pounce upon them at any moment, Price and McCulloch joined forces at Pineville, Missouri, only five miles north of the Arkansas line, to debate their next move. Price had about 7,000 troops at this point, while McCulloch commanded but 5,743 effectives. Outnumbered almost three to one, they worried that Frémont might seize the occasion for the decisive battle of the West. [17]

In such a perilous situation it was imperative that the two Rebel commanders maintain the most rigorous standards of alertness, since their very survival depended upon it. As it turned out, however, their scouting forays were generally ineffective, illustrating a third great deficiency in the Confederate command: inadequate intelligence. Since McCulloch's main force was camped seventy-two miles southwest of the Yankee concentration at Springfield, the general sent units of Greer's regiment forward to probe the Union positions. Every few days, selected companies of the Third Texas Cavalry were detailed to reconnoiter the situation. But by the time these scouts had ridden forward to find the enemy and then returned to report to their commander, the information they had gathered was already stale and useless.

About all they collected were some stirring war stories. At the end of October, for example, Cumby's and Mabry's companies reconnoitered to the outskirts of Springfield. While Cumby remained behind with the troops, Mabry and a single companion, Captain Alf Johnson, of the unattached Confederate spy company, then stole into town on foot. They first rewarded their cunning with a fine dinner at the home of a "well-known Southern lady." Thus fortified for their scouting duties, Mabry and Johnson emerged from the house to find themselves surrounded by a yard full of Yankees. The two officers brawled their way out of the trap with Bowie knife and shotgun and returned to the regiment, though Mabry's right arm was shattered in the affray and Johnson was wounded in the hip. It was a colorful escapade, but they learned very little of the Union dispositions or intentions.[18]

In the end, Frémont's blunders rather than their own vigilance saved the armies of Price and McCulloch from potential disaster. Finally persuaded of Frémont's incompetence, Lincoln removed "The Pathfinder of the West" from command and ordered his successor to evacuate Springfield on November 8. The Federal troops withdrew again to their base of supply at Rolla, missing thereby an opportunity to destroy the Rebel armies that opposed them. Indicative of the dilatory pace of his scouts, it required a week for the news of the Union withdrawal to reach McCulloch at Pineville. Though Price predictably begged him to pursue the enemy, McCulloch was clearly relieved that the immediate danger had passed. Seemingly in no hurry to tangle with the Yankee rear guard, he entered Springfield only on November 19, ten days following the Yankee departure.[19]

In fact, the last thing Ben McCulloch wanted was to catch

up with the Union army. He was too well persuaded of the in-
adequacy of his own forces to risk an engagement, and he im-
plored Price to follow a cautious policy as well. But the ardent
Missourian marched north again on his own, emboldened by the
favorable political developments of the late autumn. On November 28 the Confederate Congress admitted Governor Jackson's
itinerant Missouri government to the Confederacy, and Price
now expected more active support from President Davis.[20] Convinced that the stubborn Price had embarked upon the swift
and sure road to disaster, McCulloch withdrew his forces all
the way back into Arkansas and went into winter quarters on
December 6. While his infantry camped near Bentonville, the
cavalry took up residence at the confluence of Frog Bayou and
the Arkansas River, about twelve miles east of Van Buren.

The East Texans were determined to enjoy snug and comfortable winter quarters, since they had already suffered considerably from the chill during their prolonged surveillance of
Frémont's army. Most of the troops still lacked proper winter
clothing, and many were without blankets. Fortunately, their
quartermaster was a genius of improvisation. Captain Harris laid
out a camp that provided at least some of the comforts of home.
He selected as their campsite a grove of sweet gum trees occupying a tract of rising ground about two hundred yards from
the Arkansas River. He had rustled up a mule-powered sawmill
and had cut a quantity of sturdy planks by the time the men
rode on the scene. While Harris surveyed a regimental street
and supervised the construction of a corncrib and stables, details from each company built sixteen-foot-square cabins, each
housing ten men in relative comfort. Quartermaster Harris's devotion to duty unfortunately cost him his life, however. While
superintending the construction, he caught his clothing in the
teeth of the circle saw and was so mangled in the accident that
he died a few days later.[21]

The respite in winter quarters was to last three months. It
permitted McCulloch to reorganize and drill his forces, accumu-
late supples, and undertake some serious politicking back in
Richmond. During the fall he had called for the enlistment of
additional regiments to strengthen his command, and hundreds
of young Texans, "having but little sense," responded enthusi-

astically.[22] Four volunteer cavalry units from the Lone Star State provided the most substantial increment to McCulloch's army.

Colonel Barton W. Stone, of Dallas, raised the Sixth Texas Cavalry Regiment from companies recruited in North and Central Texas. Mustered into Confederate service on September 19, Stone and his 939 men crossed Indian Territory and reported to McCulloch's headquarters on October 20. Colonel William B. Sims organized the Ninth Texas Cavalry Regiment from North Texas volunteers and swore them into the Confederate army on October 14. They had ridden but half way across Indian Territory when they were pressed into a campaign against Union sympathizers among the Indians. Consequently, the approximately seven hundred men in the unit joined McCulloch's army only in January 1862, following that diversion.

Colonel William C. Young, the richest man in Cooke County, organized and led the 850 men of the Eleventh Texas Cavalry, who crossed the Red River about the middle of October en route to Fort Smith. Finally, Major John W. Whitfield raised a battalion of mounted riflemen from South and East Texas. This "Texas Legion" of 339 men reported to McCulloch on October 8. After being augmented to regimental strength in the spring of 1862, the legion assumed the designation of Twenty-seventh Texas Cavalry. Young's regiment later joined Major General Joseph Wheeler's Cavalry Corps in the Army of Tennessee. The other three regiments—the Sixth, the Ninth, and the Twenty-seventh—would serve as comrades in arms to the men of the Third Texas throughout most of the war. As components of Ross's Texas Brigade, they would earn battle laurels from Vicksburg to Atlanta.[23]

As these reinforcements gradually assembled near McCulloch's headquarters, and the first Christmas of the war approached, the mood in the camp of the Third Texas gradually relaxed. About 250 soldiers, including Colonel Greer himself, were granted furloughs to visit home, and the ever-ready Lieutenant Colonel Lane took over temporary command of the 747 troopers who remained. McCulloch spent most of December in Richmond, fighting a vituperative newspaper war against Sterling Price, who had accused the Texan of losing Missouri for the Confederacy by his hesitation and refusal to cooperate.

Colonel James M. McIntosh, of the Second Arkansas Mounted Riflemen, assumed command in McCulloch's absence.

With their commanders away on various errands, the East Texans unhurriedly hammered away at their cabins, adding refinements and elaborations as time permitted. Their huts were equipped with huge mud and stone fireplaces, and the men spread their blankets across broad sleeping shelves running across the interiors. Some of the wealthier men imported their own black body servants to cook, wash, and care for the horses, leaving the young gentlemen to relieve the tedium of camp with jigs and reels, horse races, and jugs of corn liquor from the copious stores at nearby Van Buren.[24] Private Americus Cartwright thought it necessary to reassure his mother that a report alleging that he and some of his comrades from San Augustine "were killing ourselves drinking whiskey," was a "base and black . . . lie."[25]

On December 17, however, the energetic Colonel McIntosh abruptly interrupted this relaxed routine on Frog Bayou. He ordered his men to break camp for a foray into Indian Territory that involved the East Texans in one of the most tragic episodes of the Civil War. Though all of the Five Civilized Tribes were formally allied with the Confederacy, intratribal feuds and ancient enmities soon led to internecine warfare among the Native Americans, almost destroying everything they had accomplished in their generation of settlement in the West. Almost all the Choctaws and Chickasaws remained loyal to the Confederacy, but the other tribes were hopelessly divided. The Union recruited about 2,200 Cherokees, while some 1,400 of these tribesmen fought with the Rebel army. Eventually, 1,575 Creeks joined the Federal forces, and 1,695 served the Southern cause. Thus was the stage set for Civil War in Indian Territory.

The curtain went up in November 1861. Opothle Yahola, an elder statesman of the Creek Nation, led a faction of his tribe who favored neutrality rather than the alliance with the Confederacy. Approximately six thousand of his followers, including warriors, their dependents, and fugitive slaves, had gathered at his camp near the North Canadian River. Confederate leaders in the territory perceived this huge concentration of dissidents not only as a threat in itself but also as a potential fifth column for a Federal invasion south from Kansas. To counter this danger, Colonel Douglas H. Cooper, the Confederate commander in Indian Territory, mobilized four Indian regiments to force Opothle Yahola's submission to Confederate authority or to drive him out of the country. On November 15, Cooper advanced upon the neutralist Creeks with fourteen hundred men, including a contingent from the Ninth Texas Cavalry. Hounded by the Rebels and having exhausted their forage, Opothle Yahola and his followers began an exodus toward safety in Union-controlled Kansas.

Opothle Yahola's refugees were compelled to fight three battles with the pursuing Confederates during the final six weeks of 1861, all within a radius of forty miles of present-day Tulsa, Oklahoma. The first was a running skirmish near the Cimarron River on November 19. On this occasion a detachment of the Ninth Texas attacked Opothle Yahola's camp, but had to beat a hasty retreat back to Cooper's main force of Indian troops. Nevertheless, the Creek neutralists abandoned most of their supplies and escaped toward the north under the cover of darkness. The second engagement occurred on December 9 as the refugees were encamped on Bird Creek. Cooper's Confederates inflicted heavy losses upon the dissidents, but Opothle Yahola's warriors held firm; still intact as a fighting force, they began to attract Cherokee defectors to their neutralist persuasion.[26]

Under these threatening circumstances Cooper appealed to McCulloch's headquarters for reinforcements. Colonel McIntosh, left in charge during McCulloch's absence in Richmond, was seventeen years younger and far more audacious than his chief, and he responded to Cooper's request with alacrity. McIntosh led 1,380 of his own men into Indian Territory and took over the direction of the campaign himself. Included in his force were units of the Sixth and the Eleventh Cavalry, Whitfield's Legion, 130 Arkansas Mounted Riflemen, and about 350 troopers from the Third Texas. With Lieutenant Colonel Lane in command, the ablest bodies of Companies A, B, E, F, and G left off with their cabin building to go fight the Indians.

The East Texans followed the Arkansas River to Fort Gibson, where they rendezvoused with Cooper's Confederate Indians on December 20. Traveling light, they had left their tents behind, though the weather was bitterly cold. The men made shelters of brush and poles, covered the floors of these lean-tos with river-bottom cane, kept huge fires blazing into the night, and slept fitfully through a blizzard that blanketed them with six inches of snow. At Fort Gibson, McIntosh proposed that his own troops march up the Verdigris River, while Cooper's Indians would advance up the Arkansas valley with the design of converging upon Opothle Yahola's fortified camp in the Osage Hills about fifteen miles north of the present site of Tulsa. In this way the Rebels could trap the old Creek chieftain and destroy his baleful influence.

Accordingly, the Third Regiment struck out to the northwest across glistening, snow-covered prairies on December 22. After fording the Grand and Verdigris rivers, they followed the west bank of the Verdigris for three days through a wintry landscape devoid of human habitation. As they approached the Osage Hills on Christmas Day, they encountered ever-increasing evidence of the hostile Indians, who awaited them in the fastness of the rocky defiles and precipitous bluffs ahead. Having tried and failed to parley with Opothle Yahola, Lieutenant Colonel Lane ordered his men into a closely guarded bivouac in a grove of blackjack, where a howling blizzard made for a miserable and sleepless night.[27]

Opothle Yahola had situated his warriors in a natural citadel: behind breastworks of boulders crowning the scrub oak thickets of a bluff that rose about three hundred feet out of the plain of Shoal Creek. Seminole braves occupied a position on the south slope of the hill, while Creek horsemen held the crest of the ridge. Their main camp, sheltering women, children, slaves, cattle, and supplies, lay in the defiles and canyons to the north.

Stiff, exhausted, and almost frozen, McIntosh's command formed up into a column on the morning of December 26 and set out toward Opothle Yahola's stronghold in the teeth of a frigid gale. Too cold to sit in the saddle, the troopers had to walk beside their mounts to keep up circulation. After seven or eight miles of this misery, they halted along the timbered banks of Shoal Creek early in the afternoon. Here the troops built fires, thawed out a bit, and deployed in a line of battle—all within full view of their enemy, less than a quarter of a mile away on

the crest of the ridge above them. The place was called Chustenahlah, meaning in Cherokee "a shoal in a stream." Without any
effort at concealment, the Indians fired off their guns, yelled like
demons, and gesticulated wildly, daring the Texans to attack
them in their rocky fortress.

McIntosh's original plan had envisioned a joint operation,
with Cooper's Indians combining with his own cavalry in a
simultaneous assault. But Cooper's march up the Arkansas had
been too slow for him to effect the planned junction of forces.
McIntosh decided to attack immediately; it was just too cold to
wait. He gazed up at the rocky bluff for a moment, the boulders
and brush of its precipitous slopes concealing hundreds of armed
Indians, and realized that it was a "desperate undertaking to
charge a position which appeared almost inaccessible."[28] But,
like many Southern commanders in similar circumstances, he
ordered a charge anyway.

In its very impulsive audacity, it worked. Forming the very
center of the Rebel line, Lane and his East Texans charged up
the bluff like "shot out of a shovel," while the Eleventh Texas
followed a defile up to the left flank of the enemy's position.[29]
Meanwhile, the Sixth Texas Cavalry circled around to the right
of the Creek chieftain's stronghold. At the sound of a bugle, "one
wild yell from a thousand throats burst upon the air, and the
living mass hurled itself upon the foe."[30]

Since the face of the bluff was too steep for horses, Companies
A and B of the Third Cavalry were ordered to dismount and
take the hill on foot, leaving every fifth man down below in the
woods to hold their mounts. So distressed was he at being detailed as a horse holder and thus deprived of the glory of the
charge, eighteen-year-old Private Henry Miller burst into tears as
he watched his comrades scramble breathlessly over the rocks,
while volleys of arrows and bullets flew past their heads. Incredibly, the young Texans reached the summit of the ridge and
stormed across Opothle Yahola's barricade of boulders. Meanwhile, McIntosh's other troopers drove into the flanks of the
stunned defenders of the hilltop fortress. It all happened so fast
that it shattered the Indians' resistance within a few minutes,
and most of them began to scatter in all directions.[31]

Not all of them yielded to the general panic, however. Private

Doug Cater remembered for the rest of his life that "some of those Indians were very brave and daring and would not leave, but continued to shoot. . . . One big feathered cap fellow stood out from the trees and continued shooting until he fell. I had shot both barrels of my gun and one of my holster pistols at him before he fell."[32] Whereas a few held firm, the bulk of Opothle Yahola's band fled northward into the hills, abandoning their camp, property, and families.

Remounting, the Texans pursued the demoralized enemy until late in the afternoon, picking them off one by one. Somewhere between their homes in the peaceful hamlets of rural Texas and the rocky bluff of Chustenahlah, they had acquired a capacity for savage warfare that did not go unnoticed by Captain Good of Dallas. "It is strange," he wrote his wife, "how blunted are our sensibilities amid the perils of war. Those who were of the most sensitive at home are perfectly callous on occasions of this kind. Men ride over the Battlefield and laugh at what would once shock them."[33] One old veteran of the clash later bragged, "I took the scalp of two Indians that day; that was all that I had time to fool with."[34]

Opothle Yahola lost perhaps 250 men in the rout, and the Texans captured 160 women and children, 21 former slaves, thirty wagons, seventy yoke of oxen, five hundred ponies, and several hundred cattle in his undefended camp. Calling off their pursuit about four o'clock in the afternoon, the victors spent the remaining hour of daylight robbing the dead Indians of whatever valuables they could find. Amongst the loot picked up from the battlefield was a medal struck in commemoration of a peace treaty between the Creeks and the British crown in 1694.[35] So far had the Creek Nation fallen from the days when it was a potent factor in the international rivalry for North America.

From the point of view of the East Texans, Chustenahlah marked a "signal and glorious victory."[36] McIntosh was persuaded that his lightning campaign had won Indian Territory permanently for the Confederacy, and at minimal cost. He had lost but fifteen killed and about forty wounded. Five of the dead belonged to the Third Texas Cavalry, including Lieutenant Ben Durham, former sheriff of Anderson County, whose thigh was shattered by a rifle ball. Since McIntosh went into action unen-

cumbered by either surgeon or medical supplies, the unfortunate Durham lay in excruciating pain for several days before he
died. Private Martin Harris, a young farmhand, and the Titus
County planter's son, Charles Hamilton, also fell. McIntosh left
Private Arch Ramey, a Shelby County teamster, to die at an Indian mission.[37]

The next morning McIntosh left some of his soldiers to guard
his booty and prisoners and led the remainder in pursuit of
Opothle Yahola's survivors as they fled toward Kansas. Throughout the bitterly cold day they succeeded in killing a few more
fugitive warriors before returning to their spartan camp. On the
following day Colonel Cooper and his Confederate Indian regiments at last appeared for their belated rendezvous, only to discover that the battle had gone on without them. Denied a share
in the glory and already resentful of McIntosh's precedence in
rank, Cooper was thoroughly disgusted with his fellow commander for not waiting for him. Now he had to content himself
with the unrewarding task of mopping up the remnants of
Opothle Yahola's shattered army. Turning over most of their
plunder to Cooper, the East Texans returned to their snug winter quarters on the Arkansas, taking with them their captured
blacks, while Cooper's Indians and elements of the Ninth Texas
chased the freezing refugees toward the Kansas border.[38]

Hounded by their pursuers, the Creek fugitives straggled into
their Kansas refuge, where they camped on the upper Verdigris
not far from the present town of Fredonia, Kansas. Many arrived half naked in the midst of a fierce blizzard; totally destitute, they were without shelter, food, or clothing. Though the
United States Army and the Office of Indian Affairs tried inef-
fectually to alleviate their suffering, they received no supplies
for almost a month. During February and March 1862, about
240 Creeks died in that camp, and more than a hundred frozen
limbs were amputated from the wretched survivors. In all, some
7,600 Indian refugees eventually crowded into the squalid encampment; they lost everything in the war. Opothle Yahola
himself died in exile in 1863.[39]

Having thus disposed of the neutralist Indians, the men of
the Third Texas returned to the routine and relative comfort of
winter quarters on the second day of January 1862. Lieutenant

Colonel Lane went off to Texas on a thirty-day leave, and Major Chilton replaced him as acting commander of the regiment. In celebration of this event—and possibly his narrow escape at Chustenahlah, where a bullet had grazed his scalp—Chilton bought the boys a barrel of liquor for a treat. He formed the whole regiment into line and passed a bucket of whiskey through the ranks, so that each man could take a drink from a tin cup. It livened up their New Year considerably.[40]

CHAPTER 6

Pea Ridge,
January–March 1862

WHILE THE Third Texas had a victory to cele-
brate at the beginning of 1862, the political and military leaders
of both the North and the South saw less cause for rejoicing.
Despite its overwhelming advantages, the Union war effort had
reached a stalemate; the fronts remained static, and hopes for a
swift suppression of the rebellion had waned. On the other side,
the early Confederate successes at Manassas and Wilson's Creek
had accomplished little. With the war less than a year old, the
South's modest resources were already stretched to the breaking
point, and not a single foreign government had recognized the
new nation. Much of the Southern borderland, its first line of
defense, had already been occupied by the enemy, and Maryland, western Virginia, and most of Kentucky were firmly in the
hands of the Union.

At the very beginning of the year the new Confederate secretary of war, Judah P. Benjamin, took steps to secure Missouri
in the Rebel fold. Though its government in exile was now recognized as a Confederate state, most of Missouri's population
centers lay under Federal control, and Benjamin's two chief
commanders in the area, Price and McCulloch, seemed incapable of collaborating toward a common goal. The Confederate
commander of the Western Department, General Albert Sidney

Johnston, was so beset with the Union threats to Kentucky and Tennessee that he could give little attention or direction to the conflict west of the Mississippi. Benjamin's response to the frustrating vacuum of authority in Missouri was to designate it part of the newly created Trans-Mississippi District and to appoint on January 10 an overall commander to direct operations there.[1]

The man he chose for this formidable task was Major General Earl Van Dorn, an aggressive, flamboyant officer with a distinguished record. Rejoicing in his appointment, Van Dorn nourished ambitious plans: a massive, lightning-fast drive to clear Missouri of the Federals. "I must have St. Louis—then Huzza!" he exclaimed in a letter to his wife.[2] Two weeks before, the Northern command had appointed Brigadier General Samuel R. Curtis as chief of the Federal army in southwestern Missouri. Thus were the forces set in motion that would ultimately collide at an obscure Ozark inn early in March. This three-day battle of Elkhorn Tavern, or Pea Ridge, as the Yankees called it, would decide the fate of Missouri.

It did not take Van Dorn long to make his presence felt at the helm of the Confederate forces in the West. He set about creating one formidable army out of three disparate and widely scattered commands: General Price at Springfield, with seven thousand men; Brigadier General Albert Pike's four regiments of Confederate Indians, posted in Indian Territory; and the soldiers under Ben McCulloch near Fort Smith and Bentonville, Arkansas. Van Dorn planned to combine the three armies into a single force, augment it to the strength of 45,000 men, and dash across southern Missouri to seize St. Louis by surprise—a bold concept indeed.[3]

The impact of Van Dorn's dynamic leadership was not immediately apparent in the daily lives of the men in winter quarters on Frog Bayou, however. To be sure, Colonel Greer had returned to his command at the end of December to impose a more rigorous military regimen upon his troopers, a routine not always punctiliously observed in the rather easy-going Confederate army. The imperatives of discipline and obedience the men found difficult to learn; given their amateur status, even key noncommissioned officers had but a vague notion of how to run an army.

As a case in point, Jim Warren had been appointed sergeant major of the Third Texas at the time of its organization. A twenty-eight-year-old Tyler lawyer, he had assumed his to be a rather exalted office, but when he tried to order officers around, he got nothing but curses and insults in return. Warren at last complained to his colonel, and the following dialogue took place:

Jim—Col. Greer, I am Sergeant Major of the 3rd Texas.
Col. Greer—Certainly you are Mr. Warren.
Jim—Well, sir, what is my rank?
Col. G.—Rank, you haven't got any rank.
Jim—Well, I resign.
Col. G.—You have nothing to resign, Mr. Warren.
Jim—Can't resign. Well, in the name of God what am I anyway?
Col. G—You are a waiting boy for headquarters, and at odd times hold the Colonel's horse.

Having learned his place in the grand scheme of things, Warren informed the colonel that he "could take the d——n little office and give it to some other fellow that wanted it." He preferred to revert to the status of private for the remainder of his tour with the regiment.[4]

Many of the troopers were already anticipating the termination of their service: they had survived half of their one-year obligation, and their thoughts dwelled constantly upon the joys of reunion at home, where a warm welcome was assured. Mrs. Amanda Cartwright cheerfully reminded her sons in Company E that "we are looking forward to the 13th of June with great pleasure. The time will soon pass off. Have your horses in good care and head home in a hurry."[5] In the meantime, the troopers were "getting along finely" in winter quarters and enjoyed a comparatively indolent existence throughout the month of January. Colonel Greer had brought his wife and children from Texas, and they set up housekeeping on the edge of the encampment, contributing to an atmosphere of peacetime garrison duty. Quarters were comfortable, officers dispensed furloughs with a liberal hand, and the men of Greer's regiment took advantage of their free time to ride out into the surrounding countryside to buy food, swap horses, or hunt game.

A considerable number of them preferred to pass their idle hours in the company of the local girls. There were frequent "entertainments" held at various farmhouses in the vicinity, and these often included a great deal of dancing, not a little drinking, and an occasional quarrel over some particularly pretty or popular girl.[6] The troopers brought their girls to these parties on horseback and sometimes danced until dawn. A participant in these youthful escapades reminisced that "along toward the close of night . . . each fellow would take his girl up behind him on his steed, and after delivering her at her house, hie himself away to camp in time to answer 'here' at roll call."[7] It was not an unpleasant life at all.

Their chivalric idyll terminated abruptly as the result of an initiative by General Curtis's Yankees, who were not content to await passively the magisterial unfolding of Van Dorn's grand offensive. On January 26, Curtis began his advance from Rolla toward Price's little army at Springfield. Forced to evacuate the town, the Missourians fell back into northern Arkansas, where McCulloch's infantry joined them. On February 23 the Rebels abandoned Fayetteville and resumed their precipitous retreat, accompanied by throngs of Southern sympathizers fleeing ahead of the Yankees. To the mortification of Cherokee County Surgeon Washington Gammage, McCulloch's soldiers despoiled the little college town of everything they could carry off: "Our own troops—men who had come . . . to protect the persons and property of the people, were actually . . . breaking open store houses, smoke houses, and even . . . private houses. . . . Stores of provisions and clothing, belonging to the Government, were thrown open, and everybody . . . invited to help themselves."[8] The Rebels burned what they could not carry away, including the courthouse, and came close to destroying the entire town. At this point it began to look like a hopeless Confederate rout.

But on March 3, Van Dorn came riding into the headquarters of Price and McCulloch south of Fayetteville and took charge. With unflagging confidence in his own abilities, the new commander of the Trans-Mississippi District regarded Curtis's offensive as an opportunity to destroy the single most formidable obstacle standing between him and St. Louis.[9] He introduced himself to the demoralized troops of McCulloch's army with the ringing salutation: "Soldiers: Behold your leader! He comes to show you the way to glory and immortal renown."[10] Van Dorn then ordered a bold counterattack against the approaching Federal army for the following day.

While their commanders conferred as to how this was to be done, the men of the Third Texas languished half frozen in a snow-covered campground about fifteen miles south of Fayetteville. Two weeks earlier they had been dragged out of their snug winter quarters and marched fifty miles northward across the icy slopes of the Boston Mountains in order to join McCulloch's infantry. It was bitterly cold, and amenities were sadly lacking. Noted Victor Rose, "The precipitous mountains rose hundreds of feet overhead, while gigantic icicles hung pendant from the overhanging rocks, like huge stalactites, and glittering in the brilliant rays of the cold winter sun, looked like the suspended spears of giants."[11] A thin cornmeal gruel took the place of the regular rations to which they had become accustomed; makeshift shelters in the lee of fallen logs made poor substitutes for their comfortable cabins. Huddled together under their saddle blankets, they kept fires burning all night long. Sleep was barely possible on the snowy ground.[12]

When the East Texans arrived at Rebel headquarters, they were attached to a brigade of cavalry commanded by recently promoted Brigadier General James McIntosh. The victor of Chustenahlah repeatedly sent his troopers out to raid Union supply points and scout the advance units of Curtis's army. On February 25, Major Lawrence S. "Sul" Ross of the Sixth Texas Cavalry led a detachment of about three hundred scouts from the Third, Sixth, and Ninth regiments all the way north into Missouri. Ross's men charged through the darkness into the village of Keetsville, shouting wildly, shooting at everything that moved, and attacked a Federal supply train. As one participant recalled his part in the exploit, "I charged up and down the street and fired my Gun and hooped, and yelled hardly having sense enough to know what I was doing, but it was sure war."[13] The Yankees were so surprised by this sudden intrusion seventy miles behind their lines that they scattered. Ross's raiders killed two of the enemy, captured a dozen others, stole sixty horses, burned eight supply wagons, and got away relatively unscathed.

More important, they located Curtis's positions athwart the Missouri-Arkansas border.[14]

Because of a shortage of forage, Curtis had dispersed his troops widely along more than seventy miles of the Telegraph Road from Fayetteville to Springfield. General Franz Sigel, still deeply embroiled in controversy over his conduct at Wilson's Creek the previous summer, commanded two of Curtis's four divisions from an advanced position at Bentonville. Curtis established his own command post on Little Sugar Creek, a stream running just south of a spur of hills called Pea Ridge, fourteen miles to the east. A third contingent bivouacked across the Missouri line, some ten miles to the north. In all, Curtis commanded about 10,500 troops, scattered along this broad front and separated from their base of supply at Rolla by upwards of two hundred miles.

The dispersal of the Union forces suggested to Van Dorn that he might defeat his foe in detail if he could but move his men speedily enough to gain the advantage of surprise. Moreover, his army outnumbered that of his adversary: McCulloch's command now included 8,384 men; Price had 6,818 soldiers; and Pike's Indian regiments would add about 1,000 more—in all, some 16,200 men. This was a far cry from the 45,000-man host that he had projected, but Van Dorn still calculated his chances as good.

Everything hinged upon speed and surprise. Consequently, the impatient general drove his men beyond the limits of human endurance. From the moment he led them out of their campgrounds at dawn on March 4, most of Van Dorn's troops would not enjoy a decent rest or a filling meal for the next ten days. They were forced to march and fight over mountainous terrain of extreme difficulty in the worst winter conditions. Bungled orders and misdirected supply trains denied the soldiers even the most basic necessities, from food to ammunition. Yet, the army of Earl Van Dorn might well have prevailed.[15]

The Rebels had four chances to defeat General Curtis. Their first opportunity lay in the fact that Sigel and his seven thousand men near Bentonville remained widely separated from the rest of Curtis's army until it was almost too late. Van Dorn's first objective was to fall upon Sigel before he could withdraw to unite his force with Curtis at Little Sugar Creek. All day Van Dorn pushed his army across the mountains through a blinding snowstorm to Fayetteville, where the troops had a dinner of hardtack and slept on the snowy ground. They spent their second day, March 5, on the road north toward Bentonville, camping about ten miles south of the town after dining upon an uncooked mush of meal and water.

In his feverish haste to overtake Sigel's command, Van Dorn roused his weary men and had them on the road north again by three o'clock the following morning. Riding forward as advance guard, the troopers of the Third Texas arrived by midmorning atop a hill from which they could gaze down upon Bentonville in the distance. From this vantage point they caught a tantalizing glimpse of a mass of bluecoats milling about the courthouse square, the burnished metal of their weapons gleaming in the bright winter sunshine, which at last was beginning to thaw the frozen ground. The glistening rifles belonged to the six hundred Yankees in Sigel's rear guard, who now withdrew rapidly towards the northeast in obedience to Curtis's order to concentrate on Little Sugar Creek.[16]

While the bulk of his force marched directly into Bentonville to occupy it in the wake of the retreating Federal troops, Van Dorn hastily dispatched McIntosh's cavalry to circle around the west of the town in an effort to cut off the enemy's withdrawal. With Lieutenant Colonel Lane at its head, the Third Texas rode in the van of this Rebel column. By the time the regiment had wound its way through the broken country north of Bentonville, however, Sigel's troops had slipped away, and the Union rear guard had set up a roadblock near an old Confederate campsite called Camp Stephens, only six miles from Curtis's headquarters. As Lane led Companies A and B down out of the ravines and onto the road, the Texans were met by a hail of rifle fire and grapeshot from a concealed Yankee battery. Sergeant Bill Isom, from Henderson, and young Sam Honey, of Hopkins County, were both killed instantly. Momentarily trapped, the cavalrymen tried to charge "up a hill so steep and rough that only a goat could have made any progress."[17] Even their doughty leader recognized the suicidal futility of the effort. "Fall back, or you will all be murdered!" Lane cried, and all were quick to obey.[18]

Thrown into confusion, the cavalry column milled about in the woods until the determined fire of Sigel's rear guard drove them back down the road toward Bentonville. Doug Cater's terrified mount ran away with him, straight toward the enemy line; Sergeant Taylor Brown's horse simply pitched his master to the ground and disappeared among the trees. At last Lane was able to extricate his men, allowing the Yankee rear guard to withdraw unmolested. The exhausted Texans returned to Camp Stephens at nightfall and rested uneasily for a few hours as they awaited the arrival of Van Dorn's main army.[19]

The warm reception they had received at the hands of Sigel's rear guard sobered the Texans considerably. The regiment lost only two men killed and nine wounded in the brief encounter, but the officers marveled that the toll had not been greater. Impressed by the Yankees' fierce resistance, Colonel Greer concluded that his cavalry vanguard had stumbled into an entire Union brigade, "4,000 or 5,000 strong," instead of the resolute 600 who actually manned it.[20] Still, many of the men were ashamed of their headlong flight in the face of the enemy. Captain Hale, of Company D, allowed as how he felt personally mortified by their hasty withdrawal. "This here regiment," he exclaimed, "are disgraced forever! I'd 'a' rather died right thar than to a give airy inch!"[21]

In their own mad dash to cut off the Union rear guard at Bentonville, Price's Missourians had fared no better than the Texans. Van Dorn had missed his first chance to defeat the enemy: he had been too slow; Sigel had just barely eluded the springing trap. Meanwhile, Curtis had dug in his troops along the terraces of rising terrain overlooking the north bank of Little Sugar Creek to face what he assumed would be the Rebel approach from the south. Throughout the afternoon of March 6, Van Dorn drove his weary men forward until they collapsed near Camp Stephens, just to the west of Curtis's outposts on the creek.

They had nothing to eat and were soon numbed by the cold. Many of the Rebels had never seen action before, and the sight

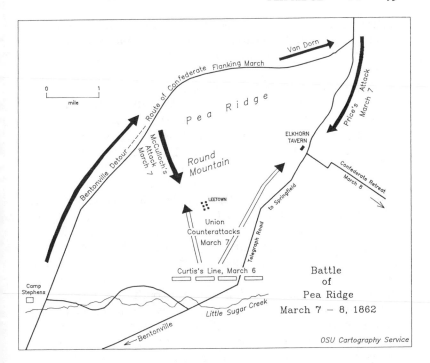

Battle
of
Pea Ridge
March 7 – 8, 1862

OSU Cartography Service

of dead and dying Yankee soldiers scattered along the roadside in the wake of Sigel's retreat further chilled their ardor on that bitterly frigid night. Though the belated arrival of General Pike's Cherokees added considerable noise and confusion to the Confederate encampment, it stirred little enthusiasm in the ranks. The soldiers knew that they would have to storm the Yankee entrenchments the following morning, and in their jaded condition they were not looking forward to the challenge.

But that evening, as their commanders conferred over their plans, McCulloch pointed out a second chance for victory without risking a frontal assault against the formidable Union line. A little-used trail called the Bentonville Detour ran north of Little Sugar Creek past Camp Stephens, looped to the east around the northern flank of Pea Ridge, and joined the Telegraph Road again above Elkhorn Tavern. Here was a possible route of about eight miles in length to the rear of the Federal lines. Instead of charging the enemy breastworks ahead, the Rebels might take the Detour, encircle the Yankees, and cut off their retreat to Springfield. Success, however, depended upon speed of execution.

Thus at 8:00 P.M., after giving his troops but three hours' rest, Van Dorn ordered them to proceed along the Detour. He and Price first led the Missourians up the dark, brush-choked trail, while McCulloch's division and McIntosh's cavalry were to follow immediately behind. It was a bold, even reckless, plan; two factors prevented its successful execution. In the first place, the detour ran through narrow gullies and defiles, and the Federals had further blocked it with felled timber and boulders. It took all night for the Missourians to cut their way through to the rear of Curtis's army. Furthermore, in their haste the Rebels neglected to bridge the creek, and McCulloch's foot soldiers barely had time to inch their way over a makeshift crossing before dawn. Instead of joining Price in the Yankee rear as planned, McCulloch's division was still south of Pea Ridge and widely separated from the Missourians when they began firing on the Union pickets north of Elkhorn Tavern about 8 A.M.

General Curtis only learned of Van Dorn's bold flanking movement shortly after daylight on March 7, and he was still unsure of the direction of attack. Cautiously, he pulled one of his divisions out of its entrenchments facing Little Sugar Creek and countermarched it three miles north up the Telegraph Road to block the passage around the eastern end of Pea Ridge. Thus, when Van Dorn and Price assaulted the Yankee positions north of Elkhorn Tavern at midmorning, Curtis was ready for them. At about the same time his scouts informed him of the presence of McCulloch's troops on the Bentonville Detour to his west. The delay in the flanking movement had persuaded Van Dorn to order these men off the Bentonville Detour; instead, they were to advance toward the Telegraph Road by a route south of Pea Ridge. Confused by this change in orders, the Rebels milled about uncertainly, while Curtis dispatched two more divisions from his entrenched line to engage McCulloch near the little hamlet of Leetown on the plateau just south of the ridge. By the skillful and timely disposition of his forces to meet his enemy on both the north and west, Curtis spoiled Van Dorn's second chance at victory.[22]

For the remainder of the day the battle of Pea Ridge assumed the character of two discrete engagements—Leetown and Elkhorn Tavern—and thereby presented Van Dorn a third opportunity for success. After all, he had clamped his adversary between the hammer of Price's Missourians north of the tavern, and the anvil of McCulloch's division near Leetown. A less resourceful commander than Curtis might have panicked and opted for retreat. But the Union general refused to abandon either of his extended wings. Using his advantage of interior lines, Curtis successively dispatched troops to reinforce his position before Leetown and then brought up additional units to strengthen his hold at Elkhorn Tavern.

In the Leetown sector the troopers of the Third Texas Cavalry were reduced to the role of unwilling spectators, while the battle raged around them all day. Stalled by the crush of infantry at the creek crossing, the East Texans spent half the night waiting in the cold for their turn to march up the Bentonville Detour. At midmorning they were still plodding around the western flank of Pea Ridge when they received the order to about-face, turn south, and confront a Federal task force of cavalry, infantry, and artillery that Curtis had sent to block McCulloch's progress around the Detour. As they debouched onto the fields north of Leetown, McCulloch ordered Greer's cavalry to remain in place to cover his artillery. McIntosh, however, deployed his other three regiments—the Sixth, the Ninth Texas, and Pike's Cherokees—into columns facing southeast, and ordered Lieutenant Colonel Lane to lead their charge against a Yankee battery about four hundred yards away across the open ground. Lane called upon his bugler, Charley Watts, to "blow the charge until you are black in the face," and led the screaming Texans down the slope toward the Yankee artillery.[23]

The men of the Third Cavalry could only look on, therefore, as their comrades slashed through the ranks of the Third Iowa Cavalry Regiment, posted to defend their cannons, and felled about two dozen men. Swarming over the Yankee battery, they captured three guns and then withdrew into the woods behind them. In their wake the Confederate Cherokees ran wild across the field and harvested eight Iowa scalps before the Union artillery drove them back to cover.[24]

McCulloch then ordered Greer's regiment to occupy and hold Round Mountain, an eminence that rose about a hundred feet above the rocky plateau south of the ridge. The East Texans dismounted, horse holders led their mounts to the rear, and the remainder of the troopers took positions on the mountain to await further instructions. But orders never came. For the entire afternoon, while the battle surged below them, the Texans remained secure as long as they kept their heads down. On one occasion the Third Louisiana Infantry Regiment mistook them for the enemy and was in the act of charging up the hill after them before the error was discovered. Fortunately, no shots were fired and no blood shed in this typical episode of battlefield confusion.

Meanwhile, Van Dorn and Price had enjoyed considerable success at the eastern end of Pea Ridge. Repeatedly assaulting Curtis's hastily improvised defenses north of Elkhorn Tavern, the Missourians ploughed relentlessly down the Telegraph Road. Each onslaught encountered ever more determined Union resistance, but at the very close of the day the Rebels took the tavern in a furious climax to the battle. They bivouacked south of the landmark that night.

More than two miles to the west, McCulloch had not been so fortunate. Emboldened by his initial success at Leetown, McIntosh mounted a second attack, but Curtis rushed reinforcements to the position and beat back the Rebel assaults with heavy artillery fire. Fighting two distinct battles, separated by miles of rough terrain controlled by the enemy, the Confederate commanders lost contact with each other. Striking power and time were wasted in pointless maneuvers, and Van Dorn forfeited the initiative.

On Round Mountain, Colonel Greer fumed over the inactivity imposed upon his regiment and made repeated attempts to reach McCulloch or McIntosh by courier. Finally, at the close of the afternoon he went himself and discovered that they were both dead. While scouting the enemy dispositions for a new assault, McCulloch had been slain by a Union sharpshooter. The impetuous McIntosh was shot as he launched still another Rebel attack. Colonel Hébert, their ranking subordinate, was captured. Leaderless, the right arm of the Confederate pincers had been paralyzed throughout much of the afternoon.[25]

As the senior officer left at his end of the battlefield, Greer turned the Third Texas over to Lieutenant Colonel Lane and assumed command of all the Rebel troops on the enemy's western flank. He was uncertain what he should do with them. He had only joined his regiment that morning, had never been apprised of Van Dorn's plans for the engagement, and was separated from his commander's headquarters at Elkhorn Tavern by the concentration of Northern troops. With the sudden and almost simultaneous demise of both McCulloch and McIntosh, uncertainty and despair began to infect the men. Greer collected the scattered Confederate units into a bivouac on the battlefield as darkness closed in.

Later that night he sent two Harrison County privates, John Coleman and Albert Blocker, on a perilous mission around enemy lines to Van Dorn's headquarters to find out what he was supposed to do now. As the two young couriers silently picked their way through the darkness of midnight toward Elkhorn Tavern, a rising moon revealed the carnage of the day before: "The dead soldiers of both armies . . . presented a most ghastly sight when the moonlight would flash out from behind a cloud onto their white upturned faces. . . . The dead soldiers and horses on every hand made the most gruesome and awful picture."[26] In the piles of the slain, Van Dorn had spent his third chance for victory.

There still remained one last forlorn hope: if Greer's troops could unite with Van Dorn before Elkhorn Tavern during the night, this reconstituted force might prove sufficient to push the Yankees off the ground. Van Dorn consequently ordered Greer to join him before sunup, and Greer's couriers dutifully informed their chief of this command. His soldiers therefore groped their way around the enemy's outposts and through the thickets of Pea Ridge to arrive at the Telegraph Road just before dawn on March 8, with the Third Texas bringing up the rear. Lane posted his regiment across the road half a mile north of Elkhorn Tavern, and the East Texans were left standing, or lying, by the roadside until the sun was high in the sky, as their commander awaited further orders.[27]

But no orders came. Van Dorn seemed incapable of seizing the initiative that morning. Through a critical blunder, his ammunition wagons had turned off toward Bentonville, and he was unable to resupply his troops. The men had eaten nothing for two days; they were past the point of exhaustion. In McCulloch and McIntosh, they had lost the commanders they trusted most. Deploying his troops across the Telegraph Road about three-fourths of a mile south of the tavern, Van Dorn awaited the Union offensive. Curtis, on the other hand, was no longer threatened by Rebels on his flank and had used the respite of darkness to strengthen his front on both sides of the road a quarter-mile farther south.

The third day's battle opened at 7:00 A.M. with a furious artillery duel. Curtis sent his infantry forward at midmorning. They hurled themselves against the center of the Confederate line, hewing huge swaths from the ranks of the tough Missourians, who bore again the brunt of the slaughter. As one young soldier remembered it, "we was like the trees in the forest [that] stand till they are cut down."[28] By noon Van Dorn's army, threatened on both flanks, stood in danger of envelopment. Though Price "begged Van Dorn with tears in his eyes to let him continue the fight," the commander gave the order to withdraw eastward toward Huntsville, and the Rebels dragged themselves off in all directions.[29] Van Dorn had consumed his fourth and final chance at victory.

Meanwhile, the men of the Third Texas had spent the morning sprawled along the road north of Elkhorn Tavern. Though grateful for the rest, the East Texans were baffled by their inactivity at what they correctly perceived to be a critical point in the battle. "This seemed to our army very wrong," reflected one of the men. "Our regiment had not fired a gun and did not know why we were not ordered forward. I could not understand this. There was no further action of McCulloch's army. Some of the command, like us, had not been used except to change positions." Gradually it dawned on them that "General Van Dorn had given up the fight."[30]

In the chaotic retreat that followed, Van Dorn assigned the

Third Texas the role of rear guard. By that time the East Texans were not only famished and exhausted but also demoralized by their defeat and ashamed of their inactivity during the battle. They lamented the loss of their two most popular leaders, and they blamed Van Dorn for what they considered his premature withdrawal. The entire Rebel army degenerated into a shattered throng of leaderless men, straggling through the innumerable draws and hollows of the Ozarks. Haunted by hunger, they could find little sustenance in that wild, wintry, and wooded country.

They devoured everything they could lay their hands on. At a deserted house "stood a slop barrel, nearly full of refuse. . . . It was upset, and the men scrambled for the decayed contents like a drove of hogs."[31] After two days of fasting, a Rusk County private found a couple of apples that revived him as though they had been a feast. Occasionally, some of the troops were lucky enough to shoot a hog in the woods. Slicing off a ham, they "march[ed] on eating the raw bloody pork without bread or salt."[32]

Fortunately for the fleeing Rebels, the Yankees were as jaded as they were: They found it difficult to locate their beaten enemy and mounted no sustained pursuit. Gradually the Confederates drifted south toward their winter quarters in the Arkansas valley. After four days of stumbling through the mountains, the Third Cavalry had reached a point east of Fayetteville when they were ordered north again to rescue twenty-four pieces of artillery that had mistakenly retreated into Missouri. Recovering their guns, the regiment finally returned to Frog Bayou on March 15.[33]

Van Dorn's reports of the debacle at Pea Ridge provide a devastating commentary upon his character. The supreme egotist, he absolved himself of all responsibility for his defeat and attributed it to the incompetence of others. "I was not defeated," he reported, "but only failed in my intentions." "A series of accidents, entirely unforeseen and not under my control, and a badly-disciplined army" were to blame. To Richmond he complained "of the crudeness of the material with which I have to deal in organizing an army out here."[34] Despite his dash and initiative, Van Dorn deserved to lose: contemptuous of everyone but himself, he gave little thought to the needs of his men, neglected to reveal his plans to his key officers, and largely ignored the intentions of his enemy.

In partial mitigation of these faults, however, Van Dorn had at least not killed very many of his men: only 185, according to one estimate. About a thousand of his soldiers, or about 6 percent of his forces engaged at Pea Ridge, were killed, wounded, or captured. Curtis incurred 1,384 casualties, or 13 percent of his command. Because the regiment watched the entire battle from the sidelines, the Third Texas lost not a single man killed, and only a dozen soldiers were wounded in the main engagement.[35] The Texans did not know whether to feel lucky or embarrassed. But they did know they had been beaten. In its defeat at Pea Ridge, the Confederacy lost whatever claim it had on the state of Missouri.

CHAPTER 7

Corinth, April–May 1862

VAN DORN enjoyed little leisure to ponder the lessons of Pea Ridge. On March 19, 1862, General Pierre G. T. Beauregard, Confederate commander on the Mississippi front, urged him to hasten eastward, where Union Brigadier General Ulysses S. Grant had just breached the Confederate first line of defense in northern Tennessee. In February his troops captured Forts Henry and Donelson, which guarded the lower reaches of the Tennessee and Cumberland rivers, respectively. It was the first substantial Union victory after ten months of discouragement, and with these strongpoints in Federal hands, Union gunboats might now ply the two rivers, outflank the Confederate defenses on the Mississippi, and split Tennessee in twain. Grant's astounding victory forced the Confederacy to abandon its foothold in Kentucky and evacuate most of Tennessee.[1]

Meanwhile, an even greater disaster threatened as the Confederate hold on the vital Mississippi waterway began to slip. Early in March the Federals laid siege to Island Number 10, a Rebel stronghold on the upper river. It fell on April 7, opening the Mississippi as far south as Memphis to the free passage of Union gunboats. Flag Officer David G. Farragut captured New Orleans, the greatest city of the South, later in the same month. The compounded agony of this succession of defeats appeared to portend the imminent destruction of the Confederacy, and the Northern press exulted somewhat prematurely that "the monster is already clutched and in his death struggle."[2]

Stunned by the loss of Forts Henry and Donelson, General Albert Sidney Johnston, commander of the Confederate Department of the West, hastily threw up a second barrier to the Northern advance. Pulling his troops out of Kentucky and western Tennessee, he concentrated almost fifty thousand men around the little northeastern Mississippi town of Corinth. Normally an insignificant place of some five hundred inhabitants, Corinth lay in the broad valley of the Tuscumbia River, with rugged, forested hills flanking it on both the east and west. Twenty miles to the east, the Tennessee River cut a great swath across northern Alabama, offering the only major natural obstacle to a further Union penetration of the region.

But it was the railroad that made Corinth a prize. Within the town the Mobile and Ohio Railroad, running from Illinois to the Gulf, crossed the tracks of the Memphis and Charleston line. The latter was the only major east-west railway in the Confederacy, linking the banks of the Mississippi with the Atlantic seaboard. This railroad constituted "the vertebrae of the Confederacy"; sever it, and the South would fall.[3] Consequently, the Confederate War Department rushed every man it could spare to Johnston at Corinth. In the meantime, Johnston and his second-in-command, Beauregard, desperately reorganized their defenses along the Tennessee River in anticipation of the Union attack they expected at any moment.

By the middle of March a race for life had developed between the Union and Confederate forces, with Corinth as the goal. Grant had shipped his 42,000-man force up the Tennessee River to Pittsburg Landing, Tennessee, only twenty-two miles north of the Rebel concentration at Corinth. At that point he halted to await reinforcements in the form of Brigadier General Don Carlos Buell's army of 21,000 men from Kentucky. Johnston and Beauregard resolved to attack Grant before he could be reinforced. In order to win, they sorely needed Van Dorn's veterans of Pea Ridge, who were at that moment enjoying a brief respite at their winter quarters near Van Buren. It was to serve this purpose that Beauregard summoned Van Dorn to the east on March 19.[4]

To his credit, Van Dorn complied as soon as he got the order, but it took a month before he could complete the massive movement of troops that Beauregard demanded. On March 21 he roused his still weary troops out of winter quarters and started them on their five-hundred-mile journey to Corinth. To the credit of his men, they realized that the war had reached a point of crisis that required new exertions. "The time has come," wrote Americus Cartwright, "for every man in the South . . . to buckle on his armor and march forth to the field of action to meet the blackhearted fiends and drive them from our country."[5]

As though in answer to this appeal, hundreds of new recruits had joined Van Dorn's army during the winter, and he hurriedly integrated these men into the ranks depleted by the battle at Elkhorn Tavern and by the attrition of winter diseases. For its part, the Third Cavalry gained 122 green volunteers during the fall and winter, most of whom had ridden up from Texas to join brothers or cousins already in the army. Epamanondas and Lycurgus, the eighteen-year-old Jarvis twins from Smith County, for example, joined their brothers in Company K. The Keahey boys from Cherokee County enrolled belatedly in Company C, and the Upshur County Rogers brothers entered Company H. Yet in addition to those felled by combat or disease, 150 men had been dropped from the regimental rolls for various disabilities or reassignment during the same period. Other dozens of sick soldiers were left behind at winter quarters under the care of Surgeon Isaac K. Frazer.[6]

In all, Van Dorn hastily cobbled together an army of seven brigades totalling some 22,000 men, who were shipped across the Mississippi to meet the Yankee threat at Corinth. The boys in the ranks had no idea of their destination; they knew only that they were winding their way eastward across Arkansas in the rain. "I never had enny idea of a soldier's life before," complained Private Richard Creswell in a letter home. "They have a terrible time, but I think I can stand it if enny of the rest of them can."[7] The Third Texas slogged through the Arkansas valley for a week before reaching Little Rock on April 5. Shortly after their departure from winter quarters, Brigadier General Joseph L. Hogg, who was slated to take the place of the slain McIntosh as their brigade commander, fell in with the riders. Fresh from civilian life, he and his staff had just come up from Texas. Most of these men were prominent Cherokee Countians of sedentary occupation and middle-age constitution; all were strangers to the hard life of a soldier. Though a veteran of the Mexican War, Hogg had not even found time to acquire a uniform. Instead, he attired his spare frame in garb more appropriate to the presiding judge that he was than to the rough campaigning which lay ahead.[8]

With characteristic insolence the veterans of the Third Cavalry delighted in ragging the greenhorns, officers or not. In his Prince Albert coat, stiff-collared white shirt, and tall silk hat, Hogg was the most conspicuous of the newcomers and inspired the most good-natured ridicule from the men. He presented "rather the appearance of a professor of languages or a preacher of the old school Presbyterian type, than that of a military officer."[9] The boys called General Hogg "Professor" or "Parson" to his face and made fun of his hat. The general seems to have endured it all with good humor.

After passing through Little Rock, Van Dorn's column struck out overland toward De Valls Bluff on the White River, fifty miles to the east. The general had requisitioned twenty steamboats out of Memphis, which were to meet his army at that point and transport the men down the White River and up the Mississippi to Memphis. Spring rains sent streams roaring out of their banks, and the primitive trails that they followed turned into sloughs and quagmires. The Third Regiment spent an entire day wading across a broad prairie so perfectly flat that water stood two or three inches deep on the ground. In addition to the unfavorable weather, Van Dorn faced a shortage of wagons and equipment, as well as the unanimous indignation of the people of Arkansas for abandoning the state to the tender mercies of the enemy. But Van Dorn was eventually able to assemble his army at De Valls Bluff and Des Arc, another port a few miles upriver, for embarkation aboard the steamboats.

When they learned of their destination, the East Texans were dismayed by the prospect of putting the giant Mississippi be-

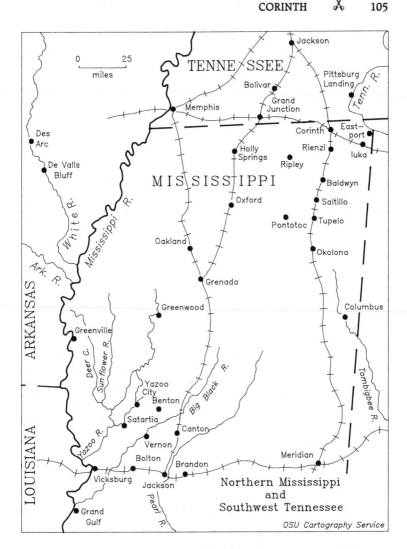

Northern Mississippi
and
Southwest Tennessee

OSU Cartography Service

tween them and their homes. As they muttered with apprehension over this concern, they were appalled to learn that Van Dorn had decreed that his cavalrymen were to give up their horses. There were simply too many cavalrymen in the Rebel army; infantry were needed to defend Corinth. Besides, there was no room aboard the riverboats for a herd of horses. Offering vague assurances that men and horses would be reunited later, the officers appointed details to lead the mounts back across the Ozarks to the Texas farms whence they had come.[10]

The erstwhile cavalrymen bitterly watched as their most precious possessions were led away, hardly able to bear the humiliation of being forced to fight on foot. As the Texas governor had explained to the secretary of war shortly before, Texans had a great aversion to serving in the infantry: "Efficient cavalry . . . can be obtained from this state almost to the extent of the male population, but infantry is difficult to furnish."[11] Like their comrades in the other Texas regiments, Greer's troopers regarded this deprivation as a breach of contract; having grown wise to the ways of the army, most despaired of ever seeing their mounts again.

For some, the sudden loss of their horses was mitigated by the anticipation of their first steamboat excursion. On April 11 the entire Third Regiment, with all accouterments, descended De Valls Bluff and crowded aboard the little side-wheeler *Scotland*, which had come to ferry them to Memphis. The first stage of their journey took them a hundred miles down the surging waters of the White River, then in flood. Fascinated by the enormous paddle wheels and the huge, throbbing engine, the men were astounded at the speed and power of their novel conveyance. One first-time river traveler recorded his amazement that the little craft was not torn apart as its engine drove it through the great boughs of a pecan tree that had fallen into the stream. Snags were not their only hazard, for the *Scotland* was so overloaded that it repeatedly threatened to capsize. To prevent the shifting of weight on board, each company was ordered to remain stationary on deck, but sometimes natural inquisitiveness overcame caution. Then the crowd would shift "from one side to the other to see some curiosity and make the boat dip water [until] it was in danger of sinking."[12]

As the *Scotland* passed out of the mouth of the White River and steered upstream against the swollen current of the Mississippi, the vessel slowed to a crawl. It required several days to navigate the two hundred miles of river up to the destination. Along much of its course, the great river had inundated the lowlands. Huge snags and rotting animal carcasses swept past the voyagers as they peered out over a drowned landscape of flooded farmhouses and ruined fields. Crowded on the deck of the *Scotland*, their bellies cramped from the diarrhea brought on by bad food and worse water, the men of the Third Cavalry at last spied the lights of the Memphis bluffs twinkling out of the twilight on April 15.

Memphis, with some 25,000 inhabitants, was by far the largest city that most of the men had ever seen. It was a seething metropolis compared to the sleepy little farming towns of East Texas. The men were forbidden to leave the *Scotland* that night, but they were understandably curious to sample whatever nocturnal delights might await them amid the bustling docks and crowded streets. Some of the more adventurous passengers escaped their confinement and explored the city. The next morning, after an uncommon treat of store-bought bread for breakfast, Greer's regiment marched through town and followed Poplar Avenue out about three miles to their campground.[13]

By this time they had already missed their date with destiny by ten days. Without waiting for Van Dorn's troops, who were still slogging through the sloughs of Arkansas, Confederate General Johnston had ordered a surprise attack against Grant's army at Pittsburg Landing on April 6. In the wild melee that ensued, the Rebels gained the initial advantage but lost their commanding general to a Yankee Minie ball. Beauregard took charge of the battle on the second day, as Buell's reinforcements arrived to enlarge Grant's army to 62,000 men. Overwhelmed by superior numbers and fatigue, the mangled Rebel army retired to the fortifications of Corinth on April 8.

That horrendous battle of Shiloh, or Pittsburg Landing, was the biggest and bloodiest of the war to date—it came very close to turning into a disaster for the Union—but ultimately it gave the Federals the advantage: Shiloh broke the second Confederate line of defense, consolidated Union gains in the West, and opened new possibilities for deeper penetration of the Southern heartland. With Shiloh, the first phase of the war in the West was over.[14]

Had Van Dorn's 22,000 men been present on the field, the outcome at Shiloh might well have been otherwise. Though the great battle had been fought and lost without them, their presence was still urgently required at Corinth, one hundred miles east of Memphis, since an enormous Federal army under Major General Henry W. Halleck was poised to attack the Rebel stronghold from the northeast. Beauregard's tattered troops required all the assistance they could muster. Heeding Beauregard's summons to "hurry up the movement," Van Dorn reordered his forces and rushed his men ahead by rail.[15]

As they piled aboard a train bound for Corinth, most of the men of the Third Texas were delighted by the novelty: some of them had never even seen a train before, and now they would get to ride in one. Besides, it would save the recently dismounted cavalrymen a hundred miles of dreary marching. So it was with a sense of anticipation that the Texans loaded their mules and equipment into boxcars of the Memphis and Charleston line and crammed themselves in the few passenger cars provided for the regimental transport.[16]

The anticipated treat, like most things in war, turned out to be an ordeal. Their train pulled smartly out of Memphis, but at the first ascending grade the locomotive blew out a cylinder head, and this entailed a wait for another engine to arrive to push them over the hill. Assisted in this way, they reached the midway point of their journey in about twelve hours. But new delays continued to impede their progress. During the middle of the night, a coupling broke, leaving the passenger cars at the rear of the train stalled at the bottom of a forty-foot cut, while the engine sped on ahead with their supplies. Lieutenant Colonel Lane had the presence of mind to mount a lantern at the rear of the uncoupled coaches to alert approaching locomotives. He also ordered his charges to evacuate the cars just in case the warning light failed to work as intended.

The Texans hurriedly crawled out of their coaches into the mud and pouring rain, scrambled up the slick sides of the cut, and perched on its rim "like swallows on a chimney."[17] From this vantage point they enjoyed an unobstructed view of the onrushing engine that soon bore down upon the rear of their train in the darkness. Its engineer braked the monster a few feet short of collision, and the muddy soldiers, drenched to the skin, piled into their coaches again for another long wait. At last the conductor of their own train discovered that he had left half his cars behind, backed up, recoupled, and renewed the tedious journey toward Corinth.

Throughout the following day the train was sidetracked at almost every station to let more urgent traffic pass. It approached Corinth late in the day, but was sidetracked repeatedly, causing several hours' delay. Lane became uneasy at this point, fearing that the train crew was sabotaging their movement or setting them up for capture by Yankee raiders. When he communicated his misgivings to General Hogg, the latter, "an irritable man [whose] suspicions were easily aroused," concurred in this anxiety and ordered Lane to arrest both the conductor and engineer.[18]

Lane executed this order with malevolent relish and instructed the train crew to proceed at full speed to Corinth, on pain of being shot as spies. When the conductor stubbornly insisted, "Colonel, suppose we meet the passenger train, what shall we do?" Lane tersely replied, "By God, Sir, if they don't get out of the way, run over them!"[19] The cars rolled along smartly then until within three miles of Corinth. By this time it was almost dark, and the rain was falling steadily.

The train halted again, with its engine facing another approaching locomotive. Out jumped a major, who furiously berated Lane for blocking General Beauregard's express by not remaining sidetracked back down the line. With his accustomed vigor of expression, Lane warned the major to back his engine the three miles to Corinth, or he would have him arrested. Threatening dire consequences, the intimidated officer complied. At last arriving at the outskirts of town, Lane unloaded his men beside the tracks, where they set up camp as best they could after a thirty-hour ride.

The next morning Beauregard summoned Hogg and Lane to his office for an explanation of why the two had obstructed his dispatch train out of Corinth. Calling upon his native Irish eloquence, Lane explained that their fault lay in their excessive zeal for the Southern cause. Having heard firing around Corinth, the Third Texas was determined to forge ahead to the scene of action in spite of all obstacles in order to participate in the battle.

Instead of a reprimand, Beauregard extended his compliments for their patriotic fervor, and Lane departed the interview much pleased with himself.[20]

As the East Texans gloomily surveyed the town on the morning of April 27, most wondered why there was any reason to fight for the place. By this time Corinth had become a muddy pesthole crowded with ragged Rebels and mired commissary wagons. "The whole earth seemed to be teeming with soldiers," marveled a Cherokee County surgeon. "The roads for miles around were crammed and jammed with wagons, carts, ambulances, caissons and artillery carriages."[21] When the Third Cavalry's quartermaster sergeant tried to haul supplies to his regiment, he found the miserable roads so choked with mud and throngs of troops that he could not get his wagons through. "There were more headquarters, more sentinels, and more red tape here than I had ever dreamed of," he grumbled.[22]

In fact, Beauregard had concentrated two armies—the Army of Mississippi under General Braxton Bragg, and Van Dorn's Army of the West—in and around the little railroad town. He deployed his 53,000 men near the railway junction and dug them in behind a line of earthworks that extended in a crescent around the northern and eastern limits of Corinth. The Third Texas, now attached to Hogg's Brigade, took a position on this fortified line about three miles east of the center of town. Hardly had they established their camp when the 707 men still present for duty began to succumb to the epidemic diseases that made the name of Corinth synonymous with suffering and squalor.

Many of the 8,000 Rebels wounded at Shiloh still crowded the churches, hotels, and schools that had been converted to hospitals. Tetanus and gangrene carried off hundreds of men, and a growing pile of amputated limbs in the yard of the Tishomingo Hotel presented a shocking testimony to the horrors of war. With the onset of warmer weather during the late spring, the litany of misery lengthened as the effects of bad food, foul water, and overcrowding became more pronounced.[23]

If a Rebel soldier got a few hard biscuits and a slice of unpalatable pickled beef to gnaw on, he counted himself lucky. For water, the men dug their own wells. The soil was so moist and spongy that at first water could be reached by scraping out a hole about two feet deep. Gradually, as the ground dried out, the troops had to dig deeper, but the water did not improve. It was so polluted that it stank; horses refused to drink it. "With every pint of fluid one has to drink a half ounce of dirt," reported a Richmond correspondent attached to the Confederate command. "You feel it scrape the throat as it goes down, and after it gets to the stomach it lays as heavy and indigestible as a bed of mortar."[24]

As a consequence of this utterly foul water, dysentery and typhoid raged throughout the Confederate camps. In some units half the men were struck down by disease. Since there was little that could be done for them in Corinth, the sick were hauled south to various villages along the railroad. A Texas cavalrymen rode in one of these "hospital trains" for two and a half days and left a vivid description of the experience. Thrown into a boxcar with thirty other sufferers, with no attending physician or medical supplies available, the stricken soldier soon found himself lying in "a mess and a mixture of things" as rain poured through the leaky roof and pooled on the floor of the car. While halted at a switch, the men piled fence rails into the car to raise themselves out of the water. "I was pretty sick," the trooper remembered, "but not so much so but what I could puke and help work."[25]

The lucky men who made such journeys from Corinth were unloaded at village crossings and found tender care at farmhouses along the way, where they either slowly recovered or at least succumbed in relatively comfortable circumstances. Others less fortunate were left to lie without water or medical care on depot platforms or under clumps of trees, where they perished by the hundreds. As many soldiers died from disease during their seven weeks' encampment at Corinth as were slain in the preceding battle of Shiloh.[26]

Typhoid and dysentery struck most savagely at the new recruits still unseasoned by the rigors of war. Many of those who had come up from Texas with General Hogg became ill and discouraged, and most of the new officers who had joined his staff resigned their commissions before they ever tasted combat. Hogg himself died on May 16 and, still in civilian clothes, was buried in a lonely grave about four miles west of the town. He was merely among the first of the East Texans to fall victim to the epidemic. In the Third Texas Cavalry alone fifty soldiers perished from the lethal fevers and infections contracted at Corinth. Observing all this, Surgeon Washington Gammage struggled to find words of reassurance for the "wives, mothers and sisters who . . . tremble for those who . . . discharge the glorious duties of war. Calm your fears," he counseled, for "*science and charity are watching over those whom you love!*"[27]

The appalling condition of Beauregard's camp and the diseases that racked his men's bodies were not, however, the general's chief concern. For only a few miles to the northeast lurked a gargantuan enemy, ponderously but inexorably bearing down upon Beauregard's defenses. After Shiloh, General Halleck had assumed personal command over the Federal army at Pittsburg Landing, a force that outnumbered Corinth's defenders more than two to one. But Halleck, a recognized authority on field fortifications, applied all his accumulated expertise to advance on his enemy at a rate of less than a mile per day.

Considering the vast disparity between his own force and that of his adversary, he should have moved faster. After their victories at Island Number 10, New Orleans, and Shiloh, the Yankees held the initiative in the spring of 1862, as they drew a noose ever more tightly around the South's Mississippi artery. Yet Halleck crawled along, requiring a month to move his ponderous host the twenty-odd miles between Pittsburg Landing and the Confederate earthworks before Corinth. Beauregard thus enjoyed plenty of time to strengthen his defenses and even to reorganize his army.[28]

The reorganization was made necessary by the provisions of the Confederate Conscription Act of April 16. A truly revolutionary measure, this legislation placed the life of every white male Southerner between the ages of eighteen and thirty-five at the disposal of the Confederate commander in chief. All men subject to conscription were drafted for three years' service, or the duration of the war. This meant that one-year volunteers such as the troops of the Third Cavalry still owed the South at least two more years, an exceedingly somber prospect to many.[29]

Having experienced almost a year of the hardships of service, even the most resolute soldiers were heartily weary of the ordeal and longed for its end. In a letter to his sister, John Long confessed, "I study a great deal about going home now."[30] Many of the men were still aggrieved that they were reduced to fighting on foot; others resented service so far away from home. A Tarrant County private summed it up: "If we could just get back to the other side of Miss. River and get our horses, I think we would be the happiest boys that ever walked the earth."[31] Some of the men declared openly that they intended to go home anyway when their one-year enlistment was up.

Yet there were also those in the regiment who would have echoed the sentiments of Lon Cartwright, when he avowed to his mother that "our country at this critical moment demands the service of every one of her brave sons to uphold and maintain her noble cause," though few could have expressed them so eloquently.[32] "If we all stay and those at home come out . . . , we will be able to maintain ourselves and prove to [the Yankees] that the idea of subjugation is absurd and that they had as well cease to fight us."[33] Cartwright could easily have afforded to hire a substitute to serve in his place; he chose not to do so.

But many of his fellow East Texans decided to take advantage of other provisions of the Conscription Act. The law required a reorganization of the Confederate army, provided for new elections of officers, and gave those men too old or too young for the draft the honorable option of returning home as soon as they were relieved by fresh troops. Like the other units in Beauregard's army, Greer's regiment underwent a reorganization during the middle of May that left it a much smaller and essentially different body of men than at its inception. Two hundred seven members of the regiment availed themselves of the opportunity for discharge as overage, underage, or disabled, and went home.

In Company A, for example, Albert Blocker and some others were discharged as underage, while Company C released the Acker brothers, Christopher and Peter, because they were too old for the draft. The Reverend Williamson Milburn, already fifty-four, returned to his flock of Baptists in Smith County, only to be slain in a quarrel with a neighbor over a dog. Many of the older men had accumulated various injuries or maladies and were given medical discharges. A few of the wealthier soldiers took advantage of the provisions of the conscription law to hire substitutes and went home to look after their families.

Some of those discharged never found their way back to Texas. As a case in point, former Sergeant Howell Harris blundered into a confrontation with a trigger-happy comrade and ended his days in Mississippi. Apparently drunk, Harris spent the night of May 15 wandering from tent to tent in the regimental campground until Private Ed Wallace of Company C shot him dead as a suspected thief. A court of inquiry ruled Wallace's deed to be justifiable homicide.[34]

By no means were all the men released at reorganization forever lost to the Confederate war effort. Most of the younger men spent a few months at home and then reenlisted in the regiment or joined some other Texas unit being formed at the time. For example, Americus Cartwright and three other young lieutenants all signed on with the First Texas Partisan Rangers and fought the war in Arkansas and Louisiana. Five overage privates from Company G enlisted in Terrell's Texas Cavalry. Doug Cater transferred to his brother's regiment from Louisiana.

Besides releasing more than two hundred men through discharge, the reorganization radically altered the entire command structure of the Third Texas: new men replaced the whole regimental staff, all the company commanders, and most of the lieutenants and sergeants. Officers left the unit for three basic reasons. Some were simply not reelected by their men. Other officers found that chronic physical disabilities precluded their active service in the field. Captain Bryan of Company I, for instance, was already forty-two years old, and his inguinal hernia had been aggravated by hard campaigning. He therefore opted for discharge and went home. With an average age of twenty-eight, the new officers elected to replace their middle-aged predecessors were almost a decade younger and presumably more fit to endure the rigors of soldiering.[35]

Finally, some officers resigned out of dissatisfaction with their current assignments or ambition for a higher command. Colonel Greer had been offended by Van Dorn's self-serving report on the battle of Pea Ridge; besides, his "mind was too much bent on a brigadier's stars."[36] He resigned, went home to

CO.	NAME	RANK	AGE	STATE OF BIRTH	COUNTY	OCCUPATION	WEALTH ($)	SLAVES
				Regimental Command and Staff				
	R. H. Cumby	Col.	36	Va.	Rusk	Farmer	$60,600	30
	H. P. Mabry	Lt. Col.	32	Ga.	Marion	Lawyer	17,000	2
	J. J. A. Barker	Maj.	26	S.C.	Cherokee	Lawyer	5,400	0
	O. N. Hollingsworth. Adj.	Capt.	26	Ala.	Rusk	Gentleman	2,100	0
	E. P. Hill, Q.M.	Capt.	23	Tex.	Harrison	Lawyer	15,000	7
	J. N. Coleman, Com.	Capt.	26	Ga.	Harrison	Merchant	11,250	0
				Company Commanders				
A	A. B. Stone, Jr.	Capt.	29	Ala.	Harrison	Gentleman	61,455	57
B	J. S. Boggess	Capt.	35	Tenn.	Rusk	Gentleman	9,000	7
C	J. A. Jones	Capt.	27	Miss.	Cherokee	Carpenter	300	0
D	R. S. Dabney	Capt.	26	Tenn.	Fannin	Clerk	15,000	7
E	P. B. Word	Capt.	23	Ga.	San Augustine			
F	R. F. Dunn	Capt.	31	Ky.	Henderson	Lawyer	10,000	0
G	S. E. Noble	Capt.	36	Miss.	Kaufman	Farmer	1,500	1
H	J. W. Lee	Capt.	23	Ala.	Upshur	Teacher	40,000	16
I	W. G. Green	Capt.	33	Miss.	Brazos	Farmer	1,000	0
K	S. S. Johnson	Capt.	22	Miss.	Cherokee	Editor	1,200	0
	Mean		28				$16,720	8

Sources: U.S. National Archives. Compiled Service Records of Confederate Soldiers Who Served in Organizations from the State of Texas (Washington, D.C., 1960). M No. 323, Rolls 18–23; U.S. National Archives. Population Schedules of the Eighth Census of the United States. 1860 (Washington. D.C.. 1967). M No. 653. Rolls 1287–1308.

Marshall, and found a general's desk job in Texas. In Greer's place, the men elected Captain Cumby of Company B, the wealthy planter from Henderson, as their new commander. Lieutenant Colonel Lane, always restless, had been dissatisfied ever since the regiment was dismounted in Arkansas: he had not joined the army to command a rabble of foot soldiers. Lane resigned his commission, organized the First Texas Partisan Rangers, and became a brigadier general as well.

Despite his eloquence and verve, Major Chilton failed at re-election. He returned to Texas and became division ordnance officer at Brownsville. Captain James Armstrong, regimental commissary officer, went home to run for district judge. Adjutant Ector had already attracted the favorable notice of the higher brass and had joined General Hogg's staff upon his arrival at Memphis. Shortly thereafter, he became the commander of the Fourteenth Texas Cavalry and was a brigadier general before the summer was over. Thus the old order gave way to the new.[37]

The men of the Third Regiment were still in the throes of their elections on May 8 when the order came down for a sortie against the enemy at Farmington, a little village about five miles east of Corinth on the Union line of advance. Major General John Pope's wing of Halleck's army had driven ahead of the main Federal host, and Beauregard ordered Van Dorn to attack Pope, cut him off, and destroy him. Having just been chosen to command the Third Texas that very morning, Captain Cumby felt too ill and unprepared to lead it immediately into battle. He was plagued with chronic diarrhea; besides, he confessed that "he did not know a thing about handling a regiment."[38] Although slated for discharge, Lieutenant Colonel Lane therefore agreed to step into the breach and assume temporary command of the regiment until the process of reorganization was completed.[39]

As it turned out, the East Texans were held in reserve and never became seriously involved in the comparatively light skirmishing that broke out at Farmington the following day. Van Dorn attempted to fling his army around the enemy's flank and trap him, but Pope cautiously withdrew before the Rebel force could pin him down. Swampy terrain and deep ravines hindered the progress of Van Dorn's troops, and after marching "about twenty miles through the worst thicket you ever saw," the Third Cavalry arrived upon the scene just as Pope's rear guard withdrew.[40] The next morning the East Texans were so "sore and weak that [they] could hardly get about."[41] Until the very end of May the two contending armies continued to menace each other; they feinted and bluffed but never came to serious blows.

As Halleck's army crawled ever closer, Beauregard recognized that his position at fever-ridden Corinth was untenable and concluded that a retreat was inevitable and necessary if his army were to survive. A master of deception, he planned the evacuation of the beleaguered stronghold with the utmost care and cunning. He sent small detachments forward to skirmish with the enemy so that the anxious Halleck would assume that the Rebels were preparing to attack. Then, on the night of May 29, Beauregard stealthily loaded his troops and supplies on trains and slipped them out of town toward the south. He left a handful of men behind to keep campfires burning; soldiers were ordered to cheer the departing trains as though reinforcements were arriving; his drummers beat reveille at the usual hour. By the morning of May 30, when the Federals at last discovered that Corinth was empty of defenders, the Rebels had stolen away to Tupelo, fifty miles to the south. Beauregard's evacuation of Corinth "was the greatest hoax of the war."[42]

The Third Texas played an important role in this deception. On the morning before the evacuation, Beauregard ordered Van Dorn to mount a demonstration against the enemy to mask the retreat. Van Dorn dispatched Lane and his East Texans to advance at sunrise toward the enemy's earthworks and draw out the Yankee skirmishers. With hundreds lying ill and many others detailed for other duties, Lane could collect only 246 men for this hazardous enterprise. He led his little band on the double-quick several hundred yards through the abatis of felled timber to within fifty paces of the Union picket line. Whether intentionally or not, Lane placed his troops in a position where they would have to either fight or die—or both—since a retreat would trap them in the labyrinth of the abatis.

Drawing fire from the entrenched Yankee pickets, the Texans dodged behind whatever cover the ground afforded. Noted Tom

Hogg, "Each man took his tree, and, after discharging his fire-lock and reloading in that position, would advance to the next cover and repeat the performance."[43] Then, assuming that he "would lose fewer men by charging the enemy than by fighting at long range," Lane ordered his men to charge.[44] Screaming like demons, the Texans drove the Union pickets out of their holes and into their own earthworks some four hundred yards to the rear.

All day long Lane's little detachment held this position against three regiments of the enemy, while Beauregard evacuated Corinth. Fearing that he might be enveloped on both wings, Lane dispatched videttes to his flanks to warn of an attack. Posted on the left wing, Private Newton Smith, a Waco resident who had just joined Company B at Memphis three weeks earlier, dashed forward so recklessly that he jumped right on top of a Yankee picket hidden in a clump of hazel bushes. The two grappled with each other for a moment, and the enemy soldier stunned Smith with a blow to the face. He drew down on the impetuous Rebel in an instant and, when Smith refused to give up, he fired, shattering his arm above the elbow with a buck and ball cartridge. Smith lost his arm but gained an official commendation and a medical discharge. Newly promoted Major James Barker was not so lucky. Mounted upon his horse, he made too easy a target for Federal sharpshooters and expired in the arms of two of his comrades from Cherokee County. In all, the regiment lost eight killed and nine wounded in this diversionary action.[45]

At nightfall Lane ordered his exhausted troopers to hold their position until midnight while Beauregard completed his evacuation. He then pulled them back to serve as the rear guard of the retreating Southern army, and the troops from East Texas stole noiselessly away in the darkness, passed through the now deserted streets of Corinth, and struck the road south toward Tupelo. Utterly spent, the Third Cavalry could at least derive the consolation of success from their perilous duty as rear guard.

"Old Brains" Halleck had indeed been fooled. He entered Corinth on the following morning to find the town's fortifications abandoned and the quarry already safe beyond the Tuscumbia River. To honor the East Texans for their part in the huge deception, Beauregard issued a general order hailing their "brave, skillful and gallant conduct."[46] After their long journey from Arkansas, the raging fevers of Corinth, and their courageous stand during Beauregard's withdrawal, the men of the Third Texas required rest and recuperation. Thanks to Union General Halleck, they got the much-needed respite.

Though he had failed to destroy Beauregard's army, Halleck at least succeeded in capturing Corinth and its vital railroad junction, thereby forcing the Rebels to abandon Fort Pillow on the Mississippi and the strategic port of Memphis. To President Lincoln and Secretary of War Stanton, the fall of Corinth opened up the prospect of the immediate conquest of the lower Mississippi, and they urged Halleck to move ahead quickly to maintain the initiative. He commanded an army of 128,315 men at or near Corinth: He might have struck south toward Mobile; he could have concentrated his forces against Chattanooga; or he had the choice of marching on Vicksburg, the last major Rebel stronghold on the Mississippi.

But he took none of those courses. Absorbed by minutiae, Halleck spent the splendid campaigning season of early summer shoring up his defenses, garrisoning his newly occupied territories, and maintaining his railway network. He split his army in two, leaving Grant with 63,000 men to defend Northern gains between Corinth and Memphis; meanwhile, Buell plodded eastward toward Chattanooga with an army exceeding 30,000.[47]

What transpired therefore, was not the rapid Union drive to victory that Washington wanted in that summer of 1862, but rather a long hiatus which deprived the North of its momentum and gave the South a few months of precious breathing space. Meanwhile, rumors of European intervention to enforce a compromise peace contributed to a renewed resolve even in the lowest Rebel ranks. "I am confident they can not beat us if the war should last five years," Lon Cartwright declared.[48]

CHAPTER 8

Iuka, June–October 1862

FEDERAL INACTION in the West early in the summer of 1862 was partially a consequence of Union changes in command following General George B. McClellan's failure to defeat Robert E. Lee's Confederates in the East. After Lee's remarkable victory in the Seven Days' Campaign before Richmond, Lincoln named Halleck general-in-chief on July 11. When Halleck went to Washington, Grant assumed command of the Union troops on the Mississippi front. Because Halleck had dispersed his once great army, however, Grant was unable to thwart the main Confederate objectives in the West, which were to fortify Vicksburg to the point of impregnability, to secure Chattanooga as a base of operations against eastern Tennessee and Kentucky, and to immobilize Grant's own army on the line between Memphis and Corinth.[1]

Though granted a temporary reprieve from onrushing Yankees, the Confederacy suffered from command problems of its own. As often in the war, its commanders wasted precious weeks of respite in advancing competing strategies, pursuing personal vendettas, or defending themselves against their numerous critics. Beauregard tried to explain to Richmond and the world at large that his evacuation of Corinth was in fact a mas-

terpiece of military genius—"equivalent to a brilliant victory,"
as he put it—but President Jefferson Davis was not impressed.[2]
On the pretext of Beauregard's ill health, Davis relieved him
of his command and appointed General Braxton Bragg as his
successor on June 17. The Confederate War Department also
transferred Van Dorn to head the garrison at Vicksburg, leaving
Sterling Price to command the Army of the West in northern
Mississippi. For his part, the imperious Price consumed the entire month of June in a vituperative quarrel with President Davis
over Price's desire to return his Missouri troops to their home
state. Frustrated in this effort, the Missourian rejoined his army
at Tupelo, Mississippi, on June 27, while Bragg led the bulk of
the Confederate forces toward Chattanooga. Since they were
all virtually independent commanders, Van Dorn at Vicksburg,
Price at Tupelo, and Bragg in eastern Tennessee found effective
cooperation always difficult and often impossible.[3]

Assembling an army of about fifteen thousand men, Price intended to recapture Corinth and then launch an invasion of
western Tennessee. He organized his Army of the West into
two divisions of infantry and a single cavalry brigade. Brigadier
General Hébert, exchanged since his capture at Pea Ridge, commanded one of the four brigades in the First Division of infantry,
and the troops of the Third Texas Cavalry, still dismounted,
formed part of his command. Though two dozen new recruits
joined the regiment during the summer, attrition from disease
and the provisions of the Conscription Act took a heavy toll of
its numbers. A veteran of Company E complained that while
additional men had joined his unit, "a great many of them have
not been worth a cent to the Confederacy as far as service is
concerned. Two have died, three have been discharged and the
remainder are sick . . . nearly all the time."[4]

By the end of the summer the regiment had only 388 men fit
for duty on its rolls. More officers resigned, and others were
promoted to take their place. Still plagued by sickness, Colonel
Cumby left the service, and Lieutenant Colonel Mabry took over
as regimental commander. Captain Boggess, of Company B,
succeeded the slain Major Barker and subsequently became
Mabry's second-in-command.[5] By this time most of the men left

in the regiment were hardened veterans, and they had three full months of relative inactivity in which to get to know their new officers.

During the summer the East Texans convalesced from the maladies contracted at Corinth and practiced incessantly the detested infantry drills. After camping for two months near Tupelo, the regiment then moved north to Saltillo and Baldwyn in preparation for Price's projected attack on the Federal forces occupying Corinth. Gradually most of the men recovered their health after the ordeal of the spring.

Their improvement was primarily the result of adequate sources of good water, plenty of rest, and the hospitality afforded the Texans by local citizens. Sick men were usually able to board themselves out in the homes of farm families of the area for several weeks. Since most of their hosts had sons of their own serving elsewhere, the convalescents were often treated like members of the family. Sam Barron, for instance, found a hospitable haven in the home of the Dunn family of Pontotoc County. His hosts had lost a son in the war, and they plied the young Texan, emaciated and weak from fever and dysentery, with nourishing food, and lavished upon him all the comforts that their prosperous farm could afford. Within a month, Barron was well enough to return to the regiment.[6]

The army medical service had little to do with the improved health of the men. Military surgeons, though well intentioned, were still groping around in a fog of ignorance, and by this time pharmaceutical supplies were all but nonexistent in the Confederate army. Dr. Dan Shaw, the genial surgeon of the Third Regiment, did what he could to assuage the effects of the chronic diarrhea that still afflicted many of the men, but his impact was minimal, inasmuch as his entire pharmacopoeia consisted of opium. At sick call, he would carve out a lump of opium "as big as a cannonball," roll out a supply of pills, and dispense these to the men in line according to their various complaints such as "a pain in my back, a hurting in my stomach, ... a misery in my head, or . . . a chill last night."[7] Whatever the symptoms, the prescription was the same. Surgeon Shaw soon fell sick himself and, after almost a year of failing health, obtained a discharge.

General Hébert, the brigade commander, was a notorious

martinet, and he subjected the former cavalrymen to the most rigorous discipline of their lives, including two hours of infantry drill in the morning and dress parade every evening. Each Sunday they altered this routine to the extent that Hébert's brigade joined in a general review for Price and his officers. In full field equipment, with their tunics buttoned up to their chins, the East Texans marched five miles under the broiling sun and through the stifling dust of a Mississippi summer so that their officers could appraise their progress toward the status of infantrymen. The verdict was favorable. Major General William J. Hardee, one of Bragg's corps commanders and supreme authority on tactics and drill, pronounced Price's army the "most efficient, best drilled and most thoroughly disciplined body of troops" in Mississippi.[8] By the beginning of September the men of the Third Texas, though depleted to a third of their original strength and reduced to the humble station of foot soldiers, were infused by a renewed optimism that reflected the recent success of Southern arms.

The Confederacy had drawn upon its dwindling resources to embark upon two major counteroffensives as the summer waned. During the last days of August, General Lee had won the second battle of Manassas only thirty miles from the Federal capital. He then launched an ambitious drive into Maryland with an eye toward winning a negotiated peace. Meanwhile, in the West, General Bragg struck deep into Kentucky with the objective of recovering the border states to the Confederate cause and persuading neutral Britain to recognize Southern independence.[9] Americus Cartwright eloquently summed up the mood of his comrades in the Third Texas when he declared that "the tide now sets in our favor, and those that are in authority should use every effort to take it at its flood and thus bring this unholy war to an end."[10] The men in the ranks were ready for action when Price at last terminated their "summer vacation" on September 5 and marched them north to give battle.[11]

Price's initiative was designed to assist Bragg, whose advance toward the Ohio River menaced the whole Union position in the West. General Buell, Bragg's Yankee adversary, waited near Nashville for a chance to attack the onrushing Rebels, and Grant's forces in northern Mississippi threatened to reinforce Buell.

Consequently, Bragg appealed to Price to engage Grant's army and keep it occupied. Grant's subordinate, Brigadier General William S. Rosecrans, commanded a force of some ten thousand men near Iuka, a small resort town about twenty miles southeast of Corinth. Assuming that Rosecrans was on his way to reinforce Buell, Price ordered a forced march to Iuka to cut him off. Still bemoaning their absent horses and carrying all their worldly goods on their backs, the men of the Third Texas trudged up the dusty roads as fast as their burning feet would carry them.

Marching night and day, they entered Iuka on the morning of September 14 to discover that Rosecrans's army had retreated to Corinth in such haste that it abandoned immense quantities of supplies. The exhausted Rebels had no time to enjoy this unexpected windfall, however. They were in a perilous situation and were too busy preparing themselves for an anticipated counterthrust to do more than catch brief snatches of sleep. Rosecrans's army still lurked somewhere to the west, and Price expected an attack along one of three approaches to Iuka. Consequently, he kept his troops almost constantly in the line of battle and frequently shifted them from one point to another according to the exigencies of the moment.[12]

For four days the Missouri general hesitated at Iuka, uncertain which course to take. Grant's army of 45,000 men was dispersed along the Tennessee-Mississippi border, but more than half of them were in forward positions where they might fall upon the Rebels at any time. Price, moreover, was the victim of contradictory advice from his fellow generals. While Bragg dispatched urgent telegrams importuning Price to join him in Kentucky, Van Dorn, now moving north from Vicksburg, requested the Missourian to fall back to the west and collaborate with him in an attack against the Federal forces in western Tennessee. Finally, on September 19, after Jefferson Davis had intervened to give Van Dorn authority over Price, the commander of the Army of the West committed himself to join Van Dorn. He completed his preparations to withdraw from Iuka that very afternoon.[13]

It was at this point that the Yankees struck. Grant projected a two-pronged attack against the Confederates in Iuka. Rose-

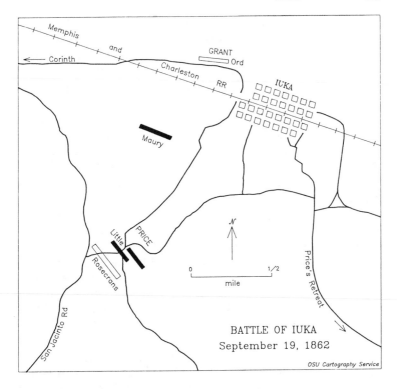

BATTLE OF IUKA
September 19, 1862

OSU Cartography Service

crans, with nine thousand troops, was to swing out and fall upon Price from the southwest. At the sound of his guns, Grant, with a column of eight thousand Union soldiers led by Major General Edward O. C. Ord, would then strike Price's flank from the northwest. After some delay, Rosecrans mounted his assault as planned about 2:30 in the afternoon of September 19. But for a freakish northwest wind, Grant's carefully conceived pincers movement would have shattered the Rebel army. The unusual atmospheric conditions muffled the thunder of Rosecrans's artillery, however, and hearing no firing on its right, Grant's column rested on its arms a few miles away. Meanwhile, Rosecrans's troops bore the full brunt of fierce Southern resistance for the entire afternoon. "Where in the name of God is Grant?" Rosecrans wondered aloud.[14]

In the rough and broken terrain about a mile south of Iuka,

the battle developed into a bloody melee between the Rebel infantry and Rosecrans's artillery. Price had posted one of his divisions west of the town to confront Grant's approaching army, while Brigadier General Henry Little's division, to which the Third Texas belonged, had to deal with Rosecrans alone. On the evening of the previous day, the East Texans had marched four miles west of Iuka in preparation for Price's planned evacuation. They lay in line of battle all that night and most of the following day, until about four o'clock. At that time, a courier alerted them that Rosecrans was advancing from the south. The troopers then doubled-timed back through the town to confront the approaching enemy and formed up on a slope facing the southwest. Across a narrow valley, Rosecrans had concealed his nine cannons behind the crest of the hill beyond.

Failing at first to spot the Yankee artillery, Price ordered the Third Texas to deploy forward as skirmishers down the steep slope ahead of them. As the men scrambled across a ravine at the bottom, the Union gunners opened up on the startled Rebels from a range of 150 yards "like lightning from a clear sky."[15] Trapped in the declivity, the skirmishers dropped to the ground, while a hailstorm of grape and canister roared over their heads. "Steady boys, steady," Captain Will Green called out to his terrified men in Company I and rose to his knees. At that moment a cannonball decapitated him.[16] When his lieutenant, D. J. Ingram, arose to check the flight of a panicky private, both he and the fleeing soldier were cut in two by grapeshot. Sergeant Victor Rose glanced up from the ground long enough to glimpse a little dog "trotting along in advance of the line, apparently oblivious to the thunders of artillery, the rattle of rifles, and the whizzing of missiles that literally filled the air."[17] It may well have been Mephistopheles in disguise, for there was the devil to pay that afternoon in Iuka.

For two and a half hours the two armies contended in what Price called "the hardest-fought fight which I have ever witnessed."[18] Bringing up their own four guns, the Rebels responded to the Union barrage with canister shot. Then Hébert gave the order to assault the Yankee artillery emplacements, and the Texans charged up the slope with a shout. At first their own artillery gave them some support, but as the attackers plunged forward toward the murderous muzzles of the Union guns, the Confederate artillerymen had to cease firing to avoid hitting their own men. Unhindered, the Yankee cannoneers poured grape and canister into the gray masses rising in front of them. Private John Sherrod died instantly when grapeshot tore through his body. Will Bonner, the regimental color bearer, was cut down a few feet in front of a Federal battery, the Confederate battle flag still clutched firmly in his hands.

Grapeshot and musketry riddled their ranks, but the East Texans pressed on. At the head of the charge, Lieutenant Dan Alley raced up the hill, crying "Come on Boys!" at the top of his voice.[19] With sabers, ramrods, and gun butts, the attackers grappled fiercely with the enemy artillerymen on the crest of the hill. Most conspicuous on the field was Private Rush Wallace, son of a San Augustine judge. Hopelessly surrounded at one point in the action, he refused to surrender but fought his way out of the trap and back to his own lines. Though hard pressed by the Indiana and Iowa infantrymen defending their guns, the Texans sustained their assault and captured six of the Yankee cannons. They had driven the enemy some six hundred yards to the rear when descending darkness at last put an end to the carnage.

All night long the Rebels lay under arms within two hundred yards of the Union line, the moaning of the wounded clearly audible in the dark. Casualties had been extremely heavy. Of the 388 soldiers in the Third Texas Cavalry, 22 were killed outright, and 74 were wounded; one of every four men on the line fell that day, by far the heaviest losses sustained by the regiment in any single engagement during the war. The uphill struggle for the Yankee guns was particularly lethal for the new officers elected in May. Besides Captain Green and Lieutenant Ingram, Lieutenants W. W. Hannah, of Company H, and M. J. Odell, of Company G, died in action. Colonel Mabry, the regimental commander, was himself wounded three times; wounds also incapacitated three company commanders and seven lieutenants. In all, Price's army lost about 1,500 men, including General Little, the division commander, while some 800 of the enemy became casualties.[20]

Despite his losses, and seemingly unconcerned that his troops were still trapped between Grant and Rosecrans, Price was eager to reopen the battle the following morning. "We'll wade through him, sir, in the morning," he assured his commanders.[21] But fortunately for his men, Price's generals persuaded the fiery Missourian that discretion was the better part of valor, and he reluctantly ordered a retreat. Leaving its wounded men behind, the Third Texas stole out of Iuka with the remainder of Price's army before sunrise. About four dozen of its wretched wounded were promptly captured when Rosecrans's troops entered the town later in the day.

At this stage of the war, prisoners from western battlefields were regularly exchanged at Vicksburg under the provisions of the cartel signed between the Union and Confederate governments the previous July. Consequently, the captured Texans, though suffering grievously from their wounds, were not confronted by the dismal prospect of indeterminate incarceration in the squalid prison camps that proliferated later. According to the cartel arrangements, the exchange was supposed to be effected within ten days after capture. Privates were traded man for man, while officers counted for more points in the human barter system: a general was worth sixty privates, a lieutenant four, and so on.

In order to take advantage of this arrangement, each prisoner of war was required to sign a parole under which he pledged not to take up arms against his captors until officially exchanged. Then he might in all good conscience fall to fighting again as his respective government expected him to do. But as the men in the ranks became accustomed to the cumbersome system, the temptation to get themselves captured, sign a parole, neglect to return to their regiment upon release from captivity, and sit out the war at home grew ever more attractive to some. Both the Confederacy and the Union took a dim view of this drain on their manpower and took steps to assure that released prisoners would rejoin their units forthwith, but many parolees never returned to duty.

The wounded men at Iuka were well cared for by their regimental surgeon and the local women who had been recruited as nurses. As soon as they were able to travel, most happily signed their paroles and were set free. But Colonel Mabry's sensitive patriotism bridled at putting his name to a parole that referred to his government as the "so-called" Confederate States of America and refused to sign. For this refractory attitude, Mabry and his like-minded subordinate, Captain Jim Lee, were sent to the Federal prison at Camp Douglas, Illinois, until they were exchanged later in the fall. During Mabry's imprisonment and convalescence, Jiles Boggess was promoted to lieutenant colonel and succeeded him as acting commander of the Third Texas.[22]

The East Texans served as the vanguard for Price's army on its hasty retreat south from Iuka. Though Rosecrans set off in pursuit early on the morning of September 20, the withdrawing Rebels moved so fast that they eluded his patrols among the wooded hills of northeastern Mississippi. The men marched twenty-five miles that day, much of the distance at double-quick time, and reached Baldwyn three days later. On September 28, Price's army linked up with Van Dorn, whom President Davis had at last put in charge of his armies in Mississippi. This at least cleared up one of the major problems of command, even if it did place the resentful Price under a general for whom he had little respect or trust. As ever devoted to "Old Pap" Price, many of the Texans shared his low opinion of Van Dorn.

The gentleman in question, however, was still brimming with confidence, eager for action, and full of grandiose plans. Assuming command of his and Price's combined forces, which together numbered about 22,000 men, Van Dorn styled his host the Army of West Tennessee, in allusion to the objective he now set before himself. He planned to dash across the Tennessee border, only twenty miles to the north, to support the apparently victorious invasion of Kentucky by Bragg. During the first three weeks of September, Bragg's army had driven deep into the Bluegrass State, while the forces of his coordinate commander, Major General Edmund Kirby Smith, were spreading havoc as far north as the Ohio River. To take Louisville, Kentucky, Bragg desperately needed Van Dorn's support. Moreover, a Confederate reconquest of western Tennessee might undo the damage done to the Southern cause at Fort Donelson and Shiloh and simultaneously outflank the Federal garrisons along the east bank of the Mississippi. The vision of the great valley liberated and Confederate soldiers marching into Ohio animated Van Dorn's calculations as he planned his next battle. If successful, he could reverse the balance of the war in the West.

The odds he faced were formidable. About half of Grant's troops in western Tennessee were available along the Mississippi border where they could hold the line against a Rebel advance. Rosecrans had fifteen thousand troops in heavily fortified Corinth, while some eighteen thousand more potential reinforcements were garrisoned at various points along the Tennessee line. From his command post at Ripley, Mississippi, Van Dorn might move against either Corinth, Memphis, or Bolivar, Tennessee, and keep his enemies guessing which one until the moment of attack.

The aggressive Rebel commander chose Corinth as his target. He knew the area and its fortifications; it still commanded the vital railway junction so fiercely contested four months earlier; its defender, Rosecrans, had been Van Dorn's classmate at West Point. By exploiting the elements of speed and surprise, the Army of West Tennessee might feint due north toward Bolivar, then cut back toward the southeast and attack Corinth from an unanticipated direction, cutting off its defenders from Grant's reinforcements and driving them south toward surrender. Keeping his own counsel as usual, Van Dorn led his troops out of Ripley on September 29.[23] "No army ever marched to battle with prouder steps, more hopeful countenances, or with more courage than marched the Army of West Tennessee . . . on its way to Corinth," he reported.[24]

For the first two days his troops made rapid progress, reaching the Tennessee border by the night of September 30, while the enemy was still unsure of the direction of the attack. Rosecrans found it difficult to believe that a commander familiar with the elaborate fortifications of Corinth would risk storming them. Only when Van Dorn's army abruptly turned east along the border did the objective of his assault become clear. By the second of October the Confederate general had lost the advantage of surprise, however, and Rosecrans began preparations to receive his adversary northwest of the town.

The pace of the Confederate advance slackened as well. The

route to Corinth crossed two rivers, the Hatchie and the Tuscumbia, only five miles apart, and the bridges that spanned both streams had been rendered impassable. Van Dorn consumed all of October 2 in bridge repair, while his stalled troops fanned out through the river bottoms to gorge themselves on papaws and muscadine grapes. Furthermore, when belatedly apprised of the objective of their march, several of Van Dorn's commanders expressed dismay that their chief intended a frontal assault against the massive earthworks of Corinth. That night the Confederate army bivouacked at the village of Chewalla, Tennessee, only ten miles northwest of their goal.

For the next two days Van Dorn's army would beat itself to death against the stoutly defended redoubts of Corinth. Its fortifications, strengthened substantially during the Union occupation, extended in three concentric arcs around the town. The outermost ring consisted of the old Confederate earthworks that formed a semicircle about three miles out from the city center. Entrenchments and gun emplacements covering Corinth's northwest quadrant provided a second barrier about a mile and a half from the railroad junction, while the last stronghold consisted of a forbidding circle of artillery redoubts in the heart of town. To penetrate these defenses, Van Dorn organized his force into three divisions, commanded respectively by General Hébert, Brigadier General Dabney H. Maury, and Major General Mansfield Lovell. Hébert's division consisted of four brigades. Colonel W. Bruce Colbert commanded the Second Brigade, in which the still dismounted Third Texas Cavalry comprised one of six regiments.[25]

In sharp contrast to Halleck's stately and deliberate investment of Corinth the previous spring, Van Dorn sent his troops plunging headlong into its earthworks and palisades. The Rebels began their advance on the town at 4:00 A.M., Friday, October 3. As the men of the Third Texas marched down the road at daybreak, three distinct shocks of an earthquake lent an even more ominous tone to their already perilous undertaking. Some recognized in the rumbling earth a harbinger of disaster, and many of the boys threw away their playing cards, entrusted their cherished possessions to comrades, and placed Bibles in

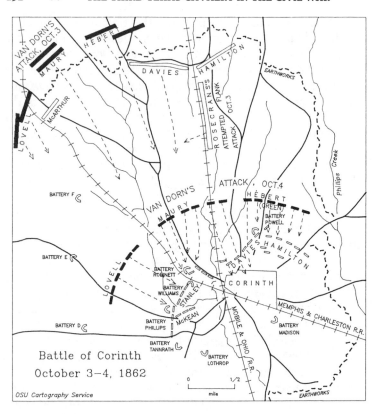

Battle of Corinth
October 3–4, 1862

OSU Cartography Service

breast pockets. By midmorning the carnage had begun, as their advance columns came in contact with the Yankee pickets posted around the outer ring of earthworks.

The Rebel general had deployed his divisions in an arc northwest of the city, with Lovell's troops on the right wing, Maury in the center, and Hébert on the left. So widely dispersed were these three commands (about four miles from wing to wing) that Van Dorn soon lost control of his men in the confusion of battle, and the struggle took on the character of three separate engagements. As the pace of the Confederate advance quickened, Colbert's brigade was placed in reserve. Thus the East Texans witnessed but did not participate in the worst of the bloodletting, as Rebel infantrymen charged around abatises of fallen timber and through a hail of rifle fire, funnelling themselves ever nearer to the deadly guns mounted in the ring of redoubts at the core of the Federal defenses.[26] Just as Rosecrans had planned, the artillery fire took a frightful toll of Confederate lives as the men struggled through the timber. "The whole air seemed to be litterally filled with grape shot and shell," wrote one Texan. "Our ranks were fearfully thined, the boys falling in every direction. . . . The trees were tumbling in every direction and the limbs fly through the air. The ground bursting into holes and ditches by the mighty force of the cannon balls."[27]

The Confederate right wing first surmounted the outermost ring of earthworks, and Maury's and Hébert's divisions soon followed. By the middle of the afternoon the Rebels had penetrated to the second line of redoubts within a mile or so of the town, as heavy fighting continued all day. The temperature stood in the nineties, canteens were empty, ammunition was in short supply, and the men were past exhaustion. As the sun set, the Yankees pulled back to their interior redoubts, while Van Dorn broke off the action and withdrew his troops a short distance to bivouac for the night. Characteristically, the Rebel general attributed his failure to conclude the battle victoriously to the perversity of the laws of nature: the earth refused to suspend its revolutions. "One hour more of daylight and victory would have soothed our grief for the loss of the gallant dead," he reported.[28] This was a highly unlikely conclusion, since Rosecrans still had more than ten thousand men in reserve.

Eager to renew the contest the following morning, Van Dorn opened up with an artillery barrage at 4:00 A.M. against the fortified redoubts along the northwestern edge of Corinth, where Rosecrans had concentrated his defenders. The Yankees replied in kind and, as one Texan reported, "The whole heavens were at once lit up with belching volcanoes of fire and smoke. Bursting shells filled the air and shrieking solid shot plowed into the deep forest behind us, bringing the tall oaks down with a continus crash."[29] The far superior Union artillery soon silenced the Rebel guns, and dawn broke upon a battlefield eerily still.

During the night Van Dorn had ordered Hébert to begin the infantry assault at daybreak, with the other two divisions to follow his lead. But at the appointed hour Hébert's division did not move, and its commander could not be found. About seven o'clock Hébert appeared at Van Dorn's headquarters to report that he was too sick to take the field. Most likely this sudden indisposition was brought on by his unwillingness to subject his men to the suicidal frontal assault that Van Dorn had planned for them. Whatever his reasons, Hébert's delay threw the Confederate battle plan into disarray and cost the Rebels any slim chance they might have had for a victory.

But the attendant confusion also saved the lives of a large number of troopers in the ranks of the Third Texas: in the process of redeployment they were shifted from the center stage of the bloody drama to the wings. Abruptly ordered to assume command of Hébert's division, Brigadier General Martin E. Green was so bewildered by his new responsibilities that he spent an hour deploying his troops. He first called his Second Brigade, to which the Third Texas was attached, out of reserve and positioned it near the center of his line. Then, to avert a Yankee flanking maneuver, Green marched the brigade to the extreme left wing of Van Dorn's army. When the heavy fighting began about midmorning, the brigade advanced upon the enemy as ordered, but the terrain over which it marched was so rough and uneven, and the distance it had to cover so great, that the men never reached the Union entrenchments where the most fearful slaughter occurred.[30] Thus by fortuitous circumstance, the men of the Third Texas lived to fight another day.

In the meantime, the Rebels in the center had plunged forward into battle. By 9:30 A.M., two of Van Dorn's divisions had closed with the enemy and were plowing ahead in the face of murderous fire from the Union batteries. The Yankees immediately to the east of the Mobile and Ohio Railroad tracks fell back under the assault, as units from both Maury's and Green's divisions broke through into the very streets of Corinth. Hastily reinforcing his center, Rosecrans poured a curtain of flanking fire into his attackers. Trapped, their ammunition gone, hundreds of Southern soldiers surrendered. West of the railroad the fighting focused upon Battery Robinett, the key redoubt in the Federal defensive core. Wave after wave of Confederates assaulted this position, only to be mown down by the score. "It reminded me," recalled a witness, "of a man cutting heavy grain, striking at a thick place."[31] By noon Van Dorn realized that "the day was lost."[32] Without waiting to commit General Lovell's still untested division, he called off the attack and ordered a general retreat. Through inadequate reconnaissance, defective coordination of his forces, and reckless assault, Van Dorn had failed again.

Now he had to extricate his exhausted troops before Grant's reinforcements could descend upon them from Tennessee and hammer them to pieces against the fortifications of Corinth. It was still early in the afternoon when the dazed Rebels began straggling westward along the road by which they had come; they bivouacked for the night just north of the Tennessee line. Fortunately for them, Rosecrans delayed pursuing his beaten foe until he could rest and resupply his men, and thereby allowed Van Dorn to escape. The Rebel commander at first wanted to launch one last desperate assault on Corinth from a new direction, but during the night his senior officers persuaded him of the folly of this plan, and the army resumed its retreat toward Holly Springs the following day.[33]

The Confederates were still by no means out of danger, however. By this time Grant had dispatched five thousand troops to intercept the retreating column, and they had occupied the bridge across the Hatchie River. While the Rebels successfully crossed the Tuscumbia on October 5, they found themselves trapped between the impassable Hatchie, Grant's army bearing down upon them from the north, and Rosecrans in belated pursuit in their rear. True to his reckless character, Van Dorn had burned the only other possible crossing, Crum's Bridge, six miles to the south. There seemed to be no exit available, and the Rebels parked their supply train with a view toward torching the wagons and swimming the river as they might.

There was one way out, but it involved a dangerous detour. An obscure trail called the Boneyard Road intersected the route of retreat about two and a half miles east of the Hatchie and then ran southwest directly to Crum's Bridge. Though the bridge itself was in ruins, a mill dam nearby might still serve as a makeshift crossing. To escape the Yankee pincers closing in upon them, Van Dorn's men consequently retraced their steps and turned south on the Boneyard Road, while their rear guard gallantly fought off a determined enemy attack at the Hatchie bridge. It required the entire afternoon and most of the night for the weary Rebels to pick their way over the perilous crossing at the mill. The men hurriedly reinforced and widened the dam with timbers and stones from the mill, and it was long after midnight before the last of their wagons rolled over the rickety structure by the light of bonfires built along the riverbank.[34]

The troops had gone without food or proper rest for days. Almost fifty years later Sam Barron recalled his dinner that night and the lucky discovery that made it possible: a half-gallon of corn meal that had spilled out on the road. Barron mixed the meal with river water, spread his dough on a board, and cooked it over General Price's campfire. He remembered it as "the most delicious piece of bread I have ever tasted."[35] Toward morning, the last of Van Dorn's army stumbled across the dam and scurried pell-mell along the road westward without any semblance of order; it was a veritable rout. "The enemy can boast of a victory," admitted Lon Cartwright, "for our troops were whipped."[36]

Reaching Ripley, the retreating Rebels paused only long enough to form a roadblock to ward off the Yankees in their rear. But Grant had elected not to pursue Van Dorn's disorganized army, and the Confederates withdrew unmolested all the way to Holly Springs, begging food from farmhouses along the route. The last of Van Dorn's men straggled into town on October 13, as a wet norther descended upon them to compound their misery. Here they halted to reorganize and recuperate.

Corinth was a Confederate disaster. Van Dorn's projected invasion of western Tennessee came to naught, Bragg remained unsupported in Kentucky, and now Grant perceived an opportunity to move against Vicksburg from the north. His Rebel adversaries were demoralized and decimated. They had suffered appalling losses. Almost five thousand men, or about one-quarter of the Army of West Tennessee, were killed, wounded, captured, or missing, while Union casualties ran to half their number. The brigade to which the Third Texas belonged, emerged comparatively sound, however, since it had been held in reserve during the first day of the battle and never reached the murderous Yankee redoubts on the second. The East Texans came out of Corinth very lucky indeed, considering the general carnage. Seven men were killed, including Captain James Jones, of Company C, who died of his wounds in a Yankee prison. Sixteen soldiers of the Third Texas were wounded, and all of them became prisoners of war as well.[37]

The debacle at Corinth prompted a court of inquiry regarding Van Dorn's conduct of the campaign. Though it concluded with his exoneration, the Confederate War Department transferred the general to less cerebral duties commanding a cavalry division. Lovell and Hébert were also relieved of their commands and placed on the sidelines. For the Confederacy as a whole, Corinth was but one of three staggering blows that autumn which dashed its high hopes for a successful counteroffensive. Lee's invasion of Maryland had been turned back at Antietam on September 17, and Bragg abandoned his Kentucky campaign after the battle of Perryville on October 8.

The autumn of 1862 had marked the high tide of Confederate aspirations, but the preponderance of the enemy's resources had stultified the Rebels' major aims. The South failed in its bid to reconquer the border states; its military achievements did not earn the fervently desired recognition by Britain; nor did its valor and sacrifice extinguished the Northern will to fight. To be sure, the elections of November struck a stinging blow at Lincoln's administration, as disillusioned voters in five of the most populous Northern states spurned his party. Yet the president retained a narrow majority in both the House and the Senate and successfully weathered a direct challenge to his leadership. The mood in Richmond was one of disappointment and frustration. The Confederate secretary of war, George W. Randolph, resigned in a dispute with his chief, and the principal commanders in the West still seemed incapable of effective cooperation with each other. The South faced the second winter of the war desperate for some favorable sign that its fortunes might change with the new year.[38]

CHAPTER 9

Holly Springs, November 1862– January 1863

JAMES A. SEDDON, the new Confederate secretary of war, faced his assigned duties with justifiable anxiety. His resources were already stretched so thin that he could not cover all his fronts simultaneously, while in spite of the looming winter Union commanders were preparing major offensives all along the line. In Tennessee, the Federal War Department replaced the methodical General Buell with the popular and energetic Rosecrans, who immediately set about reorganizing his army at Nashville with a view toward crushing Bragg's Rebels at Murfreesboro. On the Virginia front, Major General Ambrose E. Burnside began deploying his Army of the Potomac for a thrust across the Rappahannock against Lee's embattled Southerners. In Mississippi, Van Dorn's recent debacle at Corinth placed Grant in a position to launch a decisive drive on Vicksburg along the Mississippi Central Railroad, which ran from Jackson, Tennessee, to Jackson, Mississippi. Any one of these three projected onslaughts might prove fatal for the South.[1]

Consequently, from the time of his appointment in November, Seddon assiduously shifted his corps, divisions, and brigades all around the map to what appeared to be the next point of maximum peril. Ordinary Rebel foot soldiers and cavalrymen, pawns in the deadly strategic game, found themselves marching hundreds of miles to meet a perceived threat in one direction, only to be transferred back to their starting point to plug a new hole that had opened in that quarter. Thus, the men of the Third Texas Cavalry were treated to an extended tour of Dixie—from the Mississippi Valley to the Cumberland Plateau—during the following six months. While the men who engaged in all this marching and countermarching clung to their chief and unwavering purpose of staying alive, the strategists who dispatched them on fatiguing travels had other objectives in mind: to thwart the aggressive plans of General Grant, then those of Rosecrans, and finally, those of Grant again.

After Corinth it was clear to all that Grant posed the most immediate threat. As he now commanded an army of more than 100,000 along the Tennessee border, little stood between him and Vicksburg but Van Dorn's force of some 21,000 soldiers camped in and around Holly Springs. Lieutenant General John C. Pemberton, commander of the newly created Confederate Department of Mississippi and East Louisiana, bore responsibility for the defense of Vicksburg, and he began accumulating reinforcements and deploying his troops to resist Grant's anticipated offensive against the vital river stronghold.

In the process of this deployment, the Third Texas Cavalry joined Van Dorn's corps. Reinforced by some three dozen new recruits, and with about fifty of its sick and wounded returned to duty, the regiment now carried 437 soldiers on its rolls. Lieutenant Colonel Boggess held temporary command, and his men joined the Sixth, Ninth, and Twenty-seventh Texas Cavalry regiments to form the Texas Brigade under Lieutenant Colonel John S. Griffith.[2]

The ordered symmetry of Pemberton's dispositions for the defense of Vicksburg looked very good on paper, but it also masked divided counsels and dissension among the officers and men. In the camp of the Texas Brigade near Holly Springs, all was not well. For one thing, the example set by the commanders was one of self-concern rather than uncomplaining sacrifice for the cause. The court of inquiry into Van Dorn's conduct at Corinth left him embittered and mistrustful; Price had hardly waited for the cannonade at Corinth to subside before mounting a renewed clamor for his Missourians to be transferred to their native state. For months the Price controversy raged in and out of the newspapers and infected his troops, most of whom could imagine no finer fate than to be sent back across the Mississippi River.[3]

Winter struck early that year, and the soldiers of the Third Cavalry were even more miserable than usual. By October 25 snow lay two or three inches upon the ground; it was bitterly cold, and there were too few tents and not enough blankets to go around. Yet what aggrieved the men most was the continued absence of their horses. Since taking command of the department, General Pemberton had ordered the remounting of the regiments in the Texas Brigade, and details had already begun leading the animals back from Texas. Then he appeared to revoke the order, and confusion arose over the issue. A few horses began to straggle into camp, but most of the men received nothing beyond rumors of their mounts' impending arrival. Resentment almost to the point of mutiny was spreading among the ranks when Grant launched his army southward at the beginning of November.

As the rest of the Rebel army withdrew ahead of the advancing Yankees, it appeared for a moment that the Texas Brigade, though assembled for departure, would refuse to march without their mounts. The men staged an impromptu strike on the parade ground and stood stubbornly immobile as their comrades filed off toward the south. By prearrangement, the aggrieved men took up a thundering chant of "HORSES! HORSES!" that drowned out the nervous appeals of both their brigade and divisional commanders.[4] At length their officers finally prevailed upon the men to march. In any case, the defiant cavalrymen regained their treasured horses on November 5 and 6, and the threatened mutiny was averted. One trooper later recalled "how bully I felt when I got on my horse. . . . Our horses were not in good fix at all. . . . But a pair of ribs between ones legs felt very wholesome at the time."[5] With their morale remarkably improved, the Third Texas joined their division in retreat.

Grant's first objective on the road to Vicksburg was Holly Springs, where he intended to set up a base of supply. Faced by Grant's superiority in numbers, Van Dorn had no recourse but to withdraw slowly down the railroad ahead of the Yankees.

By November 12 he had evacuated Holly Springs, and units of Grant's command occupied the place on the following day. Pemberton then ordered Van Dorn to concentrate behind the Yalobusha River at Grenada, seventy-five miles to the south. For the next three weeks the Confederates gradually pulled back to this position while skirmishing sporadically with advanced units of the Union army.

Two major obstacles retarded the pace of Grant's advance. In the first place, he found it difficult to supply his marching column, owing to a shortage of locomotives and rolling stock. Moreover, there existed considerable uncertainty on the part of the Union commanders about how to proceed against Vicksburg. Should Grant act alone and assault the Confederate bastion by land, or should the main attack be mounted by an amphibious force shipped down the river from Memphis, with the Federal advance down the railroad merely serving as a diversion? While Grant in Mississippi and Halleck in Washington debated their various options by long-distance telegraph, the delay proved sufficient to allow the outnumbered Rebels to elude their sluggish enemy.[6]

Meanwhile, the newly remounted Third Texas Cavalry ranged along the Tallahatchie River south of Holly Springs, fending off repeated attempts by the enemy to outflank the Rebels and block their withdrawal. Most of this duty involved no more than scouting expeditions and light skirmishing. The pace of the Federal advance quickened toward the end of November, however, and the East Texans found themselves fighting a pitched battle. Union Brigadier General Cadwallader C. Washburn had ferried the 1,925 men of his cavalry column across the Mississippi River from Helena, Arkansas, and struck deep behind the Confederate lines with the objective of cutting off the Rebel retreat by destroying the railroads and bridges north of Grenada. For a week his raiders rampaged up and down the tracks, burning trestles and ripping up rails. With most of his mission accomplished, Washburn approached the little town of Oakland, twenty miles north of Grenada, on the morning of December 3.

There he found most of the Texas Brigade waiting for him. Upon learning of Washburn's expedition, Van Dorn had ordered

Lieutenant Colonel Griffith to lead 1,264 cavalrymen and a four-gun battery to intercept the enemy raiders and drive them off. Through torrential rains, Griffith's detachment had chased the Yankees across the countryside for four days before pinning them down at Oakland. The engagement there lasted just a little less than an hour. While most of the Third Regiment was deployed on the flank and did not come under fire, Company C was detached to form part of the advance squadron that drove directly into the center of the Federal line. Though met with a barrage of artillery fire, the Texans charged the battery "with a wild, defiant shout" and seized it.[7] At this point another Union battery on their right opened a deadly enfilade upon the Rebels. Outflanked on his left as well, Griffith withdrew his command. Still, the fight lasted long enough for Sergeant Tom Cellum and his thirty men to haul off several wagonloads of Union supplies. Griffith lost only eight men wounded.

Washburn remained in Oakland that night, but withdrew toward the Mississippi to reembark his men for Arkansas the following day. While his raid had seriously alarmed the Confederate commanders, the Texas Brigade drove him off before he could block their retreat. The last of Van Dorn's artillery rumbled unmolested on to Grenada, and by December 6 Pemberton's entire army had retired safely beyond the marshes of the Yalobusha.

By this time also the shifting Union strategy against Vicksburg had temporarily crystallized into a grandiose plan of startling dimensions. Grant, with forty thousand men, was to march directly overland against the river city, while Major Generals John A. McClernand and William T. Sherman, in command of an amphibious force of some thirty thousand, would steam downstream from Memphis and attack Vicksburg from the river. As these two commanders moved, Major General Nathaniel P. Banks was to drive upriver from New Orleans to assail the Confederate bastion from the south. On paper, the project appeared promising.

To coordinate the Confederate defenses in Mississippi and Tennessee, Jefferson Davis created a new Department of the West on November 24 and appointed General Joseph E. Johnston as its overall commander. Johnston established his headquarters at Jackson, Mississippi. To oppose Grant's three-pronged offensive against Vicksburg, Johnston had only 5,500 men at Port Hudson, twenty miles north of Baton Rouge, 21,000 troops under Van Dorn and Price at Grenada, and Pemberton's 5,900 defenders within the ramparts of Vicksburg. How could these outmanned Rebel forces confound the ambitious plans of their adversaries?[8]

Both Grant and his opponents recognized that the most questionable element in his design for conquest was his dependence upon the 180-mile-long railway supply line running, as he himself admitted, "through territory occupied by a people terribly embittered and hostile" in western Tennessee and northern Mississippi.[9] The railroad was the Achilles heel of Union strategy, and Rebel commanders launched two audacious and concurrent cavalry raids designed to sever it. Bragg ordered Brigadier General Nathan Bedford Forrest to penetrate to the rear of Grant's lines in western Tennessee and disrupt his communications and supplies before the combined Union forces could converge upon Vicksburg. On December 11, Forrest set out on this first of his famous raids. For two weeks, his 2,500 marauders ranged widely throughout western Tennessee, captured millions of dollars' worth of Federal supplies, cut Grant's supply lines, and severely disrupted Union preparations.[10]

Meanwhile in Mississippi, Rebel cavalry commanders devised a similar and simultaneous stroke of their own. Shortly after the Oakland engagement, Griffith, Boggess, and the other regimental officers of the Texas Brigade petitioned General Pemberton to let them raid Holly Springs and disrupt railroad traffic between this crucial Union supply point and Memphis. Holly Springs, a bustling little city of five thousand, was noted for its rifle factory and for its opulent homes, which reflected the affluence of citizens enriched by the cotton trade. Grant had accumulated thousands of tons of supplies in the town, and his officers had requisitioned some of the finest dwellings for their quarters.

Pemberton liked the idea for the raid. He ordered Van Dorn to assemble some 3,500 cavalrymen at Grenada for a wild ride north, and three brigades were selected to participate in the enterprise: Colonel William H. "Red" Jackson's Tennesseans; Colonel Robert McCullough's Missouri and Mississippi troopers;

and Griffith's Texans. By the middle of December these seasoned soldiers had assembled at Grenada. Each was issued three days' rations and sixty rounds of ammunition, as well as matches and turpentine to facilitate the incendiary business anticipated for the expedition.[11]

In order to conceal his objective, Van Dorn chose a circuitous route for his march against Holly Springs; only such battle-hardened veterans as those of the Third Texas could have withstood the rigors it entailed. After camping in a cold rain on the bank of the Yalobusha during the night of December 15, the troopers rode eastward the following day, covering forty-five miles before halting for bivouac. When the column reached the village of Houston on December 17, its commander abruptly turned north, pausing only briefly to rest men and horses. Early the next morning the riders trotted through the streets of Pontotoc, to the cheers of its partisan inhabitants. Though the ladies of the town brought out baskets of food for the famished riders, Van Dorn refused to slacken his pace, so the troopers gratefully bolted down the welcome delicacies even as they swayed in their saddles.

Van Dorn had revealed his presence to the troops only at their point of departure, and while received with enthusiastic cheers, he kept his own counsel as to their eventual destination. The men had no inkling of their objective; they knew only that they were about some dangerous and exciting enterprise. After the bitter experience of Corinth and the tedious withdrawal in the face of Grant's army, the prospect of action on horseback again infused a new spirit in the ranks.[12]

Though the Rebel column was already deep inside Union lines, the Yankees were not yet aware of its presence. Shortly after Van Dorn departed Pontotoc, however, a Federal cavalry patrol of eight hundred men happened upon the Rebel column as it marched northward and trailed it for several miles. Since Van Dorn refused to be distracted by the smaller enemy force, the Yankee commanding officer sent couriers racing for Grant's headquarters at Oxford, Mississippi, to report what he had seen. But the messengers became lost in the Yockna River bottom, and Grant learned of Van Dorn's approach only on the following day. He immediately notified his various commanders, including Colonel R. C. Murphy, in charge of the Union garrison at Holly Springs, of the threat of an impending raid. But neither Grant nor his subordinates took full account of the speed and cunning of their adversary.[13]

Still concealing his objective from local residents as well as from stray Yankee patrols, Van Dorn deliberately bypassed the cutoff toward Holly Springs. He bivouacked his weary men amidst a drenching rainstorm on the road toward Ripley. Cold and hungry, they set out again at sunrise on December 19. About noon, their chief turned abruptly to the west and followed a rough trail leading across the country toward the objective, still some twenty-five miles away. As night fell, the Rebel column crept stealthily through the woods, posting guards at the few isolated farmhouses they passed. It was after midnight when the raiders camped about five miles east of Holly Springs. Bitterly cold as it was, campfires were forbidden. Though Van Dorn sent scouts ahead to round up the Yankee pickets, at least one of them had spied the approaching riders and got away in time to warn Colonel Murphy of a possible attack. Yet he took no serious measures to prepare for the assault and failed to alert his subordinates.[14]

Thus, when the raiders pounced upon the town at dawn on December 20, they found both its citizens and its Federal garrison fast asleep. Approaching the outskirts of Holly Springs, the Texans broke into a gallop and rent the chill silence of early morning with their wild Rebel yell. A local matron later remembered the sound in the distance as it awoke her like the "singing of a wood fire."[15] Almost instantly, the distant roar became a wild cacophony of galloping hooves, clanking sabers, and the chatter of small-arms fire.

Colonel Murphy had billeted his men in three concentrations. While about 500 Yankee infantrymen occupied the courthouse and camped around the depot a half mile to the east, six companies of Illinois cavalry had bivouacked at the fairgrounds on the northern edge of town. To deal with these dispersed units simultaneously, Van Dorn divided his raiders into two columns: his Mississippians charged Holly Springs from the northeast and struck the Yankee cavalry; the Texas Brigade approached from the east, swept through the infantry camp at the depot, and dashed on into the heart of town. As the East Texans poured across the enemy campground near the depot, the terrified Yankees dashed out of their tents in their underwear, and finding themselves surrounded, surrendered without firing a shot. The raiders circled the courthouse, captured its occupants, and began to look around them in the early morning light.

Their first sensation was one of wonderment at the mountains of Federal stores they had captured. At that very moment a long train loaded with rations and clothing was getting up steam in the railroad yard, and the raiders burned it where it stood. Heaps upon heaps of boots, blankets, and clothing were stored in buildings all over town. Whiskey, cigars, and canned goods were piled everywhere. A livery stable near the courthouse was full of still unopened cases of carbines and pistols, and artillery ammunition filled a large brick house nearby. Hundreds of bales of cotton lined the courthouse square. Long accustomed to the privations of Confederate military life, the East Texans could hardly believe their eyes.

Their second indelible impression was the hysterical reaction of the white population of Holly Springs to what they assumed was a permanent deliverance from their despised Yankee occupiers. Citizens rushed out of their houses shouting, "Hurrah for Van Dorn! Hurrah for the Confederacy!! Hurrah for Jeff. Davis!!!"[16] Otherwise dignified matrons ran into the street in their nightgowns, screaming, "Kill them, kill them!"[17] The quiet little town turned into a frantic, shouting mass of humanity, torn between fear and exultation.

The actual fighting lasted less than an hour, but the work of destruction went on all day. While the Union infantry offered little resistance, the Illinois cavalry at the fairgrounds put up a stiff, though brief, struggle. About 130 of them escaped by cutting their way through Van Dorn's attackers. Then for about ten hours the Rebels ran wild in the streets. They burned warehouses and supply depots; the explosion of the ammunition dumps helped spread the fires into civilian quarters as well. To the justifiable indignation of Union authorities, the raiders destroyed the Federal hospital after evicting its patients.[18] Van Dorn reported hurriedly but no less jubilantly that he had "surprised the enemy . . . at daylight this morning; burned up all the quartermaster's stores . . . [and] many trains; took a great many arms and about 1,500 prisoners."[19]

His men meanwhile gave themselves over to an orgy of looting. To the ragged and half-starved Rebel troopers, the sight of so much open plunder was too great a temptation to resist. Discipline broke down, and the officers lost control of the men. The Texans had been posted to guard the town square, but emboldened by huge draughts of Yankee whiskey, they soon joined the Missourians and Mississippians in sacking up as much booty as they could from the Yankee stores. They opened the local jail, and erstwhile Federal prisoners as well as black refugees joined in the pillaging. Many Rebel soldiers took advantage of the confusion to exchange their emaciated mounts for sleek, fresh horses. Ragged privates paraded around hilariously in Federal officers' garb, complete with plumed hats. Various hangers-on as well as discharged troops who had never gone home used the occasion to collect a little plunder. Former sergeant Bill Pennington, of Rusk County, discovered $20,000 in greenbacks, which he hawked around for $5 in silver. Former Private B. L. Thomas, a discharged veteran of Company A, became uproariously drunk and regaled his old comrades with his incessant Irish blather. Until late in the afternoon Holly Springs presented a picture of utter chaos.[20]

Had a substantial Federal force descended upon the town and caught the raiders in their drunken abandon, it might have massacred them to the last man. But the Union commanders were slow to react to their humiliation. Disgusted over the fiasco at Holly Springs, Grant ordered out a formidable detachment of cavalry to attack Van Dorn's marauders early on the morning of the raid. The colonel in charge of this expedition carried out his orders with such extreme circumspection, however, that his relieving force only reached the town shortly before noon on the following day. Grant angrily suspended him from his command. By this time Van Dorn's men were well out of reach, having departed Holly Springs at daylight.[21]

While the Federal pursuers chafed impatiently for another twenty-four hours awaiting new orders and reinforcements, the Rebel raiders were dashing northward on another and more difficult mission. To protect his vital rail network against just such an attack, Grant had earlier fortified important crossings and bridges along the Tennessee-Mississippi border with improvised blockhouses manned by small garrisons. Eighteen miles north of Holly Springs stood Davis' Mills, on the Wolf River. Here a Yankee garrison of 250 Indiana infantrymen under the command of Colonel William H. Morgan had converted an old sawmill into a formidable blockhouse to guard the railway trestle across the river. Arriving on the spot about noon on December 21, Van Dorn resolved to storm the blockhouse from across the stream. He ordered the men of the Texas Brigade to dismount and attack the stronghold on foot.

Though outnumbered more than ten to one, the Indianans were well fortified in their blockhouse, some sixty yards above the river, and they also occupied a hastily constructed earthworks covering the bridge. While the attackers had to dash across the beams of the trestle or expose themselves by wading the slough beneath it, the defenders, barricaded behind their breastworks of crossties and cotton bales, could pick them off with impunity. Three times the Texans attacked, but on each occasion Federal marksmen knocked them off the bridge or pinned them to the river bank below.[22] Private George Stringfellow, of Company H, for example, had advanced in front of the regiment, and a Yankee sharpshooter shot him through the head. Though his comrades knew that Stringfellow "had 5 or 600 dollars in his pocket, . . . [his] position was so exposed, none would dare venture to him."[23]

In the course of several hours of futile and confused fighting, the Texas Brigade lost twenty-two dead and thirty wounded without ever reaching the blockhouse. Among those killed from the Third Texas was Private Sam Meeks, a schoolteacher from Cass County. Lieutenants William Creswell, Company F, and Samuel Graham, Company I, were both wounded. Fearing that thousands of Union cavalry might be right behind him, Van Dorn finally called off the suicidal attack late in the afternoon and bivouacked his men for the night a few miles from the mill.[24]

Early the next morning the troopers struck northward across the Tennessee border to raid the Memphis and Charleston Railroad, burn its trestles, and tear up its track for miles. Veering west, Van Dorn's cavalry galloped through the little hamlet of Moscow, Tennessee, and then north again to Somerville, where they found to their delight that a Union mass meeting was in progress. Whether out of prudent concern for their own necks or genuine sympathy for the Confederate cause, the inhabitants received the Rebel troops with cheers and generous gifts of food. That night, "much Jaded but *enthusiastic* from the joyous reception," the troopers camped north of Somerville.[25]

Now they were flirting with extreme peril. Less than twenty miles to the east lay the huge Federal concentration at Bolivar, and a powerful Union cavalry column had at last struck Van Dorn's trail. But the Yankee command in western Tennessee was still confused: Forrest's Confederate cavalry had been raiding the railroad towns fifty miles or so to the north, and the Union officers were hard pressed to cover all their exposed supply points simultaneously. Taking advantage of this uncertainty, Van Dorn led his column almost as far north as Brownsville before swinging southeast again toward Bolivar. At dawn on December 24 the raiders brushed past the town's outskirts, captured thirty Yankee pickets, and headed back down the railroad toward the Mississippi line.[26]

The Texans spent most of Christmas Eve morning in a vain attempt to dislodge 115 Yankees who had barricaded themselves in the brick buildings of Middleburg, Tennessee. Because there were so few defenders, the raiders believed that they "would have an easy Victory—Oh sad mistake." When the Texans approached the fortified buildings on foot, "the whole Fort seemed a living sheet of flame, so rapidly did they pour the leaden hail into our ranks. . . . Our men sunk away like stubble before a fire."[27] Among others, the Third Texas lost Lieutenant William Logan, a former Tyler law student and aspiring poet, who was killed while leading a charge. Ed Lewis, the twenty-year-old son of a prominent Henderson lawyer, also died in the attack, as did Alva Box, of Rusk, and F. M. Parish, whose leg wound eventually lost him his life. At last, warned of the approach of a Yankee cavalry column from Bolivar, Van Dorn broke off the action and left the defenders of Middleburg to savor their hard-earned victory. That night the raiders camped near the Mississippi border, only two miles ahead of their pursuers. They had ridden forty-seven miles that day.[28]

The real race was only beginning, however. Van Dorn's sanctuary at Grenada still lay more than than a hundred miles to the south, and thousands of Yankees stood between him and safety. Since Colonel Benjamin H. Grierson's Union cavalry was hard on his heels, and Grant's garrisons all over northern Mississippi were set to trap him, the Rebel general was forced to follow a circuitous course along obscure trails in order to evade his would-be captors. Christmas Day afforded no respite for celebration, as Van Dorn's troopers galloped south all morning, hotly pursued by Grierson. Their Christmas dinner consisted of parched corn bolted down on the run.

At Ripley, Van Dorn ordered the Ninth Texas to hold up the Union advance while he led the main body of his detachment on toward Grenada. This Rebel rear guard fought so fiercely that the Yankee commander was led to believe that he faced Van Dorn's entire force. Consequently, instead of continuing their pursuit into the night, the Union soldiers camped outside Ripley to prepare for a pitched battle on the morrow. This delay allowed Van Dorn to escape. His rear guard, having done its duty, scurried on south to join him. Disappointed, exhausted, and drenched to the skin, the Federals broke off the chase on December 27, and Van Dorn's raiders straggled into the comparative safety of Grenada the following day. They had ridden more than five hundred miles during the previous fortnight.[29]

Combined with Forrest's foray into western Tennessee, the Holly Springs raid had inflicted incalculable damage upon the enemy and set back his timetable for victory in the West by at least half a year. By disrupting Grant's transportation system and destroying his supplies, the twin incursions had crippled the Union commander at a crucial juncture. In the bitter summation of General McClernand, Grant's chief critic of the hour, "The golden moment for the reduction of Vicksburg was allowed to pass unimproved."[30] Instead of supporting Sherman's river-borne strike against the Rebel citadel, Grant was forced to fall back on his bases in northern Mississippi. Consequently, when Sherman's amphibious army tried to storm the outer defenses of Vicksburg on December 29, they met with a bloody repulse at the hands of the entrenched Confederates. Sherman suspended his assault and reembarked his men. The raids of Forrest and Van Dorn thus kept a vital stretch of the Mississippi under Rebel control for another six months.[31]

Lacking the advantage of hindsight, of course, the Confederate leaders did not at first realize that they had been given a reprieve. General Pemberton anxiously strengthened his fortifications at Vicksburg and appealed to General Johnston for reinforcements. Especially necessary, he insisted, were seasoned cavalrymen to operate against the enemy's flanks on the Yazoo River above Vicksburg. "With the Texas cavalry I can do," he wrote.[32] On the first day of the new year, Johnston obliged him by ordering the Texas Brigade out of its bivouac near Grenada to engage the enemy north of Vicksburg.

After only four days to rest in camp after the extraordinary exertions of the Holly Springs raid, the Texans set out at sunrise on January 2 for the beleaguered river fortress. For the next three days they slogged fifty miles south through pelting rain and waterlogged creek bottoms, leaving their wagons mired in the mud. At this point, Johnston ordered them to halt, about-face, and return to Grenada for a new assignment, since it was now clear that the immediate danger on the Vicksburg front had passed. Wearily, the troopers retraced their steps through Grenada and up the railroad, probing for any signs of a renewed offensive by Grant. Soon the almost continuous rain turned to snow, and separated from their baggage train by their rapid marches, the Texans had no tents to protect them from the frigid nights.[33]

For a week or so, while the men bivouacked in the cold, Johnston could not decide how to use his cavalry. In overall command of the Confederate armies in the West, he was faced with the task of allocating his ever dwindling resources to whichever of the two major fronts—Vicksburg or middle Tennessee—appeared most pregnant of disaster. The choice was rendered yet more difficult by the ominous quiet that descended upon both areas of contention as the new year opened. After the collapse of his first strike against Vicksburg, Grant would require four months of elaborate preparation before he could position his men for a renewed assault on the vital stronghold. In the meantime, the armies in northern Mississippi remained comparatively inactive.

In middle Tennessee, some 350 miles to the northeast, the war also reached a temporary stalemate. The year had begun with the great battle at Murfreesboro, or Stone's River, but by the end of this bloody yet inconclusive contest on January 3, neither antagonist had achieved a breakthrough. The front remained static for another six months. General Bragg extended the Confederate defensive line some seventy miles along the Duck River to block an anticipated Federal thrust toward Chattanooga, the key to the Southern heartland. Across the river Bragg's Rebels were faced by a superior force under the command of General Rosecrans, who was reluctant to attack until an accumulation of supplies and manpower, as well as favorable weather, made success a certainty. As a result, the two great armies spent half a year glaring at each other across the Duck River and foraging the farms in its fertile valley.

In spite of the stabilization of the front after Murfreesboro, Bragg clamored for all the troops Johnston could send him to counter the threat posed by Rosecrans's powerful army. Johnston responded on January 11 by creating a new cavalry corps under Van Dorn, which was to march to Tennessee and reinforce Bragg's defensive line. The success of Forrest and Van Dorn in thwarting Grant's offensive in Mississippi had been duly noted, and Johnston hoped that similarly bold cavalry raids might cut Rosecrans's supply lines as effectively as they had interdicted Grant's transportation system the month before. Johnston therefore ordered Van Dorn to concentrate his dispersed cavalry units and lead them to middle Tennessee.[34]

Colonel Elkanah B. Greer, Third Texas Cavalry Regiment. *Used with permission of Jane Judge Greer, Tyler, Texas.*

Lieutenant Colonel Walter P. Lane, Third Texas Cavalry Regiment.
Used with permission of Hill Junior College Press, Hillsboro, Texas.

Bugler Albert B. Blocker, Company A, Third Texas Cavalry Regiment.
Used with permission of Max S. Lale, Fort Worth.

Lieutenant Williamson Milburn, Company K, Third Texas Cavalry Regiment. *Used with permission of D. Judson Milburn, Stillwater, Oklahoma.*

Private Ben T. Roberts, Company E, Third Texas Cavalry Regiment.
Used with permission of David D. Jackson, Dallas.

Private Lon Cartwright, Company E, Third Texas Cavalry Regiment. *Used with permission of David D. Jackson, Dallas.*

CHAPTER 10

Thompson's Station, January–May 1863

VAN DORN accepted his assignment to Bragg's command with his customary enthusiasm. For the expedition to Tennessee he organized his cavalry corps into two divisions of two brigades each, with Brigadier General William H. "Red" Jackson, a native Tennessean, in charge of the Second Division. It included the Texas Brigade, under the authority of Colonel John W. Whitfield, formerly of the Twenty-seventh Texas Cavalry. Since Colonel Mabry was still recuperating from his wounds, and Lieutenant Colonel Boggess had obtained an extended leave, Major Absolom B. Stone served as temporary commanding officer for the Third Texas. General Price had at last persuaded his superiors to transfer him back to the Trans-Mississippi Department. Thus relieved of Price's blustering presence, and his own somewhat tarnished reputation having been refurbished by the success of the Holly Springs raid, Van Dorn was now eager to lead his independent command upon new paths of glory in Tennessee.[1]

The men in the ranks also seemed anxious to escape the mud of Mississippi under any pretext, but the route of march to middle Tennessee would take them through oceans of the stuff before they reached their destination. Fortified by a diet of sweet potatoes, the troopers of the Third Texas set out across the sloughs and rivers of northern Mississippi on January 26. Though at first frozen by the intense cold, the ground soon thawed into an almost impassable morass. Because the horses tried to step in the same spot as the animal ahead, they dragged the mud into ridges across the trail. As the mire slowly solidified, the horses had to step over these bumps in the road as though walking over logs, making for a most uncomfortable ride. Slogging again through rain and snow, the Texans camped during the first week of February near Okolona, Mississippi, where they were joined by scattered units straggling in from far-flung picket duty.[2]

Among these strays returning to the fold was venturesome Private John Long, eager to regale his delighted comrades in Company C with his escapades since his capture at Corinth five months before. Through Masonic connections with a Union officer, he had arranged comfortable quarters for himself during his incarceration at Memphis. Then, as Long recounted it, a young lady had befriended him: she helped him slip away from his guards, drove him out of the city in her buggy, and concealed him at her country home. She procured new clothes and a fast horse for the fugitive and sent him on a flight through the Yankee-infested countryside of southern Tennessee by means of a network of Confederate patriots, who identified Long by the password "hunting for a brindled cow." At length, he found the Third Texas just before its departure for Tennessee.[3]

Having organized his corps and gotten his men on the road, Van Dorn issued Order No. 5, which minutely prescribed the regulations for his new command and concluded with the ringing admonition: "Cavalry knows no danger—knows no failure; *what it is ordered to do, it must do!*"[4] With that, he led his men across the hills of northwest Alabama and down into the Tennessee Valley. Ferrying his troops across the turbulent river near Florence, Alabama, on February 16, Van Dorn kept a wary eye out for Yankee patrols on his flanks. The scattered Federal pickets could hardly contest the passage of the little army, but they burned bridges, set up roadblocks, and imposed time-consuming delays, nonetheless. As the men rode north into Tennessee, conditions became even worse. Flooded streams blocked their trail, and the weather continued wet and cold.

Eighteen-year-old Private Jim Thomas, who had been in the army only a few months, complained that "the water run in my boots . . . and I came very near freezing."[5] Under constantly dripping skies, the troopers at last slogged their way into the Confederate camp near Columbia, Tennessee, on the evening of February 21. "Perfectly saturated & . . . benumbed with cold," the men suffered "more intently than heretofore at any time."[6] It had required almost a month for them to cover the 250 miles from their old campground at Grenada.

Had their restless commander gotten his way, the men in the ranks would not have had time to dry their blankets before he drove them forth on another hazardous escapade. Eager for action, Van Dorn dreamed of hard-charging cavalry raids to strike fear in the Northern heartland. On the day after his arrival at Columbia, he informed General Johnston of his readiness to operate "on the banks of the Ohio" immediately, or "to make any movement you may desire."[7] Johnston tactfully but firmly replied that the first priority of the cavalry corps was that of guarding Bragg's left wing against Federal attack; only after that duty had been served would raids deep into the interior be appropriate. Yet, as though to double the audacity factor among the Rebel horsemen, Johnston assigned the troopers of that equally bold chieftain General Forrest to Van Dorn's command, thus augmenting his effective force to 6,300 men. A few days later the cavalry corps clattered across a pontoon bridge over the Duck River at Columbia and into camp near Spring Hill, a little town on the Nashville Turnpike eleven miles farther up the road.[8]

This placed Van Dorn on the extreme left wing of the Confederate army. Bragg's infantry was concentrated south of the Duck River some forty miles south of Nashville, while his two cavalry wings, under Van Dorn and Major General Joseph Wheeler, curved away to the left and right to form a total front about eighty miles long. This defensive line ran through rolling blue-grass prairie country that gave way here and there to wooded ridges and knobs. Farms rich in corn, wheat, and cattle dotted the broad valley of Duck River; the countryside, with its well-maintained turnpikes radiating south from Nashville, presented an aspect of bucolic prosperity but slightly clouded by the rav-

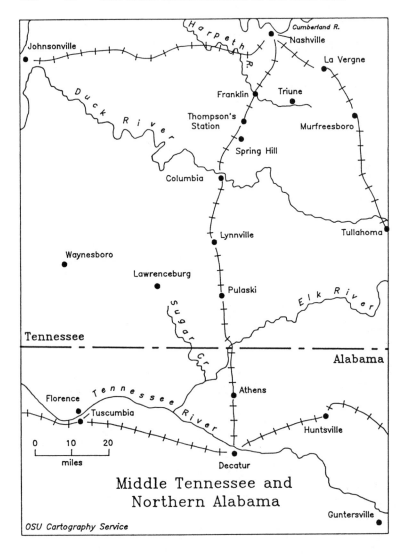

Middle Tennessee and
Northern Alabama

OSU Cartography Service

ages of winter and war. To the soldiers from East Texas, so long accustomed to privation and empty bellies, the landscape south of Nashville looked like "a land of plenty." There was, marveled one, "corn to feed the cavalry horses, corn for the mules, great houses of corn, and bacon shoulders . . . and . . . enough of hams to get a full ration of ham for all—even the privates. . . . After crossing the Tennessee River we had plenty, . . . our effectiveness was never better."[9]

Since early January the armies of Rosecrans and Bragg had stood facing each other, but neither antagonist had undertaken a major effort to break the stalemate. As a Marion County private reported to his sister: "No talk of fighting hear now. I think that Mr. ABE lincoln has got tired of us by now and we will have Peace shortly."[10] Most of the Confederate soldiers spent their days foraging for food, listlessly enduring the squalor and boredom of camp life, and grumbling about the war. Only the men in the cavalry seemed immune from this general lethargy. Since the battle of Murfreesboro, Bragg's horsemen had occupied themselves with sporadic foraging expeditions into the hospitable countryside or in aimless raids against isolated Yankee outposts and shipping points behind enemy lines.

With the arrival of Van Dorn's contingent Bragg resolved to employ his cavalry more systematically. As the springtime sun shone more brightly, the swollen rivers subsided, and the emaciated Texas ponies began to fatten on Tennessee clover. The Confederate commander sent bands of Rebel horsemen roving continually through the hills and across the streams between Nashville and Columbia, raiding supply trains and fighting brief but furious skirmishes with their Union counterparts. Like a pair of boxers, Confederate and Federal cavalry detachments stalked each other warily, jabbed, feinted, and parried, and then fell to pummeling each other until one adversary or the other backed off to gather strength, await a point of vantage, and begin probing the opponent's defenses all over again. Though much blood flowed, and the punishment sustained on both sides was painful and severe, neither side could score a knockout. In this way Van Dorn's cavalry corps fought five strenuous but indecisive rounds during its three months' sojourn in middle Tennessee.

The first set-to resulted in a clear Rebel victory. The town of Franklin, only thirteen miles north of Van Dorn's camp at Spring Hill, was one of the most active points on the Union line. Bragg expected an attack from that sector momentarily, and both Rebel and Yankee cavalry patrols frequently scouted the land between their lines. On March 4 the Union commander at Franklin sent Colonel John Coburn with a brigade of Indiana, Wisconsin, and Michigan infantry, about six hundred cavalry, and a battery of artillery down the pike toward Spring Hill. In all, Coburn's column consisted of 2,837 men and some one hundred wagons, because he was charged with foraging through the area as well as reconnoitering the Rebel lines.[11]

At about the same time that Coburn left Franklin, Van Dorn ordered General "Red" Jackson's division northward on a reconnaissance of its own. Cantering smartly up the hard-packed turnpike some four miles, Jackson arrived around midmorning at the village of Thompson's Station, on the Decatur and Nashville Railroad. Here he discovered, to his surprise, that Coburn's Yankees were entering the north side of the village even as his own riders were approaching it from the opposite direction. Immediately notifying Van Dorn of his catch, Jackson dismounted his men, deployed them in a roadblock across the turnpike, and turned his ordnance upon the enemy. Coburn halted, posted his own guns atop a knoll just east of the road, and returned the Rebel fire. For more than an hour, the two antagonists hurled grapeshot at each other across a broad field on the edge of town.

About noon Coburn impulsively ordered a cavalry charge against the Rebel positions, and Jackson pulled back to establish a longer and more secure defensive line in the broken ground south of Thompson's Station. This formidable front halted Coburn's advance, and the Yankees beat a hasty retreat back to their original positions. At this point, Van Dorn himself arrived upon the scene with his main force, which, with Jackson's advance guard, amounted to some six thousand men, more than twice the number in Coburn's command. But confronted by well-aimed Yankee cannon fire, which had already killed fifteen of his men, and suspecting that Coburn's column was part of a larger army, Van Dorn remained stationary south of Thompson's Station until the end of the day. Meanwhile, Coburn tried to extricate his wagon train and send it back to Franklin. The Confederates replied with such a telling artillery barrage, however, that only thirty-nine wagons escaped before the Federal column was pinned down in the hills north of the village. That night the two adversaries bivouacked about four miles apart on either side of town.

During the hours of darkness Van Dorn's scouts soon established that the foe they faced was much smaller than they were. Encouraged by this intelligence, their commander devised a crushing blow for the morrow. The next morning, March 5, Van Dorn posted Forrest's cavalry brigade on a hill at the extreme right, dismounted most of his other horsemen, and deployed them in a line about a mile long at the southern end of Thompson's Station. General Jackson ordered Colonel Whitfield's Texas Brigade to take cover behind a long stone wall just south of the village. Under the command of Major Stone, the men of the Third Texas crouched behind their rock barrier to await whatever was about to happen on the other side.[12]

Colonel Coburn, the Union commander, belatedly realized that he was now trapped by a superior enemy force. Still, he resolved to plunge ahead, having, as he said, "no option in the matter."[13] In response to an inquiry by one of his officers as to his intentions, Coburn curtly replied that "I must go on or show cowardice."[14] Consequently, at about 10:00 A.M. he launched an attack all along the line. The Confederate guns in the hills south of the village met this assault with a devastating volley of grapeshot. Failing to dislodge the Rebel cannoneers, Coburn then personally led an infantry attack across the open ground in front of the Texans' position behind their stone wall. While the wall protected them, it also obstructed their view, and the East Texans were naturally curious about the Yankee infantry bearing down upon them. They crowded around the few apertures that had been dug out of the wall at various points along its length and jostled each other out of the way to get a better look at the advancing wave of blue.

As the Federal troops approached within two hundred yards of their position, the officers of the Third Texas ordered their men to fire and charge the enemy at the same moment. Unloosing a shattering volley upon the advancing ranks of Indiana infantrymen, the Texans checked and repulsed the attack. The surviving Yankees then began a stubborn withdrawal under cover of the scattered buildings near the village depot and back into the wooded hills to the north, as the Rebels took the offensive. Bounding out of their cover behind the stone wall, the Texans mounted three separate assaults through thickets of scrub cedar toward the crest of the hill where Coburn had dug in his troops. Twice the Confederate cavalrymen almost attained the summit, only to be driven down again by Yankee bayonets or rifle fire—and not without cost.[15]

Lon Cartwright, "Bully" Polk, and Hugh Leslie, all privates from Company E, advanced together in the second assault against the Union skirmish line on the hilltop, taking whatever cover they could find among the cedars. As Polk aimed at a Yankee on his left, another enemy skirmisher rose up twenty paces ahead and drew a bead on the Rebel. Cartwright leveled his rifle at this new assailant, but the weapon misfired, and, as Cartwright recounted it, "in an instant he shot Bully dead, the bullet entering the uper lip and coming out through the top of the head. In an instant more, Hugh Leslie shot the Fedl." Heartsick at his failure to protect his lifelong friend, Cartwright tried to find some consolation in the fact that his assailant was slain, and that Polk "fell in front of his Regt. bravely discharging his duty."[16]

As witnesses to the ebb and flow of battle, a number of women had collected in the houses overlooking the village and formed an impromptu Confederate cheering section. At a Rebel advance, they clapped their hands and shouted encouragement; as their side fell back, they would hide their eyes and weep, "alternately shouting and crying all day."[17] One young woman performed a more conspicuous service for the Southern cause. On the second Rebel charge up the hill, an Arkansas regiment lost its color guard to a Yankee volley. Seventeen-year-old Alice Thompson thereupon rushed from the house where she had taken shelter, raised the flag, and rallied the wavering regiment. The Third Texas lost its flag, too—that banner received from the Choctaw maidens in Indian Territory a year and a half before—but unfortunately found no similar rescuer. A Yankee bullet cut the flagstaff in two, and though its bearer retrieved the flag, his escape through a plum thicket left it torn to ribbons among the tangled branches.[18]

Sweating profusely in the unseasonable heat—with canteens empty and throats dry—the Texans experienced increasing frustration in their apparent inability to take Coburn's hilltop. It was left to General Forrest to decide the fate of the day. From the extreme right of the Rebel line he led two regiments of riders around the Union left flank. Dismounting, they attacked the Yankee redoubt from the rear about four o'clock in the afternoon. Simultaneously, the Texas Brigade charged up the hill to assault Coburn's front for a third and final time. Defending their position tenaciously, the Yankees fired in all directions. But, recognizing that he was surrounded and his ammunition almost exhausted, Coburn at last surrendered.

It was a welcome victory for the Rebels. Van Dorn's command captured 1,151 prisoners that day, including 75 officers. In addition, Coburn listed 377 of his men as dead or wounded. The arms and equipment that fell to the victors were a valuable addition to the always inadequate store of Confederate supplies. The destitute Rebels also stripped their fallen enemies of shoes, clothing, and other personal articles before they consigned the victims to mass graves, much to the disgust of the captured Union officers.

Van Dorn lost 357 of his own men killed, wounded, or missing in the two-day battle. Twenty-four members of the Third Cavalry were wounded, including two lieutenants and five sergeants, while ten men were killed outright or died from their wounds. Among the dead were Lieutenant Reuben Tunnell, a twenty-six-year-old former clerk from Smith County. Besides Bully Polk, San Augustine lost Private Dan Nicholson, the son of the county assessor. Also slain were Private Rufus Allen, a Kaufman County blacksmith, and Private John Anderson, of Rusk County. Private William R. Campbell, who left a wife and three small children, and Private Beecher C. Donald, a former student at Larissa College, died from their wounds within the month.[19]

Their sacrifice accomplished little. The battle of Thompson's Station held no strategic significance: it failed to alter the balance in middle Tennessee and merely served to delay the inevitable Union advance against Bragg's outnumbered army. The battle lines remained static, and only the Confederate cavalry seriously engaged the enemy. For the next two months, Brigadier General John Hunt Morgan and Major General Joseph Wheeler, as well as Forrest and Van Dorn, embellished their reputations as bold cavaliers by launching their various commands across the countryside to attack enemy supply points and skirmish with Yankee pickets.

A Federal counterthrust soon initiated the second round of sparring for the Third Texas, almost trapping the East Texans against the swollen torrent of the Duck River, just north of Columbia. After his victory at Thompson's Station, Van Dorn pulled his troops back to Spring Hill, correctly anticipating a Yankee counterstroke at any moment. It came from two directions. Major General Philip H. Sheridan first led a Union advance on Columbia from the northeast, and Van Dorn's troopers located that column in the Harpeth River basin and attacked it. Encountering the enemy near Triune on March 8, the Rebels withdrew after a sharp skirmish. The following day, Sheridan's detachment joined forces with another under the command of Major General Gordon Granger to advance down the turnpike from Franklin toward Columbia. Recognizing that the approaching Union columns were far superior to his own, Van Dorn gave ground before them. His men dug in on the banks of Rutherford's Creek, only a few miles north of the Duck River crossing at Columbia.

The Yankees believed that they had pinned the elusive Van Dorn into a position from which there was no escape. Heavy rains had swollen the river at his back, and when his cavalrymen tried to fling a pontoon bridge across the stream, it washed away. Yet the deluge had swamped the bottoms of Rutherford Creek as well, and the impassable ground delayed the Federal pursuit sufficiently for Van Dorn to extricate his men. On March 11 he led his troopers on a twenty-mile detour eastward and found a ramshackle bridge still intact. With the Third Texas as vanguard and Forrest's brigade covering its rear, the cavalry corps dashed across the river to safety. When General Granger finally attacked across Rutherford Creek, he discovered that his quarry had flown. Unwilling to try their fortunes across the flooded river plain, the Yankees returned to Franklin, while

Van Dorn's troops, delighted that they had outwitted their pursuers, retired to camp at Columbia.[20]

Saddlesore and sodden, the Confederate cavalrymen rested for almost a week in camp before coming out for the third round. After so much dashing about, Van Dorn's horses were exhausted. Moreover, they needed shoeing. The Third Texas scoured the countryside in search of farriers with enough iron and muscle to do the job. At last, as the turgid waters of Duck River subsided, Van Dorn threw another pontoon bridge across the stream and marched his men back to Spring Hill on March 20. Bragg had ordered him to harass the Yankee strongpoint at Franklin and attack it, if the opportunity presented itself.

These Rebel demonstrations south of Franklin persuaded the Union commanders to draw in their pickets from the east, leaving their line a bit thin just below Nashville. There General Forrest, operating on Van Dorn's right flank, found the opening he needed. On March 25 he led his raiders into Brentwood, only nine miles from the Tennessee capital, captured almost eight hundred Yankees, and confiscated hundreds of rifles, which he distributed to his men. The wily Forrest then scurried back down to Columbia before Federal forces could catch him.[21]

Meanwhile, the remainder of Van Dorn's corps performed picket duty and foraged for food among the hospitable farmsteads north of Spring Hill. "The best folks in the world live here in Tennessee," exclaimed a grateful San Augustine private.[22] The foragers usually found a generous handout and a warm place to sleep in the homes of the valley, and occasionally some of the men located enough whiskey to relieve the tedium of camp life. Their work, though generally routine, could also be dangerous. As a case in point, a Union cavalry column surrounded and captured one of Van Dorn's patrols on April 2 before the Texas Brigade could be rushed to the rescue.[23]

After almost three weeks of forage and scouting duty, the brigade moved back into Spring Hill to prepare for a grand review on April 8. On this occasion six thousand mounted men paraded for the edification of visiting officers, admiring ladies, and members of the press. A correspondent for the Mobile *Register and Advertiser* was properly dazzled by the spectacle of "thousands of horses formed in line. . . , the high-spirited boys, . . . the gleaming guns and glistening sabres." The Texas cavalry he portrayed as "rollicking, rascally, brave . . . singular looking customers . . . , with their large brimmed hats, dark features, shaggy Mexican mustangs, and a *lariet* . . . around the pummel of their saddles."[24] For the benefit of his readers, the reporter sketched a stirring portrait of the heroes of the hour, Van Dorn and Forrest, galloping together across the parade ground. The men in the midst of all this pageantry, on the other hand, seemed more intent upon appraising the quality of the female spectators present. "I don't think they are as good looking as our girls," observed one East Texan, "though some of them are quite handsome."[25] Others regarded the review as just one more instance of useless military drudgery. While agreeing that "the scene was beautiful to the spectable," Jim Thomas noted sourly that "the heat and dust was very oppressive to the poor privates."[26]

Two days later the fourth round of action between Van Dorn and his adversaries opened with what might have become a major battle. General Bragg had heard rumors that the Federals were preparing to evacuate Franklin, and he ordered Van Dorn to undertake a reconnaissance in force to establish the strength of the garrison there. He found it very strong indeed. Situated eighteen miles south of Nashville on the shallow Harpeth River, Franklin was garrisoned by almost eight thousand Union troops under the command of General Granger. They had dug in on the bluffs lining the north bank of the river, under the guns of a half-completed fort that overlooked the entire town.

Leading a force of 3,700 troopers, Van Dorn set out on the main road north from Spring Hill on the morning of April 10. About three miles south of Franklin he divided his corps so that Forrest's column of 2,535 men would approach the town from the southeast while Jackson's division entered the place from the south. Just after noon, as Van Dorn's two columns of Rebel horsemen struck Franklin a strong Southern wind drove heavy clouds of dust before them, obscuring visibility long enough for the raiders to secure a lodgment. The Union garrison slowly retired from Franklin and went back into their fortified positions on the north bank of the Harpeth. By 2:30 P.M., what had begun as a reconnaissance in force by the cavalry corps had turned into a full-fledged assault against a very strong position held by a Federal contingent more than twice the strength of the attackers.[27]

Van Dorn had taken a terrible risk, for his adversary now saw a chance to use his superior manpower to encircle his foe as the two Rebel columns converged on Franklin. "I am extremely anxious to whip Van Dorn," Granger had earlier avowed, "and settle up accounts with him contracted at Thompson's Station and Brentwood."[28] Now, it would appear, the Union general saw his chance. Unfortunately for his plans, however, Granger had sent his most potent cavalry unit back toward Nashville in response to false reports of a Rebel concentration in that area. Moreover, Granger's remaining cavalry attacked prematurely, before Forrest was in the bag, and the Union infantry moved too slowly to surround the Rebel horsemen in Jackson's division. Alerted to Granger's tactics of encirclement, Van Dorn called a halt to the developing battle and sped back to Spring Hill before the Yankees could effectively pursue him. This first battle of Franklin accomplished nothing besides revealing to the Confederate command that the Union forces were still determined to hold the place—information won at the cost of forty men dead and eighty-one wounded on both sides. Like so much else in the war, it had been a pointless exercise. Fortunately for the East Texans, their position in reserve allowed them to escape unscathed.[29]

Forrest and Van Dorn worked well together in battle, and they must have made an inspiring picture galloping side by side on review. By this time, however, the two generals had come to detest each other cordially. It was perhaps inevitable: Van Dorn, the vain and pompous West Pointer, still agonizing over the damage done his reputation by the bloody debacle at Corinth, confronted by the blunt and ruthless Forrest, whose burgeoning acclaim as a cavalry chief had already begun to outshine that of his commanding officer. Violent and impetuous by nature, each was quick to resent real or imagined affronts to his honor. Soon the smoldering resentment flared into an angry encounter that might well have ended with the two hotspurs killing each other, had they both not been seized by a passing fit of restraint.

Whatever the effects of this confrontation upon their relationship, they soon parted for good. On the night of April 23, General Bragg ordered Forrest and his brigade detached from Van Dorn's corps in order to repel a Union cavalry raid in northern Alabama. Forrest set out on his mission before daylight the following morning.[30]

Forrest's departure left Van Dorn with a corps of 3,748 effectives. They began their fifth round of sparring with the Yankees by taking a severe blow to the body. Toward the end of April the Twenty-seventh Texas Cavalry relieved the Third Regiment from picket duty on the Carter Creek Pike, about five miles west of Spring Hill. As nothing very exciting had occurred at this post for almost a month, the troops became careless. At dawn on April 27 two regiments of Yankee cavalry swooped down on the slumbering Rebel camp and captured or destroyed everything in it. The Union raiders drove off three hundred horses and made captives of 112 men and 9 officers. Alerted by the few stragglers who had escaped the debacle, the remainder of the Texas Brigade dashed off belatedly in pursuit of the Yankee horsemen, who withdrew successfully to Franklin with their prisoners. Properly chastened by this humiliating blow, and increasingly conscious of a major Union buildup to the north, the men of the Third spent the following week on the alert and in the saddle.[31]

Then, on the afternoon of May 7, the men in camp learned of the death of their commanding officer earlier that day. As though unwilling to depart this life under less than melodramatic circumstances, the daring Van Dorn contrived to get himself shot at the age of forty-two by a jealous husband. Once chided by a fellow officer as "the only man I ever saw who loves danger for its own sake,"[32] the general had become romantically involved with Jessie Peters, the young wife of a prominent Spring Hill physician. The aggrieved husband stalked Van Dorn to his headquarters and shot him dead.[33]

The reaction to Van Dorn's sudden demise was mixed. He was given an impressive military funeral, and one of his junior officers recorded at the time "a universal gloom cast over the troops—[who] now begin to feel his real worth."[34] Though a private in the Third Cavalry found the funeral ceremony "romantic, grand & solemn," he expressed no personal feelings either way about the deceased; another considered the incident hardly worth mentioning.[35] Some suspected sinister motives behind the assassination of one of the South's most celebrated generals. Others clucked reprovingly that the rakish Van Dorn had gotten exactly what he deserved. As one of the troopers in his command coldly, if ungrammatically put it, neither "the Army nor humanity lost nothing."[36] In any case, when the Confederate authorities subsequently caught Van Dorn's murderer, they let him go unpunished.

CHAPTER 11

Vicksburg and Jackson, June–August 1863

WITH THE untimely demise of Van Dorn and the departure of Forrest's troops, all that was left of the cavalry corps was a single division of 3,019 horsemen under the command of General "Red" Jackson. It comprised more than a thousand Mississippians under Brigadier General George B. Cosby and the 1,815 troopers of the Texas Brigade, consisting of the Third, Sixth, Ninth, and Twenty-seventh Cavalry regiments. Recently promoted to brigadier general, John W. Whitfield retained his command over the Texans, while Lieutenant Colonel Boggess, having returned from leave, resumed his post as temporary commanding officer of the Third Texas. With Grant's siege of Vicksburg now reaching a critical stage, General Bragg ordered Jackson to lead his division back to Mississippi to assist the defenders of the beleaguered citadel.[1]

The Third Texas set out from Spring Hill on May 19, 1863, and retraced its steps of the previous winter to the Vicksburg front. Many of the men regretted the move; now that the weather had turned pleasantly warm and the fields and forests were green, Spring Hill seemed almost like home. Moreover, according to one trooper, "the young ladies through here . . . think a great deal of the Texans and seem to be willing to tie to some of them."[2] Four months earlier, rain and frost had dogged their tracks; now they made their return journey in the midst of a late spring drought, and the hooves of their mounts raised stifling clouds of dust from the primitive roads. After a hard day's ride a soldier from Company E complained that he could "plant turnips under my eyes & blow brick out of my nose."[3] The troops rode more than 375 miles in two weeks. Their route carried them across the Tennessee River, through the barren hills of northwest Alabama, and into Mississippi at Columbus. From there they plodded across the state to Canton, about twenty-five miles north of General Johnston's headquarters at Jackson.

Riding more than thirty miles per day was grueling for both man and beast. Some of the famished horses succumbed to eating "sneezeweed," a poisonous plant from which many sickened and died. The men, too, were short on rations; had it not been for the generosity of local citizens, they would have starved. At Athens, Alabama, the women of the town brought buckets of water to the roadside to quench the soldiers' thirst. From their graceful homes above the Tombigbee River, the inhabitants of Columbus sent out two wagonloads of delicacies, enough to feed the entire regiment. The people around Starkville lined the road, passing out meat and bread to the weary riders.

Men who lost their mounts, or who were too sick or simply too tired to continue, were left behind to fend for themselves. Though most of these stragglers eventually made their way back to their respective commands, they were tempted to dally awhile amid hospitable surroundings and trade the soldier's hard life for that of a tourist. "A good many of our boys think that if they fall behind & be taken prisoners & then paroled they will get to go home," grumbled an indignant officer.[4] In other cases, men were often furloughed because of illness and remained too sick to return to duty within their allotted time. Usually the separation from their comrades was not of their own choosing, but unexpected delays often caused days of absence to become weeks and then months. Under such circumstances ten men got themselves listed as deserters on the rolls of the Third Regiment during its long march from Tennessee.[5]

The main body of Whitfield's Brigade arrived at Canton on June 3, where General Johnston reviewed them and received them into his command. He put them to work without further ado, as the fate of Vicksburg hung in more precarious balance every hour. Grant's long campaign had reached the point of crisis. In the months following the collapse of his first drive against the Rebel stronghold the previous winter, the Union commander had successively launched and then abandoned four abortive expeditions combining the strength of the Federal navy with his superiority in ground forces. The Confederate guns atop the Vicksburg bluffs dominated the main channel of the Mississippi. In order to circumvent these deadly batteries and position his troops on the high ground east of the city, Grant had resorted to massive engineering projects designed to open a new channel for his gunboats along one of the many sluggish waterways that laced the alluvial lowlands. But for one reason or another, all of those bold enterprises eventually failed.

At the end of March, while the Third Cavalry was still far away in Tennessee, Grant launched his final, and ultimately successful, campaign against Vicksburg. First he marched his men through the Louisiana swamps west of the river. These troops then rendezvoused south of Vicksburg with Union gunboats and transports that had run the gauntlet of Rebel guns along the bluffs, and the vessels ferried the soldiers to the east bank of the Mississippi. From the river Grant struck first at the railroad center of Jackson, forty-five miles to the east, in order to deny reinforcements or supplies to General Pemberton's defenders of Vicksburg. Driving Johnston's army north from Jackson, Grant then bottled up Pemberton's garrison in the Vicksburg fortifications. Having failed to take the Confederate ramparts by frontal assault on May 22, the Union commander settled down to a prolonged siege.

This was the situation when the Third Texas arrived upon the scene early in June. Determined to starve the Rebels out, Grant drew a ring of 71,000 Yankees around the Confederate earthworks east of Vicksburg. His siege guns pounded the defenders from all around the perimeter, while his gunboats shelled the city from the river. Day by day, Grant's outworks crept closer to the Rebel trenches. Many of the inhabitants of Vicksburg had taken refuge in caves; their defenders were subsisting on pea bread and mule meat. Pemberton, with 20,000 men to hold the place, counted upon Johnston to march to his relief. The help was long in coming, though Johnston gradually accumulated a force of some 30,000 Rebel soldiers near Jackson. He was reluctant to undertake a relief expedition until he felt strong enough to confront the powerful Federal army in a pitched battle, because Grant had taken precautions to ensure that his rear would not be threatened while his troops were preoccupied with hammering down Vicksburg's defenses.[6]

As the siege progressed, the upland prairies and dense forests between the Federal lines east of Vicksburg and Johnston's growing force at Jackson became the scene of almost daily cavalry raids and scouting expeditions, as each side simultaneously probed for the weak points of its adversary while shielding the movements of its own troops. The landscape across which they ranged varied from the even, slightly rolling terrain along the railroad connecting the two cities to the precipitous bluffs rising above the Yazoo River's east bank with their heavily timbered ravines and brush-choked watercourses. About a third of the way from Vicksburg to Jackson, the Big Black River followed a meandering course southward toward its confluence with the Mississippi. Though increasingly fordable as the season progressed, the stream provided a natural obstacle between the two armies.

Numerous cotton plantations and villages dotted the countryside, and several sizable towns lay alongside the railroad between Vicksburg and Jackson. Both the Union and Confederate armies drew subsistence from this fertile land. Rival foraging parties carried off what they could from the farms and villages of the area, destroyed what they could not pillage in order to deny it to the enemy, and frequently collided with each other. For the next ten months this forty-mile-wide strip of ground stretching from the Yazoo to the Pearl River was to become the principal haunt of the Third Regiment; its men would become as familiar with its creeks, crossroads, and country churches as they were with their homes in East Texas.

By the time Jackson's cavalry division arrived on the scene, General Johnston had persuaded himself that his force was too weak to raise the siege of Vicksburg. He could only save the town's beleaguered garrison by convincing Pemberton to break through the iron ring that Grant had forged around him, while Johnston staged a diversion against the Yankee rear. The most favorable point for a breakout lay on the extreme right of the Union line, where the Yazoo River passed beneath the bluffs just north of Vicksburg. While Yankee gunboats controlled the lower stretches of the river, Confederates remained entrenched at Yazoo City, forty-five miles upstream from its mouth. If the interrupted communications between the embattled Pemberton and the anxious Johnston could be reestablished, there existed a remote possibility that the trapped defenders of Vicksburg might fight their way through Grant's lines and then eastward to join Johnston's relieving army.[7]

On June 5, Johnston dispatched Jackson's cavalry to support an infantry division that was testing the feasibility of a breakout between Canton and Yazoo City. Unfortunately for Pemberton's waning hopes of deliverance, however, Grant had anticipated such a move. A week earlier he had ordered nine Union gunboats and troop-laden transports up the Yazoo to within a dozen miles of Yazoo City. From that point thousands of bluecoat raiders had fanned out across the countryside, plundering farms and villages and destroying bridges all the way to the Big Black River. The task force burned the village of Mechanicsburg, destroyed half a million bushels of corn, rounded up a thousand cattle, and brought a host of liberated African Americans back into the Union lines.

Jackson's cavalry reconnaissance toward the Yazoo consequently turned into a belated effort to intercept those Yankee raiders before they could regain their transports. The Texans left their baggage train behind on June 7 and galloped across country toward the Yazoo, scouring the countryside, hot on the Yankee trail. Owing to low water in the river, however, the Union troops had embarked downstream the previous day and thus eluded their pursuers. Following this strenuous but fruitless exercise, Jackson's cavalrymen pulled back to the east bank of the Big Black River.[8]

Meanwhile, the authorities at Richmond continued to urge Johnston to take immediate action in relief of Pemberton's beleaguered men, despite the risks involved. "It is better to fail nobly daring than, through prudence even, to be inactive," Secretary of War Seddon lectured him from a distance of almost a thousand miles.[9] With his options rapidly diminishing, Johnston cast about for an opening. If he and Pemberton could mount a simultaneous attack from opposite sides against the same point in Grant's siege line, Pemberton's forces might be extricated. Pursuant to this goal, Johnston ordered Jackson's cavalry to patrol the area between the Yazoo and the Vicksburg-Jackson railroad, seek out possible approaches to Vicksburg, and prevent the Yankees from establishing bridgeheads on the east bank of the Big Black. Jackson posted Cosby's Mississippi cavalry to picket the northern end of this front and assigned the Texas Brigade to guard a sector some twenty miles wide astride the railroad.[10]

While their commander set up his headquarters at Bolton Station, twenty-five miles east of Vicksburg, the Texans bivouacked at various campsites above the Big Black River. For three weeks they took turns patrolling the river crossings for Union foraging detachments or raiding parties, without major incident. Though often within earshot of the cannonade at Vicksburg, the men enjoyed an interlude of relative quiet, feasting on wild plums and roasting ears and striking up acquaintances among the hospitable villagers of the area, who maintained a remarkably normal existence while dwelling precariously between two hostile armies.

The most noteworthy aspect of the relationship between the Texans and the civilian population was its general amity, for despite their shared political sympathies, farmers and soldiers were natural enemies to each other. The Confederate troops lived by "foraging," a euphemism that essentially meant stealing everything they could—from chickens to horses—from the people they had ostensibly enlisted to protect. Individual and informal theft of this nature went on throughout the war; its incidence depended upon the discipline imposed by regimental commanders to discourage it. Unit quartermasters, on the other hand, were empowered by law to impress supplies and provisions from the civilian population in return for Confederate scrip or promissory notes. By the summer of 1863, however, the Confederate dollar was worth only one-tenth of its value at the beginning of the war, and the payments farmers received for their livestock and produce were usually far below their market value.[11]

As a result, the inhabitants dreaded a visit from their own cavalry as much as they feared a Yankee foraging party. Owing to their greater mobility and freedom from higher echelons of control, Rebel cavalrymen in particular had earned a reputation as rakes and thieves. One Mississippian complained that the mounted troops spent their time at "gaming parties, drunkenness, marrying, horse-racing, and stealing," while the residents of Grenada petitioned Jefferson Davis to relieve them of their garrison of Rebel horsemen, who "plunder and rob the citizens, burn fences, kill stock, steal horses, destroy provisions and intrude rudely upon private families."[12]

Expecting far worse from a band of unruly Texans, the inhabitants of the little villages between Vicksburg and Jackson were pleasantly surprised by the good behavior and general decorum exhibited by the fellows from East Texas. One genteel Mississippi matron confided to a Texas lieutenant that she was "very much surprised indeed with us Texians at finding so much *civilization* in our portion of the army where they thought us all border ruffians."[13] Some Texas troopers formed romantic attachments in the area that outlasted the war and eventuated in marriage; others went into business there at the close of hostilities.

A possible explanation for the warm reception afforded some of the Texans by the civilians was their rank. While officers were normally welcomed on the assumption that they were gentlemen, an Upshur County soldier complained that "a private is so little thought of" that the local citizens would not even give him a drink of water.[14] Another common cause for the good relations between the Texans and their host population was that many rural Mississippians first encountered the soldiers in church.

Beginning late in the summer of 1863, an extraordinary wave of religious revivalism swept through the Confederate encampments on the Vicksburg front. After a long spate of backsliding from their pious upbringing, many of the men were roused to a pitch of spiritual enthusiasm. They flocked in droves to the local churches, and their chaplains took advantage of this rekindled piety to encourage the troops to at least an outward show of faith.[15] One of Jackson's chaplains, for instance, gathered his Sunday congregations by touring the card games in camp and rounding up the players. "Come on now, we are going to preaching," he would order, and the men obediently threw down their cards and followed him.[16] Under the impact of this revivalism, their heightened sense of mortality, and the growing realization that the war had entered a critical phase, soldiers' letters home took on an ever more pious tone. "While lying in the deep swamps and woods" near Yazoo City, Private J. R. White urged his wife back in Upshur County "to pray for me and teach the children virtue and truth and the importance of religion."[17]

Those relatively quiet days with time for reflection came to an abrupt end on June 29, when General Johnston reluctantly ordered his 31,000 men to advance from Jackson toward the Yankee lines. Pemberton's Vicksburg garrison was starving, and many of his troops were on the point of mutiny. In a petition signed by "Many Soldiers," they had warned him that "if you can't feed us, you had better surrender us."[18] Johnston had to act at this point, or never. Moving his army cautiously to the Big Black, he ordered his cavalry to probe the Union lines for a possible opening. On July 1 units of the Texas Brigade trapped a Federal patrol where the railroad crossed the river near Edwards Depot, but after a sharp skirmish the Yankees escaped beyond the stream. Three days later the Texans intercepted another patrol a few miles to the north. A brisk firefight ensued, and the Rebels established control of the river crossing at that point. Johnston's troops "were in the finest spirits," reported a Cherokee Countian, and "were only waiting for the hour appointed to move forward" across the Big Black River and into the enemy's rear.[19]

But it was too late. After forty-seven days under siege, Pemberton surrendered his army and his stronghold at Vicksburg on July 4, 1863. It was a sweeping triumph for the North: Grant captured 172 cannons and 60,000 stands of small arms, while almost 30,000 Rebel soldiers became prisoners of war, though they were soon paroled. In the aftermath of the Vicksburg surrender the Confederacy abandoned Port Hudson, its one remaining bastion on the Mississippi, and, as Lincoln proudly observed, "the Father of Waters again goes unvexed to the sea."[20]

With the control of the great river safely in hand, the primary goal of Union strategy in the West had been achieved. The vast resources of Texas, Louisiana, and Arkansas were henceforth irretrievably lost to the remaining states of the Confederacy. Almost simultaneously, the Federals had turned back Lee's desperate invasion of Pennsylvania on the bloody ridge at Gettysburg. All signs now pointed to an ultimate Union victory. At the Confederate capitol in Richmond, the more perceptive Southern strategists discarded any remaining illusions about the outcome of the war. "The Confederacy totters to its destruction," one of these officers intoned upon hearing the news from Vicksburg.[21]

Johnston's Rebels, poised on the banks of the Big Black River, had no time for such lugubrious reflections, for they were in extreme peril. General Sherman and his force of 46,000 victorious Union soldiers had already completed preparations to strike Johnston's army of deliverance at the moment of Vicksburg's fall, and they wasted no time. On the dawn of Independence Day, Sherman roused his cheering troops out of their encampments before Vicksburg and sent them in three mighty columns on a dash to the Big Black. Having received news of Pemberton's surrender only on the morning after it occurred, Johnston hastily set about withdrawing his troops from their exposed positions before they were engulfed by Sherman's bluecoat tide. He instructed his four divisions of infantry, now "oppressed by a gloom and a despondency," to fall back on Jackson, and he ordered his cavalry to screen their retreat.[22] Cosby's Mississippians were to guard the Rebel flank between the Yazoo and the Big Black; the men of Whitfield's brigade were allotted the perilous mission of delaying the Union onslaught in the center of the line until their infantry comrades could reach their entrenchments at Jackson.

Sherman's northern spearhead approached the Big Black River at Birdsong Ferry, about eight miles north of the Vicksburg-Jackson railway, on July 5. Hidden amid the underbrush on the opposite bank of the stream, a small force of Texans contested the crossing with the Yankees. Aided by recent rains that had raised the level of the river by four feet, the cavalrymen held up the Union advance for two days. In the meantime, Sherman's central column forced a bridgehead across the river at Messenger's

Ford, about four miles north of the railroad, against determined resistance by troops of the Third, the Ninth, and the Twenty-seventh Texas Cavalry. The Yankee spearhead to the south drove across the Big Black near the railroad itself. With the river barrier breached, there was little the Rebel horsemen could do but harass the enemy and delay his advance as long as they could.

For four days and nights the men of the Texas Brigade ranged up and down the line, disputing the ground with the foe. They covered up to twenty-five miles a day in this running fight, attacking the enemy vanguard, then falling back under the pressure of their offensive. Until dispersed by artillery fire, the brigade held up the Union forces for a full day outside Clinton, only eight miles from Jackson. They had also been given the task of destroying all the cotton and livestock in the path of the Federal army. The Texans drove herds of cattle into the ponds and cisterns ahead of the enemy's line of march and slaughtered the frantic animals in the water in order to render it unfit for drinking. Undeterred, the thirsty Yankees dragged the already rotting carcasses aside and drank the fetid water anyway.[23]

On the evening of July 9, Johnston pulled his cavalry back into the defenses of Jackson. Before Sherman's destructive sweep through the place the previous May, Mississippi's capital city had held a population of almost five thousand, their homes crowning a bluff on the west bank of the Pearl River. Johnston had employed his infantry as well as gangs of impressed slaves to extend earthworks in a rough semicircle embracing the entire town all the way down to the river landing. His artillerymen mounted heavy guns to command the main approaches from the west, and embrasures for field artillery were constructed along the perimeter. To the 28,000 troops he had left to defend the city from the onrushing Federals, he issued a grandiloquent order of the day, which enjoined them "to chastise and expel from the soil of Mississippi" the "insolent foe, flushed with hope by his recent successes at Vicksburg."[24]

Sherman knew that Johnston would put up a stubborn fight for the Mississippi capital, and he ordered his troops to close around the defensive perimeter of the city to invest it from three sides. The Confederate defenders, their backs to the Pearl

River, occupied a narrow salient about two and a half miles deep and two miles wide around what was left of the town. Union artillery proceeded to pulverize their positions; in one hour alone on July 12, Yankee cannoneers pumped three thousand rounds into the beleaguered capital. In the interim the Union commander dispatched a fourth infantry column northward to drive across the Pearl and take Jackson from the rear. Federal cavalrymen destroyed the railroad north to Canton, stripped the surrounding countryside of the cattle still left alive, and laid waste the fields of ripening corn. As Sherman observed with saturnine satisfaction, "the wholesale destruction to which this country is now being subjected is . . . the scourge of war, to which ambitious men have appealed, rather than [to] the judgement of the learned and pure tribunals which our forefathers had provided." [25]

Johnston deployed his Texas Brigade at the extreme north-eastern end of the defensive line, where the Confederate entrenchments rested upon the riverbank. Dismounted, the Third Regiment engaged advancing enemy sharpshooters and artillery in the thick brush and wooded ravines adjacent to the Pearl. The troopers succeeded in stalling the Union thrust in their sector and prevented the Yankees from gaining a lodgment on the east bank of the river. They also guarded the Confederate rail connections eastward toward Meridian. Since the railway bridge over the Pearl had been destroyed, the city's defenders had to haul their meager supplies across the river by wagon. Still, for a week the Rebels clung tenaciously to their narrow salient, compelling the enemy to pay dearly for his mistakes. When a Yankee brigade ventured a rash assault against Jackson's earthworks on July 12, it was beaten back with the loss of 519 men. [26]

On July 14, Johnston gave his entire cavalry division an assignment beyond their capacity to carry out. The Union gunners before Jackson had been so extravagant in their expenditure of shells that Sherman was obliged to requisition a huge wagon train of ammunition from Vicksburg in order to continue the siege. Johnston commanded his cavalrymen to intercept this shipment and capture or destroy it. Thus charged, the Texans rode up the east side of the Pearl about twelve miles, crossed to the opposite bank, and joined forces with Cosby's Mississippi cavalry behind enemy lines. The division of some three thousand riders then bore down upon the main road to Vicksburg, where the ammunition train rumbled along between Bolton and Clinton.

Unfortunately for the Rebel raiders, Sherman had learned of their projected coup from an escaped prisoner and alerted his commanders along the route. When the Confederate horsemen descended upon Clinton on the morning of July 16, the vigilant Yankees poured such fire into their ranks that they were forced to withdraw. Later on in the day General Whitfield sent the Third and Ninth Cavalry regiments farther to the west against Bolton. Here the Texans were able to capture a Federal pioneer train, including eight wagons and eighty-three men. Though the main ammunition shipment was not far away, it was so heavily guarded that the raiders did not risk an engagement, but retired to the northeast, having ridden forty-three miles that day.[27]

They failed to cut off the Union ammunition supply, leaving Johnston no recourse but withdrawal. While the Texans were dashing around the countryside on their abortive mission, the defenders of Jackson prepared to evacuate their positions before the Yankee guns opened up in their full fury again. Throughout the night of July 16 the Confederate army filed out of the Mississippi capital across makeshift bridges over the Pearl and headed toward Brandon, twelve miles to the east. Sherman occupied Jackson the following day and set about destroying what little remained of the railroad and the abandoned Rebel stores. With the devastation wrought in the battle for the city in May, the damage done during the siege, and the desolation inflicted by Sherman's men, Jackson was left "one mass of charred ruins."[28] Mississippians began to call their capital city "Chimneyville," because that was all that remained.

Twenty miles to the north, Whitfield's Texas Brigade was almost trapped by the advancing Yankees. One of the Union commanders had sent a formidable task force consisting of cavalry, infantry, and artillery, north from Jackson toward Canton to wreck the tracks, bridges, and shops of the railroad. While thus employed on the morning of July 17, these dispersed demolition teams encountered the Texans near Canton as they made their way east to join Johnston's retreating army. The Rebel horsemen first charged the unsuspecting Yankees, provoking a sharp skirmish that lasted about two hours. Though the Texans tried to turn the flank of their foe and capture his wagon train, the Federal commander was able to consolidate his force and turn to the attack himself. Faced by this superior concentration, the Texas Brigade retreated north through Canton, crossed the Pearl about ten miles to the east, and united with Johnston's main army at Brandon on the evening of the following day.

There was no respite for them there, however, and no forage for their famished horses, which had not been fed for two days. Sherman had sent a Union column in pursuit of the retreating Rebels, and Johnston had no choice but to drive his beaten and exhausted soldiers ahead of the advancing enemy. Thunder showers turned their path into a *via dolorosa*; infantrymen dragged their heavy wagons through the mud; the heat and humidity were stifling; the road was strewn with arms and knapsacks cast aside in the desperate retreat. Yet, with Cosby's Mississippi cavalrymen fighting off his pursuers in the rear, Johnston succeeded in putting thirty miles between himself and Jackson and bivouacked his men near Morton on the evening of July 20.[29]

There they remained for a week, while Sherman's soldiers pillaged and burned in Brandon. Indignantly, the local editor denounced the Yankees as "a gang of thieves who broke open smokehouses, dairies, pantries, fowlhouses and emptied them of their contents. . . . Many families did not have provisions [left] for breakfast. . . . There was not enough chickens left to herald the dawn."[30] But instead of continuing their pursuit of the beaten foe past Brandon, the Federals returned to Jackson, a move which, viewed in hindsight, turned out to be an egregious error. The Union army possessed the power and occupied a position to run Johnston's demoralized men to ground and destroy them as a fighting force, but even such aggressive warriors as Grant and Sherman seemed to lose their sense of purpose in the scalding heat of the Mississippi summer.

Crowned by the laurels of Vicksburg, Grant was now uncertain how best to employ the host he had assembled with such prodigious effort. The prospect of using it to chase Johnston was not attractive; it was too hot; the roads were too bad. The Rebels were demoralized to the point of desertion; they would most likely disperse and evaporate on their own. Or so the Union commander believed. Other goals seemed far more compelling. Grant contemplated an amphibious attack on Mobile, the last major Confederate port in the West. He dispatched some of his troops to the Arkansas and Tennessee valleys to serve commanders who had not been so successful as he. Lincoln, moreover, was now urging Grant to reestablish Union presence on the Rio Grande to counter French intervention in revolution-torn Mexico. Bemused by such grandiose visions, Grant let Johnston's army get away. Sherman withdrew his troops to Vicksburg on July 25, and the Rebel forces reoccupied the Jackson area shortly thereafter.[31]

Johnston had been lucky; he might well have lost his army. Instead, his casualties were light: 71 men killed; 504 wounded; and 25 missing in the entire Jackson campaign. The Third Texas lost only 6 men captured, but 6 others deserted the ranks under the pounding of the Yankee guns. Four of these were Cass Countians from Company I. Another was Private George French, a poor farmer from Titus County who had already been felled by typhoid and an infected foot. He simply refused to dismount and deploy for battle in the midst of the siege and defiantly rode off the battlefield. After a month or so, when he unwisely returned to the regiment, a court martial sentenced him to be shot, but General Johnston reversed the judgment and ordered French back to duty. By this time, however, the elusive private had escaped from the guardhouse and was gone.[32]

CHAPTER 12

The Big Black and the Sunflower, August 1863–January 1864

AFTER THEIR success at Vicksburg and Jackson, the Union commanders turned their attention to broader and more distant objectives, and the focus of the war in the West shifted to Tennessee during the late summer and fall. After more than six months of relative inactivity, General Rosecrans's Union army had resumed its offensive against Bragg's lines in middle Tennessee even as events at Vicksburg and Gettysburg thundered toward a climax. Rosecrans occupied Chattanooga on September 9. As the Mississippi front slipped into the backwater of war, General Johnston was reduced simply to keeping his men alive, finding enough forage for his horses and mules, repairing what was left of the Southern railway system, and hoping that military events farther east would relieve some of the pressure on his outnumbered troops. "My purpose," he noted with resignation, "is to hold as much of the country as I can and to retire farther only when compelled to do so."[1]

After six arduous weeks of skirmishing between Vicksburg and Jackson, the troopers of the Third Texas Cavalry went into camp on July 20 at Pelahatchie, twenty-two miles east of Jackson. There they rested for a fortnight as Colonel Mabry, now recovered from the wounds inflicted at Iuka, returned to resume command of the regiment. A few supplies were slipped in by rail from Meridian; the officers found time for a parade and a ball; one man in every twenty-five received a coveted furlough. But nothing occurred to relieve the general tedium and dejection that prevailed among the troops. They had, after all, been soundly beaten. The almost incessant rain at the end of July only intensified the scalding heat. For months on end there was very little activity or excitement to relieve their boredom, and idleness began to sap their morale.

From the first of August until the very end of the year there were but four occasions when raids, skirmishes, or scouting expeditions interrupted the deadly routine of guard duty and drill in camp. The first opportunity for action arose out of General Johnston's belated concern for the dilapidated remnants of the Confederate railway system. When Sherman pulled his forces back toward Vicksburg, he left, as before, the Big Black River as a sort of rough frontier between Union-occupied territory and the Rebel hinterland. Strong Federal garrisons occupied Yazoo City and Natchez as well, and the commanders believed that they could operate with impunity against the plantations, towns, and railroads of western Mississippi whenever they chose to do so. Johnston was intent upon protecting still undevastated areas of this countryside from Yankee marauders.

But he neglected until too late an even more vital resource, and its loss at the hands of Federal raiders dealt the South a serious blow. When Grant had attacked the town of Jackson the previous May, his men had destroyed the Pearl River railroad bridge that carried the tracks of the Southern Mississippi Railroad to Meridian and on to the Confederate East. By so doing, the Yankees stranded sixty locomotives and 350 cars near Grenada, 115 miles north of Jackson. During the long siege of Vicksburg, Johnston had neglected to repair the bridge and evacuate this precious rolling stock, which thus was lost to the Southern war effort. Now, though he still failed to order the bridge repairs, he was sufficiently concerned about the fate of the locomotives to instruct his cavalry to patrol the railroad north toward Grenada to forestall Yankee raids into the area. In obedience to this command the Texas Brigade rode out of camp on August 2, spent an uneventful week scouting the Mississippi Central Railroad, and then returned to their bivouac a few miles outside of Jackson.[2]

Hardly had the Texans settled into camp routine again when the Yankees descended upon the railroad in force, determined to capture or destroy the South's precious engines and boxcars. On August 12, Grant dispatched a formidable column of cavalry down from Tennessee toward Grenada, while another Federal task force marched east out of Yazoo City to cooperate in the railway raid. Belatedly alerted to the threat posed by this two-pronged attack, the Texans rode out of their sodden campground on August 15 in an attempt to thwart the foray against Johnston's irreplaceable locomotives. They hastened north almost as far as Grenada to find the Federal wreckers hauling out all the engines and boxcars they could salvage and demolishing the rest. By burning the trestles behind the attackers, the Rebel cavalrymen prevented the enemy from escaping with much of their loot. But the Union raiders wrecked the rolling stock, roundhouses, and shops along the line, leaving heaps of smoldering junk in their wake as they withdrew toward the Tennessee line ahead of the harassing Rebels. The raid dealt a staggering blow to the Southern railway system.[3]

Humiliated by their incapacity to do more than annoy the raiders, the Texans retraced their trail to the south and went into camp again near Vernon, on a bluff overlooking the Big Black River some twenty miles north of Jackson. There they remained for a month, idle except for the normal routine of drill, picket duty, and an occasional review. On the twenty-eighth of September, General Jackson ordered the Texas Brigade into the saddle again, this time to repel a Yankee raid from Yazoo City against their own headquarters. A Union cavalry column of nine hundred men stole across the river in the dark, and captured Vernon, but discovered that the Texans had decamped ahead of them. Having seized 150 horses and mules and a few Confederate stragglers, the Federal commander retreated hastily across the Big Black, leaving a rear guard to cover his crossing. The Rebel cavalrymen chased the Union troops five miles or so toward Yazoo City, skirmished with them for a couple of hours, and then withdrew in turn. The Texans encamped above the Big Black again, where they remained for another two weeks, grumbling about the war and bickering with their officers.[4]

The fourth and final exertion of that tedious autumn had a more strategically significant purpose if a no less inconclusive outcome than the previous skirmishes. By the middle of October, General Bragg's Confederates had bottled up a Union army in Chattanooga and seemed likely to starve the Yankees into surrender. Grant dispatched Sherman and four divisions to the rescue, but the railway route from Memphis to Chattanooga quickly fell prey to the Rebel cavalry sent by Johnston to beset them. The Southerners swarmed around the railroad and tore up the track as fast as Sherman could repair it. Anxious over the delay entailed by the disruption, Grant ordered Major General James B. McPherson, commander of the Union forces in the Vicksburg area, to lead a task force of eight thousand men against Canton. This, he believed, would create a diversion in central Mississippi sufficient to prevent the Confederate cavalry from blocking Sherman's railroad and interfering with the relief of Chattanooga.

McPherson led his host across a pontoon bridge over the Big Black River on the morning of October 15. His troops made brisk progress at first, marching almost twenty miles up the Canton road before they encountered Brigadier General William Wirt Adams's tough Mississippi cavalry. Attacking boldly, Adams held up the Yankee advance for the night. By this time General Jackson had been alerted to the Yankee threat. From his headquarters fifteen miles up the road, he ordered the Texas Brigade to concentrate in front of the approaching enemy and assembled about four thousand Rebel troopers to contest the Federals' progress over the broken and rugged terrain. Thus confronted by the determined defenders, McPherson's advance on Canton slowed to a crawl when he resumed his march the following morning. Whitfield's Texans drew up on the east bank of Bogue Chitto Creek, dismounted, and took cover in the wooded ravines above the crossing. The outnumbered Rebel soldiers pinned the Yankees to the creek bottom all day with their artillery and small arms fire.

At dawn the next morning McPherson's infantry rushed the

hills overlooking the Bogue Chitto, while Jackson pulled his troops back another five miles up the road. Here the Texans set up a second defensive line, peppered the now cautious Yankees with fire, and stalled them for yet another day. Still twelve miles from Canton, the Rebel defenders bivouacked in the rain, while McPherson paused to calculate his odds. Though he actually outnumbered his combined assailants by two to one, the Union general concluded erroneously that Canton was defended by a force superior to his own and decided to retire to Vicksburg before the Confederates trapped his army. The Federals began their withdrawal at sunrise on October 18. All day long the Texas Brigade harassed the retreating enemy until it became obvious that the Union forces were giving up the fight and heading for their base. Leaving brigades of Mississippi and Arkansas cavalry to hound the Yankees back to the Big Black River, the Confederate commander recalled the Texas Brigade to its camp near Vernon, and the five-day Canton expedition was over.[5]

Through resolute and timely concentration of his limited forces, "Red" Jackson had stalled and ultimately repulsed a far superior Union task force. Yet McPherson's expedition, while not achieving its final objective—the capture of Canton—had accomplished a substantial part of its mission. In response to the threat it posed to central Mississippi, Johnston had been forced to recall many of his Rebel raiders south toward Canton, thus relieving much of the pressure on Sherman's railroad supply line. This at least McPherson achieved, losing only five of his men killed and fifteen wounded.

For the next two months the men of the Third Cavalry did little more than lie about their camp, try to stay warm during the approach of winter, and become increasingly discouraged. Idleness was usually a greater detriment to morale than danger. Their waning spirits were indicated most conspicuously by the growing rate of desertion, which by the fall of 1863 had become a critical problem in most of the armies of the South. More than one hundred thousand Rebel soldiers would desert during the course of the conflict, about half the number of men guilty of desertion from the Union army.

There were good and sufficient reasons for this conduct in both cases. As far as the Confederate soldier was concerned, the wonder is that more men did not abandon the flag sooner, considering the odds against them, their chronically inadequate rations, clothing, and equipment, and the general disorganization of the Southern war effort. Under the impact of the major setbacks at Gettysburg, Vicksburg, and Chattanooga, a pall of futility began to settle over all the Rebel armies in the field. "I am getting very tired of being a soldier," confessed an East Texas trooper to his mother. "There is no fun in it."[6]

Morale was also adversely affected by the inability of the Confederate bureaucracy to pay its troops. In theory, captains received $140, second lieutenants $90, and sergeants $20 per month, while the cavalry private earned $12 (plus an additional $12 for his horse). But pay was always in arrears by several months and often was not forthcoming at all. The men of the Third Texas had last been paid in May, after having waited half a year for their money. When their pay did come through, it bought less and less, as Confederate scrip depreciated in value with the declining fortunes of the government. By the fall of 1863 a pair of boots cost the equivalent of ten months' wages for a private; it took him four days' pay to buy a chicken and twenty-five days to earn enough to shoe his horse.[7]

In addition, the troops were becoming ever more concerned over the hardships suffered by those at home: wives and children left alone to run farms hundreds of miles away; chronic shortages of essential goods; crops impossible to harvest or market; and the toll of sickness and death. Wives or parents in Texas often labored under such anxiety that it adversely affected morale at the front. John R. Reierson, for instance, had two sons serving in the Third Cavalry, and he worried about them constantly. "I sometimes get quite disheartened," he wrote, "when I ponder on the slim probability of ever seeing my brave boys at home safe and sound. . . . I don't expect to see them before. . . . the war is ended, and God only knows how long that will be. . . . They may be dead or cripled long before that time."[8] Confronted by such somber reflections, many of the men were sincerely puzzled where the true path of duty lay: to their families and loved ones; or to a cause that seemed already lost.

Desertion had by this time become so widespread, and the measures taken to combat it so arbitrary and unpredictable, that it ceased to bear the stigma of crime or even dishonor in the minds of thousands of soldiers. At the beginning of the war Confederate military law had prescribed death or "other punishments" as determined by courts-martial as the penalty for desertion. Because of the enormous number of men who left their posts without permission, the first penalty proved ludicrously impractical, and commanders resorted ever more frequently to "other punishments" to deter desertion. While such stern disciplinarians as Stonewall Jackson or Nathan Bedford Forrest could be counted upon to shoot deserters without excessive concern for the occasional innocent man who fell afoul of their implacable decrees, most commanders were considerably more lenient. General amnesties and pardons issued from Richmond also clouded the issue, so that by the end of the war almost any penalty conceivable—from shaving the head of the miscreant to hanging—had been applied to deter desertion. The enormous numbers of men who slipped away from various Confederate armies suggest that none of the punishments worked very well.[9]

Besides the sources of general discontent shared by Rebel soldiers as a whole, the men of the Third Texas had serious grievances peculiar to themselves. The most gnawing complaint was that most of them never obtained a leave during the entire war. Their comparative inactivity that autumn amid the backwaters of central Mississippi convinced many of the Texans that they were serving no useful purpose, and some of them succumbed to their longing for home. In August, when a few furloughs had come through, the leaves had been restricted to one officer and three enlisted men per company, and none of the troopers had been permitted to travel west of the Mississippi, which was now, of course, behind Union lines. The restrictive leave policy only exacerbated the despondency of the majority of the men who were left out.

As a result, some members of the Texas Brigade began stealing away during August and September. On the night of September 3, for example, the Ninth Texas Cavalry, already notorious for its ungovernability, lost thirty-one men and one officer through desertion. The rumor had arisen that if enough men could make their perilous way through enemy lines and across the Mississippi, the entire regiment would have no recourse but to follow them there. Some of the men rationalized their action on the grounds that this was not true desertion, but merely a redeployment of forces as dictated by men in the ranks.[10]

The Third Texas was infected by the virus of desertion as well, but its men, as in most of their mischief, did not sin quite so bravely as their comrades of the Ninth. During the three months from the beginning of August to the end of October, nineteen soldiers of the Third deserted their posts. Men from the same company and locality tended to leave together for parts unknown. On the night of September 5, for example, five men from Company D, all original volunteers, departed their encampment. A week later two soldiers from Company G disappeared, and so on throughout the fall. Instead of threatening condign punishment for the deserters, the brigade commander simply dispatched a detail to Texas to retrieve the miscreants. Since President Davis had decreed that deserters would be pardoned if they returned to their units within twenty days, this action was quite in accord with Confederate policy.[11]

The rolls of the Third Cavalry list a total of ninety-three cases of desertion during the course of the war, the incidence varying widely from company to company. Company D lost twenty-seven men, or a fourth of its original complement, through desertion; Company A lost only one. Who deserted? Deserters were not distinguished from the average soldier by age nor to any significant degree by economic status. What set them apart was their regional heritage and the localities in Texas from which they came. Troopers born outside the Lower South were twice as likely to desert as those born there. Men who came from the blackland prairie region of Texas were four and one-half times more desertion prone than those who resided in the piney-woods counties farther east. Hunt County, where most of the population were immigrants from the Upper South, and where almost half the voters had opposed secession in 1861, was the home of more deserters from the Third Cavalry than any other county.[12]

Desertion was not the only symptom of deteriorating morale in the Texas Brigade. An insubordinate lot under the best of conditions, the men became ever more unruly during that dreary autumn of 1863. Many had come to believe that by threatening desertion or loudly demonstrating their displeasure, they could get rid of unpopular officers, avoid punishment for infractions of regulations, and ultimately even force their commanders to lead them home to Texas. This mutinous contention culminated in a near-riot on the night of December 9 when the contumacious troopers of the Ninth Cavalry released all the prisoners in their guardhouse and began threatening their superiors. The officers quelled the disturbance on the following morning, however, and the troops were severely reprimanded and confined to camp. By paying the men their long overdue wages and rushing in a new commanding officer, the anxious authorities at last allayed the unrest, but not before the disgruntled soldiers of the Texas Brigade had earned a reputation as one of the most unruly units in the army.[13]

Major General Stephen D. Lee, commander of Rebel cavalry in Mississippi, ascribed much of the trouble to ineffective leadership. He urged the secretary of war to relieve General Whitfield of his command over the Texas Brigade, his health being "so feeble as to incapacitate him from active duty in the field," and warned that "unless a Proper Officer is assigned to their command," the Texans would desert en masse.[14] Duly impressed, Secretary Seddon issued the orders: Whitfield departed for Texas at the end of October; Colonel Lawrence S. "Sul" Ross, the "Proper Officer" that Lee had in mind, became the permanent commander of the Texas Brigade on December 16, 1863.

Only twenty-five, Ross had been reared on the Texas frontier; almost simultaneously, he had earned a university degree and enduring fame as an Indian fighter. When the war came, Ross enlisted as a private and rapidly rose to command the Sixth Texas Cavalry Regiment. Dashing and aggressive, but seemingly impervious to the Yankee Minie balls that cut down so many of his fellow officers, he became a military celebrity, respected by his superiors and adored by his men. The Texans were so enthusiastic about their new commander that they serenaded him.[15] Henceforth they would count themselves proud members of the "Ross Brigade."

With his first utterance, Sul Ross assured his troops that he would give them something to do besides guard duty, and the shifting character of the war made it easy for him to keep his promise. During the autumn, the great battles had occurred elsewhere: late in November, Grant defeated Bragg's Confederates before Chattanooga; by Christmas the Federals held eastern Tennessee securely in their grasp. The vanquished Bragg resigned his command, and General Johnston was sent out from Mississippi to replace him. Lieutenant General Leonidas Polk, former Episcopal missionary bishop of the Southwest, took over the Confederate forces in Mississippi and Alabama. After its defeat at Chattanooga, the Rebel army retired to winter quarters in northern Georgia, while the Union commanders pondered strategy and reinforced their position in anticipation of a renewed offensive in the spring. Meanwhile, the pendulum of combat swung back to the west. For the first four months of 1864, the lower Mississippi Valley moved to center stage again.

In the brief interval between the shifting of the scenes, Colonel Ross had to find some meaningful employment for his restless Texans before idleness and boredom provoked another mutinous outburst. Fortunately, such a project lay conveniently at hand. Lieutenant General Edmund Kirby Smith, Confederate commander of the Trans-Mississippi Department, needed arms desperately. Since the fall of Vicksburg his region had been largely cut off from supplies, and about ten thousand of the thirty thousand soldiers in his department were still without guns. In response to his repeated requests, the authorities at Richmond arranged for a consignment of weapons to be shipped by rail as far as possible toward Jackson and then hauled by the wagonload to the Mississippi River, where they were to be smuggled across to Arkansas in defiance of Union gunboat patrols. For the final and most hazardous stage of the transfer Lee ordered Ross to escort the shipment to the river and effect the crossing near Greenville, Mississippi.[16]

In obedience to this command the Texas Brigade struck out from their camp above the Big Black on December 22, plodded north some seventy-five miles, turned west to cross the swollen Yazoo, and descended into the flat and marshy Mississippi Delta east of Greenville. At the rear of Ross's column, Lieutenant Colonel R. A. Duncan led a supply train of twenty-three wagons loaded with two thousand rifles destined for the Trans-Mississippi.

At this juncture, weather and terrain conspired to place in jeopardy the already risky expedition behind enemy lines. The broad delta plain was cut by numerous streams and marshes, and great stretches of its rich black soil could be instantly inundated by the most insignificant freshet. As the Ross brigade slogged across the flats, it began to rain and continued for two days. The primitive trail through the swamps turned into a quagmire, and New Year's Day of 1864 found the Texans bogged down in the flooded bottom of the Sunflower River, with their horses belly deep in mud. Then the rain turned to snow, and ice formed an inch and a half thick across the drowned lowlands. Poorly clothed, hungry, cold, and miserable, the boys huddled around their sputtering fires. But instead of succumbing to depression, they galvanized themselves into enthusiastic, even sportive, activity.

Lieutenant Colonel Duncan had already given up the project, since his arms shipment lay mired in the swamp between the Yazoo and the Sunflower, eight miles back down the road. Even the dozen yoke of oxen that Ross sent him proved incapable of pulling the heavy wagons forward. With the precious cargo of rifles frozen in the mud, Duncan elected to abandon the expedition and try to haul the weapons out the way he had come.[17] At this point, Ross put it to his men: "What shall we do, give up the expedition or take these guns on our horses and carry them through?" The troops responded briskly: "Carry them through," they yelled.[18]

In order to spare themselves the delay involved in ferrying their mounts back across the Sunflower, the men decided to walk back to the wagon train and bring the weapons forward on foot. The "walk" turned into a race: since the ice-bound supply train was strung out for miles, the first men to reach the wagons would have the shortest distance to carry their load of rifles. Some, like Private Warren Higginbotham, a sturdy farmer from Smith County, made short work of the round trip back to the wagons. But loaded down with four guns apiece, it took others all day to run the grueling relay.[19]

Encumbered with their extra rifles, the men rode west again through sleet and rain toward Gaines' Ferry on the Mississippi, about a dozen miles northwest of Greenville. At the end of a forty-mile trek in a blinding sleet storm, they reached the river-bank on the evening of January 5. Furtively avoiding the Union gunboat patrol, the Texans found a flatboat, which they dragged to the river with oxen. After it grew dark, they loaded the craft with 266 rifles, and nine hardy souls from the various regiments in the brigade volunteered to row it over to the other side. Sergeant Major Nathan Gregg, the plucky Sergeant John Long, and Private Cyrus James, a Choctaw from Indian Territory, stepped forward for the Third Texas.

As they pushed off into the night, the volunteers had to fight a swift current roiled by a gusty wind out of the north and a film of ice that extended half a mile into the river from the opposite shore. At first the boatmen were able to break through this barrier, but about 150 yards from their goal, it became too thick. Finding the water only five feet deep at this point, Long went over the stern and, aided by his comrades on board, wrestled their boat up on the ice. They then slid the clumsy craft to the shore and delivered their cargo into the waiting arms of the Confederate soldiers on the Arkansas bank of the river. The wind and current carried the returning flatboat some five miles downstream, so that it was nine o'clock the following morning before the frostbitten gunrunners returned to their comrades. Though their clothes were frozen so stiff that they could not sit down, no fires were allowed in Ross's camp for fear of alerting the Yankees.[20]

By this time the Union patrols had already been apprised of the presence of the interlopers and were searching for them. A Federal gunboat spotted their makeshift ferry and sank it. Inasmuch as the Mississippi had become a vast maze of churning ice, Ross tried to row his remaining rifles over by daylight in two small skiffs his men had found. But five hundred Yankee cavalrymen patrolled nearby Greenville, while five transports and three gunboats were stationed about thirty miles downriver from the crossing. These vessels prowled the river diligently, rendering a daytime passage impossible for the moment.

Impatient to conclude his mission, Ross sent a diversionary

squadron of riders toward the south, ordered up the one artillery piece his men had been able to drag through the mud, and deployed it on the riverbank. Boldly opening fire on the *Delta*, the first Union transport that crossed their sights, the gunners so disabled the craft that it was forced to tie up on the opposite shore. All day Rebel sharpshooters peppered the riverbank with rifle fire, preventing the *Delta*'s would-be rescuers from towing her to safety until after dark.

In the interim the weather had turned even colder. Since many of the men suffered from frostbite, and the hooves of their mounts split apart on the frozen ground, the Texans moved inland a few miles to bivouac in a sheltering thicket in the once rich valley of Deer Creek. The plantations of the area were now deserted, and the troops dined on hogs they shot in the canebrakes and on the corn gathered from the abandoned fields. Finally, on January 10, the brigade stole back to the river and smuggled one last load of rifles to their compatriots in Arkansas. With all their vast exertions, they succeeded in ferrying only about fourteen hundred weapons to the Trans-Mississippi Department.[21]

CHAPTER 13

The Yazoo and the Black Warrior, February–April 1864

EVEN AS THE Texans shoved the last boatload of guns from the bank, their old nemesis, General Sherman, was preparing to launch a far more elaborate expedition of his own. Soon to assume command of the Federal troops in the West and impatient for action, he resolved to use the early weeks of 1864 to knock Mississippi out of the war and break up those scattered Confederate units that still possessed the capacity to interfere with Yankee shipping on the river or otherwise threaten the Union supply or transportation networks. Among the most troublesome of these Rebel contingents were General Forrest's 2,500 cavalrymen lurking in the area south of Memphis.

Almost all the Confederates in Mississippi were still supplied by the railroad from Meridian to Jackson. To eliminate this lifeline and bring retribution to the still-defiant citizens of the Magnolia State, Sherman proposed to thrust a powerful column of infantry eastward from Vicksburg all the way to Meridian, destroying farms and towns and ripping up the railroad as it went. Simultaneously, Brigadier General William Sooy Smith was to lead 7,500 Yankee cavalrymen southeast from Memphis and link up with Sherman's infantry at Meridian. On his headlong dash across Mississippi, Smith expected to encounter Forrest and destroy him.[1]

Oblivious to the plans still taking form in the fertile brain of the Yankee general, the men of the Third Texas slogged back across the delta and set up their camp near Benton, about six miles east of Yazoo City. Rain and snow continued intermittantly, swollen rivers required frequent detours, and it was January 21 before the weary men arrived at their encampment. There the lucky ones received mail from home, perhaps renewed interrupted flirtations with the local girls, and danced the night away as if the war was the farthest thing from their minds.

Despite the ordeal of campaigning in the miserable weather, morale had already improved remarkably under Ross's leadership. Recently promoted to the rank of brigadier general, he was anxious to buoy up the spirit of the troops to face a whole new year of war. Like other Confederate commanders throughout the South, Ross staged a formal ceremony during which he invited his men to reenlist en masse. Though the conscription law required the continued service of the troops in any case, it was believed that a voluntary display of renewed dedication would serve to inspire the faint of heart with revived enthusiasm for the coming spring campaign. On February 1 the troopers of the Third Texas Cavalry reenlisted to a man, showing, in Ross's words, "their determination to do their duty as good and true soldiers."[2] They would soon receive a sharp reminder of their purpose in the war.

As part of his Meridian campaign, Sherman ordered Colonel James H. Coates to take twelve hundred men, five gunboats, and five transports up the Yazoo River as far north as Greenwood, Mississippi. This expedition was intended to serve as a diversion from the main thrust of the campaign, and Coates was directed also to confiscate all the cotton he could capture at the numerous landings along the river. Embarking on January 31, Colonel Coates steamed up the Yazoo as far as Satartia, about thirty miles north of Vicksburg, where his convoy encountered the Texas Brigade three days later. Ross's scouts had spotted the conspicuous Yankee task force, and the Texans set up an ambush for Coates's convoy as it rounded a bend in the tortuous stream.[3]

Throughout most of its course between Yazoo City and Vicksburg the river wound through the flat and featureless delta.

About fifteen miles south of Yazoo City, however, it passed directly beneath rugged bluffs that rose abruptly above the eastern bank by some two hundred feet. The Texas cavalrymen had concealed themselves in the brush atop the bluffs and opened fire just as the Yankee gunboats hove into view at nine o'clock on the morning of February 3. Ross deployed two artillery pieces on the heights above the river and began shelling the vessels as they passed beneath his vantage point. Unable to elevate the ordnance aboard the gunboats sufficiently to reply to this unexpected bombardment, Colonel Coates landed a contingent of his troops downstream and sent them scrambling along the east bank to attack the Rebel guns on foot.

They were not ordinary Yankee soldiers. Besides his 560 white troops, Coates had included 370 black soldiers of the Eighth Louisiana Infantry and 320 members of the First Mississippi Cavalry, African Descent, in his expedition. Among the first African-American units raised by the North, these two regiments went on to achieve distinguished records in combat. Like the other 180,000 black men who would serve the Union cause before the war was over, they had to endure not only the normal perils and hardships of military life but the inbred contempt and condescension of their own officers and white comrades as well. And when they fought against their erstwhile Rebel masters, they could expect nothing but unrelenting ferocity.[4]

Colonel Coates deployed his troops on the riverbank, with the white infantry on the left wing and the black on the right. They advanced together up the steep bluff and across rocky ravines toward Ross's position. The Texas commander withdrew his artillery, sent the Third and Twenty-seventh regiments to cover the road to Yazoo City on his flank, and dug in the Sixth and Ninth regiments behind breastworks of rocks and logs hastily thrown up to face the enemy. Early in the afternoon the Yankees charged the Texans' position and were repelled only after a furious encounter at ten to fifteen paces. While the front was thus engaged, a contingent of black soldiers attempted to dislodge the Rebels by attacking their flank, but they also were repulsed. For three hours they skirmished sharply until the Texans ran low on ammunition. Fortunately for them, Coates called off his attack at dusk and withdrew his men to their transports, which were secured for the night on the west bank of the Yazoo. Ross reported about twenty of his men killed or wounded. Since he had detached the Third Cavalry to guard the road at his rear, the regiment emerged from the fight unscathed. Coates lost four white and two black soldiers killed in action.[5]

According to Colonel Coates, his African-American troops "acquitted themselves most handsomely, displaying the courage, coolness, and discipline of the most experienced troops."[6] The Texans were not so favorably impressed, however: any black man in a blue uniform they considered fair game for slaughter, since neither Ross nor his troopers recognized blacks as soldiers subject to the rules of civilized warfare. Their implacable racism was exacerbated when black troops were accused of murdering two captives they had taken from the Sixth Cavalry during the fight on the bluffs. The battle resumed on the following morning in an atmosphere of vengeful rage.

Before dawn Coates proceeded upriver again. His transports were hastily armored with knapsacks, boxes of hardtack, and timbers, against the renewed Rebel fire from the bluffs above. His gunboats led the way as the Yankee colonel ran the blockade to a point four miles south of Yazoo City. Two men were killed and a number were wounded by the Texas sharpshooters taking aim from the heights overlooking the river. After the convoy disappeared from sight around a bend, Ross left the Sixth Regiment to guard the bluffs and dispatched the remainder of his brigade to the landing on the south edge of Yazoo City. Two gunboats, sent ahead by Coates to reconnoiter, found the Texans securely dug in before the town. They took so much punishment from the Rebel artillery that the colonel withdrew downstream again to await a more propitious occasion to attack the place.[7]

A bustling town of three thousand inhabitants, Yazoo City owed its prosperity to the cotton trade and a local boatyard. Believing themselves delivered from the imagined horrors of occupation by black troops, the citizens showered the Texans with resolutions of gratitude and lavish gifts of food and drink. "They think that one of Ross's men is Enough for Two yankees," reported a Texas trooper to the folks back home. "They treat us Like they thought we were white men and I have been Invited by at least a half dozen citizens to go and dine (you know I have a poor way of Refusing)."[8] With understandable hyperbole, the Yazoo Citians declared that the Ross Brigade was "worth a whole army."[9] But their rescuers occupied the town for only three days.

Sherman had launched his 150-mile raid from Vicksburg to Meridian on February 3, and the Texas Brigade was summoned east to head off the Yankee juggernaut as best it might. Abandoning Yazoo City to its fate, the Texans spent the next ten days hovering impotently off Sherman's left flank as his relentless Union host rolled across the state of Mississippi. Confederate units in front of Sherman's twenty thousand soldiers were too weak even to delay the advance, and the bluecoats entered Meridian on Valentine's Day, losing only twenty-one men killed in the process. The Yankees tore up the railroad, burned all the bridges, destroyed a score of locomotives, and captured about three thousand head of livestock. After five days of systematic demolition in Meridian, Sherman led his column back to Vicksburg, noting with satisfaction that "Meridian, with its depots, store-houses, arsenal, hospitals, offices, hotels, and cantonments no longer exists."[10] He boasted that his men had left "a swath of desolation 50 miles broad across the state of Mississippi, which the present generation will not forget."[11]

With fewer than nine hundred effectives, the Texas Brigade was powerless to interfere significantly with Sherman's offensive. The cavalry skulked on the Union wings, mounted a few half-hearted skirmishes against outriding Yankee raiders, and watched sullenly as the work of destruction proceeded around Meridian. Then on February 18 the Texans were abruptly ordered to hasten to the north, where further disaster threatened the Southern cause. After a late start out of Memphis, Union General Sooy Smith was now closing in on Forrest's cavalry more than a hundred miles north of Meridian, and Ross was dispatched to reinforce the embattled Forrest. The Texas Brigade covered little more than two-thirds of the distance toward its goal, however, when the commander learned that Forrest, unaided, had administered a decisive defeat to the Federals at Okolona on February 22. This Union reverse considerably soured the fruits of Sherman's own successful Meridian raid.[12]

Forrest's victory also freed the Texas Brigade to return to their post overlooking the Yazoo delta. Curious to learn what had transpired there during their absence, Ross's men rode hurriedly across Mississippi again, arriving at their old campground east of Yazoo City on the afternoon of February 28. Even before they unsaddled their horses, the Texans discovered that the situation in Yazoo City had changed completely since their departure three weeks earlier. Colonel Coates, their old adversary, had taken advantage of their absence to carry out his orders to the letter. He had occupied Yazoo City, pushed his convoy all the way upriver to Greenwood, and confiscated 1,728 bales of cotton along the way to replenish the Union war chest. Satisfied with a job well done, Coates then pulled his expedition back to Yazoo City, arriving there late on the morning of February 28 just as the Texans were approaching their campground six miles to the east. Disembarking his men from their transports, Coates sent out a patrol of forty black cavalry scouts to secure the road toward Benton. Rounding a curve in the road, the Yankees suddenly collided with the vanguard of Ross's brigade as the Texans prepared to make camp.

The African-American troopers overcame their initial surprise and fired a hastily aimed volley at the astonished Texans, who were travel-worn and bone-weary after their three-week tour of Mississippi. Ross instantly ordered his men into their saddles, however, unlimbered his field artillery, and drove the Yankee soldiers to cover. Realizing that they had stumbled on an entire Rebel brigade, the Union patrol beat a hasty retreat, but a detachment of Texas cavalrymen bounded across the fields and over the fences to the left of the road and cut the fleeing scouts off from their base. Their mules were no match for the pursuing Rebel ponies; shouting Texas horsemen charged down upon the hapless black recruits and knocked them to the ground with pistols and sabers. Ross's men took no prisoners: of the forty-man patrol that had ridden out of Yazoo City, eight were killed outright, four were wounded, and ten were listed as missing after the running fight.[13] Ross reported that "the road all the way to Yazoo City was literally strewed with their bodies."[14] Later, after Union burial details recovered the corpses, six were found to have "been brutally used," suggesting that the Texans had murdered the men after their capture.[15] Only a handful of the African-American troopers reached the safety of Yazoo City.

Coates had deployed his infantry in a line east of the town and had occupied an earthen redoubt on a bluff overlooking the Benton road. Confronting this formidable barrier, the Texans dismounted and skirmished with the defenders for the balance of the afternoon. Toward evening, Ross withdrew his men to their encampment near Benton, where they bivouacked for the night. Remarkably enough, they had incurred no casualties during their running fight with the black soldiers. But Ross took note that day of the gallant behavior of Private Henry King, a Shelby County plantation overseer in the Third Cavalry, and promoted him to sergeant on the spot.

For five days there was little movement on either side. Coates continued to fortify his positions on the river at Yazoo City and in the redoubt on the bluff above. Ross rested his men in camp and awaited reinforcements, since the Federal force occupying the town was considerably larger than his own. At length, on March 4, Colonel Robert V. Richardson marched down from Lexington with 550 Tennessee cavalrymen to cooperate with the Texans. Now commanding some thirteen hundred men, Ross felt ready to attack the Union stronghold.

Ross's troopers moved out from camp early the following morning and by ten o'clock had driven back the outlying pickets to within a mile of Yazoo City. The town itself lay low on the banks of the river but was overlooked by a two-hundred-foot bluff directly to the east, which commanded the main road to Benton. Here Coates had stationed a regiment of Illinois infantry under the command of Major George C. McKee. They occupied the redoubt, an earthen quadrangle about fifty yards square. Coates deployed his black cavalry regiment in rifle pits immediately to the right of this strongpoint, while his African-American infantry occupied the town.

Ross launched a determined assault all along the line at midmorning on March 5. His men attacked the defenders of the redoubt from the south and east, and Richardson's Tennesseans, moving in on the right flank, boldly thrust themselves into Yazoo City from the north. By early afternoon the Rebels had completely surrounded the Yankee fortifications on the bluff and were grappling house by house with the stubborn defenders of the town. Gradually the Confederate troops won control over the main part of town, and the Federals prepared to make a last stand in two brick warehouses on the waterfront, where they hoped to benefit from the covering fire of three Union gunboats on the river. But McKee's three hundred Illinoisans, still penned in their redoubt, were pounded mercilessly by the Rebel artillery. Coates had already lost 31 men killed, 121 wounded, and 31 missing; now his entire command seemed in jeopardy.[16]

With Yazoo City virtually in his grasp, Ross tried to persuade the Yankee colonel to surrender. The Texan was more soldier than diplomat, however: His tone was so menacing, and his terms were so severe, that Coates saw little advantage in giving up. Ross had already hinted darkly that the alleged murder of his men by the black troops a month earlier had set the tone for the treatment of prisoners of war. Now he went even further, informing the Union commander that he "would not recognize negroes as soldiers or guaranty them nor their officers protection as such."[17] Then he repeatedly demanded from the beleaguered Major McKee nothing less than unconditional surrender. To this demand he coupled the dire warning that, "as to the treatment of your men and yourself, I will try and have them protected if they surrender during the charge; but you may expect much bloodshed."[18] Faced with this Hobson's choice, Coates calculated that he had little to lose by continued resistance, and he turned Ross down.[19]

Some of Ross's own men were revolted by the implications of his grim warning. A Texas trooper reported that "the news got out that Ross would Show no Q[uarte]r to prisoners. . . . This caused a great deal of dissatisfaction among our boys," who were not yet ready to descend to that level of savagery. "You would hear it in Every Camp," the trooper continued, "damned if I dont Leave if this prisoner Killing is not stoped."[20]

As it turned out, the Rebels gave up and called off the fight before the Yankees did. On the morning of March 5, Coates had urgently summoned reinforcements from downriver, and two Union transports loaded with black soldiers steamed into view below Yazoo City late in the afternoon. Confronted by these fresh troops, Ross and Richardson concluded that they had done enough for one day. They had already lost eight killed and fifty-two wounded; to storm the Federal redoubt or the riverside warehouses would probably require far greater effusions of blood. Ross consequently pulled his men from the town and then, harassed by its now emboldened occupiers, withdrew all the way back to his camp. It was a wise decision, since Coates's superiors in Vicksburg ordered him to evacuate Yazoo City the following day. As the Yankees reembarked aboard their transports, the Rebels marched into town, once more to the extravagant praise and generous hospitality of its citizens.[21]

The four regiments comprising the Texas Brigade then set up separate encampments some distance from Ross's headquarters at Benton. The Yazoo valley remained quiet until the end of March, and the men confined their activity to routine patrols and camp duties. Once again, however, their comparative idleness contributed to a resurgence of disciplinary problems in the command, and Ross expended considerable effort toward the resolution of these difficulties so that they would not undermine the effectiveness of his troops.

For one thing, during their attack on Yazoo City some of his boys had "loaded themselves with plunder," much of which belonged to the townspeople they were ostensibly protecting from the Yankees.[22] To be sure, there were a few charitable souls among the local citizenry who were so charmed by the mischievous Texans that they were prepared to argue that "inasmuch as they had defended the city and county so gallantly, anything they needed or wanted belonged to them, and the taking of it without leave was not theft."[23] Most of the people who had lost property to the Texans were not so indulgent, however. Ross found it necessary to explain to his men that their loot belonged to the Confederacy and not to themselves. Moreover, he promised to punish as common thieves those troopers found in the possession of horses or mules lawfully belonging to local citizens.[24]

Then there was the more serious case involving Colonel Jack Wharton, the unpopular commander of the Sixth Texas Cavalry. Consistent with their reputation for insubordination, his men revolted against his authority and threatened to kill him if he tried to exercise his command. Though Ross reprimanded the mutinous soldiers, he also advised the officer in question to resign. The men got what they wanted: Ross's popular brother, Lieutenant Colonel Peter F. Ross, succeeded to the command of the Sixth.[25] The inadvisability of allowing the restless Texans to lie idle had been forcefully demonstrated once again. To keep them busy, Ross ordered the Third and Ninth regiments off on a raid down the Yazoo Valley on March 30.

Their target was Yankee cotton. Perhaps no other issue inspired so much greed and corruption on both sides during the Civil War as the cotton trade. While possessing little else, the South had the cotton that the North needed to supply its own textile mills and to placate English and continental manufacturers who were cut off from their normal supply of the precious fiber. Since early in the war, both sides had therefore connived at trading with the enemy. Armed with authorization from the Federal government, and operating under the protection of the Union army, Yankee traders bought Southern cotton. The proceeds from these transactions enabled the Confederacy to purchase urgently needed arms and supplies. Such an underhanded trade fostered an atmosphere of speculation and chicanery and often frustrated Northern strategy. By its contribution to the Southern war effort, the contraband trade in cotton prolonged the war by at least a year.

After the fall of Vicksburg the Mississippi Valley became the heart of this disreputable business. The Federal government developed ways to bypass the unscrupulous traders: One method was to lease out confiscated plantations in conquered territory, place reliable agents in charge of them, and protect the cotton crop until it might be grown, picked, and delivered securely into Union hands. There were such leased plantations in the Yazoo valley, and the recently recruited African-American troops were primarily responsible for their protection from marauding Rebels. Near Snyder's Bluff, which overlooked the Yazoo about ten miles north of Vicksburg, two high-ranking Union officers had been granted the lease to one such plantation. While these gentlemen were away fighting the war, their agents supervised black laborers in cultivating the cotton and sold the crop at a tidy profit.[26]

The Texans' mission was to destroy this plantation. The troopers descended out of the bluffs and onto the main valley road before dawn on March 31, and the two attacking regiments split up in order to bracket the Yankee earthworks that protected the plantation. The Third Regiment fell upon a squadron of black cavalry from the south, while the Ninth attacked them from the rear. The Rebels slaughtered about thirty of the black soldiers, forced the remainder to take cover behind breastworks, and raged unhindered around the plantation's main buildings. They destroyed all the equipment, burned the gin, and captured about one hundred mules. After a brief skirmish with the Yankee infantry nearby, the Texans rode back unscathed through the hills to their campground. (By the time news of this modest exploit reached East Texas, it had been blown into gargantuan proportions: the word back in Smith County had it that their men had captured five thousand white prisoners and three thousand blacks.)[27]

The men of the Third Texas did not know it yet, but their raid at Snyder's Bluff would account for the last blood they shed in Mississippi. The war in the West was soon to assume a more dynamic and decisive phase, and their regiment would become a part of it. On March 10, General Grant had assumed supreme command of all the armies of the Union, and henceforth the character of the conflict was determined by his strategic goals. To the Confederate commanders who had to react to these initiatives, Grant's plans remained muffled and obscure early in the spring of 1864. Would the next Yankee offensive be aimed at Mobile? Would the Northern armies march south from Chattanooga? Or would the Union forces massed in Louisiana invade Texas?

To General Polk, Confederate commander of the Department of Alabama, Mississippi, and East Louisiana, the most immediate danger appeared to lie in central Alabama, where Union troops in the Tennessee Valley threatened to drive south toward the coal and iron region vital to the Confederacy. Consequently, Polk ordered General "Red" Jackson to concentrate his cavalry near Tuscaloosa, Alabama. From there he was to send out scouting expeditions all the way to the Tennessee River, a hundred miles to the north, and establish a network of couriers to warn of the anticipated Union attack when and if it developed.[28]

The Third Cavalry took up its line of march on April 4, 1864, and established their camp on the Black Warrior River near Tuscaloosa ten days later. Jackson's division of 2,517 effectives was composed of three brigades: Mississippi and Alabama troopers under Brigadier Generals Frank C. Armstrong and Samuel W. Ferguson, and Ross's Texans. Since Colonel Mabry had been assigned to head a brigade elsewhere, Lieutenant Colonel Boggess became the permanent commander of the Third Texas. General Polk himself received the men with a welcoming speech, which, though flattering, was judged by some of the more discriminating Texans as "altogether a crude specimen of oratory for a Bishop."[29] Polk promised the war-weary soldiers a sixty-day furlough, but this proved an ill-timed commitment that raised hopes soon to be dashed at the cost of considerable disappointment to the men.

For instead of embarking upon their long-anticipated leave, the men of the Third Cavalry spent the next three weeks prowling the inhospitable hills of northern Alabama, mapping its bridges and trails and pursuing largely imaginary bands of pro-Union guerrillas. Isolated pockets of Confederate draft evaders and deserters were said to be terrorizing loyal Southerners between Tuscaloosa and the Tennessee River, and Polk was determined to root them out. He therefore charged his cavalry with the unpleasant task of suppressing dissent among the impoverished backwoods population of northwest Alabama, as a corollary to their scouting duties.

Polk exaggerated the threat posed by these presumptive Yankee sympathizers. There were indeed enclaves of defiance against the writ of the Confederacy among the poor farmers of the Alabama hill country, but they were less active supporters of the Union than they were unwilling participants in the Southern rebellion. Most of these backwoodsmen wanted little more than to be left alone, free from the intrusions of Confederate mobilization. Their chief grievance lay in the Confederate Conscription Act: it snatched up the young men from their isolated hollows and dispatched them as cannon fodder for ambitious generals to squander on the battlefields of Virginia or Tennessee. Consequently, thousands of draft evaders hid out in mountainous retreats for years. They were joined by more thousands of Confederate deserters, who found in the hills a hospitable refuge from the rigors of combat. Yankee officers succeeded in raising a regiment of cavalry from these "mossbacks," as they were called, and sometimes the deserters sustained themselves by plundering the more prosperous plantations of the Tennessee Valley.[30]

Whatever their motives, to the Confederate authorities these disaffected Southerners were all miserable traitors, and General Polk in particular was intent upon rooting out their pockets of resistance. First, he issued an offer of amnesty to all deserters from the Rebel army who would rejoin their units within ten days. As the mailed fist to stiffen the velvet glove, he then ordered his cavalry commanders to comb the hills of northwest Alabama, arrest all "Tories," draft evaders, and deserters, and "punish them with death upon the spot," if they resisted his orders.[31]

After Ross's brigade established its camp near Tuscaloosa, Colonel Dudley W. Jones organized a detachment of three hundred men from the Third, Sixth, and Ninth Texas regiments to flush out "Tories" from the barren hills to the north. The Texans proceeded cautiously up the back-country roads, since open rebellion against the Confederacy had been reported in Marion County, about half way between Tuscaloosa and the Tennessee border. Jones's detachment plodded north for two days until it was fired upon by a small body of local men home on leave from the Union army. These Tories did no damage, but scurried to safety in the hills before they could be captured. Arriving in Marion County, the Texans discovered that reports of an insurrection in that quarter had been grossly exaggerated.

To be sure, there were many armed deserters lurking in the woods, but their purpose was to avoid combat rather than provoke it. The Texas troopers occasionally searched isolated farmhouses for suspected "bushwhackers." On one such midnight visitation, a woman barred the inspecting officer from entry into her humble dwelling. Beating down the door, the searchers discovered four beds, women's clothing scattered about, and a pair of size-eleven shoes that looked suspiciously masculine. Aroused to "her worser nature," another woman sat up in bed and exclaimed, "them's my shoes and you just let them alone and get out of here," emphasizing her point by dealing the searcher a stunning blow full in the face.[32] He knocked her down, tore off the bedclothes, and found three women and five men hiding there.

After a week in the saddle, the cavalrymen succeeded in arresting only about fifty "mossbacks," so well had they concealed themselves. Deprived of forage by the barrenness of the countryside, Jones led his detachment back to Tuscaloosa and turned his prisoners over to Jackson's headquarters for trial. Despite General Polk's earnest desire to round up all the deserters in his department, such a task was clearly beyond his capacity. Moreover, the threat posed by the "Tories" to the Confederate war effort was far less significant than had been assumed.[33]

In terms of casualties, the troopers of the Third Texas posed a greater danger to themselves during their three-week sojourn in northern Alabama than did the notorious "Tories." Private Luther Grimes, a former clerk from Cherokee County, fell into an altercation with a fellow Cherokean, James Ivy, and shot him dead. No charges were filed: Grimes claimed he had shot in self-defense. Shortly before, while trying to catch fish in the Black Warrior River, Private Harvey Gregg and a fellow soldier from Company A drowned when their skiff capsized in a whirlpool. In addition, four of the men wound up in the hospital after contracting gonorrhea and syphilis.[34]

These Alabama adventures came to an abrupt closure on May 4. Urgent dispatches arrived from General Johnston's headquarters in northern Georgia to the effect that the Union offensive from Chattanooga to Atlanta had begun. President Davis ordered Polk to rush all his available forces to Rome, Georgia, to assist Johnston, and the bishop-general complied by concentrating ten thousand of his infantry and four thousand cavalry for service there. Leaving its impedimenta behind, the Third Texas rode 150 miles through the ravines and across the ridges of eastern Alabama in five days (although, for disciplinary reasons, the stern General Jackson made some of the troopers walk part of the way). Polk brought his Army of Mississippi into the Confederate defensive line with remarkable alacrity: They arrived at Rome on May 14. The next day the East Texans went into battle. They were to serve under fire continuously for the next 112 days.[35]

CHAPTER 14

The Etowah and the Chattahoochee, May–July 1864

In terms of its strategic and political significance, the prolonged Union campaign against Atlanta was the most decisive of the war. It represented the western branch of Grant's two-pronged strategy to bring the South to its knees. Soon after his assumption of overall command of the Union army in March, Grant had formulated a scheme whereby he might destroy simultaneously the two major armies of the Confederacy: General Lee's force in Virginia and General Johnston's concentration of troops in the mountains just south of Chattanooga. The first task he accepted for himself; the second he entrusted to his faithful lieutenant, General Sherman. The two offensives were synchronized to begin during the first week in May, and they were to be complemented by unremitting Union pressure all along the line.

Accordingly, Grant launched his own armies across the Virginia tidewater at the appointed time. A series of assaults carried him eighty miles nearer his goal through the shambles at the Wilderness, Spotsylvania Court House, and Cold Harbor, but his troops bogged down in the trenches before Petersburg in June. Instead of winning a decisive victory, Grant found that he had expended 64,000 men killed, wounded, or missing, and yet stood stalled and thwarted a mere twenty-five miles from the Confederate capital at Richmond.

Sherman was more successful. Grant had ordered him to break up Johnston's army and destroy Southern military resources as deep into Georgia as possible. Sherman chose to interpret these instructions to mean that he should make Atlanta his primary target. A city of only ten thousand inhabitants before the war, it had doubled in size and now possessed a threefold strategic significance: it was the principal munitions manufacturing center of the South; the railroads that connected the Atlantic seaboard to the western states of the Confederacy radiated from the city; and Atlanta lay at the end of a series of natural obstacles—rivers, ravines, and rocky ridges—that blocked the Union armies from the eastern flank of the Deep South. The city stood like a "back gate" to Rebeldom: once pushed ajar, it would expose the heart of the South to a fatal thrust.

At Chattanooga, Sherman commanded three army corps with a total effective force of 98,797 men and 254 guns. From his headquarters in Dalton, Georgia, thirty miles to the southeast, General Joseph E. Johnston opposed Sherman with about 43,000 men—less than half the Union force. Unlike their Northern adversaries, the Southern leaders had still not established a unified command structure, and it was not clear what overall grand strategy they should pursue. Lacking adequate food, clothing, and equipment for their men, Confederate commanders were sustained merely by the assumption that if they could somehow hold out until November, a war-weary Union electorate would turn Lincoln out of office and negotiate a peace acceptable to the South. Johnston therefore traded territory for time: he met the Federal onslaught with evasive maneuvers and strategic withdrawals in an effort to avoid costly pitched battles until the enemy exposed himself to a decisive counterattack.

Much of the terrain between Chattanooga and Atlanta favored Johnston's Fabian strategy. The long spine of the Appalachian Range ended in an attenuated tail in northwest Georgia, leaving a series of ridges running roughly north and south across the most direct route between the two cities. Three major streams, the Oostenaula, the Etowah, and the Chattahoochee River, also

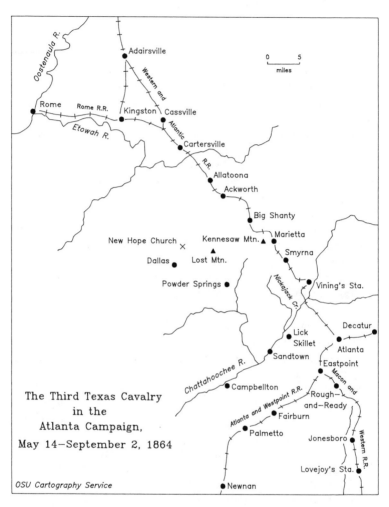

The Third Texas Cavalry
in the
Atlanta Campaign,
May 14—September 2, 1864

OSU Cartography Service

posed substantial barriers to an invader from the north. Winding across those streams and around the ridges for 138 miles were the tracks of the Western and Atlantic Railroad, which became the axis of the long fight for Atlanta. Otherwise unremarkable stations along its route—Dalton, Resaca, Allatoona, Big Shanty—took on enormous significance as indicators of Sherman's now rapid, now sluggish advance to the south.

Sherman's campaign fell into three major phases. The first, which occupied the two weeks between May 7 and 21, was already well advanced when the Third Texas arrived upon the scene with Polk's army. In a series of masterful maneuvers the Union commander drove his cautious adversary out of two strong defensive positions near the Tennessee border and down to the line of the Etowah River, some seventy miles closer to his objective at Atlanta. For his part, Johnston refused to give battle, awaiting that moment when he could lure his impatient enemy into some rash attack, then crush him in the wooded ravines that flanked the railroad. Though Sherman had driven deep into Georgia, he failed to trap Johnston and break up his army. By this time the Confederate defenders had been re-inforced to an effective strength of 62,000 men, and their casu-alties had been light. As Sherman's supply lines grew longer, Johnston's were shortened. Confident of victory, Johnston at last prepared to give battle on the banks of the Etowah on May 19.[1]

Since their arrival at Rome on the fourteenth, the soldiers of the Third Texas had been busy fending off a separate Union attack of their own. The town lay about halfway between Chattanooga and Atlanta and some dozen miles west of the main railroad between those two cities, to which it was joined by a spur of track running east and west. The site of several factories and an iron foundry, Rome was situated at the conflu-ence of the Oostenaula and Etowah rivers amid steep hills, which Johnston had turned into a link in his defensive chain. All the civilians had fled from the place, but the little town teemed with Confederate soldiers hastily throwing up their earthen fortifications. On the very day the Texans arrived, Sher-man sent two divisions against Rome in order to cut the railroad at Johnston's rear. A portion of Polk's infantry occupied the town for several days, but Johnston withdrew these troops to join his main army in anticipation of the major battle of May 19. The Texans remained behind as a rear guard.

They first encountered the scouts of the advancing Federal army while guarding the crossings of the Oostenaula River about eight miles north of Rome. After two days of light skirmishing, on May 17 the Yankees attacked the Rebel infantry still in Rome. Hastening to aid in the defense of the town, the Ross brigade took up positions about two miles north of the place that afternoon. Dismounting, the Texans charged through a narrow valley toward the positions of the advancing Yankee infantry and succeeded in driving the enemy back into the woods.

Though the engagement at Rome was but a side show, it took its toll in flesh and blood. The Third Cavalry lost two killed, seven wounded, and four captured that afternoon, with the heaviest cost falling upon Smith and Wood County men in Company K. Private Charner Gilchrist, a former farmhand, was killed outright. Sergeant Wallace Riggle, from Quitman, was shot through the knee; when the surgeon sawed off his leg, he died. Bill Perry, of Tyler, also lost a leg, but he survived. After losing as many men as he could afford in this action, Ross withdrew his troops to the shelter of Rome's breastworks for the night. The following day, while the Rebel infantry marched eastward to join Johnston at Cassville, the Texans held the Union force at bay and then retired under cover of darkness about eight miles to the southeast.[2]

On May 19, Ross's men rode twenty miles to the Etowah River, north of Allatoona, where they were supposed to guard the railroad bridge during Johnston's planned attack. But the great battle that he had hoped to initiate against the widely scattered units of Sherman's army never materialized. Lieutenant General John Bell Hood, one of Johnston's three corps commanders, had been ordered to launch the main assault, but instead of advancing, he fell back under the erroneous impression that Federal troops had penetrated to his rear. Johnston was therefore obliged to retreat to the south bank of the Etowah and make for Allatoona, where a spur of the Appalachian Range provided a strong defensive position near the railroad.

The strength of the Confederate line there persuaded Sherman to try another flanking movement rather than a headlong attack. Indeed, this indirect approach was to dominate the second phase of the Atlanta campaign: seven weeks in which most of the fighting took place between the Etowah and the Chattahoochee, which were approximately thirty miles apart. Withdrawing once again, Johnston anchored his line on the heights of Kennesaw Mountain, which overlooked the railroad at Marietta, and threw up earthworks across the rough and wooded terrain that extended westward past Lost Mountain toward the Alabama line.

During most of this phase of the campaign, the two antagonists were mired among the muddy stream banks and gullies eroded by almost incessant torrents of rain. Neither commander was willing to risk a frontal assault in the broken country. Instead, Sherman and Johnston resorted to wide flanking attacks, so that the contest resembled that of two evenly matched football teams relying more upon end runs than power plays through the middle of the line. Sherman called for such a maneuver on May 23. His intention was to sweep his army westward toward the village of Dallas, sixteen miles from the railroad at Marietta, and reach the Chattahoochee in five days.

It so happened that Ross's contingent was in position to intercept this Union drive and alert Johnston in time to head it off. During his retreat south of the Etowah, Johnston had assigned the Texans the task of protecting the pontoon bridges across which the Confederate troops withdrew. On May 21 two regiments of Yankee cavalry attacked them near the bridges but were driven off. Now on the extreme left wing of Johnston's army, the Ross brigade was ordered to patrol the creek bottoms south of the Etowah, and the wide-ranging cavalrymen informed Johnston of Sherman's intended end run almost as soon as the Yankee general set it in motion. Skirmishing continually with the enemy as they crossed the Etowah, Ross's men harassed the Union column on its way toward Dallas. The Texans reinforced the small Rebel garrison in the town, while Ross fired off urgent reports of the enemy's movements to Johnston's headquarters.[3]

Thus apprised of his adversary's intentions by his wary cavalry scouts, Johnston shifted his three corps westward to defensive positions about fifteen miles from Marietta. Occupying the center of his line, the men of General Hood's corps dug themselves in behind a hastily constructed barricade of earth and timber and mounted sixteen guns near New Hope Church, a log meetinghouse at the crossroads northeast of Dallas. Sherman's army struck this strongpoint on May 25. The Yankees peppered the Confederate defenders with artillery and small arms fire all day while probing for a weak spot in their line.[4]

Attached to Hood's corps, the troopers of the Third Texas

dismounted and deployed in a skirmish line in a grove of post oaks just west of New Hope Church. As one old Texas veteran remembered it, "the cannon balls and minnie balls rattled like hail among the oaks and the bark and splinters flew from the trees in every direction while the limbs of trees came sweeping to the ground constantly." The Methodist meetinghouse "was bored through and through by cannon shots, ... [and] was litterally stuck through [the] weather boarding with minnie balls."[5] Later in the day the roll of thunder and the crash of lightning intensified the horrendous din as the two armies grappled in the descending darkness.

The Rebels lost about three thousand men killed, wounded, and captured at New Hope Church. Their surgeons set up an improvised hospital under a brush arbor, but given the sorry state of medical service, very little could be done for the wounded. Fallen soldiers were carried to the spot and there subjected to the ministrations of the medical men on operating tables consisting of rough planks laid across posts that had been driven into the ground. The doctors arranged water-filled gourds to drip slowly over gaping wounds. Because one victim of a shot to the abdomen was unable to swallow, an orderly inserted a hollow tube of bark stripped from a tree directly into his stomach, through which water and soup were poured.

Fifteen troopers of the Third Regiment were wounded that day. Private Will Long, a Rusk County farmhand, perished within the month, and five others were left unaccounted for. Nine managed to survive both their wounds and the brush-arbor "hospital." For example, they brought in Sergeant Whit Phillips, a tough Jefferson farmer who had been shot through the lungs. The surgeon "laid him down on the table and cut out the big ball from the back and with the ball came a piece of the leather strap, gunstring, and a piece of checked shirt that had passed with the ball through his body."[6] Though he suffered terribly, Phillips survived, was sent home, and lived to a ripe old age.

Hundreds of the wounded were not so fortunate, however. Experience had already taught the burial details efficient techniques for digging mass graves. They laid the corpses across a shallow trench and, as they extended the ditch to accept more bodies, piled the excavated earth on those already interred, thus effecting "a great economy in labor."[7] In this way the grave diggers disposed of more than 700 Confederate dead at New Hope. The Yankees lost heavily as well. Sherman admitted 2,400 casualties; his men called the quiet country churchyard "the Hell Hole." Combat amid the dense timber and brush-choked ravines had proven so costly that the Union commander disengaged his troops and shifted them back eastward toward the railroad.

On May 29, Johnston tried a flank attack of his own against the eastern end of the Union line, then a similar thrust against Sherman's right flank the following day. Both failed. Recognizing that he could not prevent the Yankees from pushing back to the railroad, the Confederate general retired to a position just north of Marietta on June 4. He dug in his troops along an arc from Kennesaw Mountain, overlooking the railway, to Lost Mountain, about eight miles to the west.

Since the Ross brigade served as Johnston's rear guard during his retreat to Marietta, it was June 8 before the Texans took their positions on the left wing of the Rebel army a few miles west of Lost Mountain. It had been raining almost continually for a week, and the muddy roads were virtually impassable. Throughout these days of frantic maneuvering in the mud, Ross's men remained under fire, either in the saddle on patrol or skirmishing as infantry. Each day's action, despite its perilous uncertainty, became an exhausting routine. The troopers of the Third Texas would rise before sunup, saddle their mounts, and detail horse holders, who remained behind the lines. Each man then received his daily ration: a small pone of corn bread and three-eighths of a pound of bacon, which he bolted down during the march forward to the skirmish line. Sometimes their positions were hastily fortified; more often they were not. Normally, the men would remain under fire all day, charging forward when ordered to do so, falling back when the pressure exerted by Sherman's army became too great.

Often after nightfall the regiment would be ordered to a new position perhaps ten miles away. Had they been infantrymen, they might then have collapsed gratefully into sleep, but the Texans still had to feed their horses. This frequently involved wandering for miles through unfamiliar and dangerous territory in the rain and darkness, gathering wild peavines, crabgrass, or anything else the poor animals could eat. If one of the East Texas boys got to roll up in his sodden blankets by midnight, he considered himself fortunate.[8]

But the same wet weather that rendered their lives miserable hampered Sherman's offensive as well, and the Yankee drive stalled before Marietta for a month. Johnston fortified the slopes between Kennesaw and Lost Mountain with a series of timbered revetments and trenches about ten miles long. Moreover, Sherman's supply line to Chattanooga remained vulnerable to cavalry raids. So instead of employing the tactics of rapid maneuver favored earlier, the Yankee general was forced to resort to a tedious mobile siege warfare and satisfy himself with cutting off exposed salients in the Rebel line. Taking advantage of a brief respite from the rain, Sherman's artillery bombarded a Rebel forward redoubt on June 14. Though a lucky shot killed General Polk, the cannonade decided nothing, since Johnston merely abandoned this exposed position and tightened his hold to the rear.

Through ten days of intermittent downpour, Ross's brigade guarded the extreme left wing of Johnston's army, insuring that the Union troops of Major General John M. Schofield's Army of the Ohio would not outflank their positions west of Lost Mountain. It was miserable duty. The Texans were camped so close to the Federal lines that the Yankee reveille woke them up in the morning. They expected a major onslaught at any moment and were entangled in lethal skirmishes every day, any one of which might turn into a sustained attack. In isolated squads they picketed the waterlogged and gloomy woods in front of the Rebel line, where visibility was so limited that blackened tree stumps loomed like the blue-coated enemy amid the mists of the forest. Hungry, wet, and cold, the men of the Third Texas were hard put to maintain their martial enthusiasm.

Occasionally the insanity of it all seems to have dawned upon the individual soldiers. After a particularly harrowing skirmish atop a wooded ridge, Private Newton Keen, one of the more thoughtful of Ross's men, found the corpse of a fallen Yankee in the underbrush. In the dead man's pocket was a letter from his mother. Touched by the contents of the missive—"a motherly tender hearted letter"—Keen was moved to reflect that this youth, who was "never to see home, not even to get a soldier's burrial . . . could have been me as well as him." What if, thought Keen, it was his own shot that killed the man? "But of course I did not know, and so it was much for the best," he concluded.[9]

Occasionally the boys in the blue and the gray would momentarily step out of their assigned roles in the tragedy, cross over each other's lines, exchange newspapers, and trade for such little luxuries as coffee and tobacco. On June 9, for example, the men in Ross's skirmish line called an impromptu "armistice" for this purpose. The Texans chatted and joked amiably with their enemies like the farm boys most of them were and then resumed shooting at them again several hours later.[10] This sort of civilized behavior, of course, had no place on the battlefield.

Nor, for that matter, did the natural instinct for self-preservation. Shortly after the "armistice" episode, pickets from Captain Robert Gause's Company A of the Third Texas suddenly lost their stomach for fighting at the approach of a line of Yankee skirmishers. Like raw recruits, the Harrison County veterans scurried back to the safety of their earthworks without offering serious resistance to the advancing foe. This "disgraceful behavior" humiliated Brigadier General Ross, especially since several of his superior officers witnessed the "shameful conduct" of the company. He immediately arrested the unfortunate Gause for dereliction of duty and fired off a blistering reprimand that warned the entire brigade not to let it happen again. "Officers ordered to hold any position or to accomplish any given object must do it," he declared.[11] Having thus made his point, Ross restored Gause to his command.

The doleful stalemate in the rain lasted until the beginning of July. Johnston's ten-mile defensive front was far too long for his army to hold, and so Sherman first intensified his pressure against the projecting Rebel left wing anchored on Lost Mountain. Between June 16 and 19, therefore, the Confederate commander withdrew his entire force to positions prepared in a semicircle around the flanks and crest of Kennesaw Mountain, just west of Marietta. Ross's cavalry was charged with protecting the infantry on Johnston's left wing as it fell back into its new positions.

At this point, Sherman tried to force Johnston to stretch his line so thin that a breakthrough would be possible. Accordingly, he ordered General Schofield's Army of the Ohio into a position where it might either drive south toward the Chattahoochee or envelop the rear of the Confederate defenses on Kennesaw Mountain by marching east toward Marietta. For ten days Ross's brigade fought off Schofield's advance in daily skirmishing. On June 17 a column of Yankee infantry almost succeeded in cutting off the Texans from their rear, but the Third Cavalry held the advancing Federals in check until the brigade could withdraw. By the twentieth Jackson's cavalry had stabilized its end of the front about four miles south of Kennesaw Mountain.[12]

Having thus tried and failed to break the stalemate with another end run, Sherman next attempted a plunge directly through the middle of the Confederate line. Here Rebel ramparts on Kennesaw Mountain rose seven hundred feet above the surrounding countryside; nevertheless, the Yankee general sent his troops in a frontal assault against these fortified positions on June 27. The Union infantry dashed itself to pieces against the Confederate earthworks. By noon, when he called off the slaughter, Sherman had lost almost two thousand dead and wounded, while only 432 of Johnston's men fell on the slopes of the mountain. Sherman took consolation in the "moral effect" of this carnage, proving that he could fight as well as maneuver.

Though several miles separated Ross's cavalry on the left wing from Sherman's main attack against Kennesaw Mountain, the troopers could witness clearly the awesome dimensions of the combat to their north. One Texas trooper described the Union assault as "a wonderful sight to behold, more than 60,000 men in sight, moving . . . like a blue cloud arising."[13] The Texans were hard pressed themselves, as Schofield's infantry drove forward against their lines in support of the Federal attack in the center. Outflanked to his right and in danger of being cut off from the road to his rear, Ross pulled his brigade back by half a mile. That night Schofield's men began fortifying their new position a few hundred yards nearer the Chattahoochee.[14]

After the bloody repulse that he had sustained in his assault against Kennesaw Mountain, Sherman reverted to his previous tactics of maneuvering around his enemy's flanks. He directed

Major General James B. McPherson's Army of the Tennessee to join General Schofield in an advance south and west toward the Chattahoochee. By July 3, McPherson had led about fifteen thousand men to a point only three miles north of the river and five miles west of the railroad. Johnston, perceiving that this drive imperiled his left flank, reluctantly abandoned his stronghold atop Kennesaw Mountain and pulled his troops back to the north bank of the Chattahoochee, where he dug them in with their backs against the stream. Through the aid of the Georgia militia, he had already prepared elaborate fieldworks in front of the riverbank, and these bastions protected the six pontoon bridges in position to move his men south in the event of a Yankee breakthrough. But Johnston was confident that his troops would be able to hold the line of the Chattahoochee, and for a time they did.

As the hosts of Schofield and McPherson bore down upon the river, Ross's Texans stood directly in their path. The axis of the Yankee advance lay along a line between Powder Springs and Sandtown, a point on the Chattahoochee only ten miles west of Atlanta. As the eyes and ears of Johnston's army, the Texans had the task of reporting almost hourly on the enemy's movements, and they also had to stall the Yankees as long as possible in their race for a river crossing. For five days the Texas cavalry checked the Union advance, their skirmishers pouring such continual fire into the enemy's ranks that the Federal commanders were forced to halt and fortify their positions with earthworks and timber at the close of each day. Slowly retiring before the Union onslaught, the Texans frequently found themselves outflanked on both wings.

On July 3, Ross's men dug in on a ridge above the steep banks of Nickajack Creek, which flowed into the Chattahoochee about eight miles northwest of Atlanta. Five hundred Georgia militiamen, too old or too young for conscription and still untested in battle, reinforced their hastily fortified line along the ridge, while a Tennessee brigade stood on their right and Armstrong's Mississippi cavalry protected their left flank. Only three miles to their rear lay the still unoccupied Confederate redoubt on the north bank of the Chattahoochee, guarding one of the main approaches to Atlanta.

For two days the Texans defended their position against the combined forces of Schofield and McPherson. On the morning of Independence Day, the Federals advanced in a solid phalanx toward Nickajack Ridge, but the Ross brigade mounted a spirited charge that threw the enemy half a mile back down the road. As evening closed in, the Texans found themselves outflanked yet again and withdrew from their breastworks and down into the forests of the Chattahoochee bottom, where they could hear the Yankees on the ridge raising cheers to Lincoln, Sherman, and Schofield. The men of Ross's command and their Rebel comrades had nevertheless delayed the Federal advance sufficiently to allow Johnston to shift his infantry into the fortifications north of the river. Passing through these earthworks and across the pontoon bridge they were charged to protect, the Ross brigade retired temporarily south of the Chattahoochee on July 5.[15]

The Confederate line north of the river was still unbreached, and Sherman was disappointed to encounter the six-mile-long band of entrenchments that barred him from his goal. Though he could glimpse from afar the rooftops of Atlanta, he knew it would be costly to attempt a direct assault on the Rebel earthworks. Instead, he once again resorted to a flanking movement around a fixed obstacle. Withdrawing Schofield's corps from his right wing, he ordered it to the opposite end of his line, twenty miles to the northeast. These troops probed the extreme right of the Confederate line until they discovered two lightly defended crossing points on the Chattahoochee and began pouring around Johnston's right flank on July 8.

In order to mask this thrust by his left wing, Sherman dispatched his cavalry to create a diversion at the western end of the Rebel line. For several days the Ross brigade ranged up and down both banks of the Chattahoochee in an effort to counter the Yankee feint. Then, as Sherman concentrated his forces to exploit the bridgehead his men had established on the north, the sector of the front guarded by the Texans enjoyed a few days of relative quiet. They merely threw out pickets and patrolled along the riverbank as occasion demanded. Sometimes the troops on both sides would call an informal truce, then swim in the river and exchange opinions as to the probable outcome of the fall elections.[16]

On July 9, with the Yankees streaming around his right flank, Johnston saw no recourse but to order a retreat once more. Having foreseen this eventuality, he had earlier constructed a line of earthworks running east and west above Peachtree Creek, which flowed into the Chattahoochee only seven miles north of Atlanta. Then, as Sherman hauled his supplies forward, and Johnston directed his army into its new defensive position, a decision in distant Richmond altered fundamentally the character of the campaign. Nursing old grievances and dissatisfied with Johnston's leadership from the beginning, President Davis found his repeated pattern of defense and retreat no longer tolerable. On July 17 he informed the general that he was dismissed from his command on the grounds that he had failed to "arrest the advance of the enemy to the vicinity of Atlanta. . . . and express no confidence that you can defeat or repel him." [17]

Davis appointed General Hood to replace Johnston. Under Hood's direction, the basic strategy for the defense of Atlanta abruptly shifted from one of skillful maneuvers and withdrawals calculated to preserve the Confederate army as a force in being, to a series of sanguinary counterattacks that ultimately bled the defending army to death. Had they been consulted, the men of the Third Texas would have voted to keep Johnston. As Lieutenant A. C. Rorison, of Company B, put it at the time, "We all know that Joseph E. Johnston is by far the best General in the Confederate Army." [18] Lon Cartwright went even further, charging that Johnston's removal was "one of the worst blunders of our Pres. and greatest misfortunes of the Confederacy." [19] One of Ross's veterans summed up the situation succinctly when he recalled that "all things went all right so long as [Johnston] commanded, but when the army was put under Hood all things went wrong." [20]

CHAPTER 15

Atlanta,
July–August 1864

Hood's appointment to command the Rebel forces marked the beginning of the final stage in the Atlanta campaign. It was to last seven weeks. Hood began by launching three major battles in eight days—Peachtree Creek, Atlanta, and Ezra Church—which consumed about fifteen thousand Confederate soldiers without making any significant impact upon the huge Union army. At the end of July, Hood retired behind the miles of red clay earthworks that surrounded the city, and the initiative passed to his Northern adversary. Instead of storming Atlanta's fortifications head on, Sherman invested the place and attempted to cut off its defenders by sending forth a series of cavalry raids designed to break Atlanta's rail connections to the south and east. At last, on August 28, he flung his entire army in a great wheeling scythe around the city, forcing Hood's defenders to withdraw. Atlanta fell four days later.

The stakes at issue for both sides were enormous. The campaign was even more significant for its psychological impact on the North than for its considerable strategic consequences. Grant's offensive in Virginia stalled all summer in a series of incredibly costly encounters without destroying Lee, capturing the Confederate capital, or conspicuously altering the course of the conflict, as far as the man in the street could see. Northern morale sagged among both civilians and troops in the field. Racked by inflation and resentful of the inequitable conscription system, many thousands among the war-weary populace were ready for peace at any price. Even among some of those who had renominated him for president, Lincoln was suspected of prolonging the conflict deliberately for his own political advantage.

Unless Sherman could deliver a decisive victory on the Atlanta front, most observers, both Northern and Southern, expected that the voters would repudiate the Lincoln administration in the fall election. Down in San Augustine, Texas, canny old Matthew Cartwright predicted that "if Lincoln fails to overcome our army he probably will acknowledge our independence before he [is] voted out of office."[1] Cartwright's son in the service shared these sentiments: "I now feel more hopeful than I have since the war started," he wrote.[2]

Fully aware of the consequences of his next move, Sherman welcomed Hood's appointment to command the defense of Atlanta, for he was confident that he could beat a man already famous for the rashness of his assaults. Intent upon avoiding another shambles like that of Kennesaw Mountain, the Northern commander refused to be lured into a frontal attack against the Rebel fortifications along the Chattahoochee River and Peachtree Creek. Instead, on July 18 he tried to wheel his left wing wide around the Rebel right flank, intending to drive southeast of Atlanta and take the city from the rear. Hood met Sherman's initiative with an assault of his own, and for the next five days the two armies were locked in a bloody sequence of attack and counterattack.

At first Sherman's bold stroke appeared to be working, as his advance units swept past Decatur, seven miles east of Atlanta. But a gap opened up in the center of the Union line, and Hood lunged at this point along Peachtree Creek. Sherman's left wing then bore down upon the Confederate forces, and Hood retired behind the interior defenses of Atlanta on July 21. On the following day he ordered a renewed counterattack, this time around the left flank of the Union army and into its rear at Decatur. Once again the Yankees parried the thrust, and Hood pulled back into the safety of Atlanta's redoubts. Within five days of assuming command he had expended 13,295 of his men killed and wounded—men irreplaceable to the South.

Fortunately for the troopers of the Third Texas, they were employed almost ten miles west of this carnage. Jackson's division had the task of guarding the left flank of the Rebel line along the Chattahoochee to forestall a breakthrough by Brigadier General Edward M. McCook's Union cavalry. By now all the units in the Ross brigade were severely understrength. To be sure, there were still 596 officers and men on the rolls of the Third Cavalry, but 273 of them, or 46 percent, were absent from duty for one reason or another. Many were convalescing from wounds; dozens were too sick to fight; scores had been rendered *hors de combat* by unserviceable mounts; and some had found less hazardous jobs guarding supply depots and wagon trains. In their high rate of absenteeism the East Texas troopers were but typical of the Confederate army as a whole at this point in the war.[3]

General McCook, their particular adversary of the moment, commanded 3,600 troops; as long as this potent force of riders loomed in the wings, Ross's scouts had to watch them closely and neutralize the threat they posed to the western end of Hood's defenses. Thus, while the bloody clashes of Peachtree Creek and Atlanta were under way between July 18 and 24, the Texans merely picketed McCook's division and engaged in sporadic skirmishing along the river. By the latter date they had withdrawn some distance south of the Chattahoochee to a point six miles due west of Atlanta. Ross was particularly wary, for an ominous concentration of troops and equipment in McCook's line made him suspect that the Yankee cavalry leader was plotting a raid, or something worse.[4]

He was right, of course. After Hood retired to the inner defenses of Atlanta, his troops were forced to rely upon two railroads for their supplies. Both entered the city from the south: one ran eighty-five miles southeast to Macon, while the Atlanta and West Point line continued southwest to the Alabama border. Sherman believed that by severing these last remaining arteries he could dislodge Hood and drive him out of the city. To accomplish this, the Yankee commander mounted two major raids during the course of the following month. The first was led by General McCook and Major General George Stoneman.

On July 25, Sherman ordered McCook's cavalry to ride south from its position on the right flank of the Union army, while Stoneman's division was simultaneously to drive south from the left wing at Decatur. The two commanders were to link up at Lovejoy's Station, twenty-six miles south of Atlanta on the Macon Railroad, and systematically destroy the tracks in both directions. Then Stoneman expected to dash yet another ninety miles farther south and rescue the twenty thousand Union prisoners of war languishing in the notorious Andersonville prison. Hood's still potent army stood between these two thrusts, and exceptionally precise coordination was required to ensure the planned rendezvous of the dual columns of raiders at Lovejoy's Station. For a general who evinced but limited confidence in his cavalry, Sherman asked a great deal of it indeed.[5]

To oppose this destructive pincers movement against his rail lifeline, Hood had Major General Joseph Wheeler's cavalry corps covering the area east of Atlanta and Jackson's division on the western flank. Unfortunately for the Confederates, Jackson's cavalry scouts were not up to their usual standards of vigilance, and the first phase of McCook's raid consequently turned into a huge success. Confused and distracted, the Rebel cavalry commanders guarding the Chattahoochee west of Atlanta allowed McCook to elude their patrols. He detoured his troopers twenty miles down the west bank of the river and crossed to the eastern side unopposed on the night of July 27.

McCook's maneuver worked because for several days before their crossing the Yankees had mounted a series of feints across the river, keeping the Rebel cavalry occupied and pinning them to their fortified positions at Lick Skillet, a crossroads hamlet in the hills south of the river. Though these demonstrations—Union bands blaring, colors streaming, and artillery thundering—were only for effect, the skirmishes they provoked could be lethal for the men involved.

On July 26, for example, Yankee scouts probed to within half a mile of Ross's position at Lick Skillet. The Texans' commander ordered Captain Ewell M. Wright and Lieutenant W. T.

McClatchy, of the Ninth Cavalry, to charge these infiltrators with their two companies, and the Rebels succeeded in capturing a number of the enemy as they drove them back to the north. As McClatchy and Wright conveyed their prisoners to their lines, however, the Union artillery opened up on the area. Reluctant to become victims of their own guns, the Yankee prisoners dropped to the ground and refused to obey their captors' orders to move. Whereupon, Ross reported, "Captain Wright and his men commenced killing them. They fired all their loads from pistols and guns into them and then retired for shelter from the artillery. Captain W[right] killed two and Lieutenant McClachey fired six rounds at them."[6] Thus for the sake of a mere demonstration, ten Union soldiers died in the no man's land between the lines.

McCook's success in eluding the watchful eyes of the Rebel cavalry was also facilitated by the battle of Ezra Church, fought three miles west of Atlanta on July 28. General Hood sallied out of the city's fortifications to mount a furious but futile assault on entrenched Federal positions at that point, and the Ross brigade was ordered east to cooperate in the attack. Thus, while McCook's raiders were crossing the Chattahoochee twenty miles to the southwest, the Texans were racing in the opposite direction in a vain attempt to support their comrades at Ezra Church. Though two companies of the Third Cavalry participated in the fighting, by the time the bulk of the brigade arrived on the scene the battle was virtually over. After losing about 4,300 men while the Union lost 632, Hood broke off the engagement and pulled back into Atlanta.[7]

General Jackson was so preoccupied with the action at Ezra Church that it was late in the evening before he perceived the peril posed by McCook's cavalry far to the west. He ordered Ross to undertake a rapid countermarch back to the river and intercept the raiders, but by the time the Texans arrived at the Chattahoochee it was almost midnight. McCook had safely crossed the river earlier in the evening and enjoyed a twelve-hour head start on his pursuers, who now hurried east in an effort to catch him.

The Yankees' trail was not hard to follow, since they left a swath of destruction in their wake. McCook's men first passed through Palmetto, a village on the West Point Railroad, where they ripped up several miles of track. Then they overran the camp of the Third Texas, burned ninety-two wagons, and captured its teamsters, farriers, and chaplain. Dashing eastward another twenty miles to Lovejoy's Station, they continued their devastation. In the process, the raiders demolished two trains, destroyed or captured hundreds of wagons in a Confederate supply column, burned a thousand bales of cotton, and captured some four hundred Rebel soldiers who had been guarding or hauling these supplies. Much satisfied with his work, but uneasy that Stoneman's column had failed to rendezvous with him as ordered, McCook prepared to withdraw to the west bank of the Chattahoochee with his plunder late on the afternoon of July 29.[8]

It was at a point about a mile and a half west of Lovejoy's Station that the Rebel cavalry finally caught up with McCook, and the dashing Yankee general found himself in serious trouble. Without so much as halting from their long ride from the river, Ross's men boldly charged the raiders as soon as they caught sight of them about four o'clock in the afternoon. The Yankees received the charge of the Ninth Texas and blunted it, only to be attacked moments later by the Sixth Regiment on horseback and the Third and Twenty-seventh regiments in dismounted formation. Awaiting further orders from Jackson, the Texans hesitated in pressing their attack for about two hours, however; and McCook was able to slip around their flank and ride west again toward the river, having lost twenty men dead and wounded and fifty captured in the brief encounter. The Texans had been in the saddle for twenty-eight hours; while the men of the Third Texas dismounted long enough to feed themselves and their horses on green corn, the Ninth Regiment took up the chase again in the darkness.[9]

Meanwhile, the eastern arm of Sherman's cavalry pincers, the 5,400 men under Stoneman's command, were being led to disaster by their chief. Instead of cooperating with McCook against the Rebel railroad at Lovejoy's Station as Sherman had ordered, Stoneman hared off to the south on his own quixotic mission to liberate the Yankee prisoners at Andersonville. This well-intentioned but irresponsible deviation from his orders resulted in Stoneman's capture and the dispersal of his entire command on July 31. Since Stoneman had failed to carry out his assigned role in the operation, his adversary, General Wheeler, was freed to lead three brigades of his own cavalry to reinforce Jackson's hard-pressed troopers in their pursuit of McCook. Wheeler's men overtook the Yankees at daylight on July 30 about eight miles east of Newnan, a town on the West Point Railroad.[10]

This placed McCook in a perilous situation indeed. Pummeled by the Rebels all night, his column had fallen into a disorganized and weary retreat toward the Chattahoochee and safety. But Brigadier General Philip D. Roddey's Confederate cavalry blocked his path through Newnan, Wheeler's horsemen were dogging McCook's heels, and Jackson's riders lunged at his flanks. The Union general realized that unless he could escape to the west bank of the river, he stood in grave danger of being surrounded and cut to pieces. Skirting to the south of Newnan, McCook's troopers dashed into the thickets and ravines between the railroad and the river.

About three miles out of town they found their passage blocked by the Southerners, and McCook had no choice but make his stand in a dense grove of timber above Sandy Creek. The Texans dismounted and plunged through the thick underbrush to confront the Union horsemen of the First Tennessee Volunteer Regiment, noted for their white horses and the fact that their commander, Colonel James P. Brownlow, was the son of "Parson" W. G. Brownlow, the notorious East Tennessee Unionist. The "White Horse Cavalry" charged the Third Texas three times in a headlong effort to break out of the trap. Brownlow at last found a gap in the line and escaped to the west, but with only twenty-eight of his men. This still left the East Texans face to face with the troopers of the Eighth Iowa Cavalry, equally desperate to break through the Rebel ring that encircled them.

Because of the dense undergrowth and heavy timber, Union and Rebel units became thoroughly intermingled in the course of the struggle. Fighting hand to hand and firing at point-blank range, men captured at one moment might overwhelm their captors the next and make them prisoners in turn. That confused melee in the woods engraved itself permanently on the memory of at least two officers of the Third Cavalry. Lieutenant Sam Barron was advancing through the brush at the side of Lieutenant Sim Terrell, from Kaufman County. Suddenly, Barron glanced up to spot a Federal soldier a few feet away, taking careful aim at him through the sights of his Spencer carbine. "I looked at least two feet down his gun barrel," Barron recalled. "As quick as thought I threw up [my] carbine and fired at his face," as men from Terrell's company rushed up to dispatch another Yankee sharpshooter nearby. Now, "two dead bodies lay face downwards where a moment before, two brave soldiers had stood. . . . Somehow I could not feel glad to see these two . . . fellows killed." [11]

Lieutenant Tom Towles, of Van Zandt County, was another who never forgot that day in the woods below Newnan. The young officer was painfully wounded and he took refuge from the stifling heat under a tree, as blood saturated his clothing. While he sat there helplessly, no less a personage than General McCook himself rode up to the spot, accompanied by his staff. After assuring Towles of medical attention, he inquired of the wounded man the strength of the units that opposed him. When Towles coolly informed the general that he was surrounded by the divisions of Jackson, Wheeler, and Roddey, the now thoroughly alarmed McCook exclaimed to his officers, "We must get out of this!" and hurriedly rode away. [12]

Seeing himself encircled, McCook abandoned the spoils of his raid and ordered his regiments to disperse and make a run for the Chattahoochee wherever they could. In the process of this breakout, the Eighth Iowa Cavalry pierced the line of the Third Texas, stampeded its horses, and temporarily captured General Ross himself. Somewhat prematurely, McCook assumed that the Iowans had destroyed the Ross brigade and made a prisoner of its commander. But the Texans quickly closed up their ranks and liberated Ross before he could be led from the field. Then they proceeded to cut the Iowa regiment to pieces: of the 316 Iowans who started on McCook's raid, only 20 returned safely to Union lines.

Toward dusk, McCook and fragments of his regiments were at last able to extricate themselves from the melee and elude their Confederate pursuers. They recrossed the Chattahoochee under cover of darkness; some fled all the way to Alabama before their commander could collect the disorganized components of his division at Marietta a week later. The raid, begun with so much promise, had turned into a fiasco primarily because Stoneman failed to cooperate. McCook was forced to abandon his artillery, ambulances, hundreds of horses, and much equipment, which the delighted Rebel soldiers quickly turned to purposes of their own.[13] "It was a magnificent katch for us," one of Ross's veterans recalled.[14]

While the Federal commanders lost two-thirds of their men on the raid, the damage they inflicted upon the railroads was quickly repaired. Almost thirteen hundred Yankee prisoners were rounded up at Newnan and transferred to the prison camp at Andersonville. The Ross brigade suffered losses of only five killed and twenty-seven wounded, and in a formal address, the commanding officer proudly complimented his troops for having "nobly done your duty during the arduous service of the last four days."[15] In the midst of the inexorable erosion of the South's capacity to wage war, the failure of the Stoneman-McCook expedition came as a gleam of hope amid the general gloom in Confederate headquarters. As a Rebel staff officer recorded in his journal for August 1, "To-day deserves to be marked with a white stone; good news has flowed in from all distant points."[16]

For his part, Sherman summed up the outcome of the enterprise with unusual restraint: "On the whole, the cavalry raid is not deemed a success."[17] In the wake of this failure, he reorganized his cavalry arm by sending McCook to the rear and bringing up the 4,500 men under Brigadier General Hugh J. Kilpatrick to cover his left flank. At this point, General Hood played into his hands and offered Sherman a second chance to break down the defense of Atlanta by cutting off its supplies with a cavalry raid. Assuming that the Federal cavalry was still too disorganized to interfere, Hood ordered General Wheeler to lead eight brigades of Rebel horsemen against the Yankee supply line to Tennessee on August 10.

While he was thus absent from the Atlanta front for a month, Wheeler caused the enemy considerable trouble but inflicted no permanent damage to the Union railway system. The Wheeler raid actually benefitted Sherman, since it deprived Hood of most of his cavalry when he needed it and gave the Federal commander an occasion to turn Wheeler's absence to his own account. Though he was known to characterize General Kilpatrick as "a hell of a damned fool," Sherman respected his aggressiveness.[18] He therefore ordered Kilpatrick to drive south across the Chattahoochee, disable the West Point and Macon railroads, and thereby render Hood incapable of supplying his defenders of Atlanta.

With Wheeler's troopers ranging far to the north in Tennessee, Jackson's division was left to shoulder the responsibility for scouting west of Atlanta during the latter half of August. Still composed of the brigades of Armstrong, Ferguson, and Ross, the division had been reinforced to about 3,700 men. For more than two weeks after the Stoneman-McCook raid, the Ross brigade was employed in routine picketing and reconnaissance activity near Fairburn on the West Point Railroad; its primary mission was to guard the fords of the Chattahoochee and the vital railway. By the middle of August, Kilpatrick's cavalry division had taken up a position near the river and had begun probing the Texans' defenses preparatory to a raid. Eluding Ross's pickets, a detachment of Kilpatrick's riders swept into Fairburn and burned the depot on August 16. Concerned and wary, Ross kept an eye on his enemy's movements, but still had no inkling of the size of his force or his objective.[19] When Jackson warned of Kilpatrick's ominous concentration of troops, General Hood complacently reassured his cavalry commander that "Ross . . . can take care of them."[20]

When the blow came, the Texans were too weak to parry it. Kilpatrick struck south from his fortified position on the river at sunset on August 18. His galloping riders crashed through the pickets of the Sixth Texas guarding the bridge across Camp Creek and routed the men of Ross's other regiments from their sleep. Shortly after midnight, Ross realized that he was in the path of a major raid and, though handicapped by a shortage of ammunition, hurriedly ordered his troopers into their saddles and urged them forward through the bright moonlight to intercept the Yankee column. By early morning the Third Regiment had caught up with Kilpatrick's cavalrymen as they crossed the tracks at Fairburn and delayed their progress long enough for the other regiments of the brigade to gain the front of the enemy. Joined by Ferguson's brigade, the Texans put up a spirited resistance at the crossing of the Flint River, but by late afternoon Kilpatrick had driven the Rebels all the way through Jonesboro, eighteen miles below Atlanta. Here the Yankees fell to ripping up the railroad and burning the little town's public buildings.

As the flames and sparks from Jonesboro cast their glow over the night, Kilpatrick became aware that Jackson's three Rebel cavalry brigades were massing around him in preparation for an attack at dawn. Shortly after midnight on August 20, therefore, the Federal commander slipped his column out of town toward the east. When the Texans discovered on the following morning that their enemy had evacuated Jonesboro, they fell upon his rear again a few miles away. Kilpatrick's column then turned abruptly south to strike the railroad at Lovejoy's Station, eight miles below Jonesboro. There the Union general found the tracks defended by an Arkansas infantry brigade that had dug in under the cover of a dense wood. Behind him, the pursuing Texans were closing in. Cornered, Kilpatrick prepared to make his stand on an open hilltop a short distance east of Lovejoy's Station. As the Yankees hastily threw together a breastworks of crossties, about four hundred of Ross's men attacked the Federal position on foot. They were beaten back by artillery fire.[21]

Beset front and rear, Kilpatrick resolved to fight his way out of the impasse. He ordered Colonel Robert H. G. Minty to lead three Union regiments in a saber charge against the nearest Rebel line. This happened to be the men of the Third Texas, who, having left their horses in a grove of trees at the rear, now crouched in the open field seeking cover behind the few remnants of rail fence that remained intact across the cleared ground. As the Yankee horsemen thundered down upon them, the Texans got off one volley and then, without an order being uttered, ran for their lives. "Every officer and every man took in the whole situation at a glance: no one asked or gave advice: no one waited for orders," recalled Sam Barron. "Every one instinctively started for the horses a mile to the rear."[22]

With sabers slashing fiercely, the Union horsemen rode over Ross's brigade, "scattering horses . . . and men everywhere."[23]

The exultant Yankees cut down the fleeing Texans, seized their artillery battery, and then dashed on into the woods beyond to stampede their horses. To the Federal officers leading the charge, as well as to the frightened Rebels on the ground, it seemed that "Ross' brigade was there and then literally run over, trampled under foot, and, apparently annihilated."[24] General Kilpatrick congratulated himself for inflicting "the most perfect rout any cavalry has sustained during the war."[25]

Miraculously, however, the Third Texas survived to fight another day, although many of its members were captured. For one thing, Kilpatrick was short of ammunition and in too much of a hurry to extricate himself from his still perilous situation to follow through after the blow his troopers had dealt the Rebels. Engaging the Confederate infantry on his front just long enough to cover a retreat, the Union commander led his column back toward his own lines again before dark. Moreover, no sooner had the Yankee cavalry swept across the ground than a torrential deluge inundated the field, obscured visibility, and prevented the Federal force from pressing its advantage. Some of the East Texans merely played dead in the rain until Kilpatrick's horsemen had moved off down the road to the east. Others, like Captain Jesse Wynne, Lieutenant Tom Soape, and Sergeant Nathan Gregg, fought their way out of captivity and seized their own guards. Just before dark, when Ross and his bugler appeared on the opposite side of the field to reassemble his troops, muddy stragglers streamed in from all directions. Though humiliated by the rout and minus a precious battery of artillery, Ross had lost but two killed, twenty wounded, and thirty captured.[26]

Of all Ross's regiments, the Third Texas Cavalry suffered the most. Minty's thundering horsemen bore off their regimental battle flag, proudly inscribed with "Oak Hill," "Elk Horn," and the names of other engagements they had so far survived. Privates Will Kellum and John Hendrick, both of Rusk County, were killed. Kilpatrick's raiders bagged twenty-three members of the Third Cavalry as prisoners of war, the heaviest toll in captured levied on the regiment since Iuka. The list of captives included three company commanders, four lieutenants, two sergeants, three corporals, and eleven privates.[27]

Unlike their comrades captured at Iuka two years before, these men could not look forward to prompt repatriation under the provisions of the exchange agreement; on the contrary, they faced the woeful prospect of a lengthy incarceration in one of the Northern prison camps. The whole issue of exchanging prisoners had become clouded by controversy, and Union authorities had long since recognized that the practice was counterproductive to their war effort, inasmuch as it had the effect of periodically restoring to the South its most precious dwindling resource: men to bear arms. After Grant assumed command of the Union army, the exchange virtually ceased; instead, the United States government built more prisons and expanded those already established in order to hold its increasing thousands of captives. Between April 1864 and the end of the year, the number of Confederate soldiers in Northern prisons almost doubled, from 33,601 to 63,003. By the end of the war 214,865 Southerners had been captured and confined at one time or another.[28]

Kilpatrick's captives therefore faced a long enforced sojourn in the North. Having ridden around the entire Rebel army, the Yankee cavalry commander hurriedly withdrew his raiders along a route east of Atlanta and turned his prisoners over to Sherman's headquarters. The Federals locked their exhausted captives in a guarded enclosure for several days prior to transshipment, and fed the famished Rebels on hardtack and bacon. The crowded bull pen contained some disaffected Southerners who were understandably anxious to get out of the war as soon as possible. One of the easiest means to that end was to take the oath of allegiance to the United States provided under Lincoln's amnesty proclamation of the previous December. Though none of the Third Cavalry prisoners defected, some of the other soldiers were eager to impress their captors with their new-found loyalty to the Union and consequently gave vent to violent imprecations against the South and all it stood for. Resenting these insults to his embattled homeland, Jim Crabtree, a hot-tempered private from Greenville, tore into the turncoats of the bull pen singlehandedly and wrought general havoc until restrained by the guards.[29]

From the Atlanta front, the East Texas prisoners of war were conveyed by rail first to Nashville, and then to the transfer point at Louisville, from which they traveled on to their assigned prison camps. To maintain control over the inmates, the Federal authorities separated officers from enlisted men. The Third Cavalry officers were sent to Johnson's Island, a wind-swept spit of sand in Lake Erie, three miles north of Sandusky, Ohio. There the government had built thirteen two-story barracks enclosed within a plank stockade. When the East Texas officers arrived at their new home on September 2, they found that it contained more than 2,500 inmates.[30]

At the time of the East Texans' admission Johnson's Island seemed a fairly salubrious site, as prison camps go. Breezes off the lake kept the summer heat down; with a few exceptions, the guards were not abusive; and the health record at the prison was much better than in most other Northern camps. A Dallas lieutenant credited the prison commandant with doing "everything to make the prisoners as comfortable as possible."[31] With the coming of winter, however, the frigid gales of northern Ohio wafted freely through the cracks and knotholes of the jerry-built barracks, and there were never enough blankets or heavy clothing to keep the displaced Southerners warm. Their captors reduced food rations to a bare subsistence level in order to deflect Northern criticism that Rebels were coddled. Though the situation improved in the spring, some of the men were reduced to devouring rats and garbage. The shallow outdoor latrines constantly overflowed, and the barracks reeked with the odor of filth and uncollected refuse. With fifty to eighty men packed into each room, conditions were unbearably crowded. Deadly boredom and depression were the constant companions of the officers imprisoned there, until they were released at the end of the war.[32]

The enlisted men captured at Lovejoy's Station were interned at Camp Chase, a former training facility for Union volunteers near Columbus, Ohio. Among the largest of the twenty-three principal United States military prisons, it held almost 9,500 inmates at the height of its expansion. The men were confined to wooden barracks, each housing 198 prisoners, with 3 men to the bunk. Provisions—beef, bread, and coffee—had been adequate at first, but by the time the East Texans arrived, Yankee officials had begun to complain about "sleek, fat, comfortable looking rebels" at Camp Chase and demanded that rations be reduced to the level prevailing in Confederate prisons.[33] Until the end of the war, therefore, the inmates were always hungry and usually cold.

With the arrival of thousands of new Rebel captives at the beginning of 1865, Camp Chase became a charnel house. Many of these men were wounded, already ill, or so debilitated from their accumulated privations during the darkest days of the Confederacy that they entered the camp only to die. It was not an appropriate setting for convalescence in the best of times. Occupying low-lying ground near the Scioto River, the compound turned into a mudhole in wet weather. Open-pit latrines were sited at elevations higher than the cisterns supplying drinking water, with predictable consequences. To care for the sick there was but one surgeon, his assistant, and an assortment of more-or-less qualified medical orderlies. Smallpox, dysentery, and respiratory diseases raged through the barracks. During the last year of the war the number of deaths from disease among the enlisted men at Camp Chase reached a level thirty-eight times higher than that among the officers on Johnson's Island.

A number of men from the Third Cavalry failed to survive the Camp Chase experience. Private Reuben Chamberlain died of chronic diarrhea in November. Having once been discharged as under age, Private James Young, a farm boy from Rusk County, had reenlisted only to succumb to bronchitis at Camp Chase in December. The prison burial details were kept particularly busy the following February. During that one month alone, 499 inmates perished, while 495 others lay sick in the camp infirmary. Numbered among February's toll were Corporal Allen Nidever and Private Burrell White of the Third Texas, who thus became part of a larger statistic as two of the twenty-six thousand Confederate soldiers who died in Union captivity during the course of the war. Other members of the regiment contributed to the mortality figures from camps at Alton, Illinois, Louisville, Kentucky, and Chicago.[34]

For nine months the East Texas captives languished behind the walls of their prison, killing time by playing cards, carving fanciful figures from gutta-percha buttons, or more frequently, joining the "thousands of aimless men . . . walking around the camp like tigers, bears, and lions in their cages."[35] Then at last the interminable war ground to an end, and the captives from the Third Texas were allowed to go home in May and June 1865. They proceeded to Vicksburg by rail and steamboat, at which point they were released on parole. By July 5, Camp Chase was empty.

While their captured comrades began their long ordeal as prisoners, the remaining men in the Third Regiment pulled themselves together after their rout at Lovejoy's Station and got back into the war. Within two days after that fiasco, Ross reassembled his command and drew the troopers into line again along the West Point Railroad. Perhaps relieved that the damage had not been worse, General "Red" Jackson even saw fit to congratulate his "gallant Texans" for "resisting with the most determined courage the entire force of the enemy."[36]

Despite their undistinguished performance against Kilpatrick's cavalry, the men of the Third Texas reacted with remarkable resiliency and optimism. Lon Cartwright assured his brother that most of the men of the regiment were "now all well and in as fine spirits as ever."[37] Looking toward the fall election, Surgeon Eugene Blocker was equally encouraged. "I fully believe Sherman will have to retreat," he wrote his wife, and "that the day is not far distant when Northern Ga. will be freed from the thralldom of Lincoln's howling Soldiery. . . . The next ten days will bring forth great things for the weal or woe of our country." Blocker based his optimism upon the presumption that the Northern Democrats would nominate a peace candidate who would overwhelm Lincoln at the polls. "Everything looks cheering to me," he concluded.[38]

The Harrison County surgeon was right in his presentiment that the next ten days would be decisive for the South, but events took a course contrary to the one he anticipated. For even as Blocker penned these hopeful lines, Sherman unleashed his ultimate blow against Atlanta. During his raid south of the city, Kilpatrick had torn up fourteen miles of railroad track, but the Rebels had repaired the damage within two days. This frustration finally convinced Sherman that his cavalry "could not or would not work hard enough to disable a railroad properly."[39] If

Hood's defenders were to be dislodged from Atlanta, Sherman would have to do the job himself.

Consequently, the Union commander launched his own grand maneuver to cut off Hood's supplies to Atlanta once and for all. He wheeled his three great armies out of their trenches facing the city's northern approaches on August 26 and concentrated them along the Chattahoochee southwest of Atlanta's main defenses. Sherman then led his massive columns eastward, first across the West Point Railroad and then on to Jonesboro, where they cut the tracks from Macon to Atlanta. Reacting too slowly and uncertainly to the Yankee onslaught, Hood had no recourse but to abandon the city on the evening of September 1. In one great strategic sweep, Sherman at last accomplished in a week the objective that had eluded him for the previous four months.

After their long fight in defense of the city, the fall of Atlanta came with sudden, if anticlimactic, finality for the men of the Third Texas. In their bivouacs along the railway, Ross's cavalrymen stood directly in the path of Sherman's mighty offensive, but there were too few of them left even to monitor the Union advance, much less impede it. As some eighty thousand Yankees surged forward, the Third Cavalry could do little more than scout the enemy's movements, skirmish along his flanks, and fall back toward Jonesboro. Everything happened so quickly that even the sharp-eyed General Ross was unable to gauge the strength of the Union columns, leaving Hood unsure of Sherman's intentions until it was too late.

Spearheading the Yankee sweep, General Kilpatrick's division drove the Rebels from the railroad on August 27 and on beyond the Flint River four days later. The East Texans picketed the various stream crossings in the path of the Yankee juggernaut but fell back repeatedly after a few hours of feeble resistance. On the night of September 1 they stood under arms just east of Jonesboro, where they awaited anxiously the major assault anticipated for the morning. Then from out of the north came the distant thunder of exploding Confederate ammunition trains as Hood destroyed the supplies he could not salvage in his retreat. Shortly after midnight word came down the line that their comrades were evacuating the city they had so valiantly defended. Early on September 2, the men of the Third Texas were ordered to join the Rebel concentration at Lovejoy's Station, eight miles farther south.[40]

The Yankees occupied Atlanta the same day. Sherman's long-sought triumph restored Northern enthusiasm for the war and saved the Lincoln administration from probable defeat in the fall elections. By reviving the Union will to victory, it sealed the fate of the South. Yet even in the glow of his success, Sherman recognized that he still had not attained the main objective of his long campaign—the destruction of the Confederate army. At Lovejoy's Station, Hood had collected almost forty thousand officers and men, all "veterans inured to war."[41] So respectful was the Union commander of his defeated-yet-still-dangerous foe that he elected merely to "occupy Atlanta, enjoy a short period of rest, and . . . think well over the next step required," rather than attack Hood directly.[42] Indeed, two spectacularly destructive campaigns would be required before 1864 came to a close.

CHAPTER 16

Hell in Tennessee, September– December 1864

Sherman's sweep across Georgia and General Hood's disastrous expedition into Tennessee turned the autumn of 1864 into a season of decision. By Christmas the outcome of those two campaigns, coupled with Lincoln's victory in the November election, at last extinguished all doubt about the eventual outcome of the war. The triumph of the North was assured despite the fact that the conflict on the Virginia front remained in dreary stalemate throughout the fall as Grant's forces stood mired in the protracted siege of Petersburg.

After Sherman captured Atlanta, a month-long hiatus ensued before the war in the West resumed its normal level of violence. The Union commander spent September securing his base in the city and strengthening his defensive perimeter. With some 82,000 Federal soldiers garrisoned there, Atlanta became a huge Yankee encampment. The occupying troops seized all the property they could lay their hands on, and Sherman evacuated the civilians from the city in order to simplify the chore of occupation and expedite his subsequent operations. Having pondered his next move carefully, by the beginning of October he hit upon a bold scheme to march sixty thousand men across Georgia to capture Savannah.

At Lovejoy's Station, Hood was also considering options for

his next campaign. The forty thousand officers and men whom he now commanded were dispirited after their defeat, and their numbers would inevitably dwindle through desertion unless they were quickly employed. Hood realized that he must act soon or not at all. He first occupied himself with vindicating his own failure to hold Atlanta by casting the onus for defeat on his subordinates; then he proceeded to reorganize his army. He pleaded repeatedly with beleaguered Richmond for reinforcements, supplies, and money to pay his troops. But instead of sending military assistance (which he did not have), President Davis came out to Georgia himself, as though to encourage the troops with his dour presence. He exhorted them to "be of good cheer, for within a short while your faces will be turned homeward and your feet pressing Tennessee soil."[1]

This was welcome intelligence to Sherman, for Davis's address outlined the essence of Hood's future plans. The Confederate commander had concluded that, though he was not strong enough to recapture Atlanta itself, he might move effectively against Sherman's supply line, the long-contested railway from Chattanooga. If Yankee transport could be disrupted, Sherman might be maneuvered out of Georgia, or at least pinned down in Atlanta where he could do little additional harm. With these possibilities in mind, Hood transferred his headquarters to the West Point Railroad in mid-September. From this position about twenty miles southwest of Atlanta, he could swing to the north and threaten his enemy's communications. To prepare for his projected drive against Sherman's railroad, Hood ordered Jackson's cavalry division to probe the Union positions across the Chattahoochee.

Now augmented by five regiments of newly mounted Kentucky infantrymen, the division consisted of 3,956 effectives divided into four brigades. Ross's brigade had marched into Georgia with 1,009 men; 839 were left. The Third Texas could muster but 252 troops present for duty, of whom only 188 were armed with serviceable rifles, an inventory that included a bewildering array of models and calibers from the British Enfield .577 to the Union army issue .51. Clothing was in chronic short supply; even some of the officers were without boots or shoes and had no money to buy any. During their 112 days of action in the Atlanta campaign, the East Texans had engaged in thirty-five battles and skirmishes—about one fight every three days for three and one-half months. Way back in April the troops had been promised furloughs that never came. Many of the men were exhausted and dispirited; they longed to return to Texas.[2]

Already signs of deteriorating morale similar to those of the previous autumn began to surface with increasing frequency. Some of the troopers resorted to theft from the hard-pressed civilians of the area to fill their empty bellies. An Upshur County private lamented that "our Army is stealing, robing and burning up all that the citizens have, leaving the families of poor soldiers to starve."[3] Ross was obliged to issue repeated warnings that if any of his cavalrymen were caught stealing from civilians, they would be transferred to the infantry forthwith. A spate of relatively minor infractions in the Third Texas kept the brigade courts-martial busy. Corporal Elisha Roberts, for instance, was sentenced to carry a rail in front of regimental headquarters one hour each day for ten days and fined a month's pay, on the grounds that he had disobeyed a direct order. A court-martial found Cass County Private Nelson Higginbotham guilty of absence without leave and sentenced him to parade before the brigade in a barrel for five days.[4]

More seriously, the periodic plague of mass desertion descended once again upon the Texas Brigade. On October 5 the names of fifty-seven soldiers of the Twenty-seventh Regiment were posted as "having cowardly deserted their posts in the . . . face of the enemy."[5] Though the Third Cavalry was the best disciplined of Ross's regiments, it was by no means immune to the virus of desertion. Five Smith County troopers stole away together early in October. At about the same time, Privates Dan Turney and William Stedman crossed over Union lines and took the oath of allegiance to the United States. Ross became seriously concerned that most of his men would desert en masse unless they were assigned duties closer to home. Over the heads of his superiors, he urged former Texas Governor Francis R. Lubbock, who was passing through Georgia on his way to join President Davis's staff, to use his influence at Richmond to arrange a transfer of the Texas Brigade to the Mississippi River, where it might be possible for the men to reestablish contact with their homes. Ross's irregular request went unheeded, however.[6]

In any case, he knew that he had to find ways to keep his men busy. As part of Hood's reorganization of the army, Ross consolidated the ten understrength original companies in each of his four regiments into five companies per regiment and assigned a captain and two lieutenants to each new company. This left a surplus of several dozen young officers temporarily unemployed, and Ross detailed these men to a roster of "Brigade Scouts," for whom "pleasant and agreeable" duties were to be found.[7] A substantial number of them chose to volunteer for extra patrol duty, since it offered, in the words of one, "some recreation, or at least a diversion" from the dreary routine of camp.[8]

Forty of these "jovial, companionable fellows" organized themselves into a scouting squadron and set out one day to look for some excitement in the no-man's-land between the West Point railway and the Chattahoochee.[9] Having already fought across the war-ravaged countryside several times, they knew the area well. As the little band cantered up the road toward Campbellton, just south of the river, they passed almost total desolation: few farm animals survived; all the fences had long since been demolished for barricades or to fuel campfires; crops rotted in the fields; and the scattered population still remaining subsisted on corn bread and molasses.

At a farmhouse not far from Campbellton the scouts surprised two Yankees in the process of dressing a plundered hog. From these captives they learned that a Federal foraging party of some sixty cavalrymen was ranging just to the south off the main road to Atlanta. Concealing themselves in the woods beside the road, the Rebels set up an ambush, intending to wipe out the foragers on their way back to the Union lines. At first everything went according to plan: presently the Yankee column approached the concealed scouts, driving a herd of milch cows ahead of them and hauling two wagonloads of plunder behind. Unfortunately, one of the Texans fired too soon and spoiled the ambush, but the Rebels fell upon the head of the column nonetheless.

Within an instant, several dozen screaming Confederate horsemen sprang into the midst of the startled foragers and began firing wildly in all directions. Private "Pem" Jarvis, of Company K, lost control of his horse, which tore the pistol out of his hand as it dashed through the tangle of black jacks and plunged into the mass of milling soldiers in the middle of the road. Jarvis repeatedly found himself the target of some Yankee's carbine, but each time one of his fellow scouts picked off his assailant before he was shot. Remarkably enough, Jarvis and his Rebels comrades emerged unscathed after killing or wounding a number of the Union soldiers before the foragers fled back toward their lines. The little band of scouts then returned to their camp with a dozen prisoners, thirty or forty captured rifles, and a wagonload of booty.[10]

In the meantime, the remaining troopers of the Ross brigade probed the Yankee lines and patrolled the wooded bottomlands between the railroad and the river in preparation for the beginning of Hood's last campaign. While the Texans fanned out to the north and west to secure his bridgehead, Hood brought his main army across the Chattahoochee on September 29 and then drove northward toward the railroad at Marietta. For the next two weeks the Confederate general led a march up the railway, pausing to mount successive thrusts inward against isolated garrisons at various points along the track, then withdrawing into the broken and wooded terrain to the west again when seriously threatened by Sherman's forces. In these hit-and-run attacks, against many of the same village depots that had achieved bloody notoriety six months earlier, Hood's weary troops retraced the route of their long retreat of the previous spring. Their commander's objective was not merely to cut the Federal supply line: he wanted to entice Sherman into battle in the rough country of northwestern Georgia.[11]

For his part, Sherman was impatient to be off and running on his bold march to the sea. But he still lacked authorization from Washington for such an enterprise and was reluctantly obliged to follow Hood up the railroad. Rushing reinforcements into threatened garrisons, attempting to trap his enemy in the open country, Sherman endured the frustration of watching Hood enjoy the initiative for a change. The Yankee commander succeeded in parrying most of Hood's blows, while his engineers were kept busy repairing gaps in the rail line to Chattanooga. He was nevertheless convinced that "to pursue Hood is folly, for he can twist and turn like a fox, and wear out any army in pursuit." [12]

Ranging ahead of the Confederate army in these twists and turns, the Texas Brigade at first led in the attacks on the railroad and frequently embroiled itself in running skirmishes with the Union cavalry. Then, as Sherman accelerated his pursuit, the Texans assumed the role of rear guard to fend off his advance units. By October 14, Hood's army had marched northward to a point near the Alabama line only thirty miles south of Chattanooga. For two days its commander pondered his next move and at last decided to terminate his campaign against the railroad. Instead, he resolved to march through Alabama and advance northward toward Nashville in the vague and grandiose hope of seizing Kentucky and then driving to the east to join Lee's army near Richmond.

Such an ambitious undertaking was manifestly beyond the capacity of the Confederate army at this point in the war. Whatever remote chance the scheme may have had depended upon speed and audacity of execution. But now the redoubtable Hood, justly renowned for his boldness in the past, lapsed into an irresolute torpor that delayed his advance into Tennessee by five weeks. Mistrust developed between Hood and his nominal superior, General Beauregard, who commanded the Military District of the West, and the apparent indecision at headquarters undermined the morale of the troops. As the golden days of October gave way to the cold rains of November, Hood still dithered south of the Tennessee River, and the Union command in Tennessee enjoyed ample time to reinforce their positions against the belated Rebel attack. [13]

After his strategic decision of October 16, Hood took a month to move his army 150 miles across Alabama and establish a bridgehead at Florence, on the north bank of the Tennessee River. Sherman trailed his elusive adversary for ten more days; then almost contemptuously, he turned his army back toward Atlanta to prepare for his projected march to the Atlantic. No longer needed as rear guard, the Ross brigade received orders to join Hood's main army in preparation for its strike northward into Tennessee. The Texans picketed the main road between Decatur and Tuscumbia for more than a week, skirmishing with occasional Federal patrols as the torrential rains of early November turned the Tennessee Valley into a vast quagmire.[14]

Meanwhile, small parties of Texas scouts boldly probed north and east of the river in the direction of Huntsville. Operating stealthily by night in order to elude the Union garrisons in the towns, these raiders seized all the livestock in their path, emptied any remaining smokehouses of their contents, and begged or extorted any food they could lay their hands on. They found the Tennessee Valley in a curious state of semi-anarchy. Since Yankee gunboats patrolled the river, and Federal troops maintained order in places like Huntsville and Decatur, life in the towns and villages followed a pattern of uneasy calm, but much of the surrounding countryside had reverted to a state of nature, with every man's hand raised against every other. Wandering bands of stragglers and deserters from both armies plundered and occasionally burned the once prosperous farms of the valley. Many African Americans had long since repudiated their servitude, fled their former masters, and congregated in squalid contraband camps to await the promised fruits of freedom.

Quite naturally, these black refugees were quick to inform their Northern liberators of the presence of Rebel raiders like Ross's men, and the Texans retaliated by burning their camps and terrorizing them. On one occasion a party of Ross's scouts masqueraded as Federal officers long enough to kidnap six blacks from a contraband settlement south of Huntsville. Though two of the unfortunate captives escaped as they were being rafted across the river, the Texans shot one prisoner and hanged another of the "meddlesome blacks" on October 30.[15] Ten days later, the Ross brigade was withdrawn to the west to serve as rear guard for Hood's main army, now camped on the river just south of Florence.

For two weeks Hood remained stalled in this position until General Forrest joined him with 3,500 men out of western Tennessee. Thus reinforced, Hood's army crossed the river, and on November 21 the Rebel commander was at last ready to begin his drive against Nashville. The Yankees had not been idle, however. For a month Sherman had chafed impatiently to launch his march across Georgia, and the reelection of Lincoln on November 8 removed the last obstacle to its execution. After destroying the railroad behind him and putting Atlanta to the torch, Sherman set off toward the Atlantic Ocean on November 16. His 62,000 Union soldiers were to accomplish one of the classic campaigns of military history.

In his absence, Sherman had dispatched Major General George H. Thomas, the "Rock of Chickamauga," to defend Tennessee against Hood's anticipated onslaught. Thomas commanded 71,473 men scattered across the Cumberland Plateau and along the Tennessee River. Around his headquarters at Nashville he had posted 18,000 troops, while his subordinate, General Schofield, headed a force of about 25,000 at Pulaski, Tennessee, only thirteen miles north of the Alabama line. Thomas was confident of his capacity to hold the Rebels in check, since he enjoyed ample time to deploy his forces, which in any case outnumbered Hood's army almost two to one.

Hood departed Florence at dawn on November 21 with Nashville as his objective. He led about 37,000 men, divided into three corps of infantry and three divisions of cavalry, now united under the redoubtable Forrest. The attrition of the long Atlanta campaign and the epidemic of desertions during the fall had reduced Jackson's division to a vestige of its former strength, and the Ross brigade was down to a mere 686 men. Weeks of relative inactivity south of the Tennessee River and the unrelieved succession of miserably wet and wintry days had further undermined their spirit; some chose to desert rather than cross one more river. Thus, as the Texans set out on their last campaign, the Third Cavalry Regiment counted but 218 troops present.[16]

Yet remarkably enough, considering their condition, the long-suffering soldiers left in the ranks were animated still by an indomitable eagerness to fight. Even if one discounts the hyperbole of an old campaigner, the tribute by A. W. Sparks rings true: "The last rally of the bugle found them as ready to mount as did the first."[17] As they slogged northward through pelting sleet and half-frozen mud, the Rebel troops seemed suddenly energized and transformed. For more than a month Hood's army had drifted aimlessly through the Tennessee Valley; now, within the next twelve days, it would battle its way 115 miles to the very gates of Nashville.

To realize his objective of seizing Tennessee's capital city, Hood had to surmount three formidable obstacles that barred his way. The first consisted of Schofield's 25,000 Yankees bivouacked around Pulaski, which lay only sixteen miles east of Hood's direct line of march. Schofield was expected to strike the advancing Confederate columns on their flank, or interpose himself between Hood and Nashville, or simply fall back to join General Thomas in his defense of the city. The two other barriers were those imposed by nature: the Duck River crossing at Columbia and the passage over the Harpeth River at Franklin. As it turned out, Schofield did not seriously challenge Hood's advance from his forward position near the Alabama line. He withdrew instead to successively block the two river crossings and then retreated within the defenses of Nashville itself. On each occasion the Union commander was able to delay the Southern army but narrowly escaped entrapment and destruction himself. Hood, on the other hand, succeeded merely in wrecking his own army in his attempt to destroy Schofield.

In overall command of the Rebel cavalry, Forrest led the vanguard of Hood's army out of Florence, Alabama, toward Columbia, intending to establish a bridgehead across the Duck River before Schofield could block him. His men soon fell afoul of Yankee cavalry detachments dispatched from Pulaski to impede their progress. In the midst of a snowstorm on November 22, the advance units of Jackson's division overran a Union bivouac near Lawrenceburg, seizing as their most precious plunder the still smoldering Yankee campfires. Taking the lead on the following day, Ross's brigade pursued the enemy about twelve miles eastward toward Pulaski, where the men of the Third Texas captured the food and forage left behind by the Union rear guard as it withdrew.

By this time General Schofield had abandoned his position at Pulaski and was pushing his troops up the road toward Columbia and the Duck River. Hard on his heels, the Ross brigade intercepted Schofield's flank guard at the village of Campbellsville on November 24. While the troopers of the Third Texas attacked the enemy column on foot, Ross's other regiments bore down upon its flanks in a mounted charge. Withdrawing from the field late in the afternoon, the Yankee commander left eighty-four prisoners in the hands of the jubilant Texans, as well as a far more welcome catch of overcoats, blankets, and beef on the hoof. Ross lost five men wounded in this encounter.[18]

Meanwhile, Forrest and the other Confederate cavalry units were racing General Schofield's troops to the Duck River crossing at Columbia. The men of the North narrowly won the contest. When Hood arrived before the town with his infantry on November 27, he found it fortified and occupied by its bluecoat defenders. Rather than mount a frontal assault against the Union breastworks, Hood decided to bypass Columbia on the east, cross the river above the town, and cut off Schofield's retreat at Spring Hill, eleven miles farther up the turnpike to Nashville. Accordingly, he dispatched his cavalry to search out suitable crossing points upriver from Columbia and drive off the Federal cavalry ahead of him.

Forrest's scouts located several fords a few miles east of town, and his horsemen dashed across Duck River to pursue Brigadier General James H. Wilson's Union cavalry to the north. As the Yankee riders withdrew, the Third Texas intercepted a Federal supply train and its cavalry escort, capturing a company of enemy soldiers in the process. On the following morning, November 29, Forrest left the Texas Brigade to trail the Yankee horsemen as they retreated northward, while he led the bulk of his troopers west toward Spring Hill in an effort to seize the village before Schofield's advance guard could arrive there.

The next two days, the most crucial of the entire Tennessee campaign, substantially determined its outcome. At dawn on November 29, Hood's infantry crossed over the Duck River a few miles above Columbia and marched cross-country toward Spring Hill. By this time General Schofield had evacuated Columbia and started north himself. Marching smartly over the macadamized turnpike, the Federal vanguard was able to secure Spring Hill before Forrest's cavalry arrived in front of the town shortly before noon. When the first corps of Hood's infantry reached the scene about 4:00 P.M., they found the advanced units of the Union army pinned to the ground by Forrest's cavalry, while the bulk of Schofield's men were still strung out along the dozen miles of turnpike that separated Columbia from Spring Hill.

During the afternoon General Jackson had ordered the Ross brigade to terminate its pursuit of Wilson's cavalry and rejoin his division at Thompson's Station, four miles north of Spring Hill. Here, where they had battled so fiercely a year and a half earlier, the Texans were ordered to intercept any Union troops or supplies pulling back toward Nashville. A squadron of the Third Cavalry swooped down upon the depot, forcing the Yankees at the station to burn a trainload of ordnance and evacuate the village. At the same time other units of the brigade ambushed a train loaded with Federal soldiers, took fifty-eight captives, and burned a railway trestle. Late in the evening Ross posted his brigade about two miles from Spring Hill to await further orders.[19]

In the interim Hood's maneuvers in the area had turned into an irredeemable fiasco. It had gone well for the Confederates at first: as night descended, most of Schofield's troops were still on the road south of Spring Hill, and the Confederate infantry had moved into position to assault these columns as they hurried up the pike. A resolute and coordinated Rebel attack might have caught the enemy on the march. But the order to attack never came. Instead, an inexplicable series of ambiguous instructions and broken communications paralyzed the Rebel command, and Hood failed to exercise the leadership and initiative that the occasion demanded. Exhausted and tormented by the pain from his old wounds, he postponed the assault on Schofield until the following morning and left the Nashville Pike virtually un-guarded throughout the night. Seizing his opportunity, Schofield pushed his troops northward past the campfires of the slum-bering Confederate army, and by midafternoon on the next day he had them safely posted behind the defenses of Franklin, an-other twelve miles up the road.[20]

As the Yankees made their hasty withdrawal through the darkness, only Jackson's cavalry division was sent to bar their way. About eleven o'clock that night Hood was alerted that his enemy was slipping from his grasp. Rather offhandedly, he asked Forrest to block the turnpike with his troopers until morning.

Forrest replied that all his men were without ammunition except Jackson's division, which had captured some during the day. But he asserted, with an uncharacteristic lack of conviction, "he would do the best he could in the emergency."[21] Under orders from Forrest, Jackson dispatched the brigades of Ross and Armstrong to attack the Federal troops and wagon trains near Thompson's Station. Thus, with fewer than seven hundred men, the Ross brigade was assigned the task of blocking Schofield's entire army as it streamed northward toward Franklin.

Given the circumstances, the Texans were capable of interposing only a temporary interruption to the Yankees' hasty retreat. About midnight, Ross dismounted the Third Cavalry and two other regiments and sent them with a blood-curdling yell against a Federal baggage train as it crept up the pike through the darkness. They captured or destroyed thirty-nine of the enemy's wagons, but were able to block the road itself for only about half an hour, until a superior force of Northern infantry charged up to drive them off. Remounting, Ross's men rode up into the hills overlooking the turnpike and watched impotently as the Yankees made their getaway to Franklin during the early morning hours. This negligible delay of Schofield's retreat was the sole result of the great Confederate opportunity at Spring Hill.[22]

Having somehow assumed that his attack on Schofield could await the dawn of November 30, Hood arose that morning to discover that his enemy had eluded him during the night. Furious with his subordinates, angry that his men were apparently "unwilling to accept battle unless under the protection of breastworks," and blaming everyone but himself for the fiasco, he now drove his exhausted troops up the pike to Franklin.[23] About 3:30 P.M. his infantry arrived before the double line of earthworks guarding the southern approaches to the town. Then Hood callously ordered a direct frontal assault against Schofield's formidable fortifications. The result was a senseless slaughter of the Confederate army. On that November evening, 6,000 Rebel soldiers were either killed or wounded. Approximately 1,750 of Hood's men, including six generals, perished in this sacrifice to the wrathful obstinacy of their commander.[24]

The Third Texas fortunately belonged to the single division of Hood's army that was spared a suicidal assault against the breastworks of Franklin. Forrest brought his cavalry up on the right flank of the Rebel army, intending to sweep through to the Nashville Pike north of the town and thereby cut off Schofield's retreat. Having pursued the retreating Federals to the banks of the Harpeth during the morning, Forrest ordered Jackson's two thousand troopers to cross the river at a ford about three miles southeast of town. Thus, while Hood's serried ranks of infantry broke against the ramparts south of Franklin, the Ross brigade was attacking four thousand Yankee troopers that General Wilson had drawn up between them and Fort Granger, the Union redoubt north of the town.

The engagement began about 3:00 P.M. when Ross sent the dismounted troopers of the Ninth Texas surging up the slope north of the river for half a mile, until they encountered the main body of Wilson's cavalry deployed in the woods above. The Texans' old adversaries, Brownlow's White Horse Regiment, then came thundering down the slope as the Ninth withdrew. Standing tall in his stirrups, Ross shouted to his men, "Boys, if you don't run, they will!" and sent the Third Texas charging into the midst of the onrushing East Tennesseans.[25]

Lieutenant Colonel Boggess led his yelling troopers into the swirling mass of Yankee riders, with sabers slashing and pistols firing at point-blank range. In hand-to-hand encounters, Lieutenant Will Caven showed conspicuous daring in the assault. Private John Pritchett, a San Augustine blacksmith in civilian life, killed a Tennessee cavalryman in single combat and made off with his horse. Sergeant Tom Cellum, of Company A, took three pistol shots to the body but still slew his assailant. Bringing up the Sixth and Twenty-seventh regiments, Ross held the slope north of the Harpeth until early in the evening. But running out of ammunition and threatened with envelopment by Wilson's superior force, Forrest withdrew his men to the south bank of the river at nightfall. He had failed to sever the road to Nashville.[26]

Having withstood Hood's rash assault against Franklin and frustrated Forrest's attempt to cut off his line of retreat, Schofield withdrew his army across the Harpeth after midnight and marched his weary soldiers into the safety of Nashville, eighteen miles to the north. He added his troops to Thomas's already powerful garrison to make a total of about sixty thousand defenders. Nashville was one of the best fortified cities in America, with the loop of the Cumberland River protecting its northern and western approaches and a double line of earthworks stretching to the east and south. So shielded and so garrisoned, this was the Union stronghold that Hood, now with fewer than thirty thousand effectives, undertook to besiege during the following fortnight.

When he arrived before Nashville on December 2, winter was already upon him; from the seventh to the thirteenth, freezing rain and sleet coated the hills around the city with a slippery glaze of ice that paralyzed both armies, as movement up or down the treacherous slopes became virtually impossible. Many of the Rebels were barefoot; all were malnourished. Hood's tenuous supply line stretched all the way back to Florence, Alabama, and Federal gunboats blocked his shipping on the Cumberland. In effect, Hood had trapped himself: he could not go forward, he could not retreat. His only recourse was to embrace the vague notion that Thomas, goaded into action by his superiors in Washington, might undertake some ill-conceived sortie against his besiegers and thereby offer the Confederates an opportunity to defeat him. But even Hood himself must have recognized this as a forlorn hope. Why else, in such straits, would he have detached from his already outnumbered army his most potent arm, Forrest's cavalry, and sent these men on an expedition to Murfreesboro, thirty-five miles to the southeast?[27]

Hood's motives for staging this side show remained murky even to the generals who executed his orders. His stated goals fluctuated from that of destroying the railroad, to defeating the Yankee garrison at Murfreesboro, to merely observing the enemy and preventing his juncture with the defenders of Nashville. The general's obscure intentions were not a matter of indifference to Forrest, since Murfreesboro was defended by a Federal force estimated at eight thousand men and guarded by a system of redoubts and bastions designed to withstand the siege of a large army. These fortifications, known as Fortress Rosecrans, enclosed two hundred acres on either side of Stone's River just northwest of the town. Fifty-seven guns glowered down from its parapets, overlooking that still-littered battlefield upon which

the North and the South had battered each other to a sanguinary draw almost exactly two years earlier. It made considerable difference to Forrest and his men whether Hood wanted
this place captured or merely observed.[28]

In any case, the Confederate cavalry chieftain set out first to
destroy the railroad. Hood generously allotted Forrest two additional divisions of infantry; with his horsemen, this gave him
about 6,500 troops in all. For four days at the beginning of December, these men attacked and demolished six of the seven
blockhouses guarding the railway bridges between Nashville and
Murfreesboro. At La Vergne, a village halfway between the two
towns, the Yankees manned a small hilltop fort as well as a
blockhouse. Ross's troopers encircled the stronghold, forced its
surrender, and captured eighty prisoners in addition to a quantity of spoils.[29]

Proceeding on to Murfreesboro, Forrest's task force surrounded both the town and Fortress Rosecrans on December 6,
and the Ross brigade was assigned to patrol a broad sector to
the south and west of the perimeter. Recognizing that a direct
assault on the earthworks of the fort would be suicidal, Forrest
contented himself for ten days with harassing Federal foraging
parties and waiting to engage the enemy when he ventured out
of his citadel to challenge the Rebel besiegers. But only once did
the Yankees oblige the Confederate commander with a major
sortie outside their walls.

On December 7, Major General Robert H. Milroy led 3,325
Union soldiers out of the fortress and around its western
perimeter on a reconnaissance in force. Just southwest of the
fortifications, Milroy encountered a line of Rebel infantry and attacked them across a cotton field. Marching his column through
the woods, the Union general surprised the Southerners, found
a gap in their line, and sent them reeling backward. The foot
soldiers had "run like turkies," leaving two precious twelve-
pounder cannons behind them in the hands of the enemy.[30]
Frantically trying to rally his men, Forrest shot his own fleeing
color bearer, grabbed the flag himself, and galloped up and
down the Rebel line shouting and swearing. He hastily called
up the cavalry brigades of Armstrong and Ross, who checked
the enemy advance with a charge. Meanwhile, another detach-

ment of Forrest's infantry had marched from the east into the very heart of Murfreesboro itself, forcing Milroy to pull his troops back into Fortress Rosecrans. The Yankee general took 197 Rebel prisoners that day at the cost of 22 of his own men killed and 186 wounded.

For the next five days, operations around Murfreesboro were frost-bound by a blizzard that left middle Tennessee covered with ice, but as the ground began to thaw, sporadic skirmishing resumed. On December 14 a Federal column escorting a wagon train encountered the vedettes of the Ross brigade just south of Murfreesboro. After skirmishing with the Yankees all day, the Texans sustained but one wound in the entire command. The next day they were not so lucky: half a dozen of their number died in the novel but hazardous venture of seizing a Federal freight train. Escorted by about 220 Union troops, a locomotive and fifteen cars were returning to Murfreesboro from a supply depot on the Tennessee River with a load of rations and uniforms for the garrison at Fortress Rosecrans. Ross's brigade ambushed the train about seven miles out of Murfreesboro just after midnight. Having ripped up the tracks ahead of and behind the cars, the Ninth Texas pinned its defenders to the ground until dawn. The brigade artillery then opened up on the Yankees, while the Third and Sixth regiments charged down upon them on horseback. Some two hundred of the enemy surrendered, and the exultant Texans plundered sixty thousand rations destined for the defenders of Murfreesboro. Bushels of sugar and coffee, slabs of bacon, and "a rich harvest of overcoats" fell into their hands; the famished Texans munched on sugar and hardtack as they loaded their mounts with their loot.[31] When the Union garrison tried to save their train, they arrived too late upon the scene to prevent it from being put to the torch by Ross's men.

Even as the Texans were celebrating this minor triumph at Murfreesboro, disaster struck Hood's outmanned and outgeneraled army before Nashville. Having delayed his onslaught for two weeks, Union General Thomas delivered a crushing blow to Hood's cold, hungry, and dispirited men on December 15. Renewing his attack the following day, Thomas achieved a total victory that sent the tattered veterans of Hood's once-proud

Army of Tennessee fleeing in a disorganized mass down the pike toward Franklin. It was the sole instance of a complete rout of a major Confederate army.

Hood had neglected to summon Forrest back to the Nashville front until it was far too late for him to affect the outcome of the battle, and his horsemen were thus absent from the Rebel line that crumbled under Thomas's assault. By the night of December 16, when Forrest at last received orders to move, the Confederate debacle was already complete. All the Rebel cavalry could do then was cover the retreat of the shattered Southern army.[32]

This task they performed very well indeed. During the next twelve days, until the last of Hood's exhausted survivors straggled across the Tennessee River, the Third Texas rendered its last significant service to the Southern cause. Hard pressed by General Wilson's nine thousand Union cavalrymen, Hood ordered Forrest to rendezvous with him on the road south of Nashville and assume command of the rear guard. Chilled by rain and sleet, Forrest's men united with Hood at Columbia on December 18. In Forrest's three divisions of cavalry there remained but three thousand men. To these he added a division of infantry cobbled together from fragments of eight brigades, or about 1,850 foot soldiers altogether. Four hundred of them were without shoes. With this motley aggregation, Forrest held the Duck River crossing for two days.

Of all the components of the rear guard, the Texas Brigade posed the most substantial obstacle to the fierce pursuit by the Yankee cavalry, and its men found themselves in the middle of three bloody engagements on the eighty-mile trek south to the Tennessee River. The first occurred on Christmas Eve. Through sleet and rain, Forrest withdrew his rear guard in front of the advancing Federal column until he reached a point about twenty-five miles south of Columbia, where the open country gave way to steep, wooded ravines cut into the hillsides by the tributaries of the Tennessee. At this place, where both the turnpike to Pulaski and the Central Alabama Railroad crossed Richland Creek, Forrest threw his cavalry and infantry across the path of the Federal vanguard.

With Ross's brigade securing the right flank of their line, the

Confederates checked the enemy for about two hours. The Rebels then withdrew to a position just forward of the creek, fighting off a determined Yankee charge during the execution of this maneuver. From its new position the Rebel artillery pounded the advancing Union troops until a column of their horsemen galloped around Forrest's flank to threaten his rear. He thereupon pulled the Texas Brigade back to the south bank of Richland Creek, posted it on a hill overlooking the stream, and ordered Ross to hold the line while the remainder of his rear guard slipped on south through Pulaski in the gathering dusk. Huddled on the icy hilltop without forage or rations, these comrades from East Texas spent their last Christmas Eve of the war.[33]

Forrest celebrated Christmas by burning two trains and all the ammunition that Hood had abandoned at Pulaski. Then his retreating army left the hard-packed turnpike and began angling towards the southwest along primitive trails, since its advance units were installing a flimsy pontoon bridge over the Tennessee River a few miles east of Florence. Clogged by discarded equipment, and rendered a sea of mud as the accumulated ice began to thaw and the intermittent rain continued, these roads were almost impassable. Forrest stationed a detachment of cavalry just south of Pulaski to impede the pursuing Federals at the covered bridge across Richland Creek. Though the Rebel horsemen fired the bridge, the Union troopers doused the flames, quickly crossed the creek, and continued to hound the Confederate rear guard until about 2:00 P.M.

About seven miles southwest of Pulaski, where the road passed through a deep ravine near the crest of a ridge, Forrest prepared an ambush for the Yankees. He posted his ragged infantry behind hastily erected barricades across the road. Armstrong's cavalry guarded his left flank, and Ross stationed his men in the woods on the right. Mounted upon his war horse, Forrest took his own post amid the bare branches of an orchard a few feet to the rear, grimly prepared to sacrifice his entire command if necessary to check Wilson's pursuit. When three regiments of Yankee cavalry rode into the trap, the Rebels waited until they were sixty paces away before opening fire. Forrest's infantry charged their front, while his cavalry poured heavy volleys of musket and artillery fire into their flanks. Shocked and confused, the enemy reeled back and halted the pursuit until about five o'clock, thus giving the Rebel rear guard an opportunity to withdraw to Sugar Creek, just north of the Alabama line, where the men bivouacked for the night.

The Yankee pursuers began their attack on the Rebel camp even before sunup on December 26, but once again Forrest had prepared a surprise for them. He posted his infantry on the bank of Sugar Creek just above the ford, while his cavalrymen were stationed immediately behind on the road. The dense early-morning fog so concealed these dispositions that the Rebels were able to stun their enemy with a furious volley even as they were in the act of crossing the creek. Ross's troopers thereupon charged the flank of the Yankee column, drove it back from the creek about a mile, and captured a dozen prisoners. Thus checked for the moment at least, the Union force allowed the Confederate rear guard to withdraw unmolested. The Rebels camped that night only sixteen miles from the Tennessee River.[34]

This was the last in the series of skirmishes by which Forrest's rear guard contained the enemy long enough for Hood to pass beyond the river and thereby preserve the remainder of his army. On the following day Forrest himself reached the Tennessee. Crossing over without incident, his men took up their pontoon bridge on December 28 and camped near Tuscumbia that night. Thus ended the most extended pursuit of a beaten army during the entirety of the Civil War.

After the disaster at Nashville it appeared highly probable that the Yankees would succeed in cutting off Hood's retreat and would kill or capture his exhausted men in the confusion of their flight. But they failed, primarily because Forrest's rear guard simply refused to slacken its determination even in the face of sustained pursuit by a superior force. General Thomas, their victorious adversary, recognized as well as anyone the unshakable resolve of Forrest's men. In explaining his failure to destroy Hood's beaten army, he admitted that while most of the Rebel force "had become a disheartened and disorganized rabble of half-armed and barefooted men, who sought every opportunity to . . . desert their cause to put an end to their sufferings," Forrest's rear guard remained "undaunted and firm, and did its work bravely to the last."[35]

CHAPTER 17

The Road Back,
January–May 1865

On the first day of 1865 the men of the Third
Texas Cavalry found themselves at Eastport, Mississippi, where
the Tennessee River forms the extreme northeastern boundary
of the state. While Hood's infantry retired to Tupelo, Forrest set
up his headquarters at nearby Corinth and ordered the regiments
of the Ross brigade to picket various points along the south bank
of the river in anticipation of continued pursuit by Thomas's
cavalry.[1] Unlike Hood's main army, shattered and demoralized
by the disastrous consequences of the Tennessee campaign, the
Third Texas was still intact as a fighting force and undaunted
in defeat. Their commander made so bold as to assert to his
superiors that the campaign had left his brigade "in no worse
condition than when it started, its morale not in the least
affected nor impaired."[2]

Ross's casualties had been light: the Texas Brigade lost only
twelve men killed and seventy wounded in the entire campaign.
Of these, two of the dead were members of the Third Cavalry:
Private Jim McClure, a young merchant from Greenville, and
Private Joe Robertson, a Henderson planter's son. Twenty-four
troopers from the regiment were wounded, including Sergeant
John Long, who was shot through both thighs. A messmate
bandaged his wounds with a tow sack, stole some honey to

bolster his spirits, and rigged up a sidesaddle so that Long could keep up with his comrades. Eight members of the regiment were captured, and one was missing.[3]

In light of the appalling rate of casualties in Hood's main army, the East Texans emerged from the debacle far better off than they had any reason to expect. Ever optimistic, even with defeat staring them in the face, at least some of them took heart that General Lee had appointed their old favorite, Joseph E. Johnston, to oppose Sherman's offensive through the Carolinas. They predicted that with Johnston in charge, their army would "soon recover all that has been lost."[4]

Because it was still relatively intact, the Ross brigade was left to guard Mississippi virtually alone. What remained of Hood's army at Tupelo, some 21,000 men, were soon drawn off to reinforce other crumbling fronts. Resigning in despair, Hood was relieved by Lieutenant General Richard Taylor, who reorganized the shattered regiments before dispatching them to the Carolinas to fend off an anticipated Yankee drive in that quarter. On New Year's Day, Forrest granted twenty-day furloughs to most of his cavalrymen to enable them to obtain supplies from home. But since the Texans lived too far away to undertake a homeward journey and return within the alloted time, they were required to remain on outpost duty in Mississippi.

Ross's men patrolled the Corinth area for almost six weeks. Then they were posted to the front opposite Vicksburg, where they were to be merged with other understrength units to form a reconstituted cavalry division under General Jackson. The weary troopers drifted southwest across Mississippi, living from hand to mouth as they bivouacked at various points along their route a few days at a time. On February 25 they set up camp in their old familiar haunts above the Big Black River. Thus condemned to spend idle weeks slogging across Mississippi's still bleak and wintry landscape, denied their long-anticipated leaves, and dogged by defeat and intensifying hardships, about 180 of Ross's men deserted. The majority of these men defiantly mounted their horses in full view of brigade headquarters and struck out for the Mississippi River and home. Neither their commander nor their comrades made any serious effort to stop them.[5]

Had they waited a few more days, they might have departed under more honorable circumstances, for on February 20, Taylor at last gave Ross permission to furlough half his remaining men. He paid off these troops, granted them sixty days of leave, and enjoined the lucky ones with passes in their pockets to go home and persuade their errant comrades to return to duty under a last general amnesty for deserters. Ross released on furlough fifteen officers and about three dozen enlisted men from the Third Cavalry, and Lieutenant Colonel Boggess was placed in charge of the entire contingent of leave-takers. Clearly delighted with the prospect of home, they left behind their less fortunate comrades under the command of Major Absolom Stone.

The trip back to Texas turned into a perilous ordeal for the furloughed men as they waded across the flooded lowlands of the Mississippi Valley. Pelted by heavy rains for days on end and challenged by Union gunboats on the major rivers they crossed, they had to swim their horses across the Mississippi behind rowboats. Some Texans were captured even as they neared their homes. By following a route along the Arkansas-Louisiana border, most of them made the trip in about three weeks. By the end of March those who had made it through were basking in the affection of the folks back home. In the meantime, Ross took a ninety-day leave himself on March 13, after appointing Dudley W. Jones, the "Boy Colonel" of the Ninth Texas Cavalry, to assume temporary command of what remained of his brigade.[6]

Those who were left behind took consolation that the Yazoo City area had become almost a second home for them. The local population still held the East Texans in high regard. They gave them a warm welcome and hosted barbecues and parties for their benefit. Some of the boys resumed long-interrupted romances with the local girls, while others, succumbing to a general impulse to marry, courted new acquaintances with that end in view. They drew encouragement from the reappointment of their hero, General Johnston, and the belated decision of the Confederate government to enlist African-American soldiers in their cause. Despite the overwhelming evidence of defeat during the spring of 1865, the remaining troopers in the regiment were by no means demoralized. Three weeks before Appomattox,

Lon Cartwright reported cheerfully that all of his comrades were "enjoying good health [and] in high spirits," and that "the news from the armies is more encouraging now than for some time."[7]

But the war was almost over. During the previous November, Sherman's advancing army had swept a corridor of destruction across Georgia; he had taken Savannah on December 21, presenting the city to Lincoln as a Christmas gift. At the beginning of February the Union commander launched a drive northward across the Carolinas, and by the third week in March he stood at Goldsboro, North Carolina, 150 miles south of Richmond. At that point Sherman paused long enough to resupply his column before it marched north to join with Grant against Lee's beleaguered and now impotent defenders of the Confederate capital. The end was but a few weeks away.

In these waning days of the war General Taylor, Confederate commander of the Department of Alabama, Mississippi, and East Louisiana, faced multiple threats to his area of responsibility. All around the periphery of his department—at Memphis, Vicksburg, Baton Rouge, and Pensacola—Federal officers prepared to carry out Grant's instructions to devastate what was left of the Deep South. In the middle of March, Union Major General Edward R. S. Canby began his campaign against Mobile, and almost simultaneously Brigadier General James H. Wilson struck south from the Tennessee River toward central Alabama. Considering Wilson's thrust to be the more dangerous, Taylor ordered Forrest to concentrate his cavalry near Selma to intercept the Union column. Forrest hastily assembled most of his scattered units for the last battle and summoned his horsemen on picket duty around Vicksburg to rendezvous with him immediately.[8]

But the 550 men left in the Ross brigade remained scattered in small patrols along the Yazoo and Big Black rivers. By this time Confederate communications were ruptured and snarled. Orders sent were not always delivered; when delivered, they were not always obeyed. Everything was coming apart at once. From his headquarters at Canton, Colonel Jones was reduced to the dreary chores of rounding up deserters, pleading with his superiors for corn, and begging Taylor to send him clothing and a consignment of shoe thread for his "barefooted and naked" men.[9] All the while he remained on the alert for a Yankee drive out of Vicksburg toward Mobile, or for any targets of opportunity that might come his way.

Though sadly diminished in numbers, his Texans could still be dangerous to isolated Union parties that blundered into their lair. Some of the more cunning were not above engaging even in an act of piracy. On the night of March 9, for example, three scouts from Jones's command succeeded in talking their way on board a Yankee supply steamer, the *Monroe*, while the vessel was moored on the river south of Vicksburg. With their comrades on the shore, they then ambushed the craft, killed its crew, and confiscated its cargo.

While Jones's scouts were engaged in this and similar escapades near Vicksburg, General Wilson sent his Yankee cavalry sweeping southward from the Tennessee River. He defeated Forrest at Selma, then climaxed his victorious drive across the Deep South by capturing Jefferson Davis in Georgia. Meanwhile, General Canby advanced against Mobile from Pensacola, and after reducing the forts that guarded it, occupied this last important Southern port on April 12.

As dramatic as these developments in the West were, however, an astonishing series of events occurring east of the Appalachians eclipsed them. Grant began his final assault against the fortifications around Petersburg on March 29 and occupied Richmond five days later. Lee retreated to the west in a vain attempt to link up with General Johnston in North Carolina. But Lee's starving soldiers were overwhelmed by Grant's relentless advance, and the Southern commander capitulated at Appomattox Court House on April 9. Thus denied all hope of effecting a consolidation with Lee, and confronted by Sherman's 90,000-man army, Johnston signed a preliminary armistice at Durham on April 18, which was followed by a definitive surrender a week later. Between these two culminant capitulations, Lincoln succumbed to the assassin's bullet on April 15, throwing all political calculations into the realm of uncertainty.[10]

Given the halting pace of wartime communications, such an onrushing train of events was impossible to follow and comprehend even by the best-informed. Some Rebel commanders in the West learned of Lee's surrender within days after it occurred; others had to wait weeks for definitive word. The news of Appomattox reached Confederate headquarters in Texas only on April 20, and meanwhile, flying rumors had fed the anxiety felt by all. The victorious exultation in the North turned to rage, and the Southern despair brightened with a brief flash of hope, as tidings of Lincoln's assassination spread westward.

"The news for the past week has been a succession of wonders," marveled an East Texas editor on April 28.[11] Predictably, many of the folks back home welcomed the murder of their archenemy as a sign of divine providence. "*God grant*, that the news in regard to Old Lincoln be true," exclaimed a genteel Cherokee County lady. "I glory in the assassination. . . . [and] believe we could be victorious yet, for I believe [our] cause *is* just."[12] Editor Loughery, of Marshall, expressed the prevailing view that "the world is happily rid of a monster that disgraced the form of humanity," but warned his readers to look out for somebody even worse to take Lincoln's place.[13]

Those still on duty with the Third Texas in Mississippi first learned of Appomattox by way of returning prisoners of war; black troops guarding Vicksburg informed them of Lincoln's death. As solid, if unpleasant, facts slowly filtered out of fantastic rumors, the East Texans were caught up in the same debate and indecision that raged for a short time throughout the South: Should they continue to resist, or surrender? Some of their officers counseled stoic acceptance of the outcome of the war; others urged their men to return to Texas, where they might hold out against the Yankees forever. A member of Colonel Jones's staff offered a more devious suggestion. He predicted an imminent war between the United States and France over the future of Mexico and proposed that the men go home, take their oath to the Union, and join their erstwhile enemies in a common crusade against the French emperor.[14] No one, in fact, knew what to do.

Lesser personages might propose quixotic alternatives to capitulation, but it was up to General Taylor to dispose of the men under his command. Informed of Johnston's surrender in North Carolina, he was convinced of the futility of further resistance.

To be sure, by withdrawing across the Mississippi he might postpone the inevitable for a few more weeks, but only at an unconscionable cost in lives. Thus, "yielding. . . . to the logic of events," Taylor arranged for a truce with General Canby at a railway siding north of Mobile on April 30.[15] He advised his troops "to remain *steadfast to their colors* and be surrendered," pointing out that "we can surrender without the least dishonor," since "we would be but following the example of those we have been taught to obey."[16]

At Citronelle, Alabama, thirty miles above Mobile, Canby and Taylor signed the final terms of surrender four days later. Considering the murderous passions unleashed by the war, it was a generous peace fully in accordance with the terms previously granted Lee and Johnston. The vanquished Southerners were not forced to endure the humiliation of arrest and internment. No Yankee guards were placed over them; they remained under the command of their own officers until released from service. The Union commander permitted them to retain their horses and side arms, while their rifles, artillery, and equipment were turned over to the United States Army. Canby also agreed to furnish transportation and provisions to enable those who surrendered to reach their homes. Taylor prepared rolls of his various units, and on May 8, Canby issued blanket paroles to the 42,293 officers and men in Taylor's department on the basis of these lists.[17]

With that final act the war ended for the men of the Third Texas Cavalry. After the attrition in dead, wounded, discharged, and captured, there were but 206 of them left in Mississippi to surrender. Since the negotiations between Canby and Taylor took place some 160 miles away from their camps along the Big Black River, the soldiers of the Third Cavalry were spared the ordeal of being disarmed and ordered about by the victorious Yankees. On the contrary, they were pleasantly surprised by the kindness and generosity of their erstwhile enemies. All that remained for them was to pass their time as agreeably as possible until they could embark for home aboard a steamboat from Vicksburg. After struggling so long and valiantly, the men seemed remarkably composed. Reconciled to their defeat and the terms of surrender, they were anxious to return to Texas as soon as possible. "All were satisfied," recalled one of Ross's cavalrymen.[18]

Instead of brooding over the lost cause and plotting continued resistance, the East Texans appeared relieved to be finished with the dirty business of war; they comported themselves like tourists on a holiday from a tedious round of unrewarding labor. Some, for example, took the day off to visit Brierfield, Jefferson Davis's model plantation on the river south of Vicksburg; others made an excursion to the nearby farm operated by Old John Robinson's Southern Circus. Noted for their hospitality, the Robinsons entertained the men, treated them to a bath and dinner, and gave them a change of clothes from their ample wardrobe.

On May 5 the Texans crossed the Union lines at the Big Black River, made their way through the ramparts of Vicksburg, and camped there at the fairgrounds overnight. Then the remnant of the old Ross brigade boarded a Union transport, the *E. H. Fairchild*, and their horses were led aboard a barge made fast to the side of the vessel. While the *Fairchild* flew Old Glory from her bow, the men impudently unfurled their own flag from the stern, until Federal gunboats made them strike it. Traveling conditions were stifling hot inside the cabin and sweltering humid on deck as the transport plowed its way down the Mississippi and up into the mouth of the Red River.

Near Alexandria, Louisiana, the troops disembarked from the *Fairchild* because her master refused to steam farther up the Red River, out of fear of the mines still drifting in the channel. Marooned deep in Louisiana, the impatient Texans commandeered a Confederate transport, the *General Hodges*, which was laden with cotton and bound downriver. Over the protestations of its captain, they rolled several hundred bales onto the riverbank and compelled him to steam up to Natchitoches and Shreveport. From these points the men of the Third Texas scattered in all directions. Many found their way into Marshall just in time to arm themselves with Springfield rifles from the Confederate arsenal that the local authorities had thrown open to the public. By the end of May most of the warriors had come home.[19]

They returned to a Texas thrown temporarily into near anarchy by the consequences of the lost war and uncertainty over the future. From Lee's capitulation in April to the Federal occupation of the state in June, there ensued two months of turmoil during which the authority of government broke down, military discipline collapsed, and normal life was disrupted by wandering bands of discharged soldiers and liberated slaves thronging the roads. At first it was still not clear whether Texas would follow her sister states into submission or continue armed resistance against the Union on her own. Some of the more defiant spirits among the Confederate officer corps, as well as substantial elements of civilian leadership, refused at first to accept the successive surrenders of Lee, Johnston, and Taylor as final. Many still entertained the notion of withdrawing into a last redoubt in the Lone Star State from which they might continue the war until they could negotiate a compromise peace. Bold words and desperate proposals went for naught, however, since the Trans-Mississippi Department's command began a process of spontaneous disintegration in the middle of May.

As the dismal news from the East gradually penetrated into Texas and filtered down through the ranks, both civilians and soldiers lost heart. On paper, Kirby Smith still commanded an army of 36,000 men, but the already intolerable desertions multiplied, isolated units around the periphery of Texas began raising the white flag, and the army melted away amid sordid scenes of wholesale desertion and disorganized pillaging. The state government lost whatever authority it had once possessed, and by May 25, Kirby Smith was a general without an army. His subordinate commanders began the process of capitulation the following day, and on June 2 the department commander himself signed the terms of surrender at Galveston. Though a few scattered units held out for as long as three more weeks, there was no organized opposition when Union occupation forces began to arrive in Texas. On June 17 a regiment of Yankee infantry marched into Marshall. Two days later Major General Gordon Granger steamed into Galveston to take formal possession of the state and issue his proclamation abolishing slavery. A detachment of Illinois cavalry trooped into Tyler shortly thereafter.[20]

CHAPTER 18

East Texas Veterans

The war was over, the South had lost, and East Texans found themselves under military occupation by an enemy they had come to despise. Almost 630,000 soldiers from both sides had died in the struggle, vast reaches of the Confederacy were in a state of utter devastation, and the South's chief capital asset—property in slaves—had been wiped out with the stroke of a pen. Many white Southerners feared that the emancipation of their African-American bondsmen would unleash social and political turmoil, with the freedmen asserting primacy over their former masters under the benign auspices of Federal troops.

In the iconography of the South there is no more pervasive stereotype than the scene of the defeated Rebel soldier's homecoming: a pathetic figure, ragged and exhausted, returning to a ruined farmstead to take up the hard task of rebuilding after a shattering defeat. Though recent scholarship has revised dramatically many preconceptions about the character of the war and its aftermath, it has largely confirmed this traditional portrait of the despondent Confederate veteran, his life blighted, his ideals and values thrown into question, and his self-esteem subverted by the consequences of the war. A recent writer summed up the situation in a sentence: "For fifteen years after defeat in war, gloom and despair dominated the South."[1]

Perhaps that is an accurate representation of the mood of the Old Confederacy as a whole, but if the returning veterans of the Third Texas Cavalry shared in such paroxysms of "gloom and despair," their extant letters from the immediate postwar period do not reflect it. On the contrary, these missives are cast in an optimistic, even jaunty tone. Melancholy reflections over shattered hopes, destroyed lives, and the humiliation of defeat are notably absent. Instead, they are replete with good-humored accounts of future prospects, business plans, and romantic attachments.

After opening a law practice at Goliad, former Captain Preston Word confided to an old comrade: "I have been doing very well. . . . My prospects are bright, for I am certain that I will have a large practice. This is indeed a lovely country, and I am delighted with my situation."[2] Other veterans eagerly discussed their plans to raise a bumper cotton crop with free labor. Former Private John Armstrong plunged into the life of a traveling salesman and boasted: "I have been in Ky., Mo., Tenn., Ark., & Miss., so you see [that] I still go it. I am in [a] good business & [if I] can have such luck for two years that I had this week, I'll be willing to get married."[3]

Indeed, the immediate postwar correspondence between old messmates dwelt overwhelmingly on the prospects for connubial bliss, hardly a topic suggestive of gloom and despair. At least not former private Ben Long, who wrote his cousin that since his recent marriage, "I do not think I ever will be unhappy again. I think I have the best wife of any person in this world."[4] This preoccupation with matrimony was not merely idle talk, for many of the veterans of the Third Cavalry no sooner had returned to their homes than they trooped to the altar as quickly as possible. Within two years of the surrender, for instance, sixteen former members of the regiment found brides in Harrison County, while nineteen of their old comrades married girls in Cherokee County.[5]

One also looks in vain among these letters for expressions of cynical contempt toward earlier idealized notions of military heroism that they had brought to the war. On the contrary, the veterans of the Third Texas appeared to be as infatuated with models of courage and gallantry at the end of the conflict as they were at the beginning. When, in the aftermath of the struggle, former captain Tom Hogg penned his epic poem about the Civil War, his heroic couplets rang with sentiments as romantic as any antebellum effusion. In his *Fate of Marvin*, he could still give voice to a sanitized version of noble combat between two equally admirable antagonists:

> Two nobler, manlier forms than they
> Were not in all the Blue and Gray.[6]

Far from expressing humiliation in the aftermath of their defeat, veterans of the Third Texas projected a brazen defiance toward Federal rule, which reflected their assumption that they could perpetuate their old way of life despite a lost war and the emancipation of their slaves. "I am as strong a *rebel* as ever & expect to be forever," declared former sergeant John Long. "I don't keep back such as this, because it's nothing more or less than I would tell the Yankees. . . . [They] have behaved very well in passing through our country," he added, "or they would have been picked off at every cluster of bushes. The negroes have been giving some trouble, but by hanging & shooting one every once and a while, they have become more *docile*."[7] On the first anniversary of Lincoln's assassination Long's old messmate Eugene Williams offered a toast to John Wilkes Booth:

> Here is to the man that pulled the *Trigger*
> That killed the man that freed the *Nigger*.[8]

Why do these former soldiers of the Third Cavalry appear immune from the despondency and disillusionment that marked returning Confederate veterans as a group? Perhaps the chance survival of a few letters from the postwar period is biased in favor of the confident and successful. As Texans, they returned to a homeland unravaged by the conflict and still regarded as a land of opportunity for the energetic and enterprising. The most plausible reason for their apparently high spirits, however, is that they were not so severely traumatized by the war as were most of their Confederate comrades. Their combat experience was far less devastating than that endured by many others.

The record has shown them to be courageous and aggressive, but fortuitous circumstances shielded them from the holocaust visited upon many Rebel units during the course of the war. The Third Texas Cavalry participated in seventy-two separate engagements (or about one every three weeks), but more than a third of those were mere skirmishes. They missed the most horrific effusions of blood in the western theater at Shiloh, Chickamauga, and Stone's River. Through mere chance, they were spared the worst of the major battles in which they participated, at Pea Ridge, Corinth, and Franklin.

As a general rule, it was far less hazardous to serve in the cavalry than in the infantry: on average, battle casualties sustained by cavalry units were only about half those of the infantry. Forty-four percent of the battle deaths suffered by the Third Texas during the war were inflicted in the four and one-half months of 1862, when the unit was operating as infantry in Mississippi. One reason for these lower casualty rates was that horsemen played a relatively minor role in the conflict. In the Union army infantry regiments outnumbered cavalry regiments eight to one; Confederate recruiters raised about five infantry regiments for each one of cavalry.[9]

Despite the fame of such bold cavaliers as Forrest, Wheeler, and Van Dorn, Rebel commanders as well as their Yankee counterparts failed to exploit effectively the potential of armed horsemen. The broken and wooded terrain of the South and the lethal rifled musket inhibited resort to the classic cavalry charge, and only rarely were horsemen combined with artillery and infantry to deliver a shocking blow at the decisive point of battle. The charge of the Third Texas at Wilson's Creek, for instance, was a small-scale, impromptu affair and probably deserved the Yankee officer's derisory label as "ineffectual."[10] Neither did the various commanders in the West make effective use of their cavalry in their classic role as pursuers of a beaten foe.

Cavalrymen primarily functioned as mounted infantry. As far as Jefferson Davis was concerned, "horses are . . . no more than transportation to Riflemen."[11] Because of their superior mobility, cavalry could be thrown into the line more quickly than plodding foot soldiers, and sometimes this paid off handsomely, as in Forrest's flanking attack at Thompson's Station. Yet the advantage of mobility was frequently offset by the liabilities inherent in going to war on horseback. The necessity of using horse holders automatically reduced the number of fighting men in every company by 20 percent, the shortage of forage for their mounts stultified the best-laid plans of the generals, and horses were heir to as many ills as the men who rode them. At the beginning of the Atlanta campaign, for example, one-quarter of the men on the rolls of Companies E, H, and I of the Third Cavalry were absent from duty because they lacked serviceable mounts.[12]

The Confederate command employed horsemen extensively in only four ancillary roles, with varying degrees of success. Their most notable exploits were achieved in cavalry raids against Federal supply points and railroads. Occasionally these forays bore spectacular fruit, as in Van Dorn's Holly Springs raid. Usually, however, the damage inflicted on Union forces was limited and temporary: the results were more psychological than material. The raids, moreover, frequently dispersed scarce human resources that were needed elsewhere; thus they cost more than they yielded in benefits. The Confederacy also used its cavalry for picketing, foraging, and surveillance. As foragers, the horsemen earned a reputation as thieves; when gathering intelligence, they were not always up to the mark. It was a case in point that Ross's brigade missed catching the signals for Sherman's final onslaught against Atlanta before it was too late.[13]

The Civil War exacted but a moderate toll of killed and wounded among the Third Texas as a consequence of their good fortune in being absent from the most sanguinary of the battles in the West, the ineptitude of their commanders in employing them in other engagements, and the particular advantages inherent in cavalry service. A total of 1,340 officers and men enrolled in the regiment at one time or another in the course of the conflict. Ninety soldiers, or 7 percent, were killed in action. That battlefield mortality rate was less than half the proportion of battle deaths suffered by the infantrymen in Hood's Texas Brigade, the most famous of all the units from the state. At Iuka, the worst day in the war for the Third Texas, ninety-six of its men were either killed or wounded, a casualty rate of 25 percent. By contrast, the First Texas Infantry, Hood's brigade, lost 82 percent of its effectives in killed and wounded at the battle of Antietam two days before.[14]

The Third Texas counted 221 of its members wounded at least once: at 16 percent, that constituted a normal rate if measured against casualties in the Union army, but it was only half the casualty rate suffered by Hood's Texans. In the Third Texas, 193 members, or 14 percent of the regiment, were captured at least once, compared to 12 percent in Hood's Brigade. Only 117 soldiers, or 9 percent, of the Third Cavalry died from disease, almost half of them in and around pestiferous Corinth. That represented a low rate for any Civil War regiment. The rolls listed ninety-three troopers who deserted the unit. This desertion rate of 7 percent was well within the norm. The high level of absenteeism prevailing in the Third Texas Cavalry—46 percent of the men on the rolls were absent at the beginning of the Atlanta campaign, for instance—was no greater than that for the Confederate army as a whole.

By far the single greatest loss of manpower occurred in conjunction with the wholesale discharges granted to hundreds of men late in 1861 and during the process of reorganization the following spring, when about one-third of the regiment were formally released from service. In summary, the East Texans performed duties fraught with normal hazards for Civil War soldiers, but were healthier and more determined than most. Ranging deep into enemy territory, often stationed on isolated picket duty, they were captured with greater than normal frequency. In any case, the vast majority of the men—eight out of ten—survived the war.[15]

Most of the hallmarks of the way of life they had fought to preserve survived as well. Despite four years of war, the collapse of their Confederate nation, and a decade of Reconstruction politics, Southern conservatives eventually restored most of the distinguishing features of antebellum society except chattel slavery. Political power rapidly reverted to the same class that had exercised it before the war. White southerners gradually disenfranchised the emancipated African Americans and enforced a

Table 5. Casualties and Losses in the Third Texas Cavalry Regiment, 1861–1865

CO.	NO. ON ORIGINAL ROLL	NO. WHO JOINED LATER	TOTAL NO. EN-ROLLED	KILLED IN BATTLE[a]		WOUNDED[b]		CAPTURE	
				NO.	%	NO.	%	NO.	%
A	104	35	139	7	5	30	21	9	
B	112	31	143	14	10	22	15	16	1
C	114	21	135	13	10	23	17	11	
D	115	9	124	6	5	11	9	14	1
E	114	37	151	8	5	18	12	20	1
F	104	19	123	4	3	21	17	19	1
G	107	29	136	9	7	19	14	27	2
H	96	27	123	6	5	14	11	26	2
I	115	11	126	7	5	21	17	28	2
K[i]	110	23	133	16	12	41	31	22	1
Cmd.[j]	6	1	7	0	0	1	14	1	1
Total	1,097	243	1,340	90	7%	221	16%	193	1

[a] Includes those men killed or mortally wounded in action.
[b] Includes those wounded other than mortally at least once.
[c] Includes those captured and imprisoned, captured and paroled, and missing in action.
[d] Includes death from disease, accident, or homicide.
[e] Includes men discharged, transferred to other regiments, and dropped from roll prior to surrend
[f] Includes all listed as deserted, including those who rejoined the unit under amnesty, prior July 1, 1864.
[g] The final extent rolls for the regiment were dated June 30, 1864.

system of white supremacy and racial segregation that would endure for almost a century.[16]

Neither did a revolution occur in the economic life of the South. Despite railroads, textile mills, and urban development, the region remained predominantly agrarian in character. As late as 1900 almost two-thirds of all Texans still made their living by farming. Moreover, the old elite families, or their allies, continued to control a substantial proportion of the region's wealth. After the demise of slavery, landowners evolved the tenant farming system whereby black labor was tied to the soil, supervised, and controlled. As a result a growing proportion of the farmers, both white and black, descended to the status of sharecroppers. In 1900, seven out of ten African-American farm operators in Texas were tenants who cultivated land that was not their own. In spite of the abolition of slavery, neither the

DIED[d]		DISCHARGED[e]		DESERTED[f]		NO. ON ROLL[g] JUNE 1864	PRESENT, JUNE 1864[h]		SURRENDERED, MAY 4, 1865
NO.	%	NO.	%	NO.	%		NO.	%	
17	12	48	35	1	0.7	69	29	42	13
11	7	53	37	3	2.0	66	49	74	27
17	12	45	33	9	6.6	55	31	56	32
8	6	49	39	27	21.7	38	22	58	8
9	6	56	37	1	0.6	74	32	43	35
8	6	50	41	13	10.5	50	26	52	25
8	6	43	32	10	7.3	68	45	66	15
11	9	45	37	1	0.8	53	26	49	26
15	12	45	36	19	15.0	47	16	34	8
11	8	35	26	9	6.7	76	47	62	17
2	28	3	43	0	0.0	0	0	0	0
117	9%	472	35%	93	6.9%	596	323	54%	206

[h]The percent present represents the ratio of those present on duty with the regiment to the total number on the final roll.
[i]Companies were not normally designated as "J" because of its resemblance to the designation "I" in manuscript records.
[j]By May 1862 all the original regimental command had been replaced through resignation and promotion from within the regiment.
Source: U.S. National Archives, Compiled Service Records of Confederate Soldiers Who Served in Organizations from the State of Texas (Washington, D.C., 1960), M No. 323, Rolls 18–23.

war nor the era of Reconstruction engendered a fundamental economic transformation.[17]

There is also little evidence that defeat in war altered substantially the values and attitudes of the wartime generation. After about a decade and a half, while the mists of nostalgia enshrouded and softened the harsh realities of the conflict, former Confederate soldiers evolved a version of their wartime experience that rationalized their part in the orgy of fratricidal bloodletting. The first element in their unconscious strategy of denial was to conclude that they had not fought the war either to protect slavery or to dissolve the Union. On the contrary, the veterans generally told themselves that the purpose of their struggle had been to preserve the constitutional authority of the separate states to order their internal affairs, to enforce the benign tutelage of the white race over ignorant and improvident blacks, and to vindicate their honor. The old soldiers reassured themselves that they had not fought and bled in vain; their cause had won in the end. They tirelessly reiterated those three themes that emphasized victory in defeat—states' rights, white supremacy, and the preservation of Southern honor against overwhelming odds—to justify their war as compatible with the prevailing values of late nineteenth-century America.[18]

Actuated by those sentiments, many veterans of the Third Texas Cavalry counted themselves among the "Redeemers": those state and local leaders who resisted the Reconstruction policies of the federal government in an attempt to restore East Texas to its political and social condition in antebellum days. Some played a prominent role in the terrorism perpetrated upon African Americans who tried to exercise their newly won rights as citizens. Former corporal Iredell Thomas organized the Ku Klux Klan in San Augustine County; former sergeant John Long and four of his regimental comrades provided a similar service for Cherokee County. Long's grateful neighbors later elected him to Congress. At Tyler former private George Kennedy started a riot by attacking a black woman in the street. When arrested by a federal agent, Kennedy shot three soldiers and escaped. Tylerites made him their city marshal.[19] Walter P. Lane helped keep the peace in Marshall by warning black leaders, "This is white man's country, and must remain so. If it is your intention to raise a race riot, I am afraid there will not be a blessed negro left in Harrison County."[20]

Other veterans of the Third Texas provided more conventional leadership. In an age when a distinguished war record provided a path for political ambition, their old commander General Ross became governor. The voters sent George Chilton to the United States Congress. William S. Coleman, William W. Davis, Daniel M. Short, and Thomas J. Towles served in the state legislature. The people of their respective districts chose Mathew D. Ector and Hinche P. Mabry for the post of district judge, where the two men consistently obstructed the functions of the courts under Reconstruction. W. W. Dillard, Jonathan Russell, and Israel Spikes helped frame the new constitution of 1876 that enshrined states' rights, white supremacy, and conservative Democratic dominance in the Lone Star State. Former lieutenant Oliver N. Hollingsworth became state superintendent of public instruction.[21]

At the level of county politics, a host of former cavalrymen were much in evidence. James Dillard and David Gaines were elected to judgeships; A. W. Brown, H. A. Lewis, J. Wylie Montgomery, William Moon, John B. Reagan, and James P. Williams all applied their military experience to the office of sheriff; former captain Sid Johnson served as county attorney. Sam Barron became a perennial county clerk. William Anderson, John Arrington, John Covey, and James Fambrough were elected to the post of county assessor and collector of taxes. Of the thirty survivors on the original roll of Company K who are known to have settled in Smith County after the war, one-third were elected to county office at one time or another.[22]

As the years passed, the roster rapidly diminished, and the old soldiers came to regard their service in the war—their memories of youth—ever more as an object of pride and satisfaction. Typifying this spirit, former Sergeant Victor Rose asserted that he was "prouder of his course, during those four years [of war], than of any other period of his life." He went on to predict that the descendants of his fellow soldiers "will piously treasure the record of their services as an invaluable souvenir, and transmit it as an heir-loom to their remotest posterity."[23]

The old campaigner was at least partially right. The story of their service is indeed a valuable legacy to posterity; today's generation can only admire the exemplary record of courage, devotion to duty, and endurance demonstrated by the men of the Third Texas. They were loyal to their country, as they conceived it, to their way of life, and to their comrades. But in our admiration we should also note that their stalwart virtues were expended in the service of the pervasive racism of their age, in a cause unworthy of the sacrifices they made. We are again confronted by one of the most prevalent ironies of history: noble deeds performed in the pursuit of ignoble ends.

The young East Texans went to war in response to the rallying cry of a minority of extreme secessionists who confused their own interests with the public good. Whatever political principles or constitutional issues were invoked, these men believed at the time that they were fighting to preserve the presumed prerogative of white people to exploit the labor of African Americans. Their enthusiasm at the inception of the conflict was not merely a consequence of their youthful naïveté or their romantic assumptions regarding manliness. It was also an accurate reflection of the irrational intoxication with narrow provincial values that prevailed in Southern society.

To their credit, most of the young soldiers of the Third Cavalry remained faithful to their professed ideals even in the face of enormous suffering and privation. They discovered during the course of the war, however, that what diminished their numbers and abased their spirit was not the toll of battle but rather the inexorable attrition of disease, discouragement, and drudgery. For these men the war did not end with a rousing crescendo of violence but rather in the gradual disintegration of their capacity to fight; in the spring of 1865 they accepted defeat with resignation rather than defiance.

When they returned to their homes, they discovered that the abolition of slavery had not permanently altered their social order or their systems of authority. Many of the veterans of the regiment played prominent roles in the restoration of social attitudes and norms of behavior that had prevailed before the war. For the men of the Third Cavalry, then, the Civil War and Reconstruction did not entail a revolution in the life of their region. The war and its aftermath constituted merely a violent interlude in the fundamental continuity of their society, in a way of life whose salient characteristics were subsumed in a relationship between the races that would persist for a century after the conflict.

Notes

Abbreviations of Frequently Cited Works

AIW   Douglas J. Cater. *As It Was: Reminiscences of a Soldier of the Third Texas Cavalry and the Nineteenth Louisiana Infantry*. Austin, 1990.

AR   Walter P. Lane. *The Adventures and Recollections of General Walter P. Lane*. Marshall, Tex., 1928.

BLCW   Robert U. Johnson and Clarence C. Buel, eds. *Battles and Leaders of the Civil War*. 4 vols. 1884–1888. Reprint, Secaucus, N.J., 1983.

CBB   Washington L. Gammage. *The Camp, the Bivouac, and the Battlefield*. Selma, Ala., 1864.

CC   Cartwright Correspondence.

CCH   *Cherokee County History*.

CO   *The Chronicles of Oklahoma*.

CPA   Confederate Pension Applications.

CSC   *Chronicles of Smith County, Texas*.

CSR   U.S. National Archives and Record Service. *Compiled Service Records of Confederate Soldiers Who Served in Organizations from the State of Texas*. Washington, D.C., 1960. Microcopy No. 323, Rolls 18–23.

CV   *Confederate Veteran*.

CWH   *Civil War History*.

CWTI   *Civil War Times Illustrated*.

DAH   Demetria Ann Hill Collection.

ETHJ   *East Texas Historical Journal*.

JBL   John Benjamin Long Papers.

JSH   *Journal of Southern History.*

LSD   Samuel B. Barron. *The Lone Star Defenders: A Chronicle of the Third Texas Cavalry, Ross' Brigade.* 1908. Reprint, Washington, D.C., 1983.

MHTS   *Military History of Texas and the Southwest.*

OR   U.S. War Department. *The War of the Rebellion: A Compilation of the Official Records of the Union and Confederate Armies.* 128 vols. Washington, D.C., 1880–1901.

RTB   Victor M. Rose. *Ross' Texas Brigade.* 1881. Reprint, Kennesaw, Ga., 1960.

SHQ   *Southwestern Historical Quarterly.*

TWWG   Sidney S. Johnson. *Texans Who Wore the Gray.* Tyler, Tex., 1907.

Chapter 1. Texas Leaves the Union, 1860–1861

1. A. B. Blocker, "The Boy Bugler of the Third Texas Cavalry," ed. by Max S. Lale, *Military History of Texas and the Southwest* (hereafter cited as *MHTS*) 14, no. 2 (1978): 82–83.

2. Samuel B. Barron, *The Lone Star Defenders* (hereafter cited as *LSD*), 46.

3. Ibid., 253.

4. Marcus J. Wright, comp., *Texas in the War, 1861–1865,* ed. by Harold B. Simpson, 18–35; George H. Estes, Jr., *List of Field Officers, Regiments, and Battalions in the Confederate States Army, 1861–1865,* 60–65; E. B. Long, *The Civil War Day by Day,* 716–718; Grady McWhiney, "Who Whipped Whom? Confederate Defeat Reexamined," in John T. Hubbell, ed., *Battles Lost and Won,* 269–270; Paddy Griffith, *Battle Tactics of the Civil War,* 179–182; Fred A. Bailey, *Class and Tennessee's Confederate Generation,* 78–79, 159.

5. Ben to Eliza Long, Breckinridge, Tex., July 10, 1861, John Benjamin Long Papers (hereafter cited as JBL).

6. Lon to Matthew Cartwright, Dallas, July 6, 1861, Cartwright Correspondence (hereafter cited as CC).

7. Douglas J. Cater, *As It Was: Reminiscences of a Soldier of the Third Texas Cavalry and the Nineteenth Louisiana Infantry* (hereafter cited as *AIW*), 73.

8. Victor M. Rose, *Some Historical Facts,* 43. See also Ralph A. and Robert Wooster, "'Rarin' for a Fight'," *Southwestern Historical Quarterly* (hereafter cited as *SHQ*) 84 (Apr., 1981): 387–388; Bell I. Wiley, *The Life of Johnny Reb,* 15.

9. Barron, *LSD,* 19.

10. Quoted in Walter L. Buenger, Jr., *Secession and the Union in Texas,* 8. The following interpretation has been adapted from this work, 55–58, 122–127, 141–151, as well as from Buenger's "Secession Revisited: The Texas Experience," *Civil War History* (hereafter cited as *CWH*) 30 (Dec., 1984): 293–305, and "Texas and the Riddle of Secession," *SHQ* 87 (Oct., 1983): 151–182. See also Robin E. Baker and Dale Baum, "The Texas Voter and the

Crisis of the Union, 1859–1861," *Journal of Southern History* (hereafter cited as *JSH*) 53 (Aug., 1987): 395–420.

11. U.S. Bureau of the Census, Eighth Census, *Population, 1860*, 483–486; Otto H. Olsen, "Historians and the Extent of Slave Ownership in the Southern United States," *CWH* 18 (June, 1972): 111–112; Richard G. Lowe and Randolph B. Campbell, "Wealthholding and Political Power in Antebellum Texas," *SHQ* 79 (July, 1975): 21–30.

12. C. A. Frazier, quoted in Randolph B. Campbell, *A Southern Community in Crisis*, 144.

13. Quoted in Gay W. Allen, *Waldo Emerson*, 591. See also James M. McPherson, *Battle Cry of Freedom*, 202–213.

14. Quoted in Allan C. Ashcraft, "East Texas in the Election of 1860 and the Secession Crisis," *East Texas Historical Journal* (hereafter cited as *ETHJ*) 1 (July, 1963): 9.

15. Roy S. Dunn, "The KGC in Texas, 1860–1861," *SHQ* 70 (Apr., 1967): 543–573; Ollinger Crenshaw, "The Knights of the Golden Circle," *American Historical Review* 47 (Oct., 1941): 47–50; C. A. Bridges, "The Knights of the Golden Circle: A Filibustering Fantasy," *SHQ* 44 (Jan., 1941): 287–302; Anna I. Sandbo, "The First Session of the Secession Convention of Texas," *SHQ* 18 (Oct., 1914): 173–175; J. J. Bowden, *The Exodus of Federal Forces from Texas, 1861*, 33, 49, 83, 104; McPherson, *Battle Cry*, 103–116; Frank L. Klement, *Dark Lanterns*, 7–33.

16. A. W. Sparks, *The War Between the States as I Saw It*, 9–10; Dorman H. Winfrey, *A History of Rusk County, Texas*, 38–41; William W. White, "The Texas Slave Insurrection in 1860," *SHQ* 52 (Jan., 1949): 259–285; Wendell G. Addington, "Slave Insurrections in Texas," *Journal of Negro History* 35 (Oct., 1950): 408–434; Donald E. Reynolds, *Editors Make War*, 97–117, and Donald E. Reynolds, "Smith County and Its Neighbors During the Slave Insurrection Panic of 1860," *Chronicles of Smith County, Texas* (hereafter cited as *CSC*) 10 (Fall, 1971): 1–2, 6–7.

17. Quoted in Ashcraft, "East Texas in the Election of 1860," 9. See also Max S. Lale, "Robert W. Loughery: Rebel Editor," *ETHJ* 21, no. 2 (1983): 3–15.

18. Sparks, *War Between the States*, 10.

19. Addington, "Slave Insurrections," 421–423, 426–427; Winfrey, *Rusk County*, 40–41; Wesley Norton, "The Methodist Episcopal Church and the Civil Disturbances in North Texas in 1859 and 1860," *SHQ* 68 (Jan., 1965): 333–335; Margaret W. Brown, *Pine Grove Cumberland Presbyterian Church*, 4.

20. Quoted in Reynolds, "Smith County and Its Neighbors," 37.

21. U.S. Bureau of the Census, *Historical Statistics of the United States* 2: 1074, 1080; Ashcraft, "East Texas and the Election of 1860," 10; Joe T. Timmons, "The Referendum in Texas on the Ordinance of Secession," *ETHJ* 11 (Fall, 1973): 20.

22. Stephen B. Oates, *Visions of Glory*, 84–85; McPherson, *Battle Cry*, 234–246; Ashcraft, "East Texas in the Election of 1860," 11; Campbell, *Southern Community in Crisis*, 183–184.

23. Quoted in Dunn, "KGC in Texas," 559.

24. *Express* (Navarro, Texas), n.d., quoted in Rupert N. Richardson et al., *Texas*, 184.

25. *Texas State Gazette* (Austin), Dec. 1, 1860, quoted in Larry J. Gage, "The Texas Road to Secession and War," *SHQ* 62 (Oct., 1953): 202.

26. *Texas State Gazette* (Austin), Nov. 24, 1860, ibid.

27. Quoted in Richardson, *Texas*, 184.

28. Timmons, "Referendum in Texas," 28; Walter P. Webb, H. Bailey Carroll, and Eldon S. Branda, eds., *Handbook of Texas* 2: 587–588; Ralph A. Wooster, *The Secession Conventions of the South*, 121–135, and Ralph A. Wooster, "An Analysis of the Membership of the Texas Secession Convention," *SHQ* 62 (Jan., 1959): 322–335.

29. Ernest W. Winkler, ed., *Journal of the Secession Convention of Texas, 1861*, 64; *Texas Almanac for 1862*, 19–20.

30. *Texas Republican* (Marshall), Feb. 23, 1861, quoted in Ashcraft, "East Texas in the Election of 1860," 12.

31. *Standard* (Clarksville, Tex.), Feb. 9, 1861, quoted in Timmons, "Referendum in Texas," 27.

32. Richardson, *Texas*, 186; Buenger, *Secession and the Union in Texas*, 163–167, 174–177.

Chapter 2. Texas Goes to War, February–May 1861

1. *Texas State Gazette* (Austin), Feb. 23, 1861, quoted in Gage, "Texas Road to Secession," 209.

2. Wheeler to Roberts, n.p., Mar. 26, 1861, quoted in Timmons, "Referendum in Texas," 28.

3. *Texas Republican* (Marshall), Mar. 2, 1861, quoted in Ashcraft, "East Texas in the Election of 1860," 12.

4. Herman Hattaway and Archer Jones, *How the North Won*, 17–18; Long, *Civil War Day by Day*, 700–704, 723–726.

5. Buenger, *Secession and the Union in Texas*, 153–155; *Handbook of Texas* 1:617–618, 2:106–107; Richard Warren, "Ben McCulloch," and Morris L. Moore, "John Salmon 'Rip' Ford," in W. C. Nunn, ed., *Ten More Texans in Gray*, 1–6, 71–73; Oates, *Visions of Glory*, 91–94; Bowden, *The Exodus of Federal Forces from Texas*, 49–63; Wright, *Texas in the War*, 189–196.

6. Kenneth M. Stampp, *And the War Came*, 147–153; McPherson, *Battle Cry*, 246–264; Llerena Friend, *Sam Houston*, 338–353.

7. Ralph J. Smith, as quoted in Wooster and Wooster, "'Rarin' for a Fight'," 388.

8. U.S. War Department, *The War of the Rebellion: A Compilation of the Official Records of the Union and Confederate Armies* (hereafter cited as *OR*), Ser. 1, Vol. 1: 290–291, 623, 630–631; William R. Geise, "Texas—The First Year of the War," *MHTS* 13, no. 4 (1976): 30–34, 37–38; Oates, "Recruiting Confederate Cavalry," 465–469; Wooster and Wooster, "'Rarin' for a Fight'," 387–392; McPherson, *Battle Cry*, 273–297.

9. *Standard* (Clarksville, Tex.), May 18, 1861, quoted in Timmons, "Referendum in Texas," 28.

10. Clark to Bryan, n.p., Apr. 30, 1861, ibid.

11. Fannie Rhodes Brown Diary, entry for May 7, 1861; *Marshall News-Messenger*, July 23, 1961; *OR*, Ser. 1, Vol. 53: 678–679.

12. Angie Debo, *A History of the Indians of the United States*, 101–117, 136–140; Annie H. Abel, *The American Indian as Slaveholder and Secessionist*, 207–227; William R. Geise, "The Confederate Northwest," *MHTS* 13, no. 1 (1976): 13–16.

13. Quoted in *Marshall News-Messenger*, July 23, 1961. See also *OR*, Ser. 1, Vol. 3: 575–576, 587–588, 590–591.

14. Greer to Eugenia Holcombe, Holly Springs, Miss., Oct. 1, 1850, Greer Papers. See also Mrs. Charles A. Beehn to Mrs. Frank M. Armstrong, Marshall, Aug. 28, 1961, Greer File.

15. Ezra J. Warner, *Generals in Gray*, 118; Bridges, "Knights of the Golden Circle," 294; Crenshaw, "Knights of the Golden Circle," 38; Campbell, *Southern Community in Crisis*, 173; Sid S. Johnson, *Texans Who Wore the Gray* (hereafter cited as *TWWG*), 129–130; Jack T. Greer, *Leaves from a Family Album*, 33–37, 45–50.

16. Greer to Theodore Holcombe, Marshall, Feb. 8, 1860, Greer Papers.

17. Greer to the K.G.C., New Orleans, Jan. 26, 1860, Greer Records.

18. Cater, *AIW*, 76.

19. See Table 1. The amount of property and number of slaves held by the regimental staff and company commanders were derived from U.S. National Archives, *Population Schedules of the Eighth Census of the United States, 1860*, M 653, Rolls 1287–1308 (hereafter cited as *Population Schedules*). According to Lowe and Campbell, "Wealthholding and Political Power in Antebellum Texas," 27, the mean wealth of all white Texas households in 1860 was $6,393. For purposes of comparison, the average wealth of forty original company commanders in Parson's Texas Cavalry Brigade was $9,790. See Anne J. Bailey, *Between the Enemy and Texas*, 211–234. (I have used the terms "average" and "mean" synonymously throughout the book.)

20. The original muster rolls for the ten companies comprising the Third Texas Cavalry Regiment are found in Record Group 109, Military Records Division, U.S. National Archives and Records Administration. Abstracts of all extant rolls for the regiment are contained in U.S. National Archives, *Compiled Service Records of Confederate Soldiers Who Served in Organizations from the State of Texas*, M 323 (hereafter cited as *CSR*), Rolls 18–23. Additional data on the men in Companies A–E were derived from the *Dallas Herald*, June 19, 26, 1861; *Henderson Times*, Dec. 30, 1948; Barron, *LSD*, 23–24; Winfrey, *History of Rusk County*, 38, 43, 123, 152–154; Garland R. Farmer, *The Realm of Rusk County*, 49–54; John A. Templeton, ed., *Cherokee County History* (hereafter cited as *CCH*), 552–553; Ogreta W. Huttash, comp., *Civil War Records of Cherokee County, Texas* 1: 6–10; George L. Crocket, *Two Centuries in East Texas*, 335–336; *Handbook of Texas* 2: 99, 607; 3: 215.

21. Besides the muster rolls for Companies F–K, information was drawn from Civil War File, Smith County Historical Society Archives; "First 100 Men

to Serve in the Cass Co. Company," MS, John Arthur Bryan Papers; Johnson, *TWWG*, 314–318, and Sid S. Johnson, *Some Biographies of Old Settlers*, 252–253; Lucille B. Bullard, *Marion County, Texas, 1860–1870*, 2, 16–19; *History of Cass County People*, no. 836.

22. W. T. to J. B. Long, Rusk, Sept. 29, 1861, JBL.

23. Cater, *AIW*, 72–73; Barron, *LSD*, 20.

24. Blocker, "Boy Bugler," 73; Cater, *AIW*, 72; Mabel C. Keller, "History of Kaufman County," 137–139; Barron, *LSD*, 28; Margaret E. Hall, *A History of Van Zandt County*, 34; Bullard, *Marion County*, 6.

25. Barron, *LSD*, 61. See also Ben to Eliza Long, Breckinridge, Texas, July 10, 1861, JBL; *Handbook of Texas* 1: 541; Wright, *Texas in the War*, 77, 86; Frances T. Ingmire, comp., *Texas Rangers* 5: iv.

26. Barron, *LSD*, 29–30, 54, 58–59, 66; Victor M. Rose, *Ross' Texas Brigade* (hereafter cited as *RTB*), 30, 57.

27. Wooster and Wooster, "'Rarin' for a Fight'," 390; Vicki Betts, *Smith County, Texas, in the Civil War*, 35–36; Cater, *AIW*, 75–76; Blocker, "Boy Bugler," 73–75.

28. Quoted in Barron, *LSD*, 19. See also Robert C. Cotner, *James Stephen Hogg*, 3–4, 18–19.

29. Barron, *LSD*, 18.

Chapter 3. The Boys from East Texas, June 1861

1. Demographical and economic data on the soldiers of the regiment and their households came primarily from *Population Schedules*. The identification of individual soldiers in the *Population Schedules* involved four steps. (1) A master roll of the regiment was prepared from *CSR*, which listed 1,097 volunteers on the original roll and 243 recruits who enlisted later in the war. (2) 934 of the original enlistees (85 percent) and 159 of the subsequent recruits (65 percent) were located on the *Population Schedules*, and biographical data for each soldier so identified were recorded on a regimental roster. (Twenty-five percent of these men were living as tenants or employees in households not headed by a family member, while 75 percent were either heads of households or men living in a household headed by a family member.) (3) Using local biographical and genealogical references to supplement these data, they were then combined with the military data derived from the *CSR* to form ten separate company rosters, from which (4) a data base for the entire regiment was generated. Computations cited herein were derived from this data base. A preliminary version of this chapter appeared as "The Third Texas Cavalry: A Socioeconomic Profile of a Confederate Regiment," in *Military History of the Southwest* 19 (Spring, 1989): 1–26.

2. Counties of residence were identified from either *CSR* or *Population Schedules* for 963 original members of the regiment, or 88 percent.

3. For purposes of comparison, these categories of wealth within the population have been defined in conformity with those suggested by Bailey, *Class*

and *Tennessee's Confederate Generation,* 5, 20–44. See also Campbell, *Southern Community in Crisis,* 23–25, 31–44; Barnes F. Lathrop, "Migration into East Texas," *SHQ* 52 (July, 1948): 5; U.S. Bureau of the Census, Eighth Census, *Agriculture, 1860,* xciv, 144–145, 222, 241, *Manufactures, 1860,* 580–591, and *Population, 1860,* 481, 486–487, 656–680.

4. Randolph B. Campbell and Richard G. Lowe, "Some Economic Aspects of Antebellum Texas Agriculture," *SHQ* 82 (Apr., 1979): 351; Ralph A. Wooster, "Wealthy Texans, 1860," *SHQ* 71 (Oct., 1967): 163–165; Robert K. Peters III, "From Wilderness to War," in Robert W. Glover and Linda B. Cross, eds., *Tyler and Smith County, Texas,* 23–24; *Texas Almanac for 1862,* 31–34; Campbell, *Southern Community in Crisis,* 91–95; Vera L. Dugas, "A Social and Economic History of Texas" 1: 111–114, 121, 157, 193–194.

5. Frederick L. Olmsted, *A Journey Through Texas,* 117.

6. Kate Stone, *Brockenburn,* ed. by John Q. Anderson, 224.

7. Jennie Charlotte Smith Diary, entry for Jan. 15, 1868.

8. Peters, "Wilderness to War," 24; Frederick Eby, *The Development of Education in Texas,* 116–124; Cecil E. Evans, *The Story of Texas Schools,* 74.

9. William T. Chambers, *Texas: Its Land and People,* 23–24, 47–48; Terry G. Jordan, "Population Origins in Texas, 1850," *Geographical Review* 59 (Jan., 1969): 86–93; Terry G. Jordan, "The Imprint of the Upper and Lower South on Mid-Nineteenth Century Texas," *Annals of the Association of American Geographers* 57 (Sept., 1967): 672–688; Campbell, *Southern Community in Crisis,* 52, 98–99, 151–153, 190–197; Lathrop, "Migration into East Texas," 185–187; Wooster, "Wealthy Texans, 1860," 176; and "Notes on Texas' Largest Slaveholders, 1860," *SHQ* 65 (July, 1961): 72–79; Frank H. Smyrl, "Unionism in Texas, 1856–1861," *SHQ* 68 (Oct., 1964): 191–193; Cecil Harper, Jr., "Slavery Without Cotton: Hunt County, Texas, 1846–1864," *SHQ* 88 (Apr., 1985): 387–405; Lowe and Campbell, "Wealthholding and Political Power," 28–30; Randolph B. Campbell, "Planters and Plain Folk: Harrison County, Texas, as a Test Case, 1850–1860," *JSH* 40 (Aug., 1974): 389–392.

10. Wooster, "Wealthy Texans, 1860," 176, 178; Crocket, *Two Centuries,* 219–220; McXie Martin to author, San Augustine, Nov. 1, 1987; Templeton, *CCH,* 479; *Biographical Souvenir of the State of Texas,* 188, 676; *Confederate Veteran* (hereafter cited as *CV*) 4 (Sept., 1896): 296; *Handbook of Texas* 1: 304; 2: 383.

11. See Table 2. Average property values per household of which the individual soldiers were members were computed from the data incorporated in *Population Schedules,* Schedule 1.

12. The rates of promotion relative to economic status conform closely to those of the Tennessee soldiers studied by Bailey in *Class and Tennessee's Confederate Generation,* 78–79, 160.

13. Data on total property and slave property by county were taken from the *Texas Almanac for 1861,* 243–245, and the *Texas Almanac for 1862,* 31–34. The number of slaves owned by individual heads of household was derived from *Population Schedules,* Schedule 2.

14. Campbell Davis, quoted in George P. Rawick, ed., *The American Slave,* Vol. 4, Pt. 1, 286. On the reliability of the slave narratives collected in Rawick,

see C. Vann Woodward, "History from Slave Sources," *AHR* 79 (Apr., 1974): 470–481, and for a summary of conditions of servitude in East Texas, see Campbell, *Southern Community in Crisis,* 129–145.

15. Harrison Beckett, quoted in Rawick, *The American Slave,* Vol. 4, Pt. 1, 55.

16. Bert Strong and Will Adams, quoted in ibid., Vol. 4, Pt. 1, 1–3; and Vol. 5, Pt. 4, 70–72.

17. Green Cumby, quoted in ibid., Vol. 4, Pt. 1, 262.

18. Occupations were listed either on the *Population Schedules* or in *CSR* for 791 men, or 72 percent of the original regiment. Occupational categories are those defined by Bell I. Wiley. See McPherson, *Battle Cry,* 614; and Allan Nevins, *The War for the Union* 2: 130.

19. Helen to Oyer Funderburgh (Smith County, Tex.), July 2, 1861, in Emma H. Gayle, "James Calhoun Hill," *CSC* 8 (Fall, 1969): 63.

20. Larissa College File; Fred H. Ford and J. L. Brown, *Larissa,* 51–53; T. L. Baker, *Ghost Towns of Texas,* 81–82; Rose, *RTB,* 16; Blocker, "Boy Bugler," 87–88; *Marshall News-Messenger,* July 23, 1959; David D. Jackson and James Q. Erwin, eds., *Rebels from the Redlands,* 3.

21. Alley to Johnson, n. p., Aug. 4, 1902, quoted in Fred Tarpley, *Jefferson: Riverport to the Southwest,* 85. See also G. H. Baird, *A Brief History of Upshur County,* 14–16.

22. Dugas, "Social and Economic History of Texas" 1: 94–95; Lyder L. Unstad, "Norwegian Migration to Texas," *SHQ* 43 (Oct., 1939): 176–195. States of birth were indicated either on *Population Schedules* or *CSR* for 969 individuals, while ages at enlistment were available for 898 privates in the original regiment. For the median age of other Confederate units from Texas, see Wooster and Wooster, "'Rarin' for a Fight'," 395.

23. Glen and DeLorean Johnson, *Our Ancestors,* 9–10; Templeton, *CCH,* 38, 43, 66, 115; *Members of the Legislature of the State of Texas,* Tommy Yett, comp., 15, 23–24, 28, 34–35; *Texas Almanac for 1862,* 35; *Memorial and Biographical History of Dallas County, Texas,* 185, 278.

24. Rose, *RTB,* 59–60; Campbell, "Planters and Plain Folk," 395; Walworth Harrison, *History of Greenville and Hunt County, Texas,* 117–118; Johnson, *TWWG,* 119; William S. Speer and John H. Brown, eds., *The Encyclopedia of the New West,* 188–189; J. J. Faulk, *History of Henderson County, Texas,* 118; *The Standard* (Clarksville, Tex.), May 11, 1861.

25. *Handbook of Texas* 1: 910–911; 2: 289–290, 458, 858; 3: 789–790; Speer and Brown, *Encyclopedia of the New West,* 569–571; Johnson, *TWWG,* 47–48; *Rusk County History,* 435–436; Winfrey, *History of Rusk County,* 142; *Biographical Souvenir of the State of Texas,* 334–335; Templeton, *CCH,* 288–289; *Members of the Legislature,* 33; Marion County Family Profiles 1: 39.

26. Templeton, *CCH,* 54–55, 81, 701; A. L. Leath, "Elected County Officials, 1846–76," *CSC* 17 (Summer, 1978): 60; Speer and Brown, *Encyclopedia of the New West,* 112; *Texas Almanac for 1862,* 22–25, 37; Crocket, *Two Centuries,* 213–214; *History of Cass County People,* nos. 708, 801; Frances T. Ingmire, *Archives and Pioneers of Hunt County, Texas* 1: 42, 167–168, 397; *Biographical Souvenir of the State of Texas,* 323, 676; *Handbook of Texas* 2: 383; 3: 393; Wright, *Texas in the War,* 175–180.

27. Blocker, "Boy Bugler," 73.

28. *Dallas Herald*, quoted in *Marshall News-Messenger*, July 30, 1961.

29. Blocker, "Boy Bugler," 74–75; Rose, *RTB*, 17; Cater, *AIW*, 86–87; Barron, *LSD*, 20–23.

30. J. B. to Eliza Long, Dallas, June 22, 1861, JBL.

31. *Dallas Herald*, June 19, 26, and July 23, 1861; *Handbook of Texas* 1: 856–857; 2: 484–485; *Marshall News-Messenger*, July 16, 1961.

32. *Dallas Herald*, June 19, 1861.

33. Ibid., July 3, 1861.

34. Long, *The Civil War Day by Day*, 89; *Marshall News-Messenger*, July 16, 1961; Isaac Asimov, *Asimov's Guide to Halley's Comet*, 59–61.

35. Walter P. Lane, *The Adventures and Recollections of General Walter P. Lane* (hereafter cited as *AR*), 7–82; Warner, *Generals in Gray*, 173–174; Wright, *Texas in the War*, 86–87; Barron, *LSD*, 27; *Marshall News-Messenger*, July 23, 1961.

36. Johnson, *TWWG*, 50; *Handbook of Texas* 1: 340; Wright, *Texas in the War*, 76; Peters, "Wilderness to War," 30; Dunn, "KGC in Texas," 561.

37. Rose, *RTB*, 42.

38. John J. to Susan Good, Fort Smith, Ark., July 30, 1861, in John J. Good, *Cannon Smoke: The Letters of Captain John J. Good, Good-Douglas Texas Battery, CSA*, ed. by Lester N. Fitzhugh, 30.

39. *OR*, Ser. 1, Vol. 1: 635; Good, *Cannon Smoke*, v–viii; James P. Douglas, *Douglas's Texas Battery*, ed. by L. R. Douglas, 160; Wright, *Texas in the War*, 131–132; Johnson, *TWWG*, 395–397; *Handbook of Texas* 1: 516, 708; *Dallas Herald*, June 26, 1861; C. Alwyn Barr, "Texas' Confederate Field Artillery," *Texas Military History* 1 (Aug., 1961): 2–3.

40. Ben to Eliza Long, Breckinridge, Texas, July 10, 1861, JBL. See also Sue E. Moore, "The Life of John Benjamin Long," 16; Blocker, "Boy Bugler," 76; Cater, *AIW*, 76–77; *Marshall News-Messenger*, July 16, 1961.

41. W. T. to J. B. Long, Rusk, July 2, 1861, JBL.

42. Discrepancies appear in the accounts by participants on the character, shipment, and distribution of arms to the regiment. The narrative above is based upon the correspondence in *OR*, Ser. 1, Vol. 1: 635, Vol. 3: 607, 623, and Vol. 4: 104–105; Ben to Eliza Long, Breckinridge, Tex., July 10, 1861, JBL; Lon to Matthew and Amanda Cartwright, Dallas, July 6, 29, 1861, CC; *Dallas Herald*, July 17, 1861; Good, *Cannon Smoke*, 14–15, 47; Cater, *AIW*, 77, 82; Barron, *LSD*, 28; Rose, *RTB*, 17–18; Blocker, "Boy Bugler," 76, 89–90.

43. Douglas to White, Dallas, June 20, 1861, in Douglas, *Douglas's Texas Battery*, 2. See also John J. to Susan Good, McKinney, July 12, 1861, in Good, *Cannon Smoke*, 17–18.

Chapter 4. Wilson's Creek, July–August 1861

1. Blocker, "Boy Bugler," 76–77, 90; Barron, *LSD*, 30–31; Rose, *RTB*, 18–19; John J. to Susan Good, Colbert's Ferry, I. T., July 16, 1861, in Good, *Cannon Smoke*, 19–20; Cater, *AIW*, 78.

2. John J. to Susan Good, n.p., July 23, 1861, in Good, *Cannon Smoke*, 27.

3. Barron, *LSD*, 31–33.

4. John J. to Susan Good, Fort Smith, Aug. 1, 1861, in Good, *Cannon Smoke*, 31.

5. Rose, *RTB*, 19–20; Warner, *Generals in Gray*, 61–62; Cater, *AIW*, 79–81; McKay to Loughery, Van Buren, Aug. 2, 1861, *Texas Republican*, Aug. 17, 1861.

6. See Table 3; Lon to Matthew and Amanda Cartwright, Fort Smith, July 28, 29, 1861, CC; Farr to DeMorse, I. T., July 18, and Fort Smith, July 29, 1861, in *The Standard* (Clarksville), July 27, Aug. 17, 1861; Edwin C. Bearss, "Fort Smith Serves General McCulloch as a Supply Depot," *Arkansas Historical Quarterly* 24 (Winter, 1965): 317, 330.

7. William E. Parrish, ed., *A History of Missouri* 3: 1–25; Albert E. Castel, *General Sterling Price and the Civil War in the West*, 25–32; Ezra J. Warner, *Generals in Blue*, 35–37, 286–287, and *Generals in Gray*, 246–247.

8. *OR*, Ser. 1, Vol. 3: 39, 594–595, 606–608; Geise, "Confederate Northwest," 16–20.

9. *OR*, Ser. 1, Vol. 3: 98–99, 397, 609–610, 715.

10. Ibid., pp. 47–48, 50–52, 743–745; Castel, *General Sterling Price*, 33–39; Robert U. Johnson and Clarence C. Buel, eds., *Battles and Leaders of the Civil War* (hereafter cited as *BLCW*) 1: 271.

11. John J. to Susan Good, Lee's Creek, Ark. [Aug. 8, 1861], in Good, *Cannon Smoke*, 41. See also J. B. Long to Brother, Fort Smith, July 29, 1861, JBL; Farr to DeMorse, Fort Smith, July 29, 1861, *The Standard* (Clarksville), Aug. 17, 1861; Rose, *RTB*, 20–21.

12. Cater, *AIW*, 83. See also Barron, *LSD*, 34–35; William Baxter, *Pea Ridge and Prairie Grove*, 10; Stephen B. Oates, *Confederate Cavalry West of the River*, 16; Blocker, "Boy Bugler," 77–78.

13. Dame to Perry, Fayetteville, Aug. 6, 1861, in *Texas Republican* (Marshall), Aug. 24, 1861.

14. *BLCW* 1: 290, 298, 306; Barron, *LSD*, 36–43; Rose, *RTB*, 21–22.

15. Blocker, "Boy Bugler," 79.

16. *OR*, Ser. 1, Vol. 3: 745–746; Flournoy to Clark, Fort Smith, Aug. 16, 1861, in George M. Flournoy, "An Unofficial Account of the Battle of Wilson Creek, August 10, 1861," ed. by Willard E. Wight, *Arkansas Historical Quarterly* 15 (Winter, 1956): 363; Victor M. Rose, *The Life and Services of Gen. Ben McCulloch*, 138–139, 170–171; Castel, *General Sterling Price*, 39–41.

17. *OR*, Ser. 1, Vol. 3: 57, 60; *BLCW* 1: 304; Warner, *Generals in Blue*, 447–448; Ella Lonn, *Foreigners in the Union Army and Navy*, 107–108.

18. *BLCW* 1: 304.

19. Flournoy to Clark, Fort Smith, Aug. 16, 1861, in Flournoy, "An Unofficial Account of the Battle of Wilson Creek," 363. See also Dee Brown, "Wilson's Creek," *Civil War Times Illustrated* (hereafter cited as *CWTI*) 11 (Apr., 1972): 9–18.

20. Johnson, *TWWG*, 319; Barron, *LSD*, 43–44; Blocker, "Boy Bugler," 80–81.

21. Anonymous memoir, Greer Papers.

22. Quoted in Barron, *LSD*, 54.

23. Barron, *LSD*, 43–44; Mills to Pryor, Dallas County, Aug. 22, 1861, *Texas Republican* (Marshall), Sept. 7, 1861.

24. *OR*, Ser. 1, Vol. 3: 118–119; Cater, *AIW*, 87–89; Barron, *LSD*, 44–46.

25. *OR*, Ser. 1, Vol. 3: 119–120, Vol. 53: 425; Ector to Loughery, Round Springs, Mo., Aug. 12, 1861, *Texas Republican* (Marshall), Aug. 31, 1861; Lane, *AR*, 83–84.

26. Mills to Pryor, Dallas County, Aug. 22, 1861, *Texas Republican* (Marshall), Sept. 7, 1861. On Sigel's role at Wilson's Creek, see *OR*, Ser. 1, Vol. 3: 70–71, 95–98; *BLCW* 1:304–306; Earl J. Hess, "Sigel's Resignation: A Study in German Americanism and the Civil War," *CWH* 26 (Mar., 1980): 5–7; Castel, *General Sterling Price, 42–43*.

27. Anonymous memoir, *Greer Papers.*

28. Rose, *RTB*, 30.

29. *OR*, Ser. 1, Vol. 53: 425. See also *OR*, Ser. 1, Vol. 3: 87–88, 119.

30. Ibid., 105.

31. Blocker, "Boy Bugler," 81.

32. Barron, *LSD*, 46, 55; Mills to Pryor, Dallas County, Aug. 22, 1861, *Texas Republican* (Marshall), Sept. 7, 1861.

33. Blocker, "Boy Bugler," 81.

34. Ector to Loughery, Round Springs, Mo., Aug. 12, 1861, *Texas Republican* (Marshall), Aug. 31, 1861.

35. Barron, *LSD*, 49; A. P. to Matthew Cartwright, Springfield, Aug. 17, 1861, CC.

36. *OR*, Ser. 1, Vol. 3: 74. See also *BLCW* 1: 301.

37. *OR*, Ser. 1, Vol. 3: 119; Blocker, "Boy Bugler," 82.

38. *BLCW* 1: 303. See also *OR*, Ser. 1, Vol. 3: 67–69.

39. Barron, *LSD*, 47.

40. *OR*, Ser. 1, Vol. 3: 119; Rose, *Gen. Ben McCulloch*, 184; Castel, *General Sterling Price*, 45–46.

41. Union casualties included 258 men killed, 873 wounded, and 186 missing. See *BLCW* 1: 306; and Thomas L. Livermore, *Numbers and Losses in the Civil War*, 78.

42. Quoted in *Marshall News-Messenger*, Sept. 17, 1961.

43. Regimental casualties were derived from *Texas Republican* (Marshall), Sept. 7, 1861, and *CSR*. See also *Henderson Times*, May 19, 1938; Barron, *LSD*, 49, 62; Johnson, *TWWG*, 114; Campbell, *Southern Community in Crisis*, 203.

44. John J. to Susan Good, Mt. Vernon, Mo., Aug. 26, 1861, in Good, *Cannon Smoke*, 55–56; Lane, *AR*, 84–85; Blocker, "Boy Bugler," 83–84; Barron, *LSD*, 56–57.

Chapter 5. Chustenahlah, August–December 1861

1. Matthew to Lon Cartwright, San Augustine, Aug. 5, 1861, CC.

2. W. T. to J. B. Long, Rusk, Sept. 29, 1861, JBL.

3. Flournoy to Clark, Fort Smith, Aug. 16, 1861, in Flournoy, "An Unofficial Account of the Battle of Wilson Creek," 363.

4. Castel, *General Sterling Price*, 45–49; William R. Geise, "Divided Command in the West," *MHTS* 13, no. 3 (1976): 50–56.

5. *OR*, Ser. 1, Vol. 3: 672. See also ibid., 733–734, 747; John J. to Susan Good, Mt. Vernon, Mo., Aug. 27, 1861, in Good, *Cannon Smoke*, 57–58; *Texas Republican* (Marshall), Sept. 14, 1861; Rose, *Gen. Ben McCulloch*, 184–186. For a study of command problems in the West, see Richard M. McMurry, *Two Great Rebel Armies*, 113–132.

6. Blocker, "Boy Bugler," 84. See also *OR*, Ser. 1, Vol. 3: 690, 715–716; Castel, *General Sterling Price*, 49–50.

7. *OR*, Ser. 1, Vol. 3: 700–701, 719, 730, and Ser. 4, Vol. 1: 630; Lon to Columbus Cartwright, Carthage, Mo., Oct. 17, 1861, CC; Cater, *AIW*, 91–95; Paul E. Steiner, *Disease in the Civil War*, 9–26; Gordon W. Jones, "The Scourge of Typhoid," *American History Illustrated* 1 (Feb., 1967): 23–24; H. H. Cunningham, *Doctors in Gray*, 188–190, 194–195; Wiley, *Johnny Reb*, 244–248; James I. Robertson, Jr., *Soldiers Blue and Gray*, 147.

8. Barron, *LSD*, 57–62; Blocker, "Boy Bugler," 84–85, 149. Regimental losses from illness were taken from *CSR*.

9. W. T. to J. B. Long, Rusk, Sept. 9, 1861, JBL.

10. Ellen Ellis to J. B. Long, Rusk, Oct. 21, 1861, ibid.

11. Matthew to Lon Cartwright, San Augustine, Sept. 2, 1861, CC.

12. Quoted in Webster to Loughery, Marshall, Sept. 3, 1861, Marshall CSA File.

13. W. T. to J. B. Long, Rusk, Sept. 9, 1861, JBL. See also Greer to Citizens of East Texas, Scott's Mills, Mo., Sept. 9, 1861, *Marshall News-Messenger*, Sept. 17, 1961.

14. Anna to A. P. Cartwright, San Augustine, Oct. 10, 1861, CC. See also Susan to John J. Good, Dallas, Sept. 22, 1861, in Good, *Cannon Smoke*, 76–77; Kaufman County Commissioners' Court, Minutes 1: 76–77.

15. Quoted in Rose, *RTB*, 38. See also *OR*, Ser. 1, Vol. 3: 717–718.

16. *OR*, Ser. 1, Vol. 3: 719. See also John J. to Susan Good, Camp Jackson, Ark., Sept. 20 and Oct. 7, 1861, in Good, *Cannon Smoke*, 74, 93.

17. *OR*, Ser. 1, Vol. 3: 730, 748–749; John J. to Susan Good, Neosho, Mo., Oct. 21, 1861, in Good, *Cannon Smoke*, 100–103; Douglas, *Douglas's Texas Battery*, 12–15; Castel, *General Sterling Price*, 57–60; *BLCW* 1: 286–287.

18. *OR*, Ser. 1, Vol. 3: 730–731, 733–734, 738; Douglas, *Douglas's Texas Battery*, 11–21; Rose, *RTB*, 39–40; George T. Todd, "Commands in Hood's Texas Brigade," *CV* 20 (June, 1912): 281–282; Bailey, *Between the Enemy and Texas*, 44–45.

19. *OR*, Ser. 1, Vol. 3: 742. See also Washington L. Gammage, *The Camp, the Bivouac, and the Battlefield* (hereafter cited as *CBB*), 20; Blocker, "Boy Bugler," 85–87.

20. *OR*, Ser. 1, Vol. 3: 748–749; Parrish, *History of Missouri* 3: 30–42.

21. Rose, *RTB*, 40–42; Blocker, "Boy Bugler," 149–150.

22. Newton A. Keen, "'Such is War': The Confederate Memoirs of Newton

Asbury Keen," ed. by William C. Billingsley, *Texas Military History* 6 (Winter, 1967): 242.

23. *OR*, Ser. 1, Vol. 3: 700, 730, Vol. 8: 718–719, 728; Sparks, *War Between the States*, 14–19, 22–50; George L. Griscom, *Fighting with Ross' Texas Cavalry Brigade, C.S.A.*, ed. by Homer L. Kerr, 1–11; Garrett to Gibbard, Camp Davis, Ark., Oct. 27, 1861, David R. Garrett, *The Civil War Letters of David R. Garrett*, ed. by Max S. Lale and Hobart Key, 33; Wright, *Texas in the War*, 24–25, 28, 34, 112, 114–115; Judith A. Benner, *Sul Ross: Soldier, Statesman, Educator*, 67–72; Warner, *Generals in Gray*, 333–334; *Handbook of Texas* 2: 947–948, 3: 932; Wooster, "Wealthy Texans," 173.

24. Columbus to Lon Cartwright, San Augustine, Jan. 10, 1862, CC; Rose, *Gen. Ben McCulloch*, 164; Warner, *Generals in Gray*, 202–203; Castel, *General Sterling Price*, 63–64; Sparks, *War Between the States*, 49–50.

25. A. P. to Amanda Cartwright, Camp Wigfall, Ark., Feb. 1, 1862, CC.

26. A more detailed account of this episode appeared in my article, "Rehearsal for Civil War: The Texas Cavalry in the Indian Territory, 1861," *Chronicles of Oklahoma* (hereafter cited as *CO*) 68 (Fall, 1990): 228–265. See also Abel, *American Indian as Slaveholder*, 243–257; Dean Trickett, "The Civil War in Indian Territory," *CO* 18 (Sept., 1940): 266–280; and Edwin C. Bearss, "The Civil War Comes to Indian Territory," *Journal of the West* 11 (Jan., 1972): 9–42.

27. *OR*, Ser. 1, Vol. 8: 11–14, 22, 28–29, 709, 713, 715; Blocker, "Boy Bugler," 150–152; *Texas Republican* (Marshall), Jan. 11, 1862.

28. *OR*, Ser. 1, Vol. 8: 23. See also Muriel H. Wright and Leroy H. Fischer, "Civil War Sites in Oklahoma," *CO* 44 (Spring, 1966): 202; George H. Shirk, *Oklahoma Place Names*, 51; Blocker, "Boy Bugler," 152–153.

29. Lane, *AR*, 87.

30. *OR*, Ser. 1, Vol. 8: 23.

31. Cater, *AIW*, 103–104; H. L. Taylor, "The Indian Battle of Chaustinolla," *CV* 24 (Mar., 1916): 122.

32. Cater, *AIW*, 103.

33. John J. to Susan Good, Mount Vernon, Mo., Aug. 27, 1861, in Good, *Cannon Smoke*, 58.

34. J. T. Clower Memoir, Mar., 1919, Confederate Reminiscences, File D.

35. *OR*, Ser. 1, Vol. 8: 24; Cater, *AIW*, 105; Lane, *AR*, 88–89, 104; Johnson, *TWWG*, 307.

36. *OR*, Ser. 1, Vol. 8: 31.

37. Ibid., 25, 732; Blocker, "Boy Bugler," 154; Cater, *AIW*, 104–106; *Texas Republican* (Marshall), Jan. 11, 1862. Casualty figures were derived from *CSR*.

38. *OR*, Ser. 1, Vol. 8: 13; John J. to Susan Good, Camp Jackson, Ark., Sept. 18, 1861, in Good, *Cannon Smoke*, 71; Griscom, *Fighting with Ross'*, 10–11; D. J. Cater, "The Battle of Chustenahlah," *CV* 37 (June, 1930): 233; Sparks, *War Between the States*, 47.

39. U.S. Department of the Interior, Office of Indian Affairs, *Report of the Commissioner of Indian Affairs for the Year 1862*, 145–147, 151–154; Dean Banks, "Civil War Refugees from Indian Territory in the North, 1861–1864," *CO* 41 (Fall, 1963): 286–289, 292; Edmund J. Danziger, Jr., "The Office of In-

dian Affairs and the Problems of Civil War Indian Refugees in Kansas," *Kansas Historical Quarterly* 35 (Fall, 1969): 261–264.

40. Blocker, "Boy Bugler," 155; Cater, *AIW*, 106; Rose, *RTB*, 46, 48; Lane, *AR*, 89–90; *Marshall News-Messenger*, Feb. 25, 1962.

Chapter 6. Pea Ridge, January–March 1862

1. *OR*, Ser. 1, Vol. 8: 734; Geise, "Divided Command in the West," 53–56; Warner, *Generals in Gray*, 159–160.

2. Quoted in Robert G. Hartje, *Van Dorn*, 105. See also Warner, *Generals in Gray*, 314–315.

3. *OR*, Ser. 1, Vol. 8: 462, 748–752; Warner, *Generals in Blue*, 107–108; Hartje, *Van Dorn*, 106–111.

4. "Diary of Sam Thompson," quoted in Douglas, *Douglas's Texas Battery*, 175.

5. Amanda to A. P. and Lon Cartwright, San Augustine, Jan. 22, 1862, CC.

6. Griscom, *Fighting with Ross'*, 11–12; Douglas, *Douglas's Texas Battery*, 45; Cater, *AIW*, 107–110.

7. Blocker, "Boy Bugler," 156.

8. Gammage, *CBB*, 23. See also Baxter, *Pea Ridge and Prairie Grove*, 46–58; Rose, *Gen. Ben McCulloch*, 198–199.

9. *OR*, Ser. 1, Vol. 8: 283; Castel, *General Sterling Price*, 68–70; Hartje, *Van Dorn*, 112–120.

10. Quoted in Hartje, *Van Dorn*, 120.

11. Rose, *RTB*, 54.

12. Barron, *LSD*, 64; Keen, "'Such is War'," 246; Blocker, "Boy Bugler," 156–157.

13. Keen, "'Such is War'," 248.

14. *OR*, Ser. 1, Vol. 8: 74–76, 302; Rose, *RTB*, 55; Griscom, *Fighting with Ross'*, 13; Benner, *Sul Ross*, 72–73; Sparks, *War Between the States*, 51.

15. *OR*, Ser. 1, Vol. 8: 196–197; Rose, *Gen. Ben McCulloch*, 200–203; *BLCW* 1: 317–319; Hartje, *Van Dorn*, 122–127. For a detailed account of the action at Pea Ridge, see Michael A. Hughes, "Pea Ridge, or Elkhorn Tavern," *Blue and Gray Magazine* 5 (Jan., 1988): 8–36, 48–60.

16. Barron, *LSD*, 64–65; Baxter, *Pea Ridge and Prairie Grove*, 90–91.

17. Barron, *LSD*, 65. See also Gammage, *CBB*, 23–24.

18. Lane, *AR*, 91.

19. Cater, *AIW*, 112–115.

20. *OR*, Ser. 1, Vol. 8: 298.

21. Quoted in Barron, *LSD*, 66.

22. *OR*, Ser. 1, Vol. 8: 191–192, 209–211, 283–284; Blocker, "Boy Bugler," 157–158; Rose, *RTB*, 56–57; Griscom, *Fighting with Ross'*, 14; Keen, "'Such is War'," 249–250; Gammage, *CBB*, 24–25; Hartje, *Van Dorn*, 127–145; Annie H. Abel, *The American Indian as Participant in the Civil War*, 24–32.

23. Quoted in Barron, *LSD*, 68. See also Blocker, "Boy Bugler," 166; Lane, *AR*, 91–92.

24. *OR*, Ser. 1, Vol. 8: 206–208, 232–235, 298–299, 301, 303; Barron, *LSD*, 68–69; Griscom, *Fighting with Ross'*, 14; Garrett to Gibbard, Cantonment Washington, Ark., Mar. 20, 1862, Garrett, *Letters*, 49; Cater, *AIW*, 115–116; Sparks, *War Between the States*, 53–55; Keen, "'Such is War'," 250–251; Hartje, *Van Dorn*, 141–146; Abel, *American Indian as Participant*, 32–34; Wiley, *Johnny Reb*, 325–326.

25. *OR*, Ser. 1, Vol. 8: 283–284, 293–294, 298–299; Cater, *AIW*, 116–118; Barron, *LSD*, 69; Blocker, "Boy Bugler," 158–159; Rose, *Gen. Ben McCulloch*, 203–205; Benner, *Sul Ross*, 74–75; Hartje, *Van Dorn*, 146–150.

26. Blocker, "Boy Bugler," 161.

27. *OR*, Ser. 1, Vol. 8: 294; Blocker, "Boy Bugler," 161–162; Lane, *AR*, 92–93; Rose, *RTB*, 59–60.

28. James H. Fauntleroy, "Elk Horn to Vicksburg," ed. by Homer L. Calkin, *CWH* 2 (Mar., 1956): 13. See also Hartje, *Van Dorn*, 151–156.

29. Lon to Amanda Cartwright, Camp Wigfall, Ark., Mar. 20, 1862, CC. See also Castel, *General Sterling Price*, 76–78.

30. Cater, *AIW*, 118–119.

31. W. H. Tunnard, *A Southern Record*, 145. See also Keen, "'Such is War'," 251–252; *OR*, Ser. 1, Vol. 8: 298–301.

32. Barron, *LSD*, 73. See also Cater, *AIW*, 121.

33. Barron, *LSD*, 71–76; Blocker, "Boy Bugler," 162–163; Douglas, *Douglas's Texas Battery*, 28; Baxter, *Pea Ridge and Prairie Grove*, 98–99; Lon to Amanda Cartwright, Camp Wigfall, Ark., Mar. 20, 1862, CC.

34. *OR*, Ser. 1, Vol. 8: 787, 790. See also Hartje, *Van Dorn*, 157–160.

35. *OR*, Ser. 1, Vol. 8: 299; Gammage, *CBB*, 26; Grady McWhiney and Perry D. Jamieson, *Attack and Die*, 20; Livermore, *Numbers and Losses in the Civil War*, 79. Regimental casualty figures were taken from *CSR*.

Chapter 7. Corinth, April–May 1862

1. *OR*, Ser. 1, Vol. 8: 791; Hartje, *Van Dorn*, 166; Hattaway and Jones, *How the North Won*, 58–77; McPherson, *Battle Cry*, 395–404.

2. *New York Times*, quoted in Nevins, *The War for the Union* 2: 29.

3. Leroy P. Walker, quoted in Charles P. Roland, *Albert Sidney Johnston, Soldier of Three Republics*, 305.

4. *OR*, Ser. 1, Vol. 10, Pt. 2: 354; Roland, *Albert Sidney Johnston*, 311; T. Harry Williams, *P.G.T. Beauregard, Napoleon in Gray*, 122–125; Hattaway and Jones, *How the North Won*, 146–150, 156–158.

5. A. P. to Amanda Cartwright, Little Rock, Apr. 6, 1862, CC.

6. Sources and numbers of recruits are taken from *CSR*. See also *OR*, Ser. 1, Vol. 8: 796, Vol. 13: 818, and Vol. 53: 796–798; Blocker, "Boy Bugler," 216; Rose, *Gen. Ben McCulloch*, 165; A. P. to Amanda Cartwright, Camp Wigfall, Ark., Feb. 1, 1862, CC.

7. R. L. Creswell to Uncle, Little Rock, Apr. 25, 1862, Confederate Pension Applications (hereinafter cited as CPA), No. 23099.

8. Barron, *LSD*, 79–80; *Handbook of Texas* 1: 823; Warner, *Generals in Gray*, 139–140; John J. to Susan Good, Ozark and Des Arc, Ark., Mar. 27 and Apr. 8, 1862, in Good, *Cannon Smoke*, 174, 177.

9. Blocker, "Boy Bugler," 216.

10. *OR*, Ser. 1, Vol. 13: 813–816; Keen, "'Such is War'," 252; Griscom, *Fighting with Ross'*, 17, 35, 84; Sparks, *War Between the States*, 56–57; Rose, *RTB*, 63–64; Blocker, "Boy Bugler," 217; Barron, *LSD*, 80–81; Hartje, *Van Dorn*, 166–168.

11. *OR*, Ser. 1, Vol. 53: 784.

12. Lon to Amanda Cartwright, Memphis, Apr. 23, 1862, CC. See also Keen, "'Such is War'," 44.

13. Blocker, "Boy Bugler," 217–218; Douglas to White, Memphis, Apr. 16, 1862, in Douglas, *Douglas's Texas Battery*, 34.

14. Hattaway and Jones, *How the North Won*, 162–171; Roland, *Albert Sidney Johnston*, 316–340; Williams, *Beauregard*, 126–146; McPherson, *Battle Cry*, 406–415.

15. *OR*, Ser. 1, Vol. 10, Pt. 2: 436.

16. Keen, "'Such is War'," 46; Cater, *AIW*, 126–128.

17. Blocker, "Boy Bugler," 219.

18. Barron, *LSD*, 82.

19. Quoted in Blocker, "Boy Bugler," 220.

20. Lane, *AR*, 95–98.

21. Gammage, *CBB*, 33.

22. Barron, *LSD*, 83–84.

23. *OR*, Ser. 1, Vol. 10, Pt. 2: 462, 490, 548–551; Sparks, *War Between the States*, 255; Williams, *Beauregard*, 146, 150–151; McPherson, *Battle Cry*, 478–479.

24. Quoted in Hartje, *Van Dorn*, 180–181.

25. Keen, "'Such is War'," 47.

26. Douglas to White, Talladega, Ala., June 30, 1862, in Douglas, *Douglas's Texas Battery*, 38–39; Barron, *LSD*, 89–90; Rose, *RTB*, 65; Blocker, "Boy Bugler," 220; Wiley, *Johnny Reb*, 247.

27. Gammage, *CBB*, 133. The number of deaths from disease in the regiment were derived from CSR. See also Barron, *LSD*, 85–89; Cotner, *Hogg*, 24; Gerald F. Linderman, *Embattled Courage*, 115–116.

28. Bruce Catton, *Grant Moves South*, 265–270; Hartje, *Van Dorn*, 175–180; Williams, *Beauregard*, 151–152; Nevins, *War for the Union* 2: 111–112; Warner, *Generals in Blue*, 195–197.

29. *OR*, Ser. 4, Vol. 1: 1061–1062; Lowell H. Harrison, "Conscription and the Confederacy," *CWTI* 9 (July, 1970): 11; Stephen E. Ambrose, "Yeoman Discontent in the Confederacy," *CWH* 8 (Sept., 1962): 264–266; Nevins, *War for the Union* 2: 89–90.

30. J. B. Long to Sister, Corinth, May 17, 1862, JBL.

31. R. L. Creswell to Sister, Priceville, Miss., June 25, 1862, CPA, No. 23099.

32. Lon to Amanda Cartwright, Memphis, Apr. 23, 1862, CC.

33. Lon Cartwright to Sister, Corinth, May 6, 1862, ibid. See also A. P. to Columbus Cartwright, Camp McIntosh, Miss., May 10, 1862, ibid.

34. Discharges and reenlistments upon reorganization as well as details of the Harris case were derived from *CSR*. See also Blocker, "Boy Bugler," 22; Barron, *LSD*, 101; Cater, *AIW*, 131–132; Andrew L. Leath, "Starrville," *CSC* 23 (Sum., 1984): 17; Tim Son, "Bethel Baptist Church," *CSC* 23 (Sum., 1984): 71; *Texas Republican* (Marshall), Sept. 16, 1861; Judson Milburn, interview with author, Stillwater, Okla., Apr. 22, 1989.

35. See Table 4. Results of regimental elections and disability records were derived from *CSR*; ages of company officers were taken from *Population Schedules*.

36. Barron, *LSD*, 27. See also John J. to Susan Good, Corinth, Apr. 26, 1862, in Good, *Cannon Smoke*, 186.

37. Lane, *AR*, 98; Armstrong to Loughery, Cantonment Wigfall, Ark., Mar. 1, 1862, *Texas Republican* (Marshall), Mar. 22, 1862; Gammage, *CBB*, 118; Wright, *Texas in the War*, 9–10, 31, 76–77, 79, 85–86, 125; Warner, *Generals in Gray*, 81, 174; Winfrey, *Rusk County*, 132; Vicki Betts, "'Private and Amateur Hangings': The Lynching of W. W. Montgomery, March 15, 1863," *SHQ* 88 (Oct., 1984): 145–166.

38. Lane, *AR*, 98.

39. *OR*, Ser. 1, Vol. 10, Pt. 2: 502; Rose, *RTB*, 64–65; Barron, *LSD*, 93–94.

40. A. P. Cartwright to Brother, Camp McIntosh, Miss., May 10, 1862, CC.

41. J. B. Long to Sister, Corinth, May 17, 1862, JBL. See also *OR*, Ser. 1, Vol. 10, Pt. 1: 807–808.

42. Williams, *Beauregard*, 154. See also *OR*, Ser. 1, Vol. 10, Pt. 1: 762–765, 777–779.

43. Tom Hogg, as quoted in Rose, *RTB*, 67.

44. Lane to Cumby, Baldwyn, Miss., June 2, 1862, *Marshall News-Messenger*, July 15, 1962. See also Lane, *AR*, 99–102.

45. Casualties were derived from *CSR*. See also Barron, *LSD*, 93–95; J. W. Wynne, "Heroism of Private J. N. Smith," *CV* 14 (Aug., 1906): 353; Rose, *RTB*, 66–69; Cater, *AIW*, 134–135.

46. *OR*, Ser. 1, Vol. 10, Pt. 2: 583–584. See also Gammage, *CBB*, 36–37.

47. *OR*, Ser. 1, Vol. 10, Pt. 1: 670–671, and Vol. 17, Pt. 2: 26; Catton, *Grant Moves South*, 276–280, 300; Nevins, *War for the Union* 2: 137–138. For a more charitable view of Halleck, see McPherson, *Battle Cry*, 511–513.

48. Lon to Amanda Cartwright, Camp Priceville, Miss., June 20, 1862, CC. See also Garrett to Gibbard, Camp Maury, Miss., June 14, 1862, Garrett, *Letters*, 51.

Chapter 8. Iuka, June–October 1862

1. Nevins, *War for the Union* 2: 150–154, 275.

2. Quoted in Williams, *Beauregard*, 155.

3. Ibid., 155–165; Castel, *General Sterling Price*, 87–92; Hartje, *Van Dorn*,

182–184, 208–211; Thomas L. Connelly and Archer Jones, *The Politics of Command*, 107–108.

4. Lon to Amanda Cartwright, Camp Priceville, Miss., June 20, 1862, CC.

5. Resignations and promotions are based on *CSR*. See also *OR*, Ser. 1, Vol. 17, Pt. 1: 127; Barron, *LSD*, 101–102; Warner, *Generals in Gray*, 131.

6. Lon Cartwright to Sister, Camp Priceville, June 25, 1862, CC; Barron, *LSD*, 96–98.

7. Barron, *LSD*, 100.

8. Quoted in Castel, *General Sterling Price*, 93.

9. Nevins, *War for the Union* 2: 174–180, 215–228; McPherson, *Battle Cry*, 515–518, 526–545.

10. A. P. to Matthew Cartwright, Saltillo, Miss., Aug. 10, 1862, CC.

11. Barron, *LSD*, 104.

12. Ibid., 104–106; *OR*, Ser. 1, Vol. 17, Pt. 1: 121, 124, Pt. 2: 690, 693; *BLCW* 2: 727–731; Nevins, *War for the Union* 2: 279–282.

13. *OR*, Ser. 1, Vol. 17, Pt. 2: 696–699, 701, 708; Albert Castel, "Battle Without a Victor . . . Iuka," *CWTI* 11 (Oct., 1972): 12–14; Castel, *General Sterling Price*, 96–100.

14. Quoted in Catton, *Grant Moves South*, 311.

15. W. P. Helm, "Close Fighting at Iuka, Miss.," *CV* 24 (Apr., 1911): 171.

16. Quoted in ibid.

17. Rose, *RTB*, 70.

18. *OR*, Ser. 1, Vol. 17, Pt. 1: 123.

19. Rose, *RTB*, 71; Johnson, *TWWG*, 19.

20. Bewley and Short to Randolph, San Augustine, Oct. 28, and Shelbyville, Nov. 1, 1862, *CSR*, Roll 23; *OR*, Ser. 1, Vol. 17, Pt. 1: 72–75, 80, 121–127; Barron, *LSD*, 106–108; Castel, *General Sterling Price*, 100–102; Edwin C. Bearss, *Decision in Mississippi*, 43–49; Crocket, *Two Centuries*, 244. Casualties were taken from *CSR*.

21. Quoted in Castel, *General Sterling Price*, 103.

22. William B. Hesseltine, *Civil War Prisons*, 32–34, 69–70, 76–77; Robertson, *Soldiers Blue and Gray*, 191–192; Barron, *LSD*, 114–115.

23. *OR*, Ser. 1, Vol. 17, Pt. 1: 376–378; Lon to Matthew Cartwright, Holly Springs, Miss., Oct. 12, 1862, CC; Keen, "'Such is War'," 52; Castel, *General Sterling Price*, 104–109; Hartje, *Van Dorn*, 212–217; Glenn W. Sunderland, "The Battle of Corinth," *CWTI* 6 (Apr., 1967): 30–34.

24. *OR*, Ser. 1, Vol. 17, Pt. 1: 378.

25. Ibid., 374–375; Hartje, *Van Dorn*, 219–221; Warner, *Generals in Gray*, 194–195, 215–216.

26. *OR*, Ser. 1, Vol. 17, Pt. 1: 385–386; Rose, *RTB*, 72; Castel, *General Sterling Price*, 109–114; Hartje, *Van Dorn*, 223–227.

27. Keen, "'Such is War'," 52–53.

28. *OR*, Ser. 1, Vol. 17, Pt. 1: 379.

29. Keen, "'Such is War'," 53.

30. *OR*, Ser. 1, Vol. 17, Pt. 1: 379–382, 387–391; Hartje, *Van Dorn*, 228–229; Castel, *General Sterling Price*, 115, 123–125; Warner, *Generals in Gray*, 116–117.

31. Oscar L. Jackson, quoted in Hartje, *Van Dorn*, 232.

32. *OR*, Ser. 1, Vol. 17, Pt. 1: 380.

33. Ibid., 170, 405–406; Hartje, *Van Dorn*, 233–238; Castel, *General Sterling Price*, 117–122; Sunderland, "Corinth," 35–36.

34. Keen, "'Such is War'," 54–55; Rose, *RTB*, 74; Barron, *LSD*, 121–122; Benner, *Sul Ross*, 87.

35. Barron, *LSD*, 123.

36. Lon to Matthew Cartwright, Holly Springs, Oct. 12, 1862, CC.

37. *OR*, Ser. 1, Vol. 17, Pt. 1: 382–384; Barron, *LSD*, 124–125, 147; Keen, "'Such is War'," 55–56.

38. *OR*, Ser. 1, Vol. 17, Pt. 1: 414–459, and Pt. 2: 787, 835; Castel, *General Sterling Price*, 123–127; Hartje, *Van Dorn*, 238–246; Hattaway and Jones, *How the North Won*, 276–277; McPherson, *Battle Cry*, 523–524, 560–562.

Chapter 9. Holly Springs, November 1862–January 1863

1. Nevins, *War for the Union* 2: 343–344; Hattaway and Jones, *How the North Won*, 291–294.

2. *OR*, Ser. 1, Vol. 17, Pt. 1: 539, and Pt. 2: 716, 718, 728, 733, 787; Warner, *Generals in Gray*, 232–233.

3. *OR*, Ser. 1, Vol. 17, Pt. 2: 759, 794–796; Castel, *General Sterling Price*, 128–139; Hartje, *Van Dorn*, 247–250.

4. Rose, *RTB*, 79. While the Third, Sixth, and Twenty-seventh regiments were remounted early in November, the men of the Ninth Regiment had to wait another month for the delivery of their horses. See *OR*, Ser. 1, Vol. 17, Pt. 2: 738, 741; Keen, "'Such is War'," 56; *Texas Republican* (Marshall), Sept. 6, 1862; *Marshall News-Messenger*, Sept. 9, 1962; Garrett to Gibbard, Holly Springs, Oct. 21, 1862, Garrett, *Letters*, 69; Griscom, *Fighting with Ross'*, 49, 93.

5. Keen, "'Such is War'," 56.

6. *OR*, Ser. 1, Vol. 17, Pt. 1: 467, and Pt. 2: 750, 771; Hartje, *Van Dorn*, 250–254; Catton, *Grant Moves South*, 328–335; Hattaway and Jones, *How the North Won*, 309–311.

7. *OR*, Ser. 1, Vol. 17, Pt. 1: 540. See also ibid., Pt. 2: 779, 784–786; Barron, *LSD*, 127–131; Rose, *RTB*, 80–83.

8. *OR*, Ser. 1, Vol. 17, Pt. 2: 757–758, 800–801; Hattaway and Jones, *How the North Won*, 280–282, 300–301.

9. Quoted in Catton, *Grant Moves South*, 335.

10. *OR*, Ser. 1, Vol. 17, Pt. 1: 593–597; Robert S. Henry, *"First with the Most" Forrest*, 107–121.

11. Rose, *RTB*, 130–133; Barron, *LSD*, 131–133; Hartje, *Van Dorn*, 254–255; Wiley, *Johnny Reb*, 287; John C. Pemberton, *Pemberton: Defender of Vicksburg*, 62–63, 65–66.

12. Rose, *RTB*, 84–86; Griscom, *Fighting with Ross'*, 50–51; W. P. M'Minn, "Service with Van Dorn's Cavalry," *CV* 27 (Oct., 1919): 384; Hartje, *Van Dorn*, 255–261.

13. *OR*, Ser. 1, Vol. 17, Pt. 1: 498–499, and Pt. 2: 437, 439–440; Bruce J. Dinges, "Running Down Rebels," *CWTI* 19 (Apr., 1980): 13–14.

14. *OR*, Ser. 1, Vol. 17, Pt. 1: 515–516, and Pt. 2: 444; Griscom, *Fighting with Ross'*, 51; Barron, *LSD*, 134; W. R. Stevenson, "Capture of Holly Springs, Miss.", *CV* 9 (Mar., 1901): 134.

15. Mrs. Carrington Mason, quoted in Hartje, *Van Dorn*, 261.

16. Quoted in Rose, *RTB*, 86; and Barron, *LSD*, 135.

17. *Advertiser and Register* (Mobile), Jan. 7, 1863, quoted in Hartje, *Van Dorn*, 262. Rose, *RTB*, 86–87, includes a detailed and colorful account of General Grant's wife Julia, supposedly sojourning in Holly Springs at the time of the raid, boldly berating Lieutenant Colonel Boggess because he would "make war upon women." Other authors, including Hartje, *Van Dorn*, 264; and Hattaway and Jones, *How the North Won*, 311, repeat the story. In fact, though Mrs. Grant had stayed in the town during the previous week, she seems to have departed Holly Springs on December 19, the day before the raid, to rejoin her husband at Oxford. See Ulysses S. Grant, *The Papers of Ulysses S. Grant*, ed. by John Y. Simon, 7: 24; William S. McFeely, *Grant: A Biography*, 125–126; and Ishbel Ross, *The General's Wife: The Life of Mrs. Ulysses S. Grant*, 134–137.

18. *OR*, Ser. 1, Vol. 17, Pt. 1: 508–514.

19. Ibid., 503.

20. Rose, *RTB*, 88–90; Barron, *LSD*, 135–136; Hartje, *Van Dorn*, 263–265.

21. *OR*, Ser. 1, Vol. 17, Pt. 2: 448; Dinges, "Running Down Rebels," 14–15.

22. Barron, *LSD*, 137; Griscom, *Fighting with Ross'*, 52; Hartje, *Van Dorn*, 265–269.

23. Anonymous Memoir, 5, Demetria Ann Hill Collection (hereafter cited as DAH).

24. *OR*, Ser. 1, Vol. 17, Pt. 1: 521–523; Barron, *LSD*, 138–140; Rose, *RTB*, 91.

25. Griscom, *Fighting with Ross'*, 52.

26. Barron, *LSD*, 140–141; Rose, *RTB*, 91–92.

27. Anonymous Memoir, 7–8, DAH.

28. *OR*, Ser. 1, Vol. 17, Pt. 1: 523–524; Johnson, *TWWG*, 135–136; Griscom, *Fighting with Ross'*, 53; Dinges, "Running Down Rebels," 17–18.

29. *OR*, Ser. 1, Vol 17, Pt. 1: 518–520; Griscom, *Fighting with Ross'*, 53–54; Barron, *LSD*, 142.

30. *OR*, Ser. 1, Vol. 17, Pt. 1: 709.

31. Ibid., Pt. 2: 463. See also *BLCW* 3: 462–471; Catton, *Grant Moves South*, 340–344; Nevins, *War for the Union* 2: 381–387.

32. *OR*, Ser. 1, Vol. 17, Pt. 2: 817.

33. Ibid., 820, 827.

34. Ibid., 832–833, 838; Hartje, *Van Dorn*, 271–273; Nevins, *War for the Union* 2: 405–411.

Chapter 10. Thompson's Station, January–May 1863

1. *OR*, Ser. 1, Vol. 24, Pt. 3: 592, 614, 646; Warner, *Generals in Gray*, 12–13, 152–153; Castel, *General Sterling Price*, 138–139.
2. Griscom, *Fighting with Ross'*, 56; Barron, *LSD*, 144; Sparks, *War Between the States*, 74–75; James E. Thomas Diary, entries for Jan. 26, Feb. 6–8, 1863.
3. Moore, "The Life of John Benjamin Long," 30–36; Barron, *LSD*, 147.
4. Quoted in Rose, *RTB*, 92.
5. James E. Thomas Diary, entry for Feb. 21, 1863.
6. Griscom, *Fighting with Ross'*, 58.
7. *OR*, Ser. 1, Vol. 52, Pt. 2: 425.
8. Ibid., Vol. 23, Pt. 2: 646, 650–651; Griscom, *Fighting with Ross'*, 59; Hartje, *Van Dorn*, 275–278; Henry, *Forrest*, 128–129.
9. Sparks, *War Between the States*, 74–75.
10. J. P. Craver to Julia M. Craver, Shelbyville, Tenn., Apr. 11, 1863, Craver Correspondence.
11. *OR*, Ser. 1, Vol. 23, Pt. 1: 77–78; Keen, "'Such is War'," 58; Henry, *Forrest*, 129–131.
12. *OR*, Ser. 1, Vol. 23, Pt. 1: 80, 85–86, 113, 122–125; Barron, *LSD*, 147–148; Hartje, *Van Dorn*, 278–290.
13. *OR*, Ser. 1, Vol. 23, Pt. 1: 94.
14. Ibid., 98.
15. Ibid., 88–89, 104–105, 116–117; Barron, *LSD*, 149–150; Sparks, *War Between the States*, 76.
16. Lon to Matthew Cartwright, Thompson's Station, Mar. 22, 1863, CC.
17. Barron, *LSD*, 150.
18. Ibid., 150–151.
19. Regimental casualties were derived from *CSR*. See also *OR*, Ser. 1, Vol. 23, Pt. 1: 75, 91, 117, 119; Johnson, *TWWG*, 132; Barron, *LSD*, 149–150; Rose, *RTB*, 92–94; Griscom, *Fighting with Ross'*, 59–60; Crocket, *Two Centuries*, 213–214.
20. *OR*, Ser. 1, Vol. 23, Pt. 1: 130–131, 141–144, and Pt. 2: 119–120, 665, 669, 679, 686–687; Griscom, *Fighting with Ross'*, 60–61; Barron, *LSD*, 151–153; Rose, *RTB*, 98; Henry, *Forrest*, 131–132; Hartje, *Van Dorn*, 291–293.
21. *OR*, Ser. 1, Vol. 23, Pt. 1: 187–189; Hartje, *Van Dorn*, 293–294; Henry, *Forrest*, 132–136.
22. James E. Thomas Diary, entry for Apr. 2, 1863.
23. *OR*, Ser. 1, Vol. 23, Pt. 1: 206, and Pt. 2: 203; Griscom, *Fighting with Ross'*, 61–62.
24. Quoted in Hartje, *Van Dorn*, 295; and Benner, *Sul Ross*, 91.
25. Lon to A. P. Cartwright, Thompson's Station, Apr. 8, 1863, CC.
26. James E. Thomas Diary, entry for Apr. 8, 1863.
27. *OR*, Ser. 1, Vol. 23, Pt. 1: 222–224; Robert L. Willett, Jr., "The First Battle of Franklin," *CWTI* 7 (Feb., 1969): 16–17.
28. *OR*, Ser. 1, Vol. 23, Pt. 2: 233.
29. Ibid., Pt. 1: 224–227, 231, 239; Griscom, *Fighting with Ross'*, 63; Hartje,

Van Dorn, 297–301; Henry, *Forrest,* 136–138; Willett, "First Battle of Franklin," 17–23.

30. *OR,* Ser. 1, Vol. 23, Pt. 1: 294, and Pt. 2: 788; Hartje, *Van Dorn,* 296, 301–304; Henry, *Forrest,* 142–144.

31. *OR,* Ser. 1, Vol. 23, Pt. 1: 321–322; Barron, *LSD,* 153–154; Griscom, *Fighting with Ross',* 64–65; Hartje, *Van Dorn,* 305.

32. Dabney H. Maury, quoted in Castel, *General Sterling Price,* 120.

33. Rose, *RTB,* 99–102; Barron, *LSD,* 154–155; Hartje, *Van Dorn,* 307–323.

34. Griscom, *Fighting with Ross',* 65.

35. James E. Thomas Diary, entry for May 8, 1863. See also Lon to Matthew Cartwright, Spring Hill, May 9, 1863, CC.

36. Keen, "'Such is War'," 58.

Chapter 11. Vicksburg and Jackson, June–August 1863

1. *OR,* Ser. 1, Vol. 24., Pt. 1: 278, and Pt. 3: 947; Griscom, *Fighting with Ross',* 92, 96–97; Benner, *Sul Ross,* 91.

2. Lon to A. P. Cartwright, Thompson's Station, Apr. 8, 1863, CC.

3. James E. Thomas Diary, entry for June 5, 1863.

4. Garrett to Gibbard, Tupelo, Miss., Sept. 28, 1862, Garrett, *Letters,* 65.

5. Desertions were listed in *CSR.* See also James E. Thomas Diary, entries for May 17–31, 1863; Griscom, *Fighting with Ross',* 66–69; Barron, *LSD,* 156–161; *Texas Republican* (Marshall), Mar. 26, 1863.

6. Catton, *Grant Moves South,* 407–454, 457–462, 465–469; Lowell Harrison, "Jackson. . . . Is a Ruined Town," *CWTI* 15 (Feb., 1977): 4–6; Gilbert E. Govan and James W. Livingood, *A Different Valor: The Story of General Joseph E. Johnston, C.S.A.,* 209–213; Wiley, *Johnny Reb,* 93–94.

7. *OR,* Ser. 1, Vol. 24, Pt. 1: 242–244, and Pt. 3: 939–940, 946–947; *BLCW* 3: 480.

8. *OR,* Ser. 1, Vol. 24, Pt. 2: 435–438, 440–442; Griscom, *Fighting with Ross',* 69; *BLCW* 3: 523–524.

9. Quoted in Nevins, *War for the Union* 3: 71.

10. *OR,* Ser. 1, Vol. 24, Pt. 3: 956.

11. Keen, "'Such is War'," 60; Griscom, *Fighting with Ross',* 69–72; *Texas Almanac for 1867,* 213–214; Wiley, *Johnny Reb,* 327–328.

12. Quoted in Ambrose, "Yeoman Discontent," 262.

13. Griscom, *Fighting with Ross',* 70. See also Ben Long to J. B. Long, Vernon, Miss., Aug. 25 and Oct. 18, 1865, and J. B. Armstrong to J. B. Long, Sunflower Landing, Miss., Aug. 3, 1866, JBL.

14. J. R. White to Cynthia White, Yazoo City, June 3, 1863, *The Gilmer Mirror,* Sept. 16, 1976. See also Barron, *LSD,* 167–168.

15. Herman Norton, "Revivalism in the Confederate Armies," *CWH* 6 (Dec., 1960): 410–424; Wiley, *Johnny Reb,* 180–184; Wooster and Wooster, "'Rarin' for a Fight'," 419.

16. Sparks, *War Between the States,* 266.

17. J. R. White to Cynthia White, Yazoo City, June 3, 1863, *The Gilmer Mirror*, Sept. 16, 1976.

18. *OR*, Ser. 1, Vol. 24, Pt. 3: 983.

19. Gammage, *CBB*, 81. See also *OR*, Ser. 1, Vol. 24, Pt. 1: 244–245, Pt. 3: 987–989; Griscom, *Fighting with Ross'*, 72; Govan and Livingood, *Joseph E. Johnston*, 213.

20. Lincoln to Conkling, Washington, Aug. 26, 1863, in *Collected Works of Abraham Lincoln*, ed. by Roy P. Basler, *et al.*, 6: 409.

21. Josiah Gorgas, quoted in Samuel Carter III, *The Final Fortress: The Campaign for Vicksburg, 1862–1863*, 302. See also Catton, *Grant Moves South*, 471–483.

22. Gammage, *CBB*, 81. See also *OR*, Ser. 1, Vol. 24, Pt. 2: 521, 525, 555–556; Edwin C. Bearss, *The Siege of Jackson*, 58–60.

23. Griscom, *Fighting with Ross'*, 72–74; Barron, *LSD*, 162–163; Rose, *RTB*, 109–110; Bearss, *Siege of Jackson*, 61–68; Harrison, "Jackson . . . Is a Ruined Town," 7.

24. *OR*, Ser. 1, Vol. 24, Pt. 3: 994.

25. Ibid., Pt. 2: 526.

26. Ibid., Pt. 1: 245–246; Griscom, *Fighting with Ross'*, 74; Barron, *LSD*, 163–164; Bearss, *Siege of Jackson*, 81–82.

27. *OR*, Ser. 1, Vol. 24, Pt. 2: 535–536, 554–555, 653–654; Griscom, *Fighting with Ross'*, 75; Bearss, *Siege of Jackson*, 84, 89–91.

28. Sherman, quoted in Bearss, *Siege of Jackson*, 97. See also Govan and Livingood, *Joseph E. Johnston*, 220–222; Harrison, "Jackson . . . Is a Ruined Town," 45–47.

29. *OR*, Ser. 1, Vol. 24, Pt. 3: 1016; Griscom, *Fighting with Ross'*, 75–76.

30. *The Brandon Republican*, n.d., quoted in Bearss, *Siege of Jackson*, 102–103.

31. Ibid., 103–105, 129; Govan and Livingood, *Joseph E. Johnston*, 220–222; Bruce Catton, *Grant Takes Command*, 9–16.

32. Notes on men captured and deserted, as well as details on the French case, were included in *CSR*.

Chapter 12. The Big Black and the Sunflower, August 1863–January 1864

1. Quoted in Govan and Livingood, *Joseph E. Johnston*, 223. See also Nevins, *War for the Union* 3: 180–193.

2. *OR*, Ser. 1, Vol. 30, Pt. 4: 493–494; Lon to Mary Cartwright, Pelahatchie, Miss., Aug. 7, 1863, CC; Jeffrey N. Lash, "Joseph E. Johnston's Grenada Blunder: A Failure in Command," *CWH* 23 (June, 1977): 114–121.

3. *OR*, Ser. 1, Vol. 30, Pt. 1: 13–17, Pt. 4: 498–500, 514; Griscom, *Fighting with Ross'*, 76–80; Barron, *LSD*, 165–166; Lash, "Grenada Blunder," 122–128.

4. *OR*, Ser. 1, Vol. 30, Pt. 2: 660–661; Griscom, *Fighting with Ross'*, 81–83.

5. *OR*, Ser. 1, Vol. 30, Pt. 2: 816–817; Griscom, *Fighting with Ross'*, 101–102;

Catton, *Grant Takes Command*, 31–33, 48–49; Edwin C. Bearss, "Misfire in Mississippi: McPherson's Canton Expedition," *CWH* 8 (Dec., 1962): 401–416.

6. A. P. to Amanda Cartwright, Camp Hunter, La., Aug. 16, 1863, CC.

7. Ibid.; Lon to Matthew Cartwright, Spring Hill, Tenn., May 9, 1863, CC; Wiley, *Johnny Reb*, 131–132, 136; Harry N. Scheiber, "The Pay of Confederate Troops and Problems of Demoralization," in Hubbell, *Battles Lost and Won*, 229–239; Ambrose, "Yeoman Discontent," 266–267; Long, *Civil War Day by Day*, 714; Linderman, *Embattled Courage*, 118–124, 174–177.

8. John R. to Oscar Reierson, Prairieville, Tex., Sept. 20, 1863, Reierson Family Papers. As it turned out, the sons survived the war; the father did not.

9. Wiley, *Johnny Reb*, 225–229; Ella Lonn, *Desertion During the Civil War*, 29, 46–52, 57–61, 231; Long, *Civil War Day by Day*, 714–715.

10. Griscom, *Fighting with Ross'*, 80–81, 99; Barron, *LSD*, 165.

11. Deserters were identified in *CSR*.

12. These ratios were computed from data in *Population Schedules*, on which sixty-eight of the ninety-three deserters were identified. See Table 5.

13. *OR*, Ser. 1, Vol. 32, Pt. 3: 877–879; Mabry to Mooreman, Camp Jackson, Miss., Dec. 10, 1863, DAH; Griscom, *Fighting with Ross'*, 103.

14. Lee to Seddon, Pontotoc, Miss., Oct. 2, 1863, quoted in Griscom, *Fighting with Ross'*, 117.

15. *OR*, Ser. 1, Vol. 31, Pt. 3: 866; Griscom, *Fighting with Ross'*, 80, 92, 102–103, 116; Warner, *Generals in Gray*, 183–184, 263–264; Benner, *Sul Ross*, 96–98.

16. *OR*, Ser. 1, Vol. 31, Pt. 3: 841–842, and Vol. 34, Pt. 2: 810–811, 1000–1001; Joseph H. Parks, *General Edmund Kirby Smith*, 290–291, 324, 343–344, 352; Hattaway and Jones, *How the North Won*, 461–462, 473–474, 481–482.

17. *OR*, Ser. 1, Vol. 31, Pt. 3: 879–880, Vol. 32, Pt. 2: 823–824, and Vol. 34, Pt. 2: 810–811; Griscom, *Fighting with Ross'*, 103–105.

18. Quoted in Barron, *LSD*, 174.

19. Sparks, *War Between the States*, 72; W. A. Callaway, "Hard Service with Ross's Brigade," *CV* 28 (Sept., 1920): 328; Moore, "John Benjamin Long," 41.

20. *OR*, Ser. 1, Vol. 34, Pt. 2: 1000; Joe M. Scott, "Crossing the Mississippi in 1864," *CV* 29 (Feb., 1921): 64–65; Barron, *LSD*, 175–176.

21. U.S. Navy Department, *Official Records of the Union and Confederate Navies in the War of the Rebellion*, Ser. 1, Vol. 25: 678–679, 683; Griscom, *Fighting with Ross'*, 106–107.

Chapter 13. The Yazoo and the Black Warrior, February–April 1864

1. *OR*, Ser. 1, Vol. 32, Pt. 1: 174–175; Henry, *Forrest*, 213–220; Warner, *Generals in Blue*, 464–465; B. H. Liddell Hart, *Sherman: Soldier, Realist, American*, 223–226.

2. *OR*, Ser. 1, Vol. 32, Pt. 2: 826. See also General Orders Nos. 1–3, Benton, Jan. 20–31, 1864, DAH; *OR*, Ser. 1, Vol. 32, Pt. 2: 514, 550; Wiley, *Johnny Reb*, 132–133.

3. *OR*, Ser. 1, Vol. 32, Pt. 1: 178, 181, Pt. 2: 826–827; Griscom, *Fighting with Ross'*, 108–110.

4. Frederick H. Dyer, *A Compendium of the War of the Rebellion* 3: 1214, 1731; Ed. M. Main, *The Story of the Marches, Battles and Incidents of the Third United States Colored Cavalry*, 58–59, 93; McPherson, *Battle Cry*, 564–567; Anne J. Bailey, "A Texas Cavalry Raid: Reaction to Black Soldiers and Contrabands," *CWH* 35 (June, 1989): 150–152.

5. *OR*, Ser. 1, Vol. 32, Pt. 1: 315–317, Pt. 2: 827–830; Barron, *LSD*, 176–178; Rose, *RTB*, 104; Main, *Third United States Colored Cavalry*, 94–96.

6. *OR*, Ser. 1, Vol. 32, Pt. 1: 316.

7. Ibid., 317–318, 321–322, 326–327, 385, Pt. 2: 830–833; Wiley, *Johnny Reb*, 314–315; Ira Berlin, ed., *Freedom: A Documentary History of Emancipation, 1861–1867*, Ser. 2: 538; Main, *Third United States Colored Cavalry*, 100–102.

8. Unsigned letter to "Dear Relatives and Friends," Deasonville, Miss., Mar. 12, 1864, DAH.

9. Quoted in Griscom, *Fighting with Ross'*, 111.

10. *OR*, Ser. 1, Vol. 32, Pt. 1: 176.

11. Ibid., Pt. 2: 498.

12. Griscom, *Fighting with Ross'*, 111–112; Barron, *LSD*, 178–181; Henry, *Forrest*, 220–234.

13. *OR*, Ser. 1, Vol. 32, Pt. 1: 320, 322–323, 332, 367; Barron, *LSD*, 181–182; Griscom, *Fighting with Ross'*, 112–114; Main, *Third United States Colored Cavalry*, 113–114; Keen, "'Such is War'," 65.

14. *OR*, Ser. 1, Vol. 32, Pt. 1: 390.

15. Ibid., 327.

16. *OR*, Ser. 1, Vol. 32, Pt. 1: 323–325, 383–387, 390; Pt. 3: 875; Barron, *LSD*, 182–183; Main, *Third United States Colored Cavalry*, 116–122; Warner, *Generals in Gray*, 256–257.

17. *OR*, Ser. 1, Vol. 32, Pt. 1: 385.

18. Ibid., 328.

19. Ibid., 326–329; Main, *Third United States Colored Cavalry*, 291.

20. Unsigned letter to "Dear Relatives and Friends," Deasonville, Mar. 12, 1864, DAH.

21. *OR*, Ser. 1, Vol. 32, Pt. 1: 325–326, 384, 391; Griscom, *Fighting with Ross'*, 114.

22. *OR*, Ser. 1, Vol. 32, Pt. 1: 385.

23. Quoted in Barron, *LSD*, 185.

24. *OR*, Ser. 1, Vol. 32, Pt. 3: 875–876.

25. Ibid., 877–879; Johnson, *TWWG*, 138–139; Griscom, *Fighting with Ross'*, 112, 120; Rose, *RTB*, 151–152; Benner, *Sul Ross*, 101–102; Wiley, *Johnny Reb*, 234, 242.

26. *OR*, Ser. 1, Vol. 32, Pt. 3: 318; Griscom, *Fighting with Ross'*, 121; A. S.

Roberts, "The Federal Government and Confederate Cotton," *American Historical Review* 32 (Jan., 1927): 267–275; Nevins, *War for the Union* 3: 353–373; McPherson, *Battle Cry*, 620–625.

27. *OR*, Ser. 1, Vol. 32, Pt. 1: 653; Griscom, *Fighting with Ross'*, 115; Barron, *LSD*, 185–186; William W. Heartsill, *Fourteen Hundred and 91 Days*, ed. by Bell I. Wiley, 203; Stone, *Brokenburn*, 281.

28. *OR*, Ser. 1, Vol. 32, Pt. 3: 785–787; Joseph H. Parks, *General Leonidas Polk, CSA: The Fighting Bishop*, 370–373.

29. Griscom, *Fighting with Ross'*, 138. See also *OR*, Ser. 1, Vol. 38, Pt. 3: 645–646, Pt. 4: 691; Lee to Cooper, Canton, Mar. 29, 1864, *CSR*, Roll 21; Barron, *LSD*, 186.

30. Walter L. Fleming, *Civil War and Reconstruction in Alabama*, 112–122; Hugh C. Bailey, "Disaffection in the Alabama Hill Country, 1861," *CWH* 4 (June, 1958): 183–194; Durwood Long, "Unanimity and Disloyalty in Secessionist Alabama, *CWH* 11 (Sept., 1965): 257–273.

31. *OR*, Ser. 1, Vol. 32, Pt. 3: 825.

32. Sparks, *War Between the States*, 80–81.

33. *OR*, Ser. 1, Vol. 32, Pt. 1: 671–672, Pt. 3: 858–859; Griscom, *Fighting with Ross'*, 139–140.

34. Barron, *LSD*, 187–189; Sparks, *War Between the States*, 82. Details on the Grimes-Ivy altercation as well as hospitalization for venereal disease were recorded on the individual records in *CSR*.

35. *OR*, Ser. 1, Vol. 38, Pt. 4: 661–663, 691; Govan and Livingood, *Joseph E. Johnston*, 262; Benner, *Sul Ross*, 102–103; Griscom, *Fighting with Ross'*, 141–142, 175–176.

Chapter 14. The Etowah and the Chattahoochee, May–July 1864

1. Nevins, *War for the Union* 4: 52–57, 122–123; McPherson, *Battle Cry*, 722–743; Liddell Hart, *Sherman*, 232–252; Richard M. McMurry, "The Atlanta Campaign of 1864: A New Look," *CWH* 22 (Mar., 1976): 5–12; Govan and Livingood, *Joseph E. Johnston*, 262–278.

2. *OR*, Ser. 1, Vol. 38, Pt. 3: 962–963; Keen, "'Such is War'," 103–104, 117; Griscom, *Fighting with Ross'*, 142–144. Casualties were listed in the *Texas Republican* (Marshall), Oct. 28, 1864, and *CSR*.

3. *OR*, Ser. 1, Vol. 38, Pt. 4: 729, 731–732, 734, 737; Griscom, *Fighting with Ross'*, 144–145; Govan and Livingood, *Joseph E. Johnston*, 278–307; Liddell Hart, *Sherman*, 252–271.

4. *BLCW* 4: 269–270, 306–307; Richard H. McMurry, "'The Hell Hole': New Hope Church," *CWTI* 11 (Feb., 1973): 32–43.

5. Keen, "'Such is War'," 105.

6. Sparks, *War Between the States*, 90. Casualty figures were taken from *CSR* and *Texas Republican* (Marshall), Oct. 28, 1864. See also CPA, No. 3980 on Phillips.

7. Sparks, *War Between the States*, 87.

8. Ibid., 86; Barron, *LSD*, 194–196; Griscom, *Fighting with Ross'*, 145–147; *OR*, Ser. 1, Vol. 38, Pt. 4: 764–766, 768, 771.

9. Keen, "'Such is War'," 107–108.

10. Griscom, *Fighting with Ross'*, 148–149.

11. *OR*, Ser. 1, Vol. 38, Pt. 4: 766–767.

12. Ibid., 779–780, 783, 786–787, 790, 792–793; Griscom, *Fighting with Ross'*, 150–152; *BLCW* 4: 270–271.

13. Sparks, *War Between the States*, 97.

14. *OR*, Ser. 1, Vol. 38, Pt. 4: 799–801, 804; Griscom, *Fighting with Ross'*, 152–153; Keen, "'Such is War'," 105.

15. *OR*, Ser. 1, Vol. 38, Pt. 5: 46–47, 55–57, 859–861, 863–864, 866; Griscom, *Fighting with Ross'*, 153–155; Barron, *LSD*, 197–198; *BLCW* 4: 331–333.

16. *OR*, Ser. 1, Vol. 38, Pt. 5: 54, 872–873, 884; Barron, *LSD*, 198; Griscom, *Fighting with Ross'*, 155–158.

17. *OR*, Ser. 1, Vol. 38, Pt. 5: 885.

18. Quoted in Cater, *AIW*, 183.

19. Lon to Anna Cartwright, Mechanicsburg, Miss., Mar. 22, 1865, CC.

20. Keen, "'Such is War'," 104–105. For a discussion of the common soldiers' attitude toward Johnston and Hood, see Richard M. McMurry, "Confederate Morale in the Atlanta Campaign of 1864," *Georgia Historical Quarterly* 54 (Summer, 1970): 226–243.

Chapter 15. Atlanta, July–August 1864

1. Matthew to A. P. Cartwright, San Augustine, Aug. 6, 1864, CC. See also Liddell Hart, *Sherman*, 272–305; Hattaway and Jones, *How the North Won*, 607–613, 622–623; John P. Dyer, *The Gallant Hood*, 247–270; McPherson, *Battle Cry*, 760–773.

2. A. P. to Matthew Cartwright, Washington, La., May 23, 1864, CC.

3. The absentee rate for the regiment was derived from the rolls of May–June, 1864, in *CSR*, the last available for the war. See also Table 5, and Richard E. Beringer, et al., *Why the South Lost the Civil War*, 333.

4. *OR*, Ser. 1, Vol. 38, Pt. 5: 897, 901–902, 907; Griscom, *Fighting with Ross'*, 158–159.

5. Philip L. Secrist, "The Role of Cavalry in the Atlanta Campaign, 1864," *Georgia Historical Quarterly* 56 (Winter, 1972): 521–522; Wilbur S. Nye, "Cavalry Operations Around Atlanta," *CWTI* 3 (July, 1964): 46–50; John W. Rowell, "McCook's Raid," *CWTI* 13 (July, 1974): 5–9, 42–48; William R. Scaife, *The Campaign for Atlanta*, 77–79.

6. *OR*, Ser. 1, Vol. 38, Pt. 5: 911–912. See also Griscom, *Fighting with Ross'*, 160.

7. *OR*, Ser. 1, Vol. 38, Pt. 5: 923; Barron, *LSD*, 199; *BLCW* 4: 319–320;

J. Britt McCarley, "The Battle of Ezra Church," *Atlanta Historical Journal* 28 (Fall, 1984): 65–70.

8. *OR*, Ser. 1, Vol. 38, Pt. 2: 761–764, Pt. 3: 688; Keen, "'Such is War'," 110; Scaife, *Campaign for Atlanta*, 80–81; S. B. Barron, "Wheeler's Cavalry in Georgia Campaign," *CV* 14 (Feb., 1906): 70.

9. *OR*, Ser. 1, Vol. 38, Pt. 2: 763, Pt. 3: 963–964; Griscom, *Fighting with Ross'*, 160–161; Barron, *LSD*, 199–200.

10. Secrist, "The Role of Cavalry," 522–524; Scaife, *Campaign for Atlanta*, 86–91.

11. Barron, *LSD*, 201–202.

12. Quoted in Johnson, *TWWG*, 111.

13. *OR*, Ser. 1, Vol. 38, Pt. 2: 763, 776–777, and Pt. 3: 964–965; Sparks, *War Between the States*, 100–102; Barron, *LSD*, 200–204; Griscom, *Fighting with Ross'*, 161–162; Scaife, *Campaign for Atlanta*, 81–86, 91–92; Stephen Z. Starr, *The Union Cavalry in the Civil War* 3: 471–473.

14. Keen, "'Such is War'," 112.

15. *OR*, Ser. 1, Vol. 38, Pt. 5: 936.

16. Ibid., Pt. 3: 689.

17. Ibid., Pt. 1: 77.

18. Quoted in Warner, *Generals in Blue*, 267.

19. *OR*, Ser. 1, Vol. 38, Pt. 2: 858, Pt. 3: 683, Pt. 5: 968, 971; Griscom, *Fighting with Ross'*, 162–165.

20. *OR*, Ser. 1, Vol. 38, Pt. 5: 968.

21. Ibid., Pt. 2: 813–814, 858–859, Pt. 5: 978, 981; Griscom, *Fighting with Ross'*, 165–166; Barron, *LSD*, 205–208, 216–221; Keen, "'Such is War'," 112–117.

22. Barron, *LSD*, 209.

23. Lon to A. P. Cartwright, Rough and Ready, Ga., Aug. 24, 1864, CC.

24. Barron, *LSD*, 209.

25. *OR*, Ser. 1, Vol. 38, Pt. 2: 859.

26. Ibid., pp. 814–815.; Barron, *LSD*, 210–215, 222–227; Johnson, *TWWG*, 169; Benner, *Sul Ross*, 106.

27. *OR*, Ser. 1, Vol. 38, Pt. 1: 172; Barron, *LSD*, 214. Casualties were listed in *CSR*.

28. *OR*, Ser. 2, Vol. 8: 996–1000; William B. Hesseltine, "Civil War Prisons—Introduction," *CWH* 8 (June, 1962): 118.

29. *OR*, Ser. 1, Vol. 38, Pt. 2: 859; Rose, *RTB*, 179–180; Hesseltine, *Civil War Prisons*, 230–231.

30. *OR*, Ser. 2, Vol. 8: 998; Hesseltine, *Civil War Prisons*, 38–40, 47; Edward T. Downer, "Johnson's Island," *CWH* 8 (June, 1962): 202–217.

31. William M. Moon, quoted in *Memorial & Biographical History of Dallas County, Texas*, 954–955. See also Robertson, *Soldiers Blue and Gray*, 195; and T. B. Camp to Editor, *Texas Republican*, quoted in *Marshall News-Messenger*, July 22, 1962.

32. Hesseltine, *Civil War Prisons*, 182, 188; Henry P. Teague to E. M. Pyle, Johnson's Island, Mar. 5, 1865, *Kaufman Sun*, Jan. 8, 1885.

33. *OR*, Ser. 2, Vol. 7: 530. See also Linderman, *Embattled Courage*, 257–261.

34. *OR*, Ser. 2, Vol. 8: 581, 700–701, 996–1001; Hesseltine, *Civil War Prisons*, 52; Robertson, *Soldiers Blue and Gray*, 212. Deaths in captivity were listed in *CSR*.

35. Rose, *RTB*, 182.

36. *OR*, Ser. 1, Vol. 52, Pt. 2: 725.

37. Lon to A. P. Cartwright, Rough and Ready, Ga., Aug. 24, 1864, CC.

38. E. B. to Fannie Blocker, n.p., Aug. 27, 1864, Blocker Correspondence.

39. William T. Sherman, *Memoirs* 2: 104.

40. *OR*, Ser. 1, Vol. 38, Pt. 2: 856–857, 860–861, Pt. 5: 995–997; *Barron, LSD*, 228–230; Griscom, *Fighting with Ross'*, 167–169.

41. Sherman, in *BLCW* 4: 254.

42. Sherman, *Memoirs* 2: 110.

Chapter 16. Hell in Tennessee, September–December 1864

1. Quoted in Dyer, *Hood*, 275. See also Liddell Hart, *Sherman*, 308–316; Samuel Carter III, *The Siege of Atlanta, 1864*, 325–346; McPherson, *Battle Cry*, 807–809.

2. *OR*, Ser. 1, Vol. 39, Pt. 2: 850–851; Sykes Inspection Report, Ga., Sept. 10, 1864, U.S. National Archives and Records Service, *Inspection Reports*, M 935, Roll 6, 3–11; Richard M. McMurry, *John Bell Hood and the War for Southern Independence*, 153–157.

3. J. R. White to Cynthia White, n.p., Aug. 23, 1864, *Gilmer Mirror*, Sept. 16, 1976.

4. General Orders No. 37, Ala., Nov. 15, 1864, DAH.

5. General Orders No. 28, Ga., Oct. 5, 1864, ibid.

6. Sykes Inspection Report, Ga., Sept. 10, 1864, 9; *OR*, Ser. 1, Vol. 38, Pt. 5: 1026–1027; Benner, *Sul Ross*, 107–108; Leann C. Adams, "Francis Richard Lubbock," in William C. Nunn, ed., *Ten Texans in Gray*, 94–95. Deserters were listed in *CSR*.

7. *OR*, Ser. 1, Vol. 38, Pt. 5: 996.

8. Barron, *LSD*, 230.

9. Ibid., 231.

10. Ibid., 234–235. See also S. B. Barron, "Wade's Supernumary Scouts," *CV* 11 (Mar., 1903): 115.

11. *OR*, Ser. 1, Vol. 52, Pt. 2: 733, 747; Griscom, *Fighting with Ross'*, 169–172; McMurry, *John Bell Hood*, 159–167; Dyer, *Hood*, 279–285.

12. *OR*, Ser. 1, Vol. 39, Pt. 3: 378.

13. Ibid., Pt. 1: 729, Pt. 3: 94, and Vol. 52, Pt. 2: 749–750, 759–761; Griscom, *Fighting with Ross'*, 172–173; *BLCW* 4: 425–427; Williams, *Beauregard*, 241–245.

14. *OR*, Ser. 1, Vol. 39, Pt. 1: 713–714, and Vol. 45, Pt. 1: 767–768; Griscom, *Fighting with Ross'*, 186–188; Liddell Hart, *Sherman*, 322–329.

15. Barron, *LSD*, 239. See also Griscom, *Fighting with Ross'*, 187; Mary C.

Chadick, "Civil War Days in Huntsville," *Alabama Historical Quarterly* 9 (Sum., 1947): 280–287.

16. *OR*, Ser. 1, Vol. 45, Pt. 1: 768; Griscom, *Fighting with Ross'*, 187–189; *BLCW* 4: 441–443; Carter, *Siege of Atlanta*, 356–363; Warner, *Generals in Blue*, 500–501; Henry, *Forrest*, 384–385.

17. Sparks, *War Between the States*, 279.

18. *OR*, Ser. 1, Vol. 45, Pt. 1: 575–576, 752, 768–769; Griscom, *Fighting with Ross'*, 189–191; Henry, *Forrest*, 385–389; Warner, *Generals in Blue*, 215–216; Thomas A. Wigginton, "Cavalry Operations in the Nashville Campaign," *CWTI* 3 (Dec., 1964): 40; Moore, "Life of John Benjamin Long," 47.

19. *OR*, Ser. 1, Vol. 45, Pt. 1: 753, 769–770; Sparks, *War Between the States*, 279–283; McMurry, *John Bell Hood*, 170–171; Thomas L. Connelly, *Autumn of Glory*, 490–494; Warner, *Generals in Blue*, 566–568.

20. *OR*, Ser. 1, Vol. 45, Pt. 1: 147–149; Henry, *Forrest*, 389–394; Connelly, *Autumn of Glory*, 495–499; Hattaway and Jones, *How the North Won*, 645–646; James L. McDonough and Thomas L. Connelly, *Five Tragic Hours: The Battle of Franklin*, 46–59.

21. Quoted in Henry, *Forrest*, 393.

22. *OR*, Ser. 1, Vol. 45, Pt. 1: 770–771; Griscom, *Fighting with Ross'*, 191; J. P. Young, "Hood's Failure at Spring Hill," *CV* 16 (Jan., 1908): 40; *BLCW* 4: 445–449; Henry, *Forrest*, 394; Wigginton, "Cavalry Operations," 40–41; Nevins, *War for the Union* 4: 174–175.

23. Hood, in *BLCW* 4: 432.

24. McDonough and Connelly, *Five Tragic Hours*, 61–68, 153–154, 157–158; Henry, *Forrest*, 396–400; Connelly, *Autumn of Glory*, 502–506; Nevins, *War for the Union* 4: 175–178; McPherson, *Battle Cry*, 812–813.

25. Quoted in Rose, *RTB*, 119.

26. *OR*, Ser. 1, Vol. 45, Pt. 1: 576, 753–754, 770–771; Sparks, *War Between the States*, 283–284; Griscom, *Fighting with Ross'*, 191–192; Johnson, *TWWG*, 239–240; *BLCW* 4: 466–467; Jacob D. Cox, *The Battle of Franklin*, 172–179.

27. Dyer, *Hood*, 295–297; McMurry, *John Bell Hood*, 176–179; Connelly, *Autumn of Glory*, 506–509; Hattaway and Jones, *How the North Won*, 646–651.

28. *OR*, Ser. 1, Vol. 45, Pt. 1: 744–745, Pt. 2: 652, 666, 670, and Vol. 49, Pt. 2: 502–503; Henry, *Forrest*, 401–403.

29. *OR*, Ser. 1, Vol. 45, Pt. 1: 613, 755; Griscom, *Fighting with Ross'*, 193.

30. Griscom, *Fighting with Ross'*, 194. See also *OR*, Ser. 1, Vol. 45, Pt. 1: 613–615, 617–619, 746–747; 755; Henry, *Forrest*, 404–405; Callaway, "Hard Service with Ross's Brigade," 328.

31. Griscom, *Fighting with Ross'*, 196. See also *OR*, Ser. 1, Vol. 45, Pt. 1: 620–621, 756, 771, Pt. 2: 682; W. A. Callaway, "Hard Times with Ross's Cavalry," *CV* 28 (Dec., 1920): 447.

32. Dyer, *Hood*, 297–302; Henry, *Forrest*, 407–411; Connelly, *Autumn of Glory*, 508–512; Hattaway and Jones, *How the North Won*, 651–654; Nevins, *War for the Union* 4: 185–187.

33. *OR*, Ser. 1, Vol. 45, Pt. 1: 578, 756–758, 771; Griscom, *Fighting with Ross'*, 196–198.

34. *OR*, Ser. 1, Vol. 45, Pt. 1: 567, 603, 727–728, 758, 771–772; J. P. Young, "Christmas in Camp," MS, 5–6, DAH; Barron, *LSD*, 251–253; Henry, *Forrest*, 410–415; McMurry, *John Bell Hood*, 181.

35. *OR*, Ser. 1, Vol. 45, Pt. 1: 42.

Chapter 17. The Road Back, January–May 1865

1. *OR*, Ser. 1, Vol. 45, Pt. 2: 748; Griscom, *Fighting with Ross'*, 198, 202.

2. *OR*, Ser. 1, Vol. 45, Pt. 1: 772.

3. Ibid.; Barron, *LSD*, 275; *Daily News* (Galveston), Mar. 26, 1865; Moore, "Life of John Benjamin Long," 47.

4. Nathan Gregg, quoted in *Texas Republican* (Marshall), Jan. 27, 1865.

5. General Orders No. 1, Verona, Feb. 13, 1865, Jackson Div. Order Book, DAH; *OR*, Ser. 1, Vol. 48, Pt. 1: 973–974, and Vol. 49, Pt. 1: 791, 952–953, 972, 1015–1016; Lon to Matthew and Amanda Cartwright, Yazoo County, Miss., Feb. 20, 1865, CC; Barron, *LSD*, 268–269; Henry, *Forrest*, 418; Benner, *Sul Ross*, 112.

6. W. T. Long to J. B. Long, Rusk, Mar. 21, 1865, JBL; A. B. Stone to J. B. Long, Edward's Depot, Miss., Apr. 20, 1865, JBL; General Orders No. [ill.], Deasonville, Miss., Feb. 20, and General Orders No. 5, Vaughn Station, Miss., Feb. 29, 1865, Jackson Div. Order Book, DAH; *OR*, Ser. 1, Vol. 48, Pt. 1: 1198–1199, 1394–1395, and Vol. 49, Pt. 1: 998–999, 1026, 1061; Garrett to Gibbard, Canton, Miss., Mar. 14, 1865, in Garrett, *Letters*, 90; Barron, *LSD*, 270; Betts, "Smith County in the Civil War," 117.

7. Lon to Anna Cartwright, Mechanicsburg, Miss., Mar. 22, 1865, CC.

8. *OR*, Ser. 1, Vol. 49, Pt. 1: 1015–1016, Pt. 2: 1127; Richard Taylor, *Destruction and Reconstruction*, 267–268; James P. Jones, *Yankee Blitzkrieg*, 13–14, 21–22, 39–41, 44–52; Henry, *Forrest*, 420–425; Hattaway and Jones, *How the North Won*, 642–643, 654–658, 663–674.

9. *OR*, Ser. 1, Vol. 49, Pt. 2: 1221. See also ibid., 1150–1151, 1189, 1192–1193, 1196, 1201–1203, 1211, 1225; and *Official Records of the Union and Confederate Navies*, Ser. 1, Vol. 27: 120–121.

10. Taylor, *Destruction and Reconstruction*, 270–272; *BLCW* 4: 410–411; Henry, *Forrest*, 427–435; Jones, *Yankee Blitzkrieg*, xi–xii, 75–99, 170–179; McPherson, *Battle Cry*, 844–852.

11. *Texas Republican* (Marshall), Apr. 28, 1865. See also Heartsill, *1491 Days*, 240; William W. White, "The Disintegration of an Army," *ETHJ* 26 (1988): 41.

12. Ellen Ellis to J. B. Long, Rusk, Apr. 26, 1865, JBL.

13. *Texas Republican* (Marshall), Apr. 28, 1865.

14. Sparks, *War Between the States*, 116–117.

15. *OR*, Ser. 1, Vol. 49, Pt. 2: 1279.

16. Taylor, quoted in Jones to Stone, Jackson, Miss., May 4, 1865, JBL.

17. *OR*, Ser. 1, Vol. 49, Pt. 2: 609, 673, 1283–1284, Ser. 2, Vol. 8: 718, 828–829, and Ser. 3, Vol. 5: 532; Taylor, *Destruction and Reconstruction*,

274–276, 364–366; Max L. Heyman, Jr., *Prudent Soldier: A Biography of Major General E. R. S. Canby, 1817–1873,* 232–234.

18. Sparks, *War Between the States,* 116. See also *Texas Republican* (Marshall), May 26, 1865.

19. Sparks, *War Between the States,* 117–123; *OR,* Ser. 1, Vol. 49, Pt. 1: 880; *Official Records of the Union and Confederate Navies,* Ser. 1, Vol. 27: 230; Campbell, *Southern Community in Crisis,* 219; Max S. Lale, "The Military Occupation of Marshall, Texas," *MHTS* 13 (1976): 42–44; Moore, "Life of John Benjamin Long," 48–49.

20. White, "Disintegration of an Army," 41–44; Robert L. Kerby, *Kirby Smith's Confederacy,* 405, 410, 413–427; Charles W. Ramsdell, "Texas from the Fall of the Confederacy to the Beginning of Reconstruction," *Quarterly of the Texas State Historical Association* 11 (Jan., 1908): 199–210; Betts, "Smith County in the Civil War," 119–122; Campbell, *Southern Community in Crisis,* 219, 247.

Chapter 18. East Texas Veterans

1. Waldo W. Braden, "Repining Over an Irrevocable Past," in Braden, ed., *Oratory in the New South,* 10. See also Linderman, *Embattled Courage,* 2–3, 240–244, 249–252, 257; Reid Mitchell, *Civil War Soldiers,* 204–206; James L. Roark, *Masters Without Slaves,* 120–123, 131–135; and Gaines M. Foster, *Ghosts of the Confederacy,* 13–22.

2. Word to Lon Cartwright, Goliad, Mar. 28, 1867, CC.

3. Armstrong to J. B. Long, Sunflower Landing, Miss., Aug. 3, 1866, JBL.

4. Ben Long to J. B. Long, Vernon, Miss., Aug. 25, 1865, ibid.

5. Harrison County Marriage Records 5: 21–31; Ogreta W. Huttash, comp., *Marriage Records of Cherokee County, Texas, 1846–1880, passim.*

6. Quoted in William L. Pryor, "'The Fate of Marvin': An Epic Poem of the Civil War by a Texas Soldier," *Texas Quarterly* 20 (Sum., 1977): 12.

7. J. B. Long to Nellie and Aunt Nin, Rusk, Oct. 10, 1865, JBL.

8. E. W. Williams to J. B. Long, Pickens Station, Miss., Apr. 16, 1866, ibid.

9. Third Texas Cavalry File; William F. Fox, *Regimental Losses in the American Civil War,* 6, 8, 11–13; Long, *Civil War Day by Day,* 716–718.

10. *OR,* Ser. 1, Vol. 3: 74.

11. Quoted in Berenger, *Why the South Lost the Civil War,* 247.

12. Absentee records were derived from *CSR.*

13. These conclusions are based upon Griffith, *Battle Tactics of the Civil War,* 65–67, 69, 121–122, 179–185; Berenger, *Why the South Lost the Civil War,* 14, 169–171, 247–248; Starr, *The Union Cavalry in the Civil War* 3: 589–594; Edwin C. Fishel, "The Mythology of Civil War Intelligence," and McWhiney, "Who Whipped Whom?" in Hubbell, *Battles Lost and Won,* 94–95, 104–106, 269–270.

14. The incidence of losses in the Third Texas was derived from *CSR,* while comparative data were drawn from Harold B. Simpson, *Hood's Texas Brigade:*

A Compendium, 533–538; Earl J. Hess, "The 12th Missouri Infantry," *Missouri Historical Review* 76 (Oct., 1981): 53–77; Mark H. Dunkelman and Michael Winey, *The Hardtack Regiment*, 198–199; Long, *Civil War Day By Day*, 718.

15. See Table 5. From *CSR* and local biographical or genealogical records it was possible to ascertain the fate of 1,024 individuals among the 1,340 who served in the regiment, or 76 percent of the total. Of these 1,024 men, 817, or 79.7 percent, were known to have survived the conflict.

16. This conclusion follows the interpretations of Eric Foner, *Reconstruction*, 587–612; George C. Rable, "Bourbonism, Reconstruction, and the Persistence of Southern Distinctiveness," *CWH* 29 (June, 1983): 135–153; James T. Moore, "Redeemers Reconsidered: Change and Continuity in the Democratic South," *JSH* 44 (Aug., 1978): 357–378; Harold D. Woodman, "Sequel to Slavery: The New History Views the Postbellum South," *JSH* 43 (Nov., 1977): 523–554; Jonathan M. Wiener, "Class Structure and Economic Development in the American South, 1865–1955," *American Historical Review* 84 (Oct., 1979): 970–992; and Thomas B. Alexander, "The Dimensions of Continuity Across the Civil War," in Harry P. Owens and James J. Cooke, eds., *The Old South in the Crucible of War*, 85–94. For details on the impact of Reconstruction in East Texas, see James M. Smallwood, *Time of Hope, Time of Despair*, 24–42, 128–158; John P. Carrier, "Bullets, Ballots, and Bayonets: Reconstruction Politics and Elections in Smith County, 1866–1873," *CSC* 13 (Summer, 1974): 1–14; Gregg Cantrell, "Racial Violence and Reconstruction Politics in Texas, 1867–1868," *SHQ* 93 (July, 1989): 333–355; Campbell, *Southern Community in Crisis*, 245–364; and C. Alwyn Barr, *Reconstruction to Reform*, 193–208, 248–251. For a discussion of other perspectives on the issue, see Edgar P. Sneed, "A Historiography of Reconstruction in Texas: Some Myths and Problems," *SHQ* 72 (Apr., 1969): 435–447; and Barry A. Crouch, "'Unmanacling' Texas Reconstruction: A Twenty-Year Perspective," *SHQ* 93 (July, 1989): 275–301.

17. U.S. Bureau of the Census, Twelfth Census, *Occupations*, 392, 396, and *Agriculture*, Pt. 1, 52. This summary of the evolution of postbellum Southern agriculture is adapted from Foner, *Reconstruction*, 399–409; Roger L. Ransom and Richard Sutch, *One Kind of Freedom: The Economic Consequences of Emancipation*, 87–97, 104–105, 149–168, 177–199; and Gavin Wright, *The Political Economy of the Cotton South*, 160–184. For detailed evidence of continued economic preeminence by the old planter families in widely separated regions of the South, see Randolph B. Campbell, "Population Persistence and Social Change in Nineteenth Century Texas: Harrison County, 1850–1880," *JSH* 48 (May, 1982): 185–204; A. Jane Townes, "The Effect of Emancipation on Large Landholdings: Nelson and Goochland Counties, Virginia," *JSH* 45 (Aug., 1979): 403–412; and Jonathan M. Wiener, "Planter Persistence and Social Change: Alabama, 1850–1870," *Journal of Interdisciplinary History* 7 (Autumn, 1976): 235–260.

18. Beringer, *Why the South Lost the Civil War*, 398–417; Linderman, *Embattled Courage*, 266–297; Braden, "Repining over an Irrevocable Past," and Howard Dorgan, "Rhetoric of the United Confederate Veterans," in Braden, ed., *Oratory in the New South*, 8–37, 143–173; Charles R. Wilson, "The Religion

of the Lost Cause: Ritual and Organization of the Southern Civil Religion, 1865–1920," *JSH* 46 (May, 1980): 219–238; Patrick Gerster and Nicholas Cords, "The Northern Origins of Southern Mythology," *JSH* 43 (Nov., 1977): 567–582; and Foster, *Ghosts of the Confederacy*, 85–87, 117–126, 140–144, 156–159, 194–196.

19. Barry A. Crouch, "The Freedmen's Bureau," *CSC* 11 (Spring, 1972): 26; Barry A. Crouch, "View from Within: Letters of Gregory Barrett, Freedmen's Bureau Agent," *CSC* 12 (Winter, 1973): 20, 28; Johnson, *TWWG*, 101–102, 178–179; Robert E. Thomas, "The Thomas Family in 300 Years of American History," 87; Crocket, *Two Centuries*, 347; Sue E. Moore, "Life of John Benjamin Long," 52–55; John T. Carrier, "The Era of Reconstruction, 1865–1875," in Glover and Cross, *Tyler and Smith County*, 72–73.

20. Quoted in Lane to Vincent, Marshall, Jan., 1905, in Lane, *AR*, 137.

21. Texas, Constitutional Convention, 1875, *Journal*, 3–4; *Walsh and Pilgrim's Directory of the Officers and Members of the Constitutional Convention of the State of Texas, A.D., 1875*, 1, 3; *Members of the Legislature*, 75, 81, 90, 97; Johnson, *TWWG*, 111–112; *Handbook of Texas* 1: 340, 541, 828, 2: 76–77, 99, 607; J. E. Ericson, "The Delegates to the Convention of 1875: A Reappraisal," *SHQ* 67 (July, 1963): 25; Randolph B. Campbell, "The District Judges of Texas in 1866–1867: An Episode in the Failure of Presidential Reconstruction," *SHQ* 93 (July, 1989): 360–361, 372–373.

22. *Texas Almanac for 1867*, 238, 240–241; Leath, "Elected County Officials, 1846–76," *CSC* 17 (Summer, 1978): 60, 18 (Summer, 1979): 8–10, and 19, (Summer, 1980): 33–36; Templeton, *CCH*, 81–94, 115, 701; *Memorial and Biographical History of Dallas County, Texas*, 953–955; Rose, *RTB*, 10.

23. Rose, *RTB*, 7, 11.

Bibliography

Manuscript Sources

Blocker Correspondence. Ralph O. Harvey, Jr., Wichita Falls, Tex.
Brown, Fannie Rhodes. Diary. Mary C. Sylvester, Stillwater, Okla.
Bryan, John Arthur. Papers. Barker Texas History Center, University of Texas, Austin.
Cartwright Correspondence. David D. Jackson, Dallas.
Civil War File. Smith County Historical Society Archives, Tyler, Tex.
Confederate Pension Applications. Texas State Archives, Austin.
Confederate Reminiscences. Texas Confederate Museum, Austin.
Confederate States of America Records. Barker Texas History Center, University of Texas, Austin.
Craver Correspondence. Dorothy Craver, Jefferson, Tex.
Greer File. Special Collections, East Texas Baptist University, Marshall, Tex.
Greer Records. *Civil War Times Illustrated* Collection. U.S. Army Military History Institute, Carlisle Barracks, Pa.
Greer Papers. Jane Judge Greer, Tyler, Tex.
Harrison County Marriage Records. Jefferson Historical Museum, Jefferson, Tex.
Hill, Demetria Ann. Collection. Barker Texas History Center, University of Texas, Austin.
Kaufman County Commissioners' Court, Minutes. David D. Jackson, Dallas.
Larissa College File. Tyler Public Library, Tyler, Texas.
Long, John Benjamin. Papers. Barker Texas History Center, University of Texas, Austin.
Marion County Family Profiles. Jefferson Historical Museum, Jefferson, Tex.
Marshall C.S.A. File. Harrison County Historical Museum, Marshall, Tex.

Muster Rolls. Texas State Archives, Austin.

Reierson Family Papers. Barker Texas History Center, University of Texas, Austin.

Short, Maurice. Collection, Texas State Archives, Austin.

Smith, Jennie Charlotte. Diary. Mount Pleasant Public Library, Mount Pleasant, Tex.

Third Texas Cavalry File. Confederate Research Center and Museum, Hill College, Hillsboro, Tex.

Thomas, James E. Diary. Richard R. Hrabchak, Cranbury, N.J.

Thomas, Robert E. "The Thomas Family in 300 Years of American History." McXie Martin, San Augustine, Tex.

Government Documents

Texas. Constitutional Convention, 1866. *The Constitution, as Amended, and Ordinances of the Convention of 1866.* Austin, 1866.

————. Constitutional Convention, 1875. *Journal.* Galveston, 1875.

————. Legislature. *Members of the Legislature of the State of Texas from 1846 to 1939.* Compiled by Tommy Yett. Austin, 1939.

U.S. Bureau of the Census. Eighth Census. *Agriculture of the United States in 1860.* Washington, D.C., 1864.

————. Eighth Census. *Manufactures of the United States in 1860.* Washington, D.C., 1865.

————. Eighth Census. *Population of the United States in 1860.* Washington, D.C., 1864.

————. Eighth Census. *Statistics of the United States.* Washington, D.C., 1866.

————. Twelfth Census, 1900. *Agriculture.* Washington, D.C., 1902.

————. Twelfth Census, 1900. *Occupations.* Washington, D.C., 1904.

————. *Historical Statistics of the United States: Colonial Times to 1970.* 2 vols. Washington, D.C., 1975.

U.S. Department of the Interior. Office of Indian Affairs. *Report of the Commissioner of Indian Affairs for the Year 1862.* Washington, D.C., 1865.

U.S. National Archives and Record Service. *Compiled Service Records of Confederate Soldiers Who Served in Organizations from the State of Texas.* Washington, D.C., 1960. Microcopy No. 323, Rolls 18–23.

————. *Inspection Reports and Related Records Received by the Inspection Branch of the Confederate Adjutant and Inspector General's Office.* Washington, D.C., 1974. Microcopy No. 935, Roll 6.

————. *Population Schedules of the Eighth Census of the United States, 1860.* Washington, D.C., 1967. Microcopy No. 653, Rolls 1287–1308.

U.S. Navy Department. *Official Records of the Union and Confederate Navies in the War of the Rebellion.* 31 vols. Washington, D. C., 1894–1927.

U.S. War Department. *The War of the Rebellion: A Compilation of the Official*

Records of the Union and Confederate Armies. 128 vols. Washington, D.C., 1880–1901.

Periodicals

Daily News (Galveston), March 26, 1865.
Dallas Herald, 1861.
The Gilmer Mirror, September 16, 1976.
Henderson Times, 1938, 1948.
Marshall News-Messenger, 1961–1963.
The Sun (Kaufman), January 8, 1885.
The Standard (Clarksville), 1861.
The Texas Almanac. Galveston, 1857–1873.
Texas Republican (Marshall), 1861–1865.

Published Primary Sources

BOOKS

Barron, Samuel B. *The Lone Star Defenders: A Chronicle of the Third Texas Cavalry, Ross' Brigade.* 1908. Reprint. Washington, D.C., 1983.

Baxter, William. *Pea Ridge and Prairie Grove, or Scenes and Incidents of the War in Arkansas.* Cincinnati, 1864.

Cater, Douglas J. *As It Was: Reminiscences of a Soldier of the Third Texas Cavalry and the Nineteenth Louisiana Infantry.* Austin, 1990.

Douglas, James P. *Douglas's Texas Battery, CSA.* Edited by Lucia R. Douglas. Tyler, Tex. 1966.

Gammage, Washington L. *The Camp, the Bivouac, and the Battlefield: Being a History of the Fourth Arkansas Regiment.* Selma, Ala., 1864.

Garrett, David R. *The Civil War Letters of David R. Garrett, Detailing the Adventures of the 6th Texas Cavalry, 1861–1865.* Edited by Max S. Lale and Hobart Key, Jr. Marshall, Tex., 1967.

Good, John J. *Cannon Smoke: The Letters of Captain John J. Good, Good-Douglas Texas Battery, CSA.* Edited by Lester N. Fitzhugh. Hillsboro, Tex., 1971.

Grant, Ulysses S. *The Papers of Ulysses S. Grant.* Edited by John Y. Simon. 14 vols. Carbondale and Edwardsville, Ill., 1967–.

Griscom, George L. *Fighting with Ross' Texas Cavalry Brigade, CSA: The Diary of George L. Griscom.* Edited by Homer L. Kerr. Hillsboro, Tex., 1976.

Heartsill, William W. *Fourteen Hundred and 91 Days in the Confederate Army.* Edited by Bell I. Wiley. Jackson, Tenn., 1953.

Huttash, Ogreta W., comp. *Civil War Records of Cherokee County, Texas.* 2 vols. Jacksonville, Tex., 1982.

————. *Marriage Records of Cherokee County, Texas, 1846–1880.* Jacksonville, Tex., 1973.

Ingmire, Frances T., comp. *Archives and Pioneers of Hunt County, Texas.* 2 vols. St. Louis, 1975.

————. *Texas Rangers, 1847–1900.* 6 vols. St. Louis, 1982.

Jackson, David D., and James Q. Erwin, eds. *Rebels from the Redlands.* Dallas, 1990.

Johnson, Robert U., and Clarence C. Buel, eds. *Battles and Leaders of the Civil War.* 4 vols. 1884–1888. Reprint. Secaucus, N.J., 1983.

Johnson, Sid S. *Some Biographies of Old Settlers; Historical Personal and Reminiscent.* Tyler, Tex., 1900.

————. *Texans Who Wore the Gray.* Tyler, Tex., 1907.

Lane, Walter P. *The Adventures and Recollections of General Walter P. Lane.* 2d ed. Marshall, Tex., 1928.

Lincoln, Abraham. *The Collected Works of Abraham Lincoln.* Edited by Roy P. Basler et al. 9 vols., New Brunswick, N.J., 1953–1955.

Main, Ed. M. *The Story of the Marches, Battles and Incidents of the Third United States Colored Cavalry.* 1908. Reprint. New York, 1970.

Olmsted, Frederick L. *A Journey Through Texas, or a Saddle Trip on the Southwestern Frontier.* New York, 1857.

Rawick, George P., ed. *The American Slave: A Composite Autobiography.* 19 vols. Westport, Conn., 1972.

Rose, Victor M. *The Life and Services of Gen. Ben McCulloch.* 1883. Reprint. Austin, 1958.

————. *Ross' Texas Brigade: Being a Narrative of Events Connected with Its Service in the Late War Between the States.* 1881. Reprint. Kennesaw, Ga., 1960.

————. *Some Historical Facts in Regard to the Settlement of Victoria, Texas.* Laredo, Tex., 1883.

Sherman, William T. *Memoirs of General W. T. Sherman, Written by Himself.* 2 vols. New York, 1891.

Sparks, Allison W. *The War Between the States as I Saw It: Reminiscent, Historical and Personal.* Tyler, Tex., 1901.

Stone, Kate. *Brokenburn: The Journal of Kate Stone, 1861–1868.* Edited by John Q. Anderson. Baton Rouge, La., 1955.

Taylor, Richard. *Destruction and Reconstruction: Personal Experiences of the Late War.* Edited by Richard B. Harwell. New York, 1955.

Tunnard, W. H. *A Southern Record: The History of the Third Regiment, Louisiana Infantry.* Edited by Edwin C. Bearss. Dayton, Ohio, 1970.

Walsh and Pilgrim's Directory of the Officers and Members of the Constitutional Convention of the State of Texas, A.D. 1875. Austin, 1875.

Winkler, Ernest W., ed. *Journal of the Secession Convention of Texas, 1861.* Austin, 1912.

Yeary, Mamie, comp. *Reminiscences of the Boys in Gray, 1861–1865.* Dallas, 1912.

ARTICLES

Anderson, James W. "Writings of a Confederate Prisoner of War." Edited by George C. Osborne. *Tennessee Historical Quarterly* 10, nos. 1 and 2 (March, June, 1951): 74–90, 161–184.

Barron, Samuel B. "Wade's Supernumary [*sic*] Scouts." *Confederate Veteran* 11, no. 3 (March, 1903): 115.

———. "Wheeler's Cavalry in Georgia Campaign." *Confederate Veteran* 14, no. 2 (February, 1906): 70.

Blocker, Albert B. "The Boy Bugler of the Third Texas Cavalry: The A. B. Blocker Narrative." Edited by Max S. Lale. *Military History of Texas and the Southwest* 14, no. 2 (1978): 71–92, 147–167, 215–227; 15 (1979): 21–34.

Callaway, W. A. "Hard Service with Ross's Brigade." *Confederate Veteran* 28, no. 9 (September, 1920): 328–329.

———. "Hard Times with Ross's Cavalry." *Confederate Veteran* 28, no. 12 (December, 1920): 447–448.

Cater, Douglas J. "The Battle of Chustenahlah." *Confederate Veteran* 37, no. 6 (June, 1930): 233.

Chadick, Mary C. "Civil War Days in Huntsville." *Alabama Historical Quarterly* 9, no. 2 (Summer, 1947): 194–333.

Fauntleroy, James H. "Elk Horn to Vicksburg." Edited by Homer L. Calkin. *Civil War History* 2, no. 1 (March, 1956): 7–43.

Flournoy, George M. "An Unofficial Account of the Battle of Wilson Creek, August 10, 1861." Edited by Willard E. Wight. *Arkansas Historical Quarterly* 15, no. 4 (Winter, 1956): 360–364.

Helm, W. P. "Close Fighting at Iuka, Miss." *Confederate Veteran* 29, no. 4 (April, 1911): 171.

Hogg, Tom. "Reminiscence of the War: The Last Day at Corinth." Edited by Robert C. Cotner. *East Texas Historical Journal* 20, no. 1 (1982): 48–53.

Keen, Newton A. "'Such is War': The Confederate Memoirs of Newton Asbury Keen." Edited by William C. Billingsley. *Texas Military History* 6, no. 4 (Winter, 1967): 239–253; 7, nos. 1–3 (Spring–Fall, 1968): 44–70, 103–119, 176–194.

M'Minn, W. P. "Service with Van Dorn's Cavalry." *Confederate Veteran* 27, no. 10 (October, 1919): 384–386.

Scott, Joe M. "Crossing the Mississippi in 1864." *Confederate Veteran* 29, no. 2 (February, 1921): 64–65.

Stevenson, W. R. "Capture of Holly Springs, Miss." *Confederate Veteran* 9, no. 3 (March, 1901): 134.

Taylor, H. L. "The Indian Battle of Chaustinolla." *Confederate Veteran* 24, no. 3 (March, 1916): 122.

Terry, W. C. "Data About Third Texas Cavalry." *Confederate Veteran* 20, no. 11 (November, 1912): 521.

Todd, George T. "Commands in Hood's Texas Brigade." *Confederate Veteran* 20, no. 6 (June, 1912): 281–282.

Wynne, J. W. "Heroism of Private J. N. Smith." *Confederate Veteran* 14, no. 8 (August, 1906): 353.

Young, J. P. "Hood's Failure at Spring Hill." *Confederate Veteran* 16, no. 1 (January 1908): 25–41.

Secondary Works

BOOKS

Abel, Annie H. *The American Indian as Participant in the Civil War.* Cleveland, Ohio, 1919.

———. *The American Indian as Slaveholder and Secessionist.* Cleveland, Ohio, 1915.

Allen, Gay W. *Waldo Emerson: A Biography.* New York, 1981.

Amann, William F., ed. *Personnel of the Civil War.* 2 vols. New York, 1961.

Asimov, Isaac. *Asimov's Guide to Halley's Comet.* New York, 1985.

Bailey, Anne J. *Between the Enemy and Texas: Parson's Texas Cavalry in the Civil War.* Fort Worth, 1989.

Bailey, Fred A. *Class and Tennessee's Confederate Generation.* Chapel Hill, N.C., 1987.

Baird, G. H. *A Brief History of Upshur County.* Gilmer, Tex., 1946.

Baker, T. Lindsay. *Ghost Towns of Texas.* Norman, Okla., 1986.

Barr, C. Alwyn. *Reconstruction to Reform: Texas Politics, 1876–1906.* Austin, 1971.

Bearss, Edwin C. *Decision in Mississippi: Mississippi's Important Role in the War Between the States.* Jackson, Miss., 1962.

———. *The Siege of Jackson, July 10–17, 1863.* Baltimore, 1981.

Benner, Judith A. *Sul Ross: Soldier, Statesman, Educator.* College Station, Tex., 1983.

Beringer, Richard E., Herman Hattaway, Archer Jones, and William N. Still, Jr. *Why the South Lost the Civil War.* Athens, Ga., 1986.

Berlin, Ira, *et al.,* eds. *Freedom: A Documentary History of Emancipation, 1861–1967.* Series 2, *The Black Military Experience.* Cambridge, England, 1982.

Betts, Vicki. *Smith County, Texas, in the Civil War.* Tyler, Tex., 1978.

Biographical Souvenir of the State of Texas. Chicago, 1889.

Bowden, J. J. *The Exodus of Federal Forces from Texas, 1861.* Austin, 1986.

Braden, Waldo W., ed. *Oratory in the New South.* Baton Rouge, La., 1979.

Brown, Margaret W. *Pine Grove Cumberland Presbyterian Church.* Henderson, Tex., 1965.

Buenger, Walter L. *Secession and the Union in Texas.* Austin, 1984.

Bullard, Lucille B. *Marion County, Texas, 1860–1870.* Jefferson, Tex., 1965.

Campbell, Randolph B. *A Southern Community in Crisis: Harrison County, Texas, 1850–1880.* Austin, 1983.

Carter, Samuel III. *The Final Fortress: The Campaign for Vicksburg, 1862–1863.* New York, 1980.

————. *The Siege of Atlanta, 1864.* New York, 1973.

Castel, Albert E. *General Sterling Price and the Civil War in the West.* Baton Rouge, La., 1968.

Catton, Bruce. *Grant Moves South.* Boston, 1960.

————. *Grant Takes Command.* Boston, 1968.

Chambers, William T. *Texas: Its Land and People.* Austin, 1952.

Connelly, Thomas L. *Autumn of Glory: The Army of Tennessee, 1862–1865.* Baton Rouge, La., 1971.

Connelly, Thomas L., and Archer Jones. *The Politics of Command: Factions and Ideas in Confederate Strategy.* Baton Rouge, La., 1973.

Cotner, Robert C. *James Stephen Hogg: A Biography.* Austin, 1959.

Cox, Jacob D. *The Battle of Franklin, Tennessee.* New York, 1897.

Crocket, George L. *Two Centuries in East Texas.* Dallas, 1932.

Crute, Joseph H., Jr., comp. *Confederate Staff Officers, 1861–1865.* Powhatan, Va., 1982.

Cunningham, H. H. *Doctors in Gray: The Confederate Medical Service.* Baton Rouge, La., 1960.

Debo, Angie. *A History of the Indians of the United States.* Norman, Okla., 1970.

Dunkelman, Mark H., and Michael J. Winey. *The Hardtack Regiment: An Illustrated History of the 154th Regiment, New York State Infantry Volunteers.* London, 1981.

Dyer, Frederick H. *A Compendium of the War of the Rebellion.* 3 vols. New York, 1953.

Dyer, John P. *The Gallant Hood.* Indianapolis, Ind., 1950.

Eby, Frederick. *The Development of Education in Texas.* New York, 1925.

Estes, George H., Jr. *List of Field Officers, Regiments, and Battalions in the Confederate States Army, 1861–1865.* Macon, Ga., 1912.

Evans, Cecil E. *The Story of Texas Schools.* Austin, 1955.

Farmer, Garland R. *The Realm of Rusk County.* Henderson, Tex., 1951.

Faulk, J. J. *History of Henderson County, Texas.* Athens, Tex., 1929.

Fleming, Walter L. *Civil War and Reconstruction in Alabama.* New York, 1949.

Foner, Eric. *Reconstruction: America's Unfinished Revolution, 1863–1877.* New York, 1988.

Ford, Fred H., and J. L. Brown. *Larissa.* New Orleans, 1919.

Foster, Gaines M. *Ghosts of the Confederacy: Defeat, the Lost Cause, and the Emergence of the New South, 1865 to 1913.* New York, 1987.

Fox, William F. *Regimental Losses in the American Civil War, 1861–1865.* 1889. Reprint. Washington, D.C., 1974.

Friend, Llerena. *Sam Houston, the Great Designer.* Austin, 1954.

Glover, Robert W., and Linda B. Cross. *Tyler and Smith County, Texas: An Historical Survey.* Tyler, Tex., 1976.

Govan, Gilbert E., and James W. Livingood. *A Different Valor: The Story of General Joseph E. Johnston, C.S.A.* Indianapolis, Ind., 1956.

Greer, Jack T. *Leaves from a Family Album (Holcombe and Greer).* Waco, Tex., 1975.

Griffith, Paddy. *Battle Tactics of the Civil War.* New Haven, 1989.

Hall, Margaret E. *A History of Van Zandt County*. Austin, 1976.

Harrison, Walworth. *History of Greenville and Hunt County, Texas.* Waco, Tex., 1977.

Hartje, Robert G. *Van Dorn: The Life and Times of a Confederate General*. Nashville, 1967.

Hattaway, Herman, and Archer Jones. *How the North Won: A Military History of the Civil War*. Urbana, Ill., 1983.

Henry, Robert S. *"First With the Most" Forrest*. Indianapolis, Ind., 1944.

Hesseltine, William B. *Civil War Prisons: A Study in War Psychology*. New York, 1964.

Heyman, Max L., Jr. *Prudent Soldier: A Biography of Major General E. R. S. Canby, 1817–1873.* Glendale, Calif., 1959.

History of Cass County People. Atlanta, Tex., 1982.

Hubbell, John T. *Battles Lost and Won: Essays from Civil War History*. Westport, Conn., 1975.

Johnson, Glen, and DeLorean Johnson. *Our Ancestors*. Baltimore, 1979.

Jones, James P. *Yankee Blitzkrieg: Wilson's Raid through Alabama and Georgia*. Athens, Ga., 1976.

Jordan, Terry G., John L. Bean, Jr., and William M. Holmes. *Texas: A Geography*. Boulder, Colo., 1984.

Kerby, Robert L. *Kirby Smith's Confederacy: The Trans-Mississippi South, 1863–1865.* New York, 1972.

Klement, Frank L. *Dark Lanterns: Secret Political Societies, Conspiracies, and Treason Trials in the Civil War*. Baton Rouge, La., 1984.

Liddell Hart, Basil H. *Sherman: Soldier, Realist, American*. 1958. Reprint. Westport, Conn., 1978.

Linderman, Gerald F. *Embattled Courage: The Experience of Combat in the American Civil War*. New York, 1987.

Livermore, Thomas L. *Numbers and Losses in the Civil War in America, 1861–1865.* 1901. Reprint. Bloomington, Ind., 1957.

Long, E. B. *The Civil War Day by Day: An Almanac, 1861–1865.* Garden City, New York, 1971.

Lonn, Ella. *Desertion During the Civil War*. New York, 1928.

———. *Foreigners in the Union Army and Navy*. Baton Rouge, 1951.

McDonough, James L., and Thomas L. Connelly. *Five Tragic Hours: The Battle of Franklin*. Knoxville, Tenn., 1983.

McFeely, William S. *Grant: A Biography*. New York, 1981.

McMurry, Richard M. *John Bell Hood and the War for Southern Independence*. Lexington, Kentucky, 1982.

———. *Two Great Rebel Armies*. Chapel Hill, N.C., 1989.

McPherson, James M. *Battle Cry of Freedom: The Civil War Era*. New York, 1988.

McWhiney, Grady, and Perry D. Jamieson. *Attack and Die: Civil War Military Tactics and the Southern Heritage*. University, Ala., 1982.

Memorial and Biographical History of Dallas County, Texas. Chicago, 1892.

Mitchell, Reid. *Civil War Soldiers*. New York, 1988.

Nevins, Allan. *The War for the Union*. 4 vols. New York, 1959–1971.

Nunn, William C., ed. *Ten More Texans in Gray*. Hillsboro, Tex., 1980.
———. *Ten Texans in Gray*. Hillsboro, Texas, 1968.
Oates, Stephen B. *Confederate Cavalry West of the River*. Austin, 1961.
———. *Visions of Glory: Texans on the Southwestern Frontier*. Norman, Okla., 1970.
Owens, Harry P., and James J. Cocke, eds., *The Old South in the Crucible of War*. Jackson, Miss., 1983.
Parks, Joseph H. *General Edmund Kirby Smith, C.S.A.* Baton Rouge, La., 1954.
———. *General Leonidas Polk, CSA: The Fighting Bishop*. Baton Rouge, La., 1962.
Parrish, William E., ed. *A History of Missouri*. 3 vols. Columbia, Mo., 1971–1973.
Pemberton, John C. *Pemberton: Defender of Vicksburg*. Chapel Hill, N.C., 1942.
Ransom, Roger L., and Richard Sutch. *One Kind of Freedom: The Economic Consequences of Emancipation*. Cambridge, England, 1977.
Reynolds, Donald E. *Editors Make War: Southern Newspapers in the Secession Crisis*. Nashville, 1970.
Richardson, Rupert N., *et al. Texas: The Lone Star State*. 3d Edition. Englewood Cliffs, N.J., 1970.
Roark, James L. *Masters Without Slaves: Southern Planters in the Civil War and Reconstruction*. New York, 1977.
Robertson, James I., Jr. *Soldiers Blue and Gray*. Columbia, S.C., 1988.
Roland, Charles P. *Albert Sidney Johnston, Soldier of Three Republics*. Austin, 1964.
Ross, Ishbel. *The General's Wife: The Life of Mrs. Ulysses S. Grant*. New York, 1959.
Scaife, William R. *The Campaign for Atlanta*. Atlanta, 1985.
Shirk, George H. *Oklahoma Place Names*. 2d ed. Norman, Okla., 1974.
Simpson, Harold B. *Hood's Texas Brigade: A Compendium*. Hillsboro, Tex., 1977.
Smallwood, James M. *Time of Hope, Time of Despair: Black Texans During Reconstruction*. Port Washington, N.Y., 1981.
Speer, William S., and John H. Brown, eds. *The Encyclopedia of the New West*. Marshall, Tex., 1881.
Stampp, Kenneth M. *And the War Came: The North and the Secession Crisis, 1860–1861*. Baton Rouge, La., 1950.
Starr, Stephen Z. *The Union Cavalry in the Civil War*. 3 vols. Baton Rouge, La., 1979–1985.
Steiner, Paul E. *Disease in the Civil War*. Springfield, Ill., 1968.
Tarpley, Fred. *Jefferson: Riverport to the Southwest*. Austin, 1983.
Templeton, John A., ed. *Cherokee County History*. Jacksonville, Tex., 1986.
Warner, Ezra J. *Generals in Blue: Lives of the Union Commanders*. Baton Rouge, La., 1964.
———. *Generals in Gray: Lives of the Confederate Commanders*. Baton Rouge, La., 1959.
Webb, Walter P., H. Bailey Carroll, and Eldon S. Branda, eds. *The Handbook of Texas*. 3 vols. Austin, 1952–1976.

Wiley, Bell I. *The Life of Johnny Reb: The Common Soldier of the Confederacy.* Indianapolis, Ind., 1943.

Williams, T. Harry. *P. G. T. Beauregard: Napoleon in Gray.* Baton Rouge, La., 1955.

Winfrey, Dorman H. *A History of Rusk County, Texas.* Waco, Tex., 1961.

Wooster, Ralph A. *The Secession Conventions of the South.* Princeton, N.J., 1962.

Wright, Gavin. *The Political Economy of the Cotton South: Households, Markets, and Wealth in the Nineteenth Century.* New York, 1978.

Wright, Marcus J., comp. *Texas in the War, 1861–1865.* Edited by Harold B. Simpson. Hillsboro, Tex., 1965.

ARTICLES

Addington, Wendell G. "Slave Insurrections in Texas." *Journal of Negro History* 35, no. 4 (October, 1950): 408–434.

Ambrose, Stephen E. "Yeoman Discontent in the Confederacy." *Civil War History* 8, no. 3 (September, 1962): 259–268.

Ashcraft, Allan C. "East Texas in the Election of 1860 and the Secession Crisis." *East Texas Historical Journal* 1, no. 1 (July, 1963): 7–16.

Bailey, Anne J. "A Texas Cavalry Raid: Reaction to Black Soldiers and Contrabands." *Civil War History* 35, no. 2 (June, 1989): 138–152.

Bailey, Hugh C. "Disaffection in the Alabama Hill Country, 1861." *Civil War History* 4, no. 2 (June, 1958): 183–194.

Baker, Robin E., and Dale Baum. "The Texas Voter and the Crisis of the Union, 1859–1861." *Journal of Southern History* 53, no. 3 (August, 1987): 395–420.

Banks, Dean. "Civil War Refugees from Indian Territory in the North, 1861–1864." *Chronicles of Oklahoma* 41, no. 3 (Autumn, 1963): 286–298.

Barr, C. Alwyn. "Texas' Confederate Field Artillery." *Texas Military History* 1, no. 2 (August, 1961): 1–8.

Bearss, Edwin C. "The Civil War Comes to Indian Territory: The Flight of Opothleyoholo." *Journal of the West* 11, no. 1 (January, 1972): 9–42.

———. "Fort Smith Serves General McCulloch as a Supply Depot." *Arkansas Historical Quarterly* 24, no. 4 (Winter, 1965): 315–347.

———. "Misfire in Mississippi: McPherson's Canton Expedition." *Civil War History* 8, no. 4 (December, 1962): 401–416.

Betts, Vicki. "'Private and Amateur Hangings': The Lynching of W. W. Montgomery." *Southwestern Historical Quarterly* 88, no. 2 (October, 1984): 145–166.

Bridges, C. A. "The Knights of the Golden Circle: A Filibustering Fantasy." *Southwestern Historical Quarterly* 44, no. 3 (January, 1941): 287–302.

Brown, Dee A. "Pea Ridge." *Civil War Times Illustrated* 6, no. 6 (October, 1967): 4–11, 46–48.

———. "Wilson's Creek." *Civil War Times Illustrated* 11, no. 1 (April, 1972): 8–18.

Buenger, Walter L. "Texas and the Riddle of Secession." *Southwestern Historical Quarterly* 87, no. 2 (October, 1983): 151–182.

————. "Secession Revisited: The Texas Experience." *Civil War History* 30, no. 4 (December, 1984): 293–305.

Campbell, Randolph B. "The District Judges of Texas in 1866–1867: An Episode in the Failure of Presidential Reconstruction." *Southwestern Historical Quarterly* 93, no. 1 (July, 1989): 357–377.

————. "Planters and Plain Folk: Harrison County, Texas, as a Test Case, 1850–1860." *Journal of Southern History* 40, no. 3 (August, 1974): 369–398.

————. "Population Persistence and Social Change in Nineteenth Century Texas: Harrison County, 1850–1880." *Journal of Southern History* 48, no. 2 (May, 1982): 185–204.

Campbell, Randolph B., and Richard G. Lowe. "Some Economic Aspects of Antebellum Texas Agriculture." *Southwestern Historical Quarterly* 82, no. 4 (April, 1979): 351–378.

Cantrell, Gregg. "Racial Violence and Reconstruction Politics in Texas, 1867–1868." *Southwestern Historical Quarterly* 93, no. 1 (July, 1989): 333–355.

Carrier, John P. "Bullets, Ballots, and Bayonets: Reconstruction Politics and Elections in Smith County, 1866–1873." *Chronicles of Smith County, Texas* 13, no. 1 (Summer, 1974): 1–14.

Castel, Albert E. "Battle Without a Victor: Iuka." *Civil War Times Illustrated* 11, no. 6 (October, 1972): 12–18.

Crenshaw, Ollinger. "The Knights of the Golden Circle." *American Historical Review* 47, no. 1 (October, 1941): 23–50.

Crouch, Barry A. "The Freedmen's Bureau." *Chronicles of Smith County, Texas* 11, no. 1 (Spring, 1972): 15–30.

————. "'Unmanacling' Texas Reconstruction: A Twenty-Year Perspective." *Southwestern Historical Quarterly* 93, no. 1 (July, 1989): 275–301.

————. "View from Within: Letters of Gregory Barrett." *Chronicles of Smith County, Texas* 12, no. 2 (Winter, 1973): 13–28.

Danziger, Edmund J., Jr. "The Office of Indian Affairs and the Problems of Civil War Indian Refugees in Kansas." *Kansas Historical Quarterly* 35, no. 3 (Autumn, 1969): 257–275.

Dinges, Bruce J. "Running Down Rebels." *Civil War Times Illustrated* 19, no. 1 (April, 1980): 10–18.

Downer, Edward T. "Johnson's Island." *Civil War History* 8, no. 2 (June, 1962): 202–217.

Dunn, Roy S. "The KGC in Texas, 1860–1861." *Southwestern Historical Quarterly* 70, no. 4 (April, 1967): 543–573.

Ericson, J. E. "The Delegates to the Convention of 1875: A Reappraisal." *Southwestern Historical Quarterly* 67, no. 1 (July, 1963): 22–27.

Gage, Larry J. "The Texas Road to Secession and War: John Marshall and the *Texas State Gazette*, 1860–1861." *Southwestern Historical Quarterly* 62, no. 2 (October, 1958): 191–226.

Gayle, Emma H. "James Calhoun Hill." *Chronicles of Smith County, Texas* 8, no. 2 (Fall, 1969): 8–11, 59–67.

Geise, William R. "The Confederate Northwest, May–August, 1861." *Military History of Texas and the Southwest* 13, no. 1 (1976): 12–21.

————. "Divided Command in the West." *Military History of Texas and the Southwest* 13, no. 2 (1976): 47–54, and no. 3 (1976): 49–57.

————. "Texas—The First Year of the War." *Military History of Texas and the Southwest* 13, no. 4 (1976): 29–43.

Gerster, Patrick, and Nicholas Cords. "The Northern Origins of Southern Mythology." *Journal of Southern History* 43, no. 4 (November, 1977): 567–582.

Hale, Douglas. "Company K: A Composite Portrait of Smith County Boys in the Civil War." *Chronicles of Smith County, Texas* 27, no. 1 (1988): 1–27.

————. "Rehearsal for Civil War: The Texas Cavalry in the Indian Territory, 1861." *Chronicles of Oklahoma* 68, no. 3 (Fall, 1990): 228–265.

————. "The Third Texas Cavalry: A Socioeconomic Profile of a Confederate Regiment." *Military History of the Southwest* 19, no. 1 (Spring, 1989): 1–26.

Harper, Cecil, Jr. "Slavery without Cotton: Hunt County, Texas, 1846–1864." *Southwestern Historical Quarterly* 88, no. 4 (April, 1985): 387–405.

Harrison, Lowell H. "Conscription in the Confederacy." *Civil War Times Illustrated* 9, no. 4 (July, 1970): 10–19.

————. "Jackson . . . Is a Ruined Town." *Civil War Times Illustrated* 15, no. 10 (February, 1977): 4–7, 45–47.

Hess, Earl J. "Sigel's Resignation: A Study in German-Americanism and the Civil War." *Civil War History* 26, no. 1 (March, 1980): 5–17.

————. "The 12th Missouri Infantry: A Socio-Military Profile of a Union Regiment." *Missouri Historical Review* 76, no. 1 (October, 1981): 53–77.

Hesseltine, William B. "Civil War Prisons—Introduction." *Civil War History* 8, no. 2 (June, 1962): 117–120.

Hughes, Michael A. "Pea Ridge or Elkhorn Tavern, Arkansas—March 7–8, 1862." *Blue and Gray Magazine* 5, no. 3 (January, 1988): 8–36.

Jones, Gordon W. "The Scourge of Typhoid." *American History Illustrated* 1, no. 10 (February, 1967): 22–28.

Jordan, Terry G. "The Imprint of the Upper and Lower South on Mid-Nineteenth-Century Texas." *Annals of the Association of American Geographers* 57, no. 4 (December, 1967): 667–690.

————. "Population Origins in Texas, 1850." *Geographical Review* 59, no. 1 (January, 1969): 83–103.

Lale, Max S. "The Military Occupation of Marshall, Texas, by the 8th Illinois Volunteer Infantry, U.S.A." *Military History of Texas and the Southwest* 13 (1976): 39–47.

————. "Robert W. Loughery, Rebel Editor." *East Texas Historical Journal* 21, no. 2 (1983): 3–15.

Lash, Jeffry N. "Joseph E. Johnston's Grenada Blunder: A Failure in Command." *Civil War History* 23, no. 2 (June, 1977): 114–128.

Lathrop, Barnes F. "Migration into East Texas, 1835–1860." *Southwestern Historical Quarterly* 52, nos. 1–3 (July, 1948–January, 1949): 1–31, 184–208, 325–348.

Leath, Andrew L. "Elected County Officials [1846–1934]." *Chronicles of Smith County, Texas* 17, no. 1 (Summer, 1978): 59–61; 18, no. 1 (Summer, 1979): 8–10; 19, no. 1 (Summer, 1980): 33–36.

———. "Starrville." *Chronicles of Smith County, Texas* 23, no. 1 (Summer, 1984): 3–37.

Long, Durwood. "Unanimity and Disloyalty in Secessionist Alabama." *Civil War History* 11, no. 3 (September, 1965): 257–273.

Lowe, Richard G., and Randolph B. Campbell. "Wealthholding and Political Power in Antebellum Texas." *Southwestern Historical Quarterly* 79, no. 1 (July, 1975): 21–30.

McCarley, J. Britt. "The Battle of Ezra Church." *Atlanta Historical Journal* 28, no. 3 (Fall, 1984): 65–70.

McMurry, Richard M. "The Atlanta Campaign of 1864: A New Look." *Civil War History* 22, no. 1 (March, 1976): 5–15.

———. "Confederate Morale in the Atlanta Campaign of 1864." *Georgia Historical Quarterly* 54, no. 2 (Summer, 1970): 226–243.

———. "'The Hell Hole': New Hope Church." *Civil War Times Illustrated* 11, no. 10 (February, 1973): 32–43.

Moore, James T. "Redeemers Reconsidered: Change and Continuity in the Democratic South." *Journal of Southern History* 44, no. 3 (August, 1978): 357–378.

Norton, Herman. "Revivalism in the Confederate Armies." *Civil War History* 6, no. 4 (December, 1960): 410–424.

Norton, Wesley. "The Methodist Episcopal Church and the Civil Disturbances in North Texas in 1859 and 1860." *Southwestern Historical Quarterly* 68, no. 3 (January, 1965): 317–341.

Nye, Wilbur S. "Cavalry Operations Around Atlanta." *Civil War Times Illustrated* 3, no. 4 (July, 1964): 46–50.

Oates, Stephen B. "Recruiting Confederate Cavalry in Texas." *Southwestern Historical Quarterly* 64, no. 4 (April, 1961): 463–477.

Olsen, Otto H. "Historians and the Extent of Slave Ownership in the Southern United States." *Civil War History* 18, no. 2 (June, 1972): 101–116.

Pryor, William L. "'The Fate of Marvin': An Epic Poem of the Civil War by a Texas Soldier." *Texas Quarterly* 20, no. 2 (Summer, 1977): 7–21.

Rable, George C. "Bourbonism, Reconstruction, and the Persistence of Southern Distinctiveness." *Civil War History* 29, no. 2 (June, 1983): 135–153.

Ramsdell, Charles W. "Texas from the Fall of the Confederacy to the Beginning of Reconstruction." *Quarterly of the Texas State Historical Association* 11, no. 3 (January, 1908): 199–219.

Reynolds, Donald E. "Smith County and Its Neighbors During the Slave Insurrection Panic of 1860." *Chronicles of Smith County, Texas* 10, no. 2 (Fall, 1971): 1–8.

Roberts, A. S. "The Federal Government and Confederate Cotton." *American Historical Review* 32, no. 2 (January, 1927): 262–275.

Rowell, John W. "McCook's Raid." *Civil War Times Illustrated* 13, no. 4 (July, 1974): 4–6, 8–9, 42–48.

Sandbo, Anna I. "The First Session of the Secession Convention of Texas." *Southwestern Historical Quarterly* 18, no. 2 (October, 1914): 162–194.

Secrist, Philip L. "The Role of Cavalry in the Atlanta Campaign, 1864." *Georgia Historical Quarterly* 56, no. 4 (Winter, 1972): 510–528.

Smyrl, Frank H. "Unionism in Texas, 1856–1861." *Southwestern Historical Quarterly* 68, no. 2 (October, 1964): 172–195.

Sneed, E. P. "A Historiography of Reconstruction in Texas: Some Myths and Problems." *Southwestern Historical Quarterly* 72, no. 4 (April, 1969): 435–448.

Son, Tim. "Bethel Baptist Church." *Chronicles of Smith County, Texas* 23, no. 1 (Summer, 1984): 71–72.

Sunderland, Glenn W. "The Battle of Corinth." *Civil War Times Illustrated* 6, no. 1 (April, 1967): 28–37.

Timmons, J. T. "The Referendum in Texas on the Ordinance of Secession, February 23, 1861: The Vote." *East Texas Historical Journal* 11, no. 2 (Fall, 1973): 12–28.

Townes, A. Jane. "The Effect of Emancipation on Large Landholdings: Nelson and Goochland Counties, Virginia." *Journal of Southern History* 45, no. 3 (August, 1979): 403–412.

Trickett, Dean. "The Civil War in Indian Territory."
Chronicles of Oklahoma 18, no. 3 (September, 1940): 266–280.

Unstad, Lyder L. "Norwegian Migration to Texas." *Southwestern Historical Quarterly* 43, no. 2 (October, 1939): 176–195.

White, William W. "The Disintegration of an Army: Confederate Forces in Texas, April–June, 1865." *East Texas Historical Journal* 26, no. 2 (1988): 40–47.

———. "The Texas Slave Insurrection in 1860." *Southwestern Historical Quarterly* 52, no. 3 (January, 1949): 259–285.

Wiener, Jonathan M. "Class Structure and Economic Development in the American South, 1865–1955." *American Historical Review* 84, no. 4 (October, 1979): 970–992.

———. "Planter Persistence and Social Change: Alabama, 1850–1870." *Journal of Interdisciplinary History* 7, no. 2 (Autumn, 1976): 235–260.

Wigginton, Thomas A. "Cavalry Operations in the Nashville Campaign." *Civil War Times Illustrated* 3, no. 8 (December, 1964): 40–43.

Willett, Robert L., Jr. "The First Battle of Franklin." *Civil War Times Illustrated* 7, no. 10 (February, 1969): 16–23.

Wilson, Charles R. "The Religion of the Lost Cause: Ritual and Organization of the Southern Civil Religion, 1865–1920." *Journal of Southern History* 46, no. 2 (May, 1980): 219–238.

Woodman, Harold D. "Sequel to Slavery: The New History Views the Postbellum South." *Journal of Southern History* 43, no. 4 (November, 1977): 523–554.

Woodward, C. Vann. "History from Slave Sources." *American Historical Review* 79, no. 2 (April, 1974): 470–481.

Wooster, Ralph A. "An Analysis of the Membership of the Texas Secession Convention." *Southwestern Historical Quarterly* 62, no. 3 (January, 1959): 322–335.

———. "Notes on Texas' Largest Slaveholders, 1860."
Southwestern Historical Quarterly 65, no. 1 (July, 1961): 72–79.

————. "Wealthy Texans, 1860." *Southwestern Historical Quarterly* 71, no. 2 (October, 1967): 163–180.

Wooster, Ralph A., and Robert Wooster. "'Rarin' for a Fight': Texans in the Confederate Army." *Southwestern Historical Quarterly* 84, no. 4 (April, 1981): 387–426.

Wright, Muriel H., and LeRoy H. Fischer. "Civil War Sites in Oklahoma." *Chronicles of Oklahoma* 44, no. 2 (Summer, 1966): 158–215.

Theses and Dissertations

Ashcraft, Allan C. "Texas 1860–1866: The Lone Star State in the Civil War." Ph.D. diss., Columbia University, 1960.

Betts, Vicki. "Smith County in the Civil War." Honors thesis, University of Texas at Tyler, 1976.

Dugas, Vera L. "A Social and Economic History of Texas in the Civil War and Reconstruction Periods." 2 vols. Ph.D. diss., University of Texas at Austin, 1963.

Keller, Mabel C. "History of Kaufman County, Texas." Master's thesis, North Texas State University, Denton, 1950.

Moore, Sue E. "The Life of John Benjamin Long." Master's thesis, University of Texas at Austin, 1924.

Index